Working in Groups

SECOND EDITION

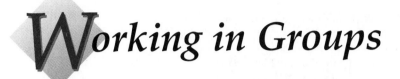

Working in Groups

Communication Principles and Strategies

Isa Engleberg
Prince George's Community College

Dianna Wynn
Midland College

Houghton Mifflin Company • Boston • New York

Senior Sponsoring Editor: George T. Hoffman
Assistant Editor: Jennifer Wall
Senior Project Editor: Kathryn Dinovo
Senior Manufacturing Coordinator: Marie Barnes
Senior Marketing Manager: Pamela J. Laskey

Cover design and illustration: Minko T. Dimov, MinkoImages

Printed in the U.S.A.

Library of Congress Catalog Card Number: 99-72003

ISBN: 0-395-96130-0

2 3 4 5 6 7 8 9-QF-03 02 01 00

Contents

CHAPTER **8**   *Conflict and Cohesion in Groups*   **157**

CHAPTER 10   *Argumentation in Groups*   217

CHAPTER **1 4**   *Agendas and Minutes*   *300*

Preface

When we wrote the first edition of *Working in Groups*, our research and writing were guided by the principle indicated by the question, "What do students enrolled in an introductory small group communication course really need to know?" We used two criteria to help us answer this question. The first was to make sure that we included both classic and current theories of small group communication that focus on "how groups work." The second was to make sure that we included practical information on small group communication skills that emphasized "how to work in groups." These criteria helped us select and balance the amount and types of theory and skills appropriate for an introductory college course in small group communication. In the second edition of *Working in Groups*, we have continued to be guided by these criteria and the overriding principle.

We are delighted by the positive and enthusiastic response to the first edition of *Working in Groups*. We are particularly gratified because both instructors and students have told us that the book is academically strong *and* useful. In our new edition, we are dedicated to preserving this balance between theory and practice. We also have included updated theory and research as well as new "methods" and "tools." As was the case with the first edition, we have employed a style that is both clear and accessible to a diverse audience of readers.

Reviewers of our first edition requested we make very few changes in order to preserve the book's many strengths. While we have heeded this recommendation, we also knew there was room for improvement. Because the quantity and quality of research and skills training in small group communication is expanding exponentially, we have improved and updated several sections but have retained the core components and spirit of the first edition. We have kept what adopters and reviewers of *Working in Groups* liked best: a balanced approach to theory, research, and practice; a clear and lively writing style; comprehensive coverage of all aspects of small group communication; and the addition of separate chapters on participation, communication apprehension, listening, argumentation, making presentations, planning and conducting meetings, agendas and minutes, and parliamentary procedure. We are particularly proud of our last-minute changes to the chapter on Technology and Groups to ensure that it is as timely as the publishing process allows.

Central Metaphor: Balance

As was the case in the first edition of *Working in Groups*, we have integrated small group theory and research into the communication practices of successful groups by relying on a central metaphor: **Balance**. Effective groups and members balance several important components of group work:

> Member Needs and Group Goals
> Participation and Leadership
> Task Functions and Maintenance Functions
> Verbal Communication and Nonverbal Communication
> Individual Expression and Team Talk
> Cohesiveness and Conflict
> Seeking Consensus and Offering Arguments
> Structured Procedures and Creative Thinking
> Shared Perceptions and Respect for Differences
> Speaking Skills and Listening Skills
> Face-to-Face Meetings and Cybermeetings

Effective groups do not just happen; conscientious members use communication strategies and skills to make what happens in groups meaningful and productive. The key to successful group communication is achieving balance between the complex and even competing elements that occur any time there is interaction among three or more interdependent people working toward a common goal.

Textbook Format and Chapters

Although some of the chapters have been reordered, *Working in Groups* continues to be organized into four major sections:

Part I: Basic Group Concepts, provides an introduction to some of the most basic theories and principles of small group communication, including the importance and nature of group communication, the formation and development of small groups, and the theories and practice of effective small group leadership and participation.

Part II: Interaction Skills, examines specific communication principles and competencies required of effective group members, including communication confidence, listening ability, verbal and nonverbal communication skills, and strategies for expressing differences and managing conflict.

Part III: Achieving Group Goals, focuses on task-specific competencies common to most work groups, including planning and conducting meetings, decision-making and problem-solving methods, argumentation in groups, and making presentations in, for, and by groups.

Part IV: Resources and Tools, serves as a "how to" section focusing on methods and tools essential for efficient and effective group action in specific settings and circumstances. Separate chapters cover planning and conducting meetings, how to write and use meeting agendas and minutes, how to follow and apply parliamentary procedure, and how to use and take advantage of communication technology in groups.

Although the chapters may be read and taught in sequence, the textbook is written so that chapters are self-contained and can be used in any order. However, given that group communication is rarely as orderly as the chapters of a book, convenient **Toolboxes** are placed in each chapter to refer readers to other sections of the textbook for a more comprehensive treatment of related subjects.

New Topics and Features

In addition to the topics and themes found in the first edition of *Working in Groups,* we have included several new features that strengthen the textbook's scholarship and usefulness. By continually asking ourselves "What do our students really need to know about small group communication?" we have added several new sections that combine our dual focus on "how groups work" and "how to work in groups."

Team Talk.   We have included Anne Donnelon's valuable research and theory on *team talk* as part of Chapter 7: Verbal and Nonverbal Communication. Team talk is more than words—it is the means we use to achieve group goals, the stimulus we use to build team relationships, and the evidence we use to assess group work. Analyzing and applying the principles of effective team talk can provide a useful tool for understanding and improving group communication.

Creative Problem Solving.   The more we work in groups, the more we have come to appreciate the value and benefits of creative thinking. Because curiosity and creativity fuel all great groups, we describe the creative problem-solving process and recommend several methods for enhancing group creativity. At the same time, we recognize that a group must work out an internal balance between creative discussions and productive research, analysis, and action.

Cybermeeting.   We are now living in an age of cybermeeting; a time in which technology is no longer separate from group communication but is becoming an integral part of the group process. There are exciting, new ways of using information technology to produce more effective forms of collaboration. Because technology is changing the way we communicate in groups, we have described and provided advice about how and when to use a variety of cybermeeting methods and tools. These techniques and technologies include teleconferences, videoconferences, and computer conferences (meetingware, groupware, group support systems, and electronic focus groups).

Instructors Resource Manual. Both users and reviewers have praised our *Instructor's Resource Manual* as being comprehensive, original, and ready-to-use. At the request of users and reviewers, we have kept a special feature for instructors adopting the textbook: a computer disk containing selected items that can be adapted and printed for classroom use. Equally important, we have added more original exercises, refined the bank of test questions, and provided more teaching tips. The *Instructor's Resource Manual* has become a valuable resource for veteran instructors and a step-by-step guide for faculty members who are teaching small group communication for the first time.

Continued Themes and Topics

In addition to several new features, we have made a concerted effort to update and improve every chapter. Significant improvements have been made to the standard subjects on small group communication, as well as to topics that are neglected in many textbooks and courses.

Leadership. Leadership is introduced early in the textbook and treated as one of the most important variables in effective group communication. We emphasize that effective leaders are able to make strategic decisions and use communication skills to mobilize group members toward a shared goal.

Participation. An entire chapter is devoted to the responsibilities and skills of effective members. In addition to including the standard functional roles of participants, we use personality theory to help readers understand and adapt to the different ways in which members perceive and make decisions about themselves and their groups. A major section is devoted to methods for dealing with the difficulties that often arise during interaction among group members.

Communication Apprehension in Groups. Because so many people experience speaking anxiety, the textbook devotes significant attention to the subject of communication apprehension and its relationship to group process and member confidence.

Listening in Groups. An entire chapter is devoted to the difficult task of listening in a group setting, including ways to improve the listening behavior of a group by capitalizing on the relationship between listening abilities and member roles.

Expressing Differences. Several approaches to dealing with differences in groups emphasize the necessity and value of constructive conflict. In addition to traditional methods of conflict management, we encourage the use of mediation as a process to help groups and their members express and resolve differences.

Decision Making and Argumentation. In addition to a major chapter on group decision making and problem solving, the textbook includes a complete chapter on argumentation designed to help group members advance their own viewpoints and analyze the views of others.

Planning and Conducting Meetings. A separate chapter is devoted to running effective meetings. In addition to highlighting the important role of chairpersons and responsible group members, we provide suggestions for dealing with many of the common duties and problems that arise before, during, and after meetings.

Agendas and Meetings. The importance of using agendas and recording accurate minutes is emphasized in a chapter that also provides sample agendas and minutes from formal and informal group meetings.

Parliamentary Procedure. Because many public and private organizations rely on parliamentary procedure to ensure civil and organized meetings, *Robert's Rules of Order, Newly Revised* is used to explain the basics of parliamentary procedure.

Gender and Cultural Differences. Because every group member brings a unique background and perspective to the group process, we devote special attention to the ways in which gender and cultural differences affect the task and social dimensions of a group. We urge all group members to make a concerted effort to understand, respect, and adapt to the rich diversity found in most groups.

Instructional Features. *Working in Groups* incorporates several features designed to help readers and instructors link the theories of small group communication (how groups work) with communication skills (how to work in groups). In some cases, theories suggest specific methods and practices; in other cases, experiential and collaborative learning exercises are used to demonstrate the value and applications of theories.

Theories, Methods, and Tools. The textbook emphasizes that the best way to study groups is to balance an understanding of theories, methods, and tools with practical experience. Without theories, group members may not understand why methods and tools work in one situation and fail in others. Without underlying theories, they may not appreciate the experiences and consequences of group communication and action.

TOOLBOXES. Toolboxes are cross-references to the theories, methods, and tools found in other chapters. Although the textbook's chapters follow a logical sequence, toolboxes help readers use other sections of the book to supplement their understanding and further develop their skills.

Graphics as Learning Guides.   Every chapter contains graphics (checklists and/or figures) that summarize and illustrate small group communication concepts. Checklists may be used to help readers chair a meeting, test the validity of evidence, or illustrate the steps in a problem-solving sequence. In many cases, the figures serve as previews or summaries of major sections in a chapter. In all cases, graphics have been designed to function as supplementary learning guides.

Summary Study Guides.   At the end of every chapter, a summary study guide helps students review the major concepts covered in that chapter. Any reader able to explain and provide examples of the summary statements in each guide should have an excellent understanding of the chapter and its content.

GroupWork.   The GroupWork in every chapter provides a group-based exercise designed to demonstrate, illustrate, or practice a principle in the chapter. Although the *Instructor's Resource Manual* includes additional class exercises, GroupWork provides a way for classroom groups to interact and to function in a collaborative learning environment.

Assessment.   The end of every chapter provides an assessment instrument or checklist that can be used to evaluate student and group understanding of concepts or mastery of skills. Other assessment instruments are provided in the *Instructor's Resource Manual.*

Recommended Readings.   Preceding the reference notes at the end of each chapter, a short, recommended reading list offers selections that an interested reader can consult for more information on topics discussed in the chapter. We have selected readings that are accessible and can be found in most libraries and in many comprehensive bookstores.

Glossary.   A large glossary at the back of the book includes every term or phrase defined in the textbook. Words, phrases, and the names of theories printed in **bold** are defined within chapters as well as in the glossary.

Instructor's Resource Manual.   We have written an Instructor's Resource Manual that contains a variety of items that can be adapted to different types of students and different course objectives. The manual features sample syllabi, chapter-by-chapter exercises, and photo-ready graphics for use as transparencies or handouts, additional GroupWork exercises and Assessment instruments, textbook-specific test questions, and instructional guides and teaching tips. A special feature of the *Instructor's Resource Manual* for instructors adopting the textbook is a computer disk containing selected items that can be adapted and printed for classroom use.

Coverage and Writing Style

We have tried to make this textbook realistic and readable. When selecting which theories and topic areas to include, we applied our overriding principle: What does a reader need to know about small group communication in order to understand how groups work as well as how to work in groups? When theory or research helped us answer this question, we included it. When a theory or topic area was more appropriate for an advanced or graduate course, we left it to the students and professors in those courses.

Throughout the writing and reviewing process, we placed special emphasis on making this textbook highly readable and user-friendly. This is a how-to textbook grounded in classic and current theory. The writing style is conversational and clear. The authors' voices are also clear. Although it would have been possible for us to write a textbook that lacked any personality, our ideas, feelings, and opinions are evident throughout.

Acknowledgments

Working in Groups has become a way of expressing our appreciation and admiration for our colleagues and students at Prince George's Community College and Midland College, who continually demonstrate the value of working in groups.

At the top of our list of acknowledgments is George Hoffman, Senior Sponsoring Editor at Houghton Mifflin Company. George's ability to separate our best and worst ideas, deal with our enthusiasm and occasional frustrations, and fulfill our hopes while calming our anxieties exemplifies our belief that "balance" is the most appropriate metaphor for working with a group—even when that group is only one senior editor and two determined, highly opinionated co-authors. We also want to thank Jennifer Wall, Assistant Editor, who joined us mid-project but quickly took over those pesky editorial responsibilities we preferred to entrust to a publishing professional.

In preparing the second edition of *Working in Groups,* we are particularly indebted to our students. Never shy nor fearful of giving us their opinions, they provided valuable suggestions and insights. Not only did they tell us when we were reaching over their heads and needs, they also suggested alternative ways of clarifying unfamiliar theories, research, and academic terminology. Special thanks go to Jillian Whittaker and Dawn Triches, students at Midland College, for suggesting ways to make parliamentary procedure easier for students to understand.

As always and above all, we are indebted to Brian Holland and Allan Kennedy. Their advice, support, and patience gave us the freedom to lock ourselves away with our text when deadlines were imminent. Again, we offer special thanks to Brian, corporate counsel at The Dialog Company, whose role as technology consultant helped us make Chapter 16 a state-of-the-art contribution to the study of small group communication.

We are particularly grateful to the following groups of conscientious reviewers whose excellent suggestions and comments helped us revise and improve the second edition of *Working in Groups:* Mark G. Borzi, Eastern Illinois University; Kurt A. Bruder, Texas Tech University; James J. Fernandez, Gallaudet University; L. Kristine Pond, Kansas State University; and Kathryn Sue Young, University of Central Arkansas.

Isa Engleberg and Dianna Wynn

*B*asic Group Concepts

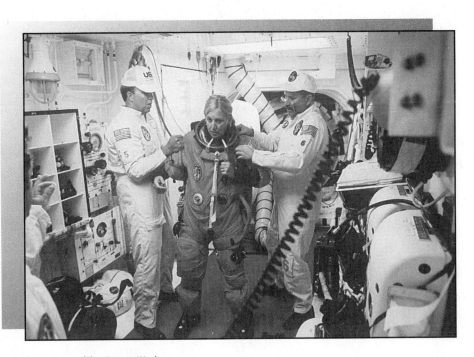

Jason Laure/The Image Works

*I*ntroduction to Small Group Communication

Inescapable Groups

You can run but you can't hide from groups. Nor should you. As a member of many groups—families, friends, teams, colleagues, businesses, institutions, and communities—you cannot escape the need to work in groups. Former Green Bay Packers coach, Vince Lombardi, put it this way: "Individual commitment to a group effort: this is what makes a team work, a company work, a society work, and a civilization work."[1] Whereas individual achievement was once the hallmark of personal success, we now live in an era in which success depends on our ability to work together.

From aboriginal clans to high-tech research teams, we move through life surrounded by and immersed in groups. When asked to describe who we are, most of us include information about the groups to which we belong. The members of an exclusive country club, a rural church, a corporate board, and Alcoholics Anonymous belong to groups in order to meet their individual and collective needs.

Not only can't you escape the influence of groups, you may be surprised by the long list of groups to which you belong. College students typically list family, friends, study groups, class project groups, car pools, roommates, volunteer groups, sports teams, staff at work, campus clubs, religious groups, and neighborhood groups. After graduation, you may add service clubs, management teams, governing boards, political committees, and professional association memberships.

Groups are fast becoming the U.S. way of doing business.

- Studies of managers show that they spend 30 percent to 80 percent of their time in meetings.[2]
- As many as 11 million meetings occur daily in the United States.[3]
- An insurance company found that the average executive spends . . . almost two out of every five working days in small group meetings.[4]
- By the year 2000, 40–50 percent of the U.S. workforce will use work teams to manage businesses, produce products, and provide services.[5]

Katzenbach and Smith observe that "most models of the organization of the future that we have heard about . . . are premised on teams surpassing individuals as the primary performance unit in the company."[6] This observation does not mean that individual performance will become unimportant. Rather, the challenge will be to balance the roles of individuals and teams.

Defining Small Group Communication

When does a collection of people become a group? Do people talking in an elevator or discussing the weather at an airport constitute a group? Should the members of a church congregation listening to a sermon or the fans cheering at a baseball game be considered a group? Although the people in these examples may look like a group, they are not working in, for, or with other members. Working in groups requires sustained and purposeful small group communication.

We define **small group communication** as the interaction of three or more interdependent people working toward a common goal. In order to better understand this definition, it is necessary to understand its essential terms.

Three or More People

A small group consists of at least three people. The phrase "two's company, three's a crowd" recognizes that a conversation between two people is quite different from a three-person discussion. When two people interact in a conversation, the interaction is limited to two possibilities: Eve communicates with Adam; Adam communicates with Eve. When a third person is added the dynamics of the situation change. A third person can change a tie vote into a two-to-one decision. A third person can be the listener who judges and influences the content and style of the conversation: All of us have had the experience of walking up to two people who immediately change the subject because we have joined them.

Although three is the minimum number of people needed for small group communication, a maximum size is more difficult to recommend. According to Wood, Phillips, and Pedersen, the ideal group size for a problem-solving discussion is five to seven members.[7] To avoid ties, an odd number of members seems to be better than an even number. Groups having more than seven members tend to divide into subgroups. Also, as groups grow larger, individual satisfaction and commitment to the group often decreases.[8] Members simply begin to feel left out or inconsequential. Yet, groups with fewer than five members often lack the resources and diversity of opinion needed for effective problem solving.

Obviously, many groups consisting of more than seven members are formed. Yet, even in large groups, there is usually a core of five to seven members who do more of the work and take on leadership functions. Beyond fifteen members, coordination and control become difficult. Members may not know one another or be able to communicate directly with other members, and discussion often requires elaborate rules and procedures in order to organize group tasks and control the flow of communication.

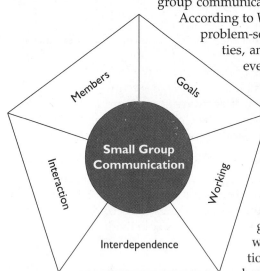

FIGURE 1.1
Components of Small Group Communication

Interaction   **Interaction** requires communication among group members who use verbal and nonverbal messages to generate meanings and establish relationships within a group context.[9] Communication is the medium through which groupwork is done. Communication allows members to share information and opinions, make decisions and solve problems, and develop interpersonal relationships. The way in which group members communicate does more than reveal group dynamics, it creates them.[10] Ellis and Fisher maintain that, in a group, "a communicative relationship develops during the process of interacting with others."[11] Group members learn which behaviors are appropriate and inappropriate, and which communication rules govern the interaction among members. Regardless of whether group members are meeting face-to-face or in cyberspace, small group communication requires interaction.

Common Goal   Group members come together for a reason. It is this collective reason or goal that defines and unifies a group. A **goal** is the purpose or objective toward which a group is directed. The label doesn't matter—goal, objective, purpose, mission, assignment, or vision statement. Without a common goal, groups would wonder: Why are we meeting? Why should we care or work hard? Where are we going?

Often a group's goal is assigned. For example, a marketing instructor may assign a semester-long project to a group of students in order to demonstrate their ability to develop a marketing campaign. A chemical company may assemble a group of employees from various departments and ask them to make recommendations for more efficient and safe storage of hazardous chemicals.

Other groups may have the freedom to choose their own goal. A gathering of neighbors may meet to discuss ways to prevent crime in their immediate neighborhood. A group of nursing students may form a study group to review course materials for an anatomy exam. Whatever the goal, effective groups understand their common goal and dedicate their efforts to the work needed to accomplish that goal.

The importance of a group's goal cannot be underestimated. If there is one single factor that separates successful from unsuccessful groups, it is having a clear goal. A study by Larson and LaFasto concluded that "in every case, without exception, where an effectively functioning team was identified, it was described . . . as having a clear understanding of its objective."[12] The most effective groups, writes Billington, "invest tremendous time and effort in exploring, shaping, and agreeing on a purpose. . . ."[13]

Interdependence   **Interdependence** means that each group member is affected and influenced by the actions of other members. An interdependent group functions as a team in which all members take responsibility for doing their part. The failure of a single group member can adversely affect the entire group. For example, if one student in a study group fails to read an assigned chapter, the entire group will be unprepared for questions related to the subject matter covered in that chapter.

When small groups interact in order to achieve a common goal, members exert influence on one another. Whether we like it or not, there are not many tasks that can be accomplished without information, advice, support, and assistance from other people.

Working

This textbook places special emphasis on groups that work together in pursuit of a common goal. Working in groups, however, is not the same as groups at work. Certainly, many of the groups that you have worked with have been at your job; however, groups that are unrelated to your job also engage in work. A church committee discussing construction plans for a new youth center is engaged in work. A family sitting around the kitchen table trying to come up with a way to divide household chores is working hard to find an equitable solution. However, friends meeting for dinner are not working. Although a group of friends may be interacting with the goal of meeting their social needs, they do not need a plan of work in order to accomplish that goal. Being with friends is not the same as working with friends.

*S*ynergistic System

When three or more interdependent people interact and work toward a common goal, they have the potential to be synergistic. **Synergy** is a term that describes the cooperative interaction of several factors that results in a combined effect greater than the total of all individual contributions. In other words, the whole is greater than the sum of its individual parts. The term *synergy* comes from the Greek word *sunergos,* meaning "working together." Synergy does not occur when people work alone; it occurs only when people work together.

Small group communication, as we have defined it, is more than a collection of individuals who talk to each other. A group is a complex system. Ellis and Fisher define a system as "a set of component parts that have relationships and are interdependent."[14] In such a system, the actions of individual members in the form of talk or behavior affect everyone in the group as well as the outcome of the group's work. The analogy of a recipe illustrates this effect. Eggs, sugar, cream, and bourbon have very different and individual tastes, but when combined properly in a recipe, the result is an irresistible and potentially intoxicating eggnog. In groups, people are the major ingredients; in the right combination, they can create a highly productive and satisfying experience.

Effective groups are synergistic. Baseball teams without superstars have won the World Series. Companies whose executives earn modest salaries have surpassed those companies in which the CEOs are paid millions of dollars. Ordinary groups have achieved extraordinary results. Synergy represents the positive energy that transforms group members into a motivated, energetic, and highly productive team. Synergy occurs when the knowledge, talents, and dedication of group members merge into a force that surpasses anything group members could have produced without cooperative interaction.

Advantages and Disadvantages of Working in Groups

If you are like most people, you have had to sit through long and boring meetings run by incompetent leaders. Perhaps you have lost patience with a group that couldn't accomplish a simple task you could do all by yourself. One study found that one-third of business meeting participants feel as though they have little or no influence on the outcome of group decisions.[15] Other studies suggest that as much as a third of the time we spend in meetings is wasted with unproductive business.[16] In the long run, however, the advantages of working in effective groups outweigh the potential disadvantages.

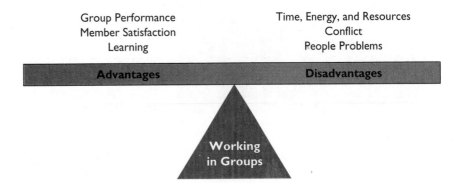

FIGURE 1.2   Advantages and Disadvantages of Working in Groups

Advantages

Although participating in groups can be time-consuming and even aggravating, the advantages are significant. Three of these advantages are that, in many situations, groups perform better than individuals working alone; members find the experience rewarding; and participants can learn more.

Group Performance. Groups make important decisions and solve many problems. They decide how businesses compete, how staff members work, how governments rule, how instructors teach, and how doctors attend to patients' needs. Poole describes how the "daily media report hundreds of decisions emanating from civic bodies, juries, boards of directors, government panels, church groups, clubs, labor caucuses, school boards, task forces, and the like."[17] The reason so many groups are doing so much that affects our daily lives is fairly simple: Groups can perform better and accomplish more

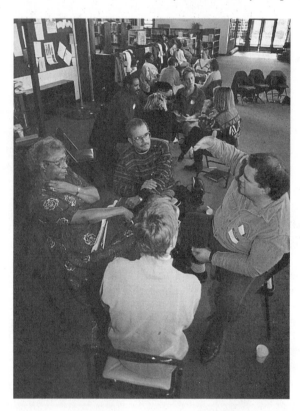

A very large group will often form smaller groups. What are the advantages of working in smaller groups rather than very large groups? (McLaughlin/The Image Works)

than individuals working alone. Katzenbach and Smith have noted that groups "outperform individuals acting alone especially when performance requires multiple skills, judgments, and experiences."[18] Senge and his colleagues claim that "if you want something really creative done, you ask a team to do it—instead of sending one person off to do it on his or her own."[19]

Despite such impressive claims about group performance, there are exceptions. If the task is fairly simple and routine (write a memo, mail a letter, total the receipts), it may be easier for individuals working alone to accomplish the task. If one person knows the answer to a question or if the task requires a specialized expert, then a single person may be better equipped to get the job done. When, however, the task is complex and the answers are unclear, a group will perform better. McClernon explains that groups have more successful outcomes because complex decisions require more perspectives and expertise than any one person might have.[20] Groups may not perform better in all situations, but when the right members are matched to an appropriate task, little can compare to the good work and success of an effective group.

Member Satisfaction. Even if groups didn't accomplish more than individuals working alone, many people would still work in groups. The social benefits can be just as important as task achievement. People belong to and work in groups because they make friends, have an opportunity to socialize, and can feel part of a unified and successful team. After reviewing the literature on group member satisfaction, Pavitt and Curtis conclude that "the greater the opportunity that people have to communicate in groups, the more satisfactory the group experience will be for them." [21] When members become good friends and valued colleagues, they look forward to working in groups. In studying the use of groups and teams in U.S. businesses, Manz and Sims conclude that team "members are generally more satisfied and experience an enhanced quality of life at work. For the most part, people like teams."[22]

Learning.   An added advantage of working in groups is the amount of learning that occurs within an effective group. Groups can enhance learning by sharing collective information, stimulating critical thinking, challenging assumptions, and even raising standards of achievement. Collaborative learning is receiving high marks and praise in public schools and in higher education. A *New York Times* article summarized the results of a Harvard University study on college learning. The report concluded that college students thrive "when they do at least some of their studying in small groups rather than logging long, solitary hours of study. . . ."[23] A review of 168 studies of college students comparing cooperative, group-based learning with traditional means indicated that collaborative learning promotes higher individual achievement in knowledge acquisition, retention, accuracy, creativity in problem solving, and higher-level reasoning.[24]

Senge and colleagues claim that, in the corporate world, "great teams are learning organizations—groups of people who, over time, enhance their capacity to create what they truly deserve to create."[25] Working in groups promotes learning because the process helps members put theories and facts into perspective while stimulating interest, clarifying ideas, and teaching individuals to cooperate.

Working in groups also gives us the opportunity to learn from and with other members. New members learn from veterans; amateurs learn from experts. Not only do group members learn more about the topics they discuss, they also learn more about how to work as a team.

Disadvantages

The advantages of working in groups most often occur when groups are working efficiently and effectively. The disadvantages are more likely to occur when a group is not the appropriate way to achieve a goal; when members do not meet their potential; or when problems interfere with group members' willingness and ability to communicate. The most common complaints about working in groups concern the amount of time, energy, and resources expended by groups and the conflict and people problems that can arise.

Time, Energy, and Resources.   Working in groups costs time, energy, and resources. Does an organization get its money's worth when executives spend two out of every five working days in meetings? The 11 million daily meetings that are held in the United States cost a lot of time and money. One survey found unproductive meeting time to be a $37 billion annual waste.[26]

The 3M corporation has tried to take into account the many factors that affect the cost of meetings, including the hourly wages of group members, the wages of those who help prepare for meetings, the cost of materials used in the meeting, and overhead costs. The conclusion was that meetings cost the 3M corporation a staggering $78.8 million annually.[27] We spend a lot of time in groups; if that time is wasted, we are throwing away valuable resources and effort.

Conflict.   Very few people enjoy or seek out conflict. Bennis, Parikh, and Lessem explain that "fear of conflict is often prevalent in the work-place because conflict is taken to spell trouble."[28] When group members work together to achieve a goal, there is always the potential for disagreement. Unfortunately, those who disagree are often seen as aggressive and disruptive. As a result, some people will do almost anything to avoid conflict and confrontation. They may even avoid working in groups. Although most researchers and writers argue that "in a good discussion, arguing our different viewpoints might lead to clarifying and reconciling them,"[29] group members often are wary of situations in which they may have to argue with others or defend their opinions. Ironically, one study found that nearly 30 percent of all meetings in corporate America are held to resolve a conflict.[30] Yet, because of apprehension about conflict, some people avoid meetings in which controversial issues are scheduled for discussion, or remain unwilling to express their opinions.

People Problems.   As much as we may want our colleagues to share our interests, viewpoints, and willingness to work, there is always the potential that individual group members will create problems. Like anyone else in our daily lives, group members can be stubborn, lazy, and even cruel. When deciding whether to work in a group, we often consider whether we want to spend time working with certain members.

Members who are not confident or well-prepared may have little to contribute. In order to avoid conflict or extra work, some members may go along with the group rather than search for the best solution to a problem. Strong, domineering members can put so much pressure on others that dissent is stifled. Although no one wants to work with a group of unpleasant members, there may be circumstances in which people problems cannot be avoided. When this situation occurs, the disadvantages of group work can overwhelm the advantages.

Types of Groups

All groups are not alike. Groups, like their individual members, have many different characteristics and concerns. We have sorted them into seven categories: primary groups, social groups, self-help groups, learning groups, ser-

Types of Groups

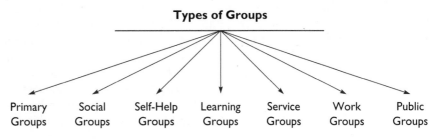

FIGURE 1.3 Types of Groups

vice groups, work groups, and public groups. These categories range from the most personal and informal types of groups to more formal types. Each type of group can be recognized by observing its setting (where and when the group meets) and its membership (who is in the group).

Primary Groups

Primary groups are composed of family members and friends who provide us affection, support, and a sense of belonging. Primary groups make us who we are. When families or close friends do not provide appropriate or sufficient support, the psychological scars can last a lifetime. When primary groups help us gain confidence, we are better prepared for all the other types of groups we encounter.

Social Groups

Social groups share common interests in a friendly setting or participate in a common activity. These groups are formed by people who enjoy interacting with others while pursuing recreational or social goals. Examples of social groups include college sororities and fraternities, athletic teams, and hobby groups (for example, stamp collecting, gardening, classic cars, or bird watching).

Self-Help Groups

Self-help groups offer support and encouragement to members who want or need support with personal problems. They are also referred to as support groups, therapy groups, personal growth groups, and encounter groups. People join self-help groups to meet and share their personal concerns with other people who are dealing with the same problems. According to Wuthnow, 40 percent of the adult population in the United States belongs to support groups.[31] In addition to private therapy groups, self-help groups include specialized organizations such as Parents Without Partners, Weight Watchers, and Alcoholics Anonymous.

Learning Groups   By sharing knowledge and experiences, **learning groups** help members acquire information and develop skills. In some cases, learning groups are designed to benefit individual members ("I want to improve my grade on the next exam.") or the group as a whole ("We need to learn how to use our e-mail system more effectively."). Learning groups can range from a postgraduate seminar at a university to a parenting class at the local hospital. Other examples include book discussion groups, religious study groups, class project groups, health and fitness classes, and professional workshops.

Service Groups   Like members of social groups, service group members may join in order to socialize with others. In addition, **service groups** are dedicated to worthy causes that help other people both within and outside the group. Many communities rely on service groups to fill the gap between self-help and government support. There are numerous examples of service groups including the Kiwanis, labor unions, business and professional women's clubs, neighborhood associations, PTAs, the American Legion, the NAACP, and fire and police auxiliary groups.

Work Groups   If you are employed, you probably belong to several work groups. You may be a member of a production team or a work crew. You may be part of a sales staff, service department, management group, or research team. In almost every case, the **work groups** you belong to are responsible for achieving specific tasks or routine duties on behalf of a company, organization, association, agency, or institution. Goodall contends that over the last twenty years, American businesses have shifted to become more group-centered; work groups have assumed responsibility for making decisions and carrying out tasks in organizations.[32] Among the many types of work groups, two deserve special attention: committees and teams.

Committees.   **Committees** form when a group is given a specific assignment by a larger group or by a person in a position of authority. Although committees are most common in the work environment, they are often used when service groups have a specific task to accomplish. Committees can take several forms. An **ad hoc committee** is formed for a very specific purpose and disbands once it has completed that assignment or task. For example, an ad hoc committee could plan a ground-breaking ceremony or high school reunion, organize a company's fund-raising campaign for a charity, or promote a community cleanup for a neighborhood.

    Standing committees remain active in order to accomplish an ongoing task. Many businesses and organizations have ongoing social committees, membership committees, program committees, and finance committees. A **task force** is a type of committee appointed to gather information and make recommendations regarding a specific issue or problem. A corporation's marketing task force could recommend a package of promotional activities. A government task force could examine the health care system or the reasons why a school system's test scores have declined.

Teams.   Work **teams** are groups given full responsibility and resources for their performance. Unlike committees, work teams are relatively permanent groups. They do not take time *from* work to meet—they unite *to* work. A health care team attends to a specific patient or group of patients. A research team is assigned a specific research project. A legal team may defend or prosecute a specific case.

The latest innovation in work groups is the self-management team. In their book *The Wisdom of Teams*, Katzenbach and Smith define a **self-management team** as "a small number of people with complementary skills who are committed to a common purpose, performance goals, and an approach for which they hold themselves mutually accountable."[33] In a self-management team, peer-led groups are formed and given complete responsibility for seeing that a task is completed. Dumaine reports that "in growing numbers of companies, self-management teams are taking over such standard supervisory duties as scheduling work, maintaining quality, even administering pay and vacations."[34] Many managers claim that teams produce higher productivity, lower labor costs, and more committed employees.[35] The following examples document the efficiency and effectiveness of self-management teams:

- At a Johnson Wax plant, a self-management team figured out how to make an operation more efficient. As a result, productivity increased 30 percent while the number of middle managers decreased.[36]
- At a weekly meeting, a team of Federal Express clerks spotted—and eventually solved—a billing problem that was costing the company $2.1 million a year.[37]
- A General Motors automobile-battery plant organized around teams reported productivity savings of 30 to 40 percent when compared with traditionally organized plants.[38]

Undoubtedly, there will be more attempts to use teams to enhance productivity and improve employee morale and product quality in all sorts of work settings.

Public Groups   Primary, social, self-help, learning, service, and work groups usually function in private. Although a group and its product may be visible to the public, members often prefer to meet, discuss, and make decisions in private.

There is, however, one type of group that is seen and heard by non-group members. **Public groups** engage in discussion in front of or for the benefit of the public. Their meetings usually occur in public settings where they are

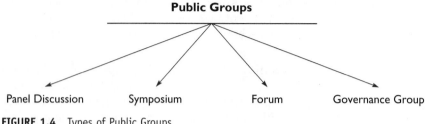

Public Groups

Panel Discussion   Symposium   Forum   Governance Group

FIGURE 1.4 Types of Public Groups

judged by an audience of listeners. Although public groups may engage in information sharing, decision making, or problem solving, they are also concerned with the impression they make on a public audience. Four different categories of public groups illustrate how these groups function.

Panel Discussion. A **panel discussion** involves several people who interact with one another about a common topic for the benefit of an audience. Panel discussions are very common on television talk shows as varied as Oprah Winfrey and Ricki Lake. These programs have presented bizarre and controversial panel discussions, while more somber discussions have been moderated on Sunday morning political discussion shows and on business programs such as *Wall $treet Week.* Regardless of whether a panel discussion is live or on television, there is usually a moderator who tries to control the flow of communication. Whatever the format, panel discussions are designed to educate, influence, or entertain an audience.

Symposium. In a **symposium,** group members present short, uninterrupted speeches on different aspects of a topic for the benefit of the public. For example, a local PTA may sponsor a drug symposium in which a physician, psychologist, police officer, and former drug addict are given uninterrupted time to inform parents about the extent of the drug problem and to recommend strategies for prevention and treatment. At election time, the League of Women Voters or a group of politicians may organize a candidates' symposium at which each candidate is given five minutes to explain why he or she should be elected to public office. What makes a symposium unique is that group members give speeches to a public audience rather than interact with other group members.

Forum. Very often a panel or symposium is followed by a **forum,** which provides an opportunity for audience members to comment or ask questions. In some cases, a forum is an open discussion in which members of the public share their concerns about a specific issue with one another. In other cases, a forum is an opportunity for members of the public to ask questions of and express concerns to elected officials and experts. A strong moderator is needed in a forum to make sure that audience members have an equal opportunity to speak.

Governance Group.   Public policy decisions are made in public by **governance groups.** State legislatures, city and county councils, and the governing boards of public agencies and educational institutions must conduct their meetings in public. The U.S. Congress cannot deny the public access to congressional debate. Unfortunately, most government watchers know that "real" decisions are often made in private and that the public debate is just for show. At the same time, though, an elected or appointed official's vote is not a secret. Governance group members know that if their votes are different from their public positions, they may be accused of pandering to voters.

The seven types of groups are not absolute categories. Many forms of groups overlap. A Girl Scout belongs to a social and learning group, whereas the adults who run a troop or form the national association would be classified as members of a service and a work group. Understanding the ways in which the types or forms of groups differ can help members work more efficiently and effectively.

How to Learn about Groups

Most of us would laugh if someone were trying to become a pilot or a chef just by reading a book. Likewise, no textbook or classroom lecture alone can teach us to become more effective group members. The way to study groups is to balance an understanding of theories, methods, and tools with practical experience.

Theories, Methods, and Tools

Theories, methods, and tools are inseparable components in the learning process. Peter Senge and his colleagues claim that the "synergy between theories, methods, and tools lies at the heart of any human endeavor that truly builds knowledge."[39] The interaction of theories, methods, and tools also lies at the heart of learning how to work in groups. To illustrate such synergy, Senge and his colleagues provide the following example:

> In medicine, the theory of cardiac functioning—how a healthy heart functions and the irregularities that indicate a heart attack—has led to a longstanding methodology for cardiac monitoring to track heart attacks in progress and to avert those that are starting. The method advanced significantly when electronic cardiac monitors were developed—a tool which enabled much more precise and extensive monitoring.[40]

THIS city council meeting is an example of a governance group. In what other situations do groups conduct their work publicly? (Nubar Alexanian/Stock Boston)

Theories. **Theories** are statements that explain how the world works. They try to explain or predict events and behavior. Karl Popper described theories as "nets to catch what we call 'the world': to rationalize, to explain, and to master it."[41] Small group communication theories have emerged from extensive observation and research. They help us understand what is occurring in a group and why a group succeeds or fails.

Throughout this textbook you will read about theories associated with names such as Bales, Bormann, Dewey, Donnellon, Fiedler, Fisher, Frey, Gouran, Hirokawa, Janis, Lewin, Maslow, Myers/Briggs, Poole, Putnam, Seibold, and Schutz. Learning about such theories, however, will not make you a more effective group member. Theories do not necessarily tell you what to do, or what is right or wrong. Moreover, many of the accepted theories of yesteryear have been disproved or have gone out of style. Yet, without theories, we would have difficulty understanding why or how a particular method or procedure affects group performance.

Methods. The word *method* comes from the Greek *methodos*—the means to pursue particular objectives.[42] **Methods** are strategies, guidelines, procedures, and techniques for dealing with the issues and problems that arise in groups. Throughout this textbook, you will read about individual and group methods—from leadership strategies to participation guidelines, from conflict-management techniques to decision-making procedures.

Learning about methods, however, is not enough. Effective methods are based on theories. Without theory, you won't know why a particular method works in one situation and fails in another. Methods based on theory provide a way to understand when, where, why, and how to use methods effectively.

Tools. Tools are devices used to perform work. Unlike handheld devices such as saws or hammers, the **tools** needed by groups are resources, rules, and skills that help carry out or achieve a group's common goal. Throughout this textbook, you will read about how to use researched information, assessment instruments, agendas, minutes, parliamentary procedure, and even technology-based tools. You also will learn about the ways in which communication skills function as the most important tools available to all group members. Hirokawa and Poole describe communication as the "primary tool of social action" that has a significant influence on decision making. "Like all tools, communication can shape both the user and the forces applied" to the group and its members.[43]

Like methods, tools are most effective when their use is based on theory. Although a master carpenter can tell you what tool to use, you may have no idea how to use it or why it works. Senge and his coauthors maintain that without an underlying theory, we may not "appreciate the limitations of a tool, or even its counterproductiveness, if used inappropriately."[44] In our eagerness to solve problems or achieve a group's goal, we may grab readymade, easy-to-use tools that do not address the causes of a problem or help us achieve the group's goal. Using tools without an understanding of methods and theories can make the process of working in groups inefficient, ineffective, and frustrating for all members.

In addition to the tools themselves, TOOLBOXES appear in every chapter.

TOOLBOX 1.1 Using Toolboxes

TOOLBOXES contain cross-references to the theories, methods, and tools you will find in other chapters. Learning how to work in groups is not a step-by-step process. Although the chapters in this textbook follow a logical sequence, you can go anywhere in the book to supplement your understanding and further develop your skills. If, for example, you want to learn how to construct a meeting agenda, you can turn to Chapter 14. If you have to plan and conduct a meeting, read Chapter 13. If you are nervous about speaking out in an important meeting, review the guidelines on communication apprehension in Chapter 5. If you want to understand the roles and responsibilities of group leadership, consult Chapter 3. TOOLBOXES are designed to remind you that theories, methods, and tools do not stand alone.

Experiential Learning

An understanding of theories, methods, and tools is necessary in learning how to achieve group goals. There is nothing, though, that can surpass the hands-on experiences that help members learn the complex skills needed to work effectively in groups.

Fortunately, you already have extensive experience working in groups. These experiences provide you with events and behavior to consider and analyze. Yet, experience alone may not improve your effectiveness in groups. Experiences can teach as many bad habits as good ones, and they can be misinterpreted. Participating in a disastrous discussion may not help you learn how to improve the effectiveness and efficiency of a group; instead, it may convince you to avoid working in groups at all costs.

Productive change in the behavior of group discussants depends on several experiential learning assumptions:

- You learn more from active participation in structured group experiences.
- You progress more rapidly by dealing with realistic problems.
- You improve performance when you can practice new skills without threat or evaluation.
- You better understand small group communication theories when they are applied to real-world experiences.[45]

When reading this textbook, we recommend that you add a simple, one-word question to the end of every concept you read about. That question is "So?" In other words, what is the significance of this idea or example? How does it apply to your experiences in groups? How can it affect and change the way you behave in groups? A theory may be interesting but of little benefit if you cannot apply it. Methods and tools may be clear but of little use if you don't try to use them.

Just reading this book will not necessarily make you a better and more effective group member. Participating in group discussions will. Like many skills, effective group participation requires both knowledge and practice. You *can* learn to become a more effective group member. All you need is a willingness to study and work in groups, along with the courage to challenge assumptions and try new strategies.

Balance: The Guiding Principle

This textbook includes small group communication theories, methods, and tools designed to help you and your group become more efficient and effective. At the heart of this book is a guiding principle that gives real-world significance to your experiences in and study of small group communication. We believe that an ideal group succeeds because it has achieved *balance*.

The concept of balance is a way of relating small group theories, methods, and tools to a group's goal and its members' needs. A clear goal is the point or supporting fulcrum on which a group must balance many factors. A group that reaches a decision or completes an assigned task is not in balance if every person in the group ends up hating everyone else. Also, a group that relies on one or two members to do all the work is not in balance. Effective groups balance task and social functions, individual and group needs, leadership and participation, conflict and cooperation, speaking and listening.

Task Functions	Social Functions
Advantages of Groups	Disadvantages of Groups
Theories	Methods and Tools

FIGURE 1.5   The Principle of Balance

The key to balancing the complex and even competing elements in a group discussion is a commitment to communicating effectively and working cooperatively toward the group's goal.

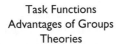

Summary Study Guide

- Working in groups is an inescapable part of life; most people spend a considerable amount of time and energy working in groups.
- Small group communication is the interaction of three or more interdependent people working toward a common goal.
- The ideal size of a small group is five to seven members.
- Group interaction requires communication among group members who use verbal and nonverbal messages to generate meanings and establish relationships within a group context.
- Communication is the medium through which group goals are accomplished.
- The most significant single factor that separates successful groups from unsuccessful ones is having a clear understanding of the group's common goal.
- Effective groups are synergistic; they combine the best qualities and talents of all members into something that surpasses anything group members could have produced without cooperative interaction.
- Three advantages of working in groups include improved performance, member satisfaction, and more learning.
- The disadvantages of working in groups include the amount of time, energy, and resources expended by groups and the interpersonal conflict and people problems that arise.
- The different types of groups can be sorted into seven group categories: primary, social, self-help, learning, service, work, and public.

- Work groups include committees and teams. Corporations have given special attention to self-management teams.
- Public groups communicate to and for the benefit of an audience. Four types of public groups are panel discussions, symposia, forums, and governance groups.
- Understanding and applying theories, methods, and tools are inseparable components in learning about the small group communication process.
- Successful groups are able to achieve balance as they confront a variety of challenges.

Groupwork *Learning about Groups in Groups*

GOAL   To establish study groups for the course.
To become acquainted with group members.

PARTICIPANTS   Groups of 5–7 members.

PROCEDURE

1. Students should arrange themselves in study groups, making sure that each group has neither too many nor too few members.
2. All members should briefly introduce themselves.
3. Group members should then address the "Study Group Issues" listed below. The group will have approximately 30 minutes to complete the discussion.
4. These groups should constitute study groups for the course. As Chapter 1 points out, individuals who study in groups tend to learn better. Groups should be encouraged to meet regularly for the remainder of the course.

Study Group Issues

- What is the goal of our group?
- How can each member best contribute to the group's goal?
- What are some frustrating experiences each member has had in other groups?
- How can the group avoid these problems?
- When and how often should we meet?
- Where should the group meet?
- How will group members contact each other outside of class?

ASSESSMENT

Basic Group Elements

Directions   Small group communication includes five basic elements: (1) group size, (2) interaction, (3) common goal, (4) interdependence, and (5) working. Think about the groups you belong to or a group that has just formed in your class or at work. Answer the following questions to assess the extent to which your group contains the basic group elements. If you can answer yes to most of the questions, your group is likely to succeed.

ELEMENTS OF SMALL GROUP COMMUNICATION

	Yes	No	Sometimes
Group Size			
1. Do group members communicate with each other directly?			
2. Does the group have enough people to achieve its goal?			
3. Can the group function effectively without forming subgroups?			
Interaction			
1. Can group members communicate with each other easily and frequently?			
2. Do members receive and respond to messages in a way that enhances communication?			
Common Goal			
1. Does the group have a clear goal?			
2. Do members understand and support the group goal?			
Interdependence			
1. Do members feel responsible for the group's actions?			
2. Do members understand their individual and group responsibilities?			
3. Do members believe "we're all in this together"?			
Working			
1. Are members ready, willing, and able to participate as active group members?			
2. Do members give the time and energy needed to achieve the group's goal?			

Recommended Readings

Katzenbach, J. R. & Smith, D. K. (1993). *The wisdom of teams: Creating the high-performance organization.* New York: HarperBusiness.

Senge, P. M., Kleiner, A., Roberts, C., Ross, R. B., & Smith, B. J. (1994). *The fifth discipline fieldbook: Strategies and tools for building a learning organization.* New York: Doubleday.

3M Meeting Management Team with J. Drew (1994). *Mastering meetings: Discovering the hidden potential of effective business meetings.* New York: McGraw-Hill.

Notes

1. Quoted in Johnson, D. W., Johnson, R. T., & Smith, K. A. (1998 July/August). "Cooperative learning returns to college." *Change,* p. 27.

2. Poole, M. S. (1991). Procedures for managing meetings: Social and technological innovation. In R. A. Swanson & B. O. Knapp (Eds.). *Innovative meeting management.* Austin, TX: Minnesota Mining & Manufacturing, p. 53.

3. McDonald, E. D. (1991). Chaos or communication: Technical barriers to effective meetings. In R. A. Swanson & B. O. Knapp (Eds.). *Innovative meeting management.* Austin, TX: Minnesota Mining & Manufacturing, p. 177.

4. Tubbs, S. L. (1995). *A systems approach to small group interaction* (5th ed.). New York: McGraw-Hill, p. 7.

5. Manz, C. C. & Sims, H. P. (1993). *Business without bosses: How self-management teams are building high-performing companies.* New York: John Wiley.

6. Katzenbach, J. R. & Smith, D. K. (1993). *The wisdom of teams: Creating the high-performance organization.* New York: HarperBusiness, p. 19.

7. Wood, J. T., Phillips, G. M., & Pedersen, D. J. (1996). Understanding the group as a system. In R. S. Cathcart, L. A. Samovar, & L. D. Henman (Eds.). *Small group communication: Theory and practice* (7th ed.). Madison, WI: Brown & Benchmark, p. 21.

8. Bonito, J. A. & Hollingshead, A. B. (1997). "Participation in small groups," In B. R. Burleson (Ed.), *Communication Yearbook 20.* Thousand Oaks, CA: Sage, p. 236.

9. Based on the Association for Communication Administration's 1995 Conference on Defining the Discipline statement that "The field of communication *focuses* on how people use verbal and nonverbal messages to generate meanings within and across various contexts, cultures, channels, and media." See *Spectra,* the official newsletter of the Speech Communication Association, October, 1995, p. 12.

10. Donnellon, A. (1996). *Team talk: The power of language in team dynamics.* Boston, MA: Harvard Business School Press.

11. Ellis, D. G. & Fisher, B. A. (1994). *Small group decision making: Communication and group process* (4th ed.). New York: McGraw-Hill, p. 88.

12. Larson, C. E. & Lafasto, F. M. J. (1989). *TeamWork: What must go right/What can go wrong.* Newbury Park, CA: Sage, p. 27.

13. Billington, J. (1997 January). "The three essentials of an effective team." *Harvard Management Update,* 2, p. 3.

14. Ellis, D. G. & Fisher, B. A. (1994). *Small group decision making: Communication and the group process.* New York: McGraw-Hill, p. 6.

15. Smith, S. M. (1991). Managing your meeting for a "bottom line payoff." In R. A. Swanson & B. O. Knapp (Eds.). *Innovative meeting management.* Austin, TX: Minnesota Mining & Manufacturing, p. 20.

16. Lazar, J. B. (1991). Ensuring productive meetings. In R. A. Swanson & B. O. Knapp (Eds.). *Innovative meeting management.* Austin, TX: Minnesota Mining & Manufacturing, p. 35.
17. Poole, p. 53.
18. Katzenbach & Smith, p. 9.
19. Senge, P. M., Kleiner, A., Roberts, C., Ross, R. B., & Smith, B. J. (1994). *The fifth discipline fieldbook: Strategies and tools for building a learning organization.* New York: Doubleday, p. 51.
20. McClernon, T. R. (1991). One hundred percent participation: Key to team effectiveness. In R. A. Swanson & B. O. Knapp (Eds.). *Innovative meeting management.* Austin, TX: Minnesota Mining & Manufacturing, p. 157.
21. Pavitt, C., & Curtis, E. (1994). *Small group discussion: A theoretical approach* (2nd ed.). Scottsdale, AZ: Gorsuch, Scarisbrick, p. 54.
22. Manz & Sims, p. 212.
23. Fiske, E. B. (March 5, 1990). How to learn in college: Group study, many tests. *The New York Times,* p. A1.
24. Johnson, Johnson, and Smith, p. 31.
25. Senge et al., p. 18.
26. Smith, p. 20.
27. 3M Meeting Management Team with J. Drew (1994). *Mastering meetings: Discovering the hidden potential of effective business meetings.* New York: McGraw-Hill, p. 12.
28. Bennis, W., Parikh, J., & Lessem, R. (1994). *Beyond leadership: Balancing economics, ethics and ecology.* Cambridge, MA: Blackwell, p. 139.
29. Bennis et al., p. 139.
30. 3M Meeting Management Team, p. 4.
31. Wuthnow, R. (1994). *Sharing the journey: Support groups and America's new quest for community.* New York: Free Press, p. 45.
32. Goodall, H. L. (1990). *Small group communication in organizations* (2nd ed.). Dubuque, IA: Wm. C. Brown.
33. Katzenbach & Smith, p. 45.
34. Dumaine, B. (February 22, 1993). The new non-manager managers. *Fortune,* p. 80.
35. Donnellon, p. 3.
36. Dumaine, p. 81.
37. Dumaine, B. (May 7, 1990). Who needs a boss? *Fortune,* p. 52.
38. Manz & Sims, p. 15.
39. Senge et al., p. 28.
40. Senge et al., pp. 28–29.
41. Popper, K. R. (1959). *The logic of scientific discovery.* New York: Basic Books, p. 59.
42. Senge et al., p. 29.
43. Hirokawa, R. Y. & Poole, M. S. (1996). *Communication and group decision making* (2nd ed.). Thousand Oaks, CA: Sage, p. 7.
44. Senge et al., p. 31.
45. See Etheridge, R. A. (1982). Conceptual approach to teaching/learning. In C. Klevins (Ed.). *Materials and methods in adult and continuing education.* Los Angeles: Klevins Publications, pp. 212–221.

$\mathcal{G}$roup Formation and Development

Why People Need Groups

Sometimes we encounter a perfect group. It has an interesting and worthwhile goal, it is composed of friendly and conscientious members, and it provides an opportunity to achieve personal goals. Without analyzing our reasons, we rush to become a member. Yet, even when a group is less than perfect, we put up with wasted time, conflict, and people problems in order to complete a task or maintain interpersonal relationships. Whether perfect or flawed, we join groups because we need them to share information, make decisions, solve problems, coordinate and implement tasks, and socialize.

Two psychological theories—Maslow's hierarchy of needs and Schutz's theory of interpersonal behavior—have made significant contributions to understanding why we join, stay in, and leave groups.

Maslow's Hierarchy of Needs

Abraham H. Maslow claims that as we move through life, some needs are more important than others. Basic survival needs must be satisfied before we can fulfill higher psychological needs. In other words, we cannot achieve personal success or meet our emotional needs if we are homeless and hungry. **Maslow's Hierarchy of Needs** ranks critical needs in the following order: physiological, safety, belongingness, esteem, and self-actualization.[1]

Although Maslow's hierarchy describes individual needs, it can be applied to the reasons people join and stay in groups. At the most basic level, people join groups to survive; at the highest level, people join groups in order to reach their own full potential.

Physiological Needs. Physiological needs are the needs of the body. A hunting/gathering clan cannot survive if members fail to work together. Families provide food, water, and shelter for both young and aging relatives. Family farms and businesses still depend on everyone's cooperative effort.

Safety Needs. Safety needs are met by groups when people join together to shelter and protect themselves. People join forces to establish police and fire departments. Unions were created to protect members from unfair labor practices. Military forces stand ready to protect our national security. Neighborhood watch groups are formed to deter crime in a community.

Belongingness Needs. Once our physical and safety needs are satisfied, belongingness needs emerge. Just about everyone wants to be liked. We create circles of friends by joining groups. Regardless of the group's purpose, people join groups to satisfy their need to belong and be loved. When teenagers try to fit in with their peers, they are pursuing a belongingness need.

Maslow's Hierarchy of Needs

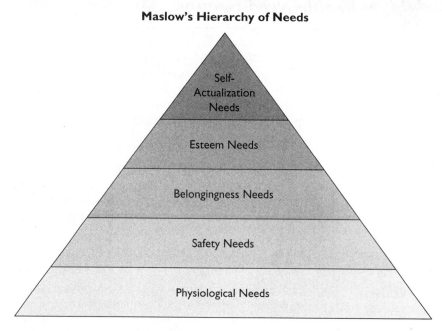

FIGURE 2.1 Maslow's Hierarchy of Needs

Esteem Needs. Esteem needs reflect our desire to feel important and valued. People who strive for group leadership are often motivated by esteem needs. Membership in certain groups can enhance a person's esteem. Being invited to join an exclusive club, being asked to serve on a prestigious task force, or being honored by a group for exceptional service are common ways in which groups satisfy our need for personal success and esteem.

Self-Actualization Needs. Our ultimate goal is what Maslow calls **self-actualization,** the need to fulfill our own human potential; the personal reward of becoming the best that we can be. Although self-actualization is an individual process, groups can enhance our ability to achieve this goal. We often join groups that we believe will help us become better individuals. Volunteering to serve meals to the needy, participating in church activities, or joining a professional organization to improve job skills are some examples of how groups can help individuals fulfill their self-actualization needs. Personal satisfaction comes from participating in a group that allows and encourages self-actualizing behavior.

Implications. Using Maslow's theory to improve a group's performance requires the translation of need satisfaction into action. For example, if members are preoccupied with issues related to job security, it may be difficult to get them to concentrate on the group's goal. If members' belongingness needs are unmet, they are likely to become more cooperative if they feel welcome and well liked. Praising and rewarding effective group behavior can satisfy esteem needs while encouraging a group to coordinate its talents and efforts toward a common goal.

There are, however, reasons to be cautious about using Maslow's hierarchy of needs to explain and predict group behavior. According to Lefton, Maslow's conclusions "seem closely tied to middle-class American cultural experience, so the theory may not be valid for all cultures or socioeconomic strata."[2]

Schutz's Theory of Interpersonal Behavior

William Schutz developed a theory of interpersonal behavior called the **Fundamental Interpersonal Relationship Orientation (FIRO)**.[3] Unlike Maslow's hierarchy of needs, FIRO concentrates on three interpersonal needs that most people share to some degree: the needs for inclusion, for control, and for affection. Schutz maintains that people join groups in order to satisfy one or more of these needs.

Inclusion.   **Inclusion** represents our need to belong, to be involved, to be accepted. For some group members, the need for inclusion is strong—they want to fit in and be appreciated by other members. For other group members, the need for inclusion may be less important—they are quite content to work without significant involvement in groups. When a group meets a member's inclusion needs, the result is what Schutz calls an **ideal social member**—a person who enjoys working with people but is comfortable working alone.

When inclusion needs are not met, members do not feel accepted; they do not fit in with the group and may engage in undersocial behavior or oversocial behavior. **Undersocial members** feel unworthy or undervalued by the group. They may withdraw and become loners. Because they believe that no one values them, they avoid being hurt by not being noticed. A quiet or unproductive member may be someone whose inclusion needs are unmet. **Oversocial members** try to attract attention to compensate for feelings of inadequacy. They seek companionship for all activities because they can't stand being alone. They try to impress other members with what and who they know.

Dealing with undersocial and oversocial members requires group behavior that satisfies inclusion needs. Making new members feel welcome and veteran members feel valued requires a careful balance between the needs of the member and the needs of the group.

Control.   **Control** refers to whether we feel competent, confident, and intelligent enough to succeed in the group. The need for control is often expressed by a member who wants to be the group's leader. For some members, the need for control is strong—they want to take charge of the group and its members. For other group members, the need for control may be less

THE members of this group working for Habitat for Humanity may have volunteered for a variety of reasons. What needs might membership in such a group fulfill? (Jim Harrison/Stock Boston)

important—they are quite content to be followers and let others lead. When a group meets a member's control need, the result is what Schutz calls a **democratic member**—a person who has no problems with power and control and who feels just as comfortable giving orders as taking them. Such members are often excellent leaders because they can exercise control when needed but put the group's goal ahead of their own needs.

Unmet control needs can result in the emergence of an abdicrat or autocrat. Both types of members have much in common, but they manifest control needs in opposite behaviors. The **abdicrat** wants control but is reluctant to pursue it. Abdicrats are often submissive members because they have no hope of having any control in the group. They will do what they are told and avoid responsibilities. The **autocrat** tries to take control by dominating the group. Autocrats may criticize other members and try to force their decisions on the group.

Dealing with abdicrats and autocrats requires granting members a sense of control appropriate to their needs. Giving members responsibility for and leadership of special projects or tasks may satisfy their need for control. For example, asking a member to chair a highly visible and important subcommittee may satisfy her or his control need.

Affection. Affection refers to the need to feel liked. Those who need affection seek close friendships, intimate relationships, and expressions of warmth from other group members. As was the case with inclusion and control, some group members have a high affection need—they want to be liked and develop strong friendships with group members. For others, the need for affection may be less important—they don't need to be liked to be a productive group member. When a group meets a member's affection needs, the result is what Schutz calls an **ideal personal member**—a person who has no emotional problems dealing with group members. While preferring to be liked, an ideal personal member is secure enough to function in a group where social interaction and affection are not high priorities.

When affection needs are not met, members do not feel liked; they become uncomfortable in the group setting. Reactions to this deficit fall into

Inclusion Needs

"I need to feel accepted by the group."

"I feel accepted by the group."

Ideal Social Member

"I don't feel accepted by
or involved in the group."

"I won't participate much
in group discussions."

Undersocial Member

"I try to gain the
group's attention."

Oversocial Member

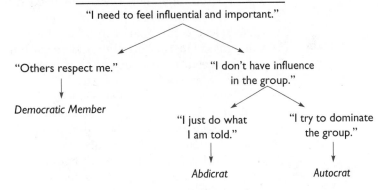

Control Needs

"I need to feel influential and important."

"Others respect me."

Democratic Member

"I don't have influence
in the group."

"I just do what
I am told."

Abdicrat

"I try to dominate
the group."

Autocrat

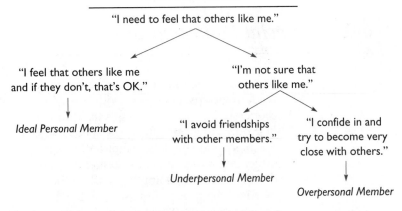

Affection Needs

"I need to feel that others like me."

"I feel that others like me
and if they don't, that's OK."

Ideal Personal Member

"I'm not sure that
others like me."

"I avoid friendships
with other members."

Underpersonal Member

"I confide in and
try to become very
close with others."

Overpersonal Member

FIGURE 2.2   Fundamental Interpersonal Relationship Orientation

two categories: underpersonal behavior and overpersonal behavior. **Underpersonal members** believe they are not liked and may establish only superficial relationships with other members. When pressed, they rarely share their honest feelings or opinions and may appear aloof and uninvolved. **Overpersonal members** try to get close to everyone. They seek intimate friendships despite the disinterest of other members. They may be too talkative, too personal, and too confiding.

Dealing with underpersonal and overpersonal members requires expressions of fondness and friendliness to those who need affection. Expressing liking to new members and taking time to communicate affection to long-standing members can take extra time but has the potential to convert unsatisfied participants into ideal personal members.

Implications.   Using Schutz's theory to improve a group's performance requires adapting to members' inclusion, control, and affection needs. For example, a member who seeks attention or tries to impress other members may have a strong inclusion need. This need can be satisfied by praising good work. When members who have strong control needs are not capable or eligible to lead a group, there may be value in assigning them to head up a special project. Just as praising and rewarding effective group behavior can satisfy esteem needs, such reinforcement can help group members feel included, competent, and well liked.

There are, however, reasons to be cautious about using FIRO theory to explain and predict group behavior. Undersocial behavior may not reflect unmet inclusion needs; the member may be quite comfortable and happy working alone. Overpersonal behavior may not reflect unmet affection needs; such behavior may be an enthusiastic attempt to create a positive social climate for the group. Moreover, Schutz's conclusions have not been fully researched for different cultures and socioeconomic groups.

Task and Social Dimensions

Beyond psychological theories, there are practical reasons why we join and work in groups. Groups provide a way to get a job done with congenial and cooperative people. A group's **task dimension** focuses on the job—the goal or product of group effort. The **social dimension** is concerned with people—the interpersonal relationships among group members. For example, a group discussing a department's budget is primarily focused on its task, or issues directly related to doing the work of the group. However, if at the end of the meeting, the group surprises a fellow member with a cake in celebration of her birthday, the focus of group interaction is the social dimension. More

> **TOOLBOX 2.1**   Task and Maintenance Roles
>
> The task and social dimensions of a group are so powerful that they have been used to analyze and predict member behavior. Task and social functions have been separated and sorted into lists of task roles, social maintenance roles, and self-centered roles that a member may assume. For example, the role of initiator assumes the task function of proposing new ideas and suggestions. A harmonizer assumes a social maintenance function by helping resolve conflicts and mediating differences among group members. Beyond the task and social dimensions, self-centered roles, such as blocker and special interest pleader, stand in the way of progress and group unity. **Chapter 4: Participation in Groups** devotes an entire section to a functional theory of participation and describes the impact of task, maintenance, and self-centered roles on group achievement and member satisfaction.

often, a group exhibits both task- and social-oriented behaviors throughout its interactions. That is, as we engage in communication that allows the group to get the job done, we do it in a way that makes others feel socially accepted and valued. The task and social dimensions of a group "exert mutual and reciprocal influences on each other and are thus virtually inseparable in practice."[4] It can be just as difficult and frustrating to work on a task when the participants do not get along with each other as it is to work with friends who don't take the task seriously.

All work and no play makes you dull. All play and no work makes you unemployed. A coordinated balance makes you more productive. While both teamwork and social work are essential to team success, getting the whole team in sync is important.[5]

How Groups Develop

Regardless of the reasons why people join and stay in groups, there are recognizable milestones in the life of most small groups. Like individuals, groups move through stages as they grow and mature. An "infant" group behaves differently from a group that has worked together for a long time and matured into an "adult." Just as there are theories to explain why people need groups, there are theories that try to explain how a group moves through several "passages" during its lifetime.

Tuckman's Stages

Tuckman claims that groups go through four basic and predictable stages of development, each of which contains both task and maintenance functions.[6]

Stage 1: Forming
Stage 2: Storming
Stage 3: Norming
Stage 4: Performing

During the **forming stage,** group members are cautious and somewhat uncomfortable about meeting a group of strangers. During this stage, group members try to define their tasks and test personal relationships. "For now, the most important job for this team is not to build a better rocket or debug a beta version of a new software product or double sales—it is to orient itself to itself."[7]

Once the group knows what it is supposed to do as well as who will be involved in the effort, the second stage begins. During the **storming stage,** groups become more argumentative and emotional as they discuss important issues and ideas. Many groups are tempted to skip this stage in an effort to avoid conflict. However, storming is a necessary part of a group's development. Without it, the group may be unsure of individual members' roles, who's in charge, or even what the group's goal is.

> Storming is . . . like internal combustion. If you place a teaspoon of gasoline on a sidewalk it quickly disperses, more or less harmlessly. Compressed in an engine cylinder, however, its vaporized particles begin to bounce into one another at supersonic speeds. Ideally, a controlled explosion occurs, and a vehicle many thousands of times the weight and size of that teaspoon of fuel begins to move. When that happens, the storm has broken. Roles clarify. A team style begins to materialize.[8]

During the **norming stage,** conflicts are resolved, and the group begins working as a team to find acceptable ways to achieve its goal. There is more order and direction during this third stage of group development.

> . . . The group itself can finally be said to have a relationship with itself. . . . [H]idden agendas covertly advanced by members during storming . . . have been unmasked or diminished in importance. . . . Information is freely shared, and the group conducts periodic agenda checks to remind itself of its goals and take note of its progress.[9]

In the **performing stage,** group members focus their energies. Decisions are reached and solutions are agreed upon.

> With the sharing of the experiences, feelings, and ideas of other team members comes a new level of consciousness—the sense of knowing where other team members are at, a sense of fierce loyalty even to members you may not be friendly with, and a willingness to find a way through nearly any challenge that arises. . . . The atmosphere is one of enthusiasm and *esprit de corps.*[10]

Fisher's Phases   B. Aubrey Fisher also describes four phases of group development.[11] However, unlike Tuckman's stages, Fisher's phases focus on decision-making groups. Fisher suggests that an ideal decision-making group will experience the following phases.

> Phase 1: Orientation
> Phase 2: Conflict
> Phase 3: Emergence
> Phase 4: Reinforcement

In the **orientation phase,** group members get to know one another and the requirements of their assigned or agreed-upon task. Often, members are hesitant to express strong opinions in this phase until they know more about how other members think and feel.

> Members clarify and agree most often at this time. . . . They do not quickly or strongly assert themselves or their opinions. . . . This stage is a period of forming opinions, not rocking the boat.[12]

During the **conflict phase,** group members express their opinions and make suggestions. Controversy and conflict are normal during this period. In the conflict phase, group members make up their minds. They argue for or against positions.

> Not only do members express less ambiguous attitudes, but they also express them more tenaciously. They now provide data and evidence to substantiate these beliefs and engage in full-fledged debate with other members.[13]

In the **emergence phase,** a search for solutions and decisions replaces argumentation. Group members seem more willing to listen to compromise suggestions and search for agreement. Uncertainty recurs. Although there may be resistance to a proposal, the opposition is weaker and appears willing to accept modifications.

> The third phase is probably the crucial stage in the group process of decision making. During this third phase the eventual outcome of group interaction becomes increasingly more apparent.[14]

Finally, during the **reinforcement phase,** group members agree upon a decision or solution. Everyone shares, supports, and justifies a common viewpoint.

> Pervading this final phase in group decision making is a spirit of unity. . . . Their interaction patterns reflect virtually no tension; rather, the members are jovial, loud, boisterous, laughing, and verbally backslapping each other.[15]

Implications   Tuckman's stages and Fisher's phases are only two of the many theories that attempt to explain the process of group development. While each theory uses different words to describe parts of the process, many of these theories are strikingly similar in their descriptions of group development. In an effort to explain group development that recognizes the observations of many of these theories, Wheelan created an integrative model that describes five distinct stages groups will experience.[16] The first stage is **dependency and inclusion.** Because members are unfamiliar with each other and the task, the group tends to depend on the leader more for direction. Group interaction tends to be tentative and polite. The second stage of **counterdependency and fight** is characterized by conflict. In stage three, **trust and structure,** members define roles and determine group procedures. **Work** is the fourth stage of group development. Having resolved much of the conflict related to group organization, members are able to perform the tasks necessary to accomplish the group goal. The final stage of **termination** describes the point at which the goal has been achieved and the group begins to disband.

Group development theories have been useful to explain why and how groups and their members behave at different points in their development. Consider how inappropriate or disruptive it would be if a member were to cast caution aside on the first day of a group's existence and demand acceptance of a particular position. What would happen if members never matured beyond either the forming stage or the orientation phase? The group would become bogged down in procedural details or polite conversation rather than dealing with its task.

One researcher who has taken a closer look at these phases is Marshall Scott Poole. He suggests that Fisher's phases are "ideal" phases but that groups often stray from the ideal path. Poole and Roth identified factors that can derail a group from an ideal sequence of phases.[17] Included in these factors are group size, the level of member cooperation, the clarity of goals, the history of conflict, the availability of information and possible solutions, and the concentration of power in the group. For example, a very large group may be unable to get past the early stages of group development. If a group's goal is unclear, the result will be wasted time, member frustration, and unproductive work. If, however, members are cooperative, a group will move through the stages much more easily.

Tuckman's Stages	Fisher's Phases	Integrative Model
Forming	Orientation	Dependency and inclusion
Storming	Conflict	Counterdependency and fight
Norming	Emergence	Trust and structure
Performing	Reinforcement	Work
		Termination

FIGURE 2.3   Phases of Group Development

Group Norms

One factor that influences a group's passage from forming to performing is the creation of norms. Patricia Andrews defines **norms** as "sets of expectations held by group members concerning what kinds of behavior or opinion are acceptable or unacceptable, good or bad, right or wrong, appropriate or inappropriate."[18] Norms are the group's rules. They determine how members behave, dress, speak, and work. For example, the norms for the members of a company's sales team might include meeting before lunch, applauding each other's successes, and wearing suits to work. Without norms, accomplishing group goals would be difficult. There would be no agreed-upon way to organize and perform work.

Some norms, however, can work against a group and its goals. If group norms place a premium on friendly and peaceful discussions, then its members may be reluctant to voice disagreement or share bad news. If group norms permit members to arrive late and leave early, there may be times when a meeting lacks enough members to make important decisions. Norms that do not support a group's goal can prevent the group from succeeding.

Identifying Norms

There are two general types of group norms—implicit and explicit. Because **explicit norms** are put in writing or are stated verbally, they are easy to recognize. Explicit norms are often imposed on a group. The group leader may have the authority to determine rules. A large group or organization may have standard procedures it expects everyone to follow; for example, the workers in a customer services department may be required to wear name

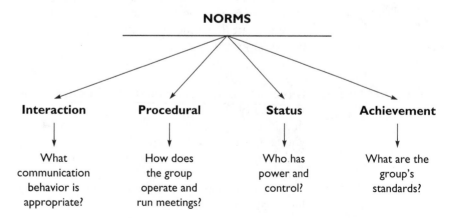

FIGURE 2.4 Types of Norms

CONFORMITY to norms is essential to the success of many groups. Why is conformity important for this group of soldiers? (Norman Rowan/Stock Boston)

badges. The staff may have recommended this rule, the supervisor may have ordered this "custom," or the company may have established a policy regarding employee identification.

Because **implicit norms** are rarely discussed or openly communicated, they are not as easy to recognize. Generally they are the result of group interaction. For example, it may take new group members several weeks to learn that meetings begin fifteen minutes later than scheduled. Even seating arrangements may be governed by implicit norms. Group members often learn about an implicit norm when it has been violated. Almost all of us have been unsettled when walking into a classroom to discover someone sitting at "our" desk. Groups rarely discuss such rules. However, offending members soon sense that an implicit norm has been violated.

Regardless of whether they are openly communicated or implicitly understood, norms can be divided into four categories: interaction norms, procedural norms, status norms, and achievement norms. **Interaction norms** determine how group members communicate with one another and will help you determine what types of communication behavior are appropriate in a group. **Procedural norms** dictate how the group will operate and will help you adapt to the rules and procedures the group typically follows. Status refers to the degree of prestige, respect, or influence a person possesses. **Status norms** identify the levels of influence among group members and how status is determined. **Achievement norms** determine the quality and quantity of work expected from group members. They can help you make decisions about how much time and energy must be devoted to working with a particular group.

Conformity and Norms

Group norms function only to the extent that members conform to them. **Conformity** requires choosing "a course of action that a majority favors or that is socially acceptable."[19] We learn the value of conformity at a very young age. In the classroom, children learn that standing in line and raising their hands are expected behaviors. On the playground, children who refuse to play by the rules may find themselves playing alone.

Although some group members may have reasons for ignoring or wanting to change norms, most groups pressure members to conform. According to Napier and Gershenfeld, you are more likely to conform to norms when one or more of the following factors are present:

- You want to continue your membership in the group.
- You have a lower status than other members and don't want to risk being seen as an upstart.
- You strongly support the group's principles and goals.
- You get along and like working with the other group members.
- You may be punished for violating norms and/or rewarded for compliance.[20]

Constructive Deviation

Members decide whether they will conform or deviate from group norms or expectations. **Deviation** occurs when a member does not conform to the expectations of the group. Although conformity to norms is essential to the functioning of a group, deviation from norms can, in some cases, improve group performance.

Members may deviate from the group when they have legitimate concerns and alternative suggestions. **Constructive deviation** occurs when a member resists a norm while still working to promote a group goal. The following statements are examples of constructive deviation:

- "I know we always ask the newest group member to take minutes during the meeting, but we may be losing the insight of an experienced member and skilled notetaker by continuing this practice."
- "I can't attend any more meetings if they're going to last for three hours."

When a member voices concerns or objections, the other members are forced to defend positions, address important issues, and explore alternatives. These discussions can lead to better decisions and discourage the hasty adoption of inferior solutions. In contrast, **destructive deviation** occurs when a member resists conformity without regard for the best interests of the group and its goal.

Deviation of either type provides a group with an opportunity to examine its norms. When members deviate, the group may have to discuss the value of a particular norm and subsequently choose to change, clarify, or continue to accept it. At the very least, deviant behavior helps members recognize and understand the norms of the group. For instance, if a member is reprimanded for criticizing an office policy, other members will learn that the boss should not be challenged. Some groups will attempt to correct nonconforming members or may change their norms as a result of constructive deviation. However, when deviation becomes highly disruptive, members may ignore or exclude the nonconforming member from the group.

TOOLBOX 2.2 Groupthink

Groupthink is a phenomenon that occurs when a group fails to sufficiently evaluate its decisions in order to achieve agreement. Pressure to conform to group norms may discourage members from expressing disagreement or questioning a group's decisions and actions. The tragic explosion of the space shuttle *Challenger* might have been avoided if NASA officials had recognized the extent to which groupthink was controlling the decision-making process. Several launch team members have admitted that pressure to conform inhibited them from expressing reservations about the launch decision. Constructive deviation can help prevent groupthink. **Chapter 8: Conflict and Cohesion in Groups** describes the symptoms of groupthink and ways to prevent it.

Dealing with Change

Although we form groups to satisfy task and social needs, the goal, membership, and norms of a group can change over time. Change may come about because some of the group's needs have been satisfied or because new needs have arisen. Change can also occur when outside demands or innovations affect a group's work. As groups evolve, their changing goals, changing membership, and changing norms can have a significant effect on their ultimate success.

Changing Goals

Group goals should be continually reexamined and changed when necessary, although doing so often requires difficult adjustments. However, groups that fail to revise their goals and meet new challenges are not likely to be very successful. For example, rather than trying to recruit more students, a college may change its goal to that of retaining and improving the graduation rate of students who are currently enrolled. The following list of suggestions can help a group adapt to changing goals:

- Continually evaluate the group's goal. Is the original goal still worth achieving?
- Use members' expertise and skills flexibly. Are members assigned to tasks that maximize their talents?

- Eliminate tasks that are no longer useful. Have some tasks become routine rather than necessary?

Just as our own needs and goals change as we mature, effective groups understand that the goals of yesterday may not serve the group of today. Groups that refuse to examine or modify their goals may miss opportunities to excel.

Changing Membership

Most people join an existing group rather than one that is forming. In fact, many groups have had a long history before a newcomer joins them. Moreland and Levine point out that "the entry of a newcomer into the group can threaten its development by forcing members to alter their relationships with one another."[21] New members are challenged to catch up and fit in.

The following tips can be helpful when joining an existing group:

- If possible, learn about the group before you join. Try to find out about its explicit and implicit norms.
- Initially, assume the role of "newcomer" by avoiding disagreement and critical comments about the group or its members.
- Seek a mentor within the group who will provide advice and guidance.

Being a new member can be an awkward and uncomfortable experience. Learning as much as you can and seeking the support of others will make your initial interactions with the group much easier.

Changing Norms

When norms no longer meet the needs of a group or its members, new ones should be established. Some norms may be too rigid or too vague. Other norms may have outlived their usefulness. Norms can be difficult to change, especially when they are implicit or unspoken. Napier and Gershenfeld identify the following ways in which changes in group norms typically occur:

- Through contagious behavior, as in dress style and speech patterns.
- Through the suggestions of high-status members.
- Through the suggestions or actions of highly confident members.
- Through the suggestions of consultants.
- Through group discussion and decision making (for explicit norms).
- Through continued interaction (for implicit norms).[22]

Some members will resist changes in norms because change can be disruptive and threatening. However, norms that are no longer useful can impede a group's progress. The natural development of most groups requires changes in goals, memberships, and norms.

Balancing Needs and Norms

Throughout the group process, members must work to balance a group's task and social needs. Placing too much emphasis on the task may create dissatisfaction among members who lack motivation to do the group's work. Too much attention to social needs may result in group members who enjoy each other's company but neglect their work. An effective group fulfills the personal needs of members, promotes positive relationships among members, and accomplishes the group's goal.

An effective group also balances its members' individual needs with the work needed to accomplish the group's goal. When a group satisfies its members' needs, it is more likely to achieve its goal. And when a group achieves its goal, members are more likely to be happy and proud of working in the group. When a group is forming, the social dimension may require more attention than the task. However, once a group has moved beyond the early stages of development, it can reduce its concentration on social needs in order to focus its time and energy on the task dimension.

As a group develops, the costs and benefits of adhering to group norms must also be balanced. If members recklessly deviate from norms, the group's equilibrium will be upset. If, on the other hand, members place too much value on conformity, the group may fail to make effective decisions. As a group develops, it also changes. Whether those changes represent the natural phases of group development or the transformation imposed by changes in goals, membership, and norms, an effective group monitors and adapts to change in order to preserve the necessary balance between the task and social dimensions of group development.

Group Formation   Group Development
Conformity to Norms   Deviation from Norms
Task Dimensions   Social Dimensions

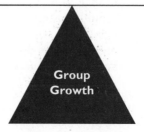

FIGURE 2.5 Group Growth

Summary Study Guide

- Maslow's hierarchy of needs consists of physiological, safety, belonging-ness, esteem, and self-actualization needs, all of which may be satisfied by participation in a group.
- Schutz's FIRO theory identifies three interpersonal needs (inclusion, control, and affection) that affect member behavior and group effectiveness.
- The ideal social member's inclusion needs are met. When inclusion needs are not met, members may engage in undersocial or oversocial behavior.
- The democratic member's control needs are met. When control needs are not met, members may become abdicrats or autocrats.
- The ideal personal member's affection needs are met. When affection needs are not met, members may engage in underpersonal or overper-sonal behavior.
- All groups have interrelated task and social dimensions that affect goal achievement and member satisfaction.
- Tuckman's stages of group development are forming, storming, norm-ing, and performing.
- Fisher's phases of group development are orientation, conflict, emer-gence, and reinforcement.
- The integrated model of group development stages are dependency and inclusion, counterdependency and fight, trust and structure, work, and termination.
- Norms are expectations held by group members concerning acceptable behavior; norms can be explicit or implicit.
- Norms can be divided into four categories: interaction norms, proce-dural norms, status norms, and achievement norms.
- Constructive deviation occurs when members resist norms while still working to promote the group's goal.
- As groups evolve, factors such as changing goals, changing member-ship, and changing norms can have a significant impact on the group's growth, development, and success.

Groupwork *Classroom Norms*

GOAL To understand the purpose and impact of implicit and explicit norms.

PARTICIPANTS Groups of 5–7 members.

PROCEDURE

1. Each group should generate a list of the implicit and explicit norms that operate in many of their classes.
   - Example of Implicit Norm: When students come in late, they tiptoe to the closest available seat near the door.
   - Example of Explicit Norm: The syllabus states that no make-up work will be allowed if students do not have legitimate, written excuses.
2. Each group should rank the norms on each list in terms of their usefulness in ensuring quality instruction and effective learning.
3. Groups should post their lists and compare them with the norms generated by other groups. The class should discuss the following questions:
   - Do any norms appear on all or most of the lists?
   - Which norms are most important?
   - Are there more implicit than explicit norms?
   - Should any of the norms be changed, strengthened, or abolished in this class?

ASSESSMENT

Group Attraction Survey

Directions   Think of an effective group in which you currently work or have worked in the past. Try to keep the group you select in mind as you complete this assessment instrument. The following 15 statements describe possible reasons why you joined or are attracted to your group. Indicate the degree to which each statement applies to you by marking whether you (5) strongly agree, (4) agree, (3) are undecided, (2) disagree, or (1) strongly disagree. Work quickly and record your first impression.

_____ 1. I like having authority and high status in the group.

_____ 2. I want the other group members to act friendly toward me.

_____ 3. Group members help each other solve personal problems.

_____ 4. I am proud when the group achieves a goal or an objective.

_____ 5. I try to be an active participant in group activities.

_____ 6. Some group members are close friends.

_____ 7. I become upset if group members waste time and effort.

_____ 8. I like to do things with group members outside the group.

_____ 9. Group members are excellent decision makers and problem solvers.

_____ 10. Group members like me.

_____ 11. I work hard to be a valuable group member.

_____ 12. I try to influence the opinions and actions of group members.

_____ 13. I like it when group members invite me to join their activities.

_____ 14. I enjoy talking to members about things unrelated to the group's goal.

_____ 15. I try to get group members to do things the way I want them done.

Scoring

Seek Task Achievement
   Add your responses to items 4, 7, and 9: _____
Seek Social Goals
   Add your responses to items 3, 8, and 14: _____
Seek Inclusion
   Add your responses to items 5, 11, and 13: _____

(continued)

(Group Attraction Survey, *continued***)**

Seek Control
    Add your responses to items 1, 12, and 15: _____
Seek Affection
    Add your responses to items 2, 6, and 10: _____

A score of 12 or above in any category indicates that this source of attraction is an important reason why you joined and stay in this group. A score of 6 or below indicates that this source of attraction was not an important factor in why you joined and not a major reason why you stay in this group. Examining your attraction to other groups in which you work may result in different scores.

Recommended Readings

Cathcart, R. S., Samovar, L. A., & Henman, L. D. (Eds.), (1996). *Small group communication: Theory and practice* (7th ed.). Madison, WI: Brown & Benchmark.

Napier, R. W. & Gershenfeld, M. K. (1993). *Groups: Theory and experience* (5th ed.). Boston: Houghton Mifflin.

Pavitt, C. & Curtis, E. (1994). *Small group discussion: A theoretical approach* (2nd ed.). Scottsdale, AZ: Gorsuch, Scarisbrick.

Robbins, H. & Finley, M. (1995). *Why teams don't work: What went wrong and how to make it right.* Princeton, NJ: Peterson's/Pacesetter Books.

Notes

1. Maslow, A. H. (1954). *Motivation and personality.* New York: Harper & Row.
2. Lefton, L. A. (1994). *Psychology* (5th ed.). Needham Heights, MA: Paramount, p. 372.
3. Schutz, W. C. (1958). *FIRO: A three-dimensional theory of interpersonal behavior.* New York: Holt, Rinehart, & Winston.
4. Ellis, D. G. & Fisher, B. A. (1994). *Small group decision making: Communication and the group process* (4th ed.). New York: McGraw-Hill, p. 51.
5. Robbins, H. & Finley, M. (1995). *Why teams don't work: What went wrong and how to make it right.* Princeton, NJ: Peterson's/Pacesetter Books, p. 26.
6. Tuckman, B. W. (1965). Developmental sequence in small groups. *Psychological Bulletin, 63*, pp. 384–399.
7. Robbins & Finley, p. 191.
8. Robbins & Finley, pp. 196–197.
9. Robbins & Finley, pp. 197–198.
10. Robbins & Finley, pp. 199–200.
11. Fisher, B. A. (1970). Decision emergence: Phases in group decision making. *Speech Monographs, 37*, pp. 53–66.
12. Ellis & Fisher, pp. 157 & 158.
13. Ellis & Fisher, p. 158.
14. Ellis & Fisher, p. 160.

15. Ellis & Fisher, p. 160.
16. Wheelan, S. A. (1994). *Group processes: A developmental perspective.* Boston: Allyn & Bacon, pp. 14–19.
17. Poole, M. S. & Roth, J. (1989). Decision development in small groups, V: Test of a contingency model. *Human Communication Research, 15,* pp. 549–589.
18. Andrews, P. H. (1996). Group conformity. In R. S. Cathcart, L. A. Samovar, & L. D. Henman (Eds.), *Small group communication: Theory and practice* (7th ed.). Madison, WI: Brown & Benchmark, p. 185.
19. Pavitt, C. & Curtis, E. (1994). *Small group discussion: A theoretical approach* (2nd ed.). Scottsdale, AZ: Gorsuch, Scarisbrick, p. 178.
20. Napier, R. W. & Gershenfeld, M. K. (1993). *Groups: Theory and experience* (5th ed.). Boston: Houghton Mifflin, pp. 152–155.
21. Moreland, R. & Levine, J. (1987). Group dynamics over time: Development and socialization in small groups. In J. McGrath (Ed.), *The social psychology of time.* Beverly Hills, CA: Sage, p. 156.
22. Napier & Gershenfeld, pp. 161–162.

*L*eadership in Groups

What Is Leadership?

All groups need leadership. Without leadership, a group may be nothing more than a collection of individuals lacking the coordination and motivation to achieve a common goal. Cathcart and Samovar maintain, "There are no successful groups without leaders. . . . Leaders lead because groups demand it and rely on leaders to satisfy needs."[1]

In his book *Certain Trumpets: The Call of Leaders,* Garry Wills offers a definition of leadership that describes what a leader does: "The leader is one who mobilizes others toward a goal shared by leader and followers. . . . Leaders, followers, and goals make up the three equally necessary supports for leadership."[2] Without willing followers and shared goals, you may possess the title of leader but still accomplish nothing.

The Wills definition, however, does not acknowledge that an effective leader needs decision-making and communication skills in order to influence and motivate group members toward achieving a goal shared by leader and followers. **Leadership,** then, can be defined as the ability to make strategic decisions and use communication to mobilize group members toward achieving a shared goal.

A leader and leadership are not the same. Leader is the title given to a person; leadership refers to the action that a leader takes to help group members achieve shared goals. Some groups have no official leader but instead have one or more members who engage in leadership behaviors. Other groups may have designated leaders who fail to behave in ways typically associated with leadership.

> Lee is the manager of our department, so he's technically our leader. Lee always follows procedures and meets deadlines for paperwork, so I guess he's a good manager. But, we don't get much guidance or motivation from

---

TOOLBOX 3.1 Chairing a Meeting

The person who chairs a meeting may not be the same person who serves as a group's leader. Although a leader often calls and conducts meetings, that responsibility may also be delegated to someone other than the leader, particularly when a group breaks into subcommittees or when a leader wants to be a more active participant in a group's deliberations. Maintaining order during a meeting and facilitating a productive discussion are the primary responsibilities of the chairperson. **Chapter 13: Planning and Conducting Meetings** describes the methods and tools available to group members who have the responsibility of planning and chairing a meeting.

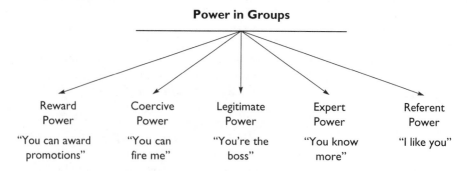

FIGURE 3.1 Power in Groups

him. I just think managing tasks and real leadership of people are somehow different. Allison supervises the other department. She seems to inspire her workers. They're more innovative and work closely with each other. We do our job, but they seem to be on a mission. I've always thought that working for Allison would be more fulfilling.

Becoming an effective group leader requires an understanding of leadership theories, methods, and tools.

Leadership and Power

It is impossible to understand effective leadership and the skills of an effective leader without understanding the importance of power. As Jesuíno has written, "The capacity of a leader to influence [group members] is another way of saying that the leader has power over the followers."[3] In the hands of a just and wise leader, power is a positive force; in the hands of an unjust and foolish leader, power can be destructive. Bennis and Nanus contend that power is "the quality without which leaders cannot lead."[4]

Power is the ability or authority to influence and motivate others. One of the traditional ways to analyze power in a group discussion is found in the categories of power developed by French and Raven.[5] They divide power into five categories: reward power, coercive power, legitimate power, expert power, and referent power.

Reward Power

Reward power derives from the leader's authority to give group members something they value. Whether the reward is a cash bonus, a promotion, or a convenient work schedule, its effectiveness depends on whether group members value the reward. Some leaders may think they have power because they control group rewards, only to discover that those rewards have little value for members. Employees may not want a promotion if the new job is less appealing than their current job. Only when the reward is worthwhile will group members respond to a leader who uses this kind of power.

Coercive Power

If the carrot approach doesn't work, a leader may resort to using a stick: **coercive power.** Another way to describe coercive power is to call it punishment power. When leaders can discipline, demote, or dismiss group members, they have coercive power. Hackman and Johnson contend that "coercion is most effective when those subject to this form of power are aware of expectations and are warned in advance about the penalties for failure to comply. . . . Leaders using coercive power must consistently carry out threatened punishments."[6] In emergency situations, coercive power may be the only way to rescue a project or safeguard a group. However, coercive power can be counterproductive. A skillful leader uses coercive power sparingly and only when all other means of influence have failed to mobilize group members toward achieving their shared goal.

Legitimate Power

Legitimate power resides in a job, position, or assignment rather than in a person. For example, elected officials have the power to vote on the public's behalf; committee chairpersons are authorized to take control of their assigned tasks; supervisors have authority over their workers. The word *legitimate* means "lawful" or "proper." Most people believe it is lawful and proper that a judge make decisions and keep order in a courtroom. Group leaders may call meetings, assign tasks, and evaluate members as part of their legitimate duties.

Expert Power

Expert power is assigned to someone who has demonstrated a particular skill or special knowledge. Just as we may accept the advice of a doctor when we're ill or that of an auto mechanic when we've broken down on the highway, we are more likely to grant power to an expert. When, however, the advice of supposed experts proves incorrect, their power will fade and even disappear. A leader can rely on expert power only if the group has recognized the leader as a well-informed and reliable authority.

Referent Power

Hackman and Johnson write that "**referent power** is role model power—the ability to influence others that arises when one person admires another."[7] Referent power is the personal power or influence held by people who are admired and respected. When certain individuals demonstrate that they are effective communicators, talented organizers, shrewd problem solvers, and good listeners, we are more likely to be influenced by them. We often feel honored to work with someone who has strong referent power. Referent or personal power is very influential because it is recognized and conferred by the group rather than by an outside source.

In most groups, a leader employs several kinds of power depending on the needs of the group and the situation. Some leaders may have the power to reward and coerce as well as having legitimate, expert, and referent power. In other groups, a leader may depend entirely on one type of power to get a group to work cooperatively toward a goal. The more power a leader has, the more carefully the use of that power must be balanced with the needs of the group. If you exert too much power, your group may lose its energy and enthusiasm. If you don't exert enough power, your group may flounder and fail. Gaining power is not the same as using it wisely.

Becoming a Leader

Anyone can become a leader. Abraham Lincoln and Harry S Truman rose from humble beginnings and hardship to become U.S. presidents. Exceptional athletes such as Arthur Ashe and Cal Ripken overcame enormous odds to become all-American heroes and spokespersons for worthy causes. Corporate executives have worked their way up from the sales force (Ross Perot) and secretarial pools (Ardis Krainik, General Director of the Lyric Opera of Chicago) to become chief executive officers. Yet, as inspiring as these examples may be, leaders are not necessarily the hardest workers or the smartest employees. The path to a leadership position can be as easy as being in the right place at the right time or being the only person willing to take on a difficult job. Becoming the leader, chairperson, or president of a group occurs in many different ways.

Designated Leaders
Designated leaders are deliberately and purposely selected by a group or an outside authority. You may be hired for a job that gives you authority over others. You may be promoted or elected to a leadership position. Your boss may create a special work team or subcommittee and assign you to be its leader. In all these cases, the selection of the leader depends on an election or an appointment. Those who choose leaders should base their decisions on a candidate's qualifications and abilities. Unfortunately, less-than-deserving people are sometimes appointed or elected to powerful positions. Electing a compromise candidate or appointing a politically connected member as a leader is too common a practice and no guarantee of leadership ability. Is it possible, then, for a designated leader to be an effective leader? Of course it is. When a leader's abilities match the needs of the group and its goal, there is a greater likelihood of success.

Unique challenges face a leader chosen by a source outside the group. When a new leader enters a well-established group, there can be a long and difficult period of adjustment for everyone. One student described this difficult process as follows:

> For five summers, I worked as a counselor at a county day camp for underprivileged children. Harry was our boss and all of us liked him. We worked hard for Harry because we knew he'd look the other way if we showed up late or left early on a Friday. As long as the kids were safe and supervised, he didn't bother us. When Harry was promoted into management at the county government office, we got Frank. The first few weeks were awful. Frank would dock us if we were late. No one could leave early. He demanded that we come up with more activities for the kids. Weekend pool parties were banned. He even made us attend a counselors' meeting every morning rather than once every couple of weeks. But, in the end, most of us had to admit that Frank was a better camp director. The camp did more for the kids and that was the point.

Both Harry and Frank were leaders with legitimate power. What made them different were the various kinds of power available to them. Because Harry had earned the admiration and respect of the staff, he could rely on his personal, or referent, power. Frank, however, had to use coercive power to establish order.

Before designated leaders can effectively lead, they must gain the group's trust by demonstrating their competence and good character. Thus, if a leader appears to have good intentions yet is viewed as incompetent, members won't have faith in the leader's abilities. Likewise, a competent person with questionable motives will lack the trust of group members.[8]

When a leader is elected or appointed from within a group, the problems can be as difficult as with a leader from outside the group. If the person who once worked next to you becomes your boss, the adjustment can be problematic. Here is the way a business executive described how difficult it was when she was promoted to vice president:

> When I was promoted, I became responsible for making decisions that affected my colleagues, many of whom were close friends. I was given the

INDIVIDUALS with ordinary backgrounds can become exceptional leaders. What events or characteristics do you believe contribute to the success of such leaders? (© Kraft/Sygma)

authority to approve projects, recommend salary increases, and grant promotions. Colleagues who had always been open and honest with me were more cautious and careful about what they said. I had to deny requests from people I cared about while approving requests from colleagues with whom I often disagreed. Even though I'm the same person I was as a manager, I was treated differently and, as a result, I behaved differently.

Being plucked from a group in order to lead it can present problems because it changes the nature of your relationship with the other group members. Your fellow group members whom you consider friends wonder if that has changed. Others fear that you will favor your friends. Some members may resent that they were not chosen to lead the group. Even though the members know you well, you still must earn their trust in your leadership abilities. Initially, try involving the group in decision making as much as possible. Discuss ground rules for interaction with friends within the group while assuring them of your continued friendship. Finally, openly and honestly addressing leadership concerns with group members and seeking their suggestions may resolve many potential problems.[9] Whether you are an outsider or a promoted member newly designated to lead a group, it takes time and energy to develop group members' trust.

Emergent Leaders

Very often, the most effective leadership occurs when a leader emerges from a group rather than being promoted, elected, or appointed. The leaders of many political, religious, and neighborhood organizations emerge. Ellis and Fisher maintain that "When people achieve leadership status gradually, the process is termed leadership emergence."[10] **Emergent leaders** gradually achieve leadership by interacting with group members and contributing to the achievement of the group's goal. The leader who emerges from within a group has significant advantages. He or she does not have to spend time learning about the group, its goals, and its norms. In addition, a leader who emerges from within a group has some assurance that the group wants him or her to be the leader rather than having to accept leadership because an election or outside authority says it must. Such leaders usually have referent power—a significant factor in mobilizing members toward the group's goal.

Strategies for Becoming a Leader

Although there is no foolproof method, there are strategies that can improve your chances of emerging or being designated as a group's leader. The following strategies require a balanced approach, one that takes advantage of opportunities without abusing the privilege of leadership:

- Talk early and often (and listen).
- Know more (and share it).
- Offer your opinion (and welcome disagreement).
- Volunteer for meaningful roles (and follow through).

Talk Early and Often (and Listen).   Of all the strategies that can help you attain the position of group leader, the most reliable have to do with when and how much you talk. According to Hollander, the person who speaks first and most often is more likely to emerge as the group's leader.[11] The number of contributions is even more important than the quality of those contributions. The quality of contributions becomes more significant after you become a leader. The link between participation and leadership "is the most consistent finding in smalll group leadership research."[12] Although talking early and often does not guarantee you a leadership position, failure to talk will keep you from being considered as a potential leader. Researchers have found that group members perceive talkative participants as "more competent, more confident, more interested in discussion, and more influential."[13] The strategy is simple: If you want to be a leader, talk early and often throughout the discussion. Don't overdo it, though. If you talk too much, members may think that you are not interested in or willing to listen to their contributions. As important as it is to talk, it is just as important to demonstrate your willingness and ability to listen to every member of the group.

Know More (and Share It).   Leaders often emerge or are appointed because they are seen as experts—people who know more about an important topic. Even if a potential leader is only able to explain ideas and information more clearly than other group members, she or he may be perceived as knowing more. Groups need well-informed leaders; they do not need know-it-alls. Know-it-alls see their own comments as most important; leaders value everyone's contributions. Knowing more than other members may require hours of advance preparation. Members who want to become leaders understand that they must demonstrate their expertise without intimidating other group members.

TOOLBOX 3.2 Listening and Leadership

Effective listening is one of the hallmarks of successful leadership. If you talk early and often but ignore or misinterpret what other group members say, you will not emerge or be highly successful as a leader. Effective leaders devote their full attention to making sure that they comprehend what is said. They also follow the golden listening rule: Listen to others as you would have them listen to you. In other words, suspend your own needs in order to listen to someone else's. **Chapter 6: Listening in Groups** offers guidelines for becoming a more effective and appreciated listener.

Talk
Know More
Offer Your Opinion
Volunteer for Meaningful Roles

Listen
Share Knowledge
Welcome Disagreement
Follow Through

FIGURE 3.2 Becoming a Leader: A Balanced Approach

Offer Your Opinion (and Welcome Disagreement). When groups are having difficulty making decisions or solving problems, they appreciate someone who can offer good ideas and informed opinions. Very often leaders will emerge when they help a group out of some difficulty. Offering ideas and opinions, however, is not the same as having those ideas accepted. Criticizing the ideas and opinions of others runs the risk of causing resentment and defensiveness. Bullying your way into a leadership position can backfire. If you are unwilling to compromise or listen to alternatives, the group may be unwilling to follow you. Effective leaders welcome constructive disagreement and discourage hostile confrontations. "They do not suppress conflict, they rise and face it."[14]

Volunteer for Meaningful Roles (and Follow Through). The person who demonstrates a willingness to take on extra jobs that help the group achieve its goals is likely to be perceived as a potential leader. There are, however, jobs with limited leadership potential. Rarely will a group's secretary, social chairperson, or the member assigned to take minutes become the leader. An aspiring leader, therefore, should avoid permanent assignment to these positions.

Volunteering, however, is not the same as follow-through. If you volunteer to write a report, the report should be well written and on time. If you volunteer to chair a subcommittee, the responsibility for that position should be taken seriously. If you volunteer but then fail to follow through, you only succeed in demonstrating why you should not become the group's leader.

Implications. The strategies for becoming a leader are not necessarily the same strategies needed for successful leadership. Once you become a leader, you may find it necessary to listen more than talk, welcome better-informed members, criticize the opinions of others, and volunteer for a job no one else wants to do. Once you have emerged as leader, your focus should shift from becoming the leader to serving the group you lead.

Regardless of how you become a leader, it is critical to understand the difference between wanting to lead and wanting power. Group members who seek leadership positions because they crave power are trying to satisfy their own selfish needs. Effective leaders put members' needs and the group's goal ahead of their own needs. Power-hungry leaders use power in a way that allows no competition or conflict; effective leaders welcome such challenges. Leadership is not a power trip; it is a commitment to uniting the separate interests of group members in the pursuit of a higher, shared goal.[15]

Leadership Theories

Leadership is a quality that seems to defy accurate measurement. Bennis and Nanus point out that "no clear and unequivocal understanding exists as to what distinguishes leaders from non-leaders, and perhaps more important, what distinguishes effective leaders from ineffective leaders. . . ."[16] Despite such inconclusive results, there is a lot to be learned from the many theories of leadership. In the following sections, we explain four different theoretical approaches to leadership.

Trait Theory

The trait theory is often called the "Great Man" theory. It is based on what many people now believe is a myth—that leaders are born, not made. **Trait theory** attempts to identify and prescribe individual characteristics and behaviors needed for effective leadership.

Think of some of the leaders you most admire. What traits do they have? Most of us can come up with a list of desirable leadership traits that includes intelligence, ability to communicate, confidence, enthusiasm, organizational talent, and good listening skills. Most of us would gladly follow a leader with

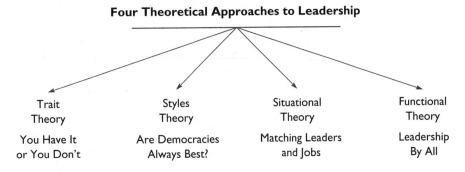

Four Theoretical Approaches to Leadership

Trait Theory	Styles Theory	Situational Theory	Functional Theory
You Have It or You Don't	Are Democracies Always Best?	Matching Leaders and Jobs	Leadership By All

FIGURE 3.3 Leadership Theories

these qualities. The problem is that there is no guarantee that someone possessing these traits will be an effective leader. Furthermore, there are many effective leaders who possess only a few of these traits. Harriet Tubman, an illiterate runaway slave, did little talking but led hundreds of her people from bondage in the South to freedom in the North. Ross Perot, a little guy with big ears and a squeaky voice, became a business leader and serious contender for the U.S. presidency. Depending on the group and its circumstances, one set of traits may be less effective than another. Yet, some important implications of this theory are of value to anyone seeking and gaining a leadership position.

Implications of Trait Theory.   According to one contemporary psychological theory, there is such a thing as a born or natural leader. Psychological type theory has produced a survey instrument called the **Myers-Briggs Type Indicator®,** the most widely used, nonclinical personality inventory. Based on the idea that different kinds of people think differently and are interested in different things, psychological type theorists claim that they can identify "life's natural leaders" or "extroverted thinkers" who use reasoning ability to control and direct those around them.[17] These people are usually enthusiastic, decisive, confident, organized, logical, and argumentative. They love to lead and can be excellent communicators. Although they often assume or win leadership positions, they may not necessarily be effective leaders.

Extroverted thinkers may intimidate and overpower others. They may be insensitive to the personal feelings and needs of group members. Women with such traits, moreover, are often perceived as arrogant and confrontational. Although many extroverted thinkers become leaders, they may need a less intense, more balanced approach in order to be effective leaders.

Styles Theory

As a way of expanding the trait approach to the study of leadership, researchers began reexamining the traits they had collected. Rather than looking for individual leadership traits, they developed the **styles theory** of leadership—a collection of specific behaviors that could be identified as unique leadership styles. Actors work in different styles—tough or gentle, comic or tragic. Even sports teams differ in style; the South American soccer teams are known for their speed and grace, the European teams for their technical skill and aggressiveness. Different styles are attributed to leaders, too.

One of the first attempts to describe different leadership styles yielded three categories: autocratic, democratic, and laissez-faire.[18]

An autocrat is a person who has a great deal of power and authority, someone who maintains strict control over the group and its discussion. The **autocratic leader** tries to control the direction and outcome of a discussion, makes many of the group's decisions, gives orders, expects followers to obey orders, focuses on achieving the group's task, and takes responsibility for the results.

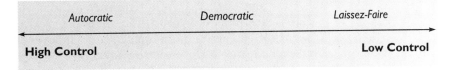

FIGURE 3.4   The Leadership Style Continuum

A **democratic leader** promotes the interests of group members and believes in and practices social equality. This type of leader shares decision making with the group, helps the group plan a course of action, focuses on the group's morale as well as on the task, and gives the entire group credit for success.

Laissez-faire is a French phrase that means "to let people do as they choose." A **laissez-faire leader** lets the group take charge of all decisions and actions. In mature and highly productive groups, a laissez-faire leader may be a perfect match for the group. Such a laid-back leadership style can generate a climate in which open communication is encouraged and rewarded. Unfortunately, there are laissez-faire leaders who do little or nothing to help a group when it needs decisive leadership.

Implications of Styles Theory.   Many people assume that democratic leadership is always the best. There are, however, circumstances in which an autocratic style may be more effective. During a serious crisis there may not be enough time to discuss issues or consider the wishes of all members. In an emergency, a group may want its leader to take total responsibility.

Although groups led by autocratic leaders may be more efficient and, in the short run, more effective, democratic leadership has significant advantages. In groups with democratic leadership, members are often more satisfied with the group experience, more loyal to the leader, and more productive in the long run. Whereas members often fear or distrust an autocratic leader, they usually enjoy working with a democratic leader. Autocratic leaders may stifle critical opinions and creativity whereas a democratic leader can create a climate in which members' opinions and ideas are welcome. Not surprisingly, groups led by democratic leaders exhibit lower levels of stress and conflict along with higher levels of innovation and creative problem solving.[19]

It may be worthwhile to assess your own leadership style. If you have a tendency to interrupt group members who seem to be wasting time, to start meetings on time regardless of the social interaction occurring in the group, or to confront members with terse questions, you may be more of an autocratic than a democratic leader. There are costs to using the autocratic approach. By exerting excessive control, autocratic leaders may lower group morale and sacrifice long-term productivity. Unfortunately, many autocratic leaders defend such authoritarian actions by arguing that the group can't get the job done without the strict control of the leader.

Dr. Sandy Faber, a world-renowned astronomer, wrote about her experience as the leader of a group of six astronomers who developed a new theory about the expansion of the universe. An unfortunate back injury made her take a new look at her leadership style:

> My usual style would have been to take center stage . . . and control the process. My back problem was at its worst . . . and instead I found myself lying flat on a portable cot in Donald's office. It is very hard to lead a group of people from a prone position. My energies were at a low ebb anyway. I found it very comfortable to lie back and avoid taking central responsibility. . . . It was the best thing that could have happened to us. The resultant power vacuum allowed each of us to quietly find our own best way to contribute. This lesson has stood me in good stead since. I now think that in small groups of able and motivated individuals, giving orders or setting up a well-defined hierarchy may generate more friction than it is designed to cure. If a good spirit of teamwork prevails, team leadership can be quite diffuse.[20]

If you have a tendency to ask open and general questions of the group as a whole, encourage participation from all members regardless of their status, and avoid dominating the group with your own opinion, you may be a democratic leader. Here, too, there are costs. Democratic leaders may sacrifice productivity by avoiding direct leadership. Many democratic leaders defend this approach by arguing that, regardless of the circumstance, the only way to make a good decision is to involve all group members. However, by failing to take charge in a crisis or curb a discussion when final decisions are needed, democratic leaders may be perceived as weak or indecisive by their followers.

Laissez-faire leaders are most effective in groups with very mature and productive members. Whether for lack of leadership skill or interest, laissez-faire leaders avoid taking charge or taking the time to prepare for complex and lengthy discussions. They can, however, assume procedural responsibilities that allow a group to speed up its progress and effectiveness.

Knowing whether your primary leadership style is autocratic, democratic, or laissez-faire is helpful only if you also understand the ways in which that style affects the members of your group and the goal your group is working to achieve. Effective leadership cannot be classified like a chemical molecule or a style of automobile. Effective leaders must seek a balance between their natural traits or instinctive style and their ability to use other leadership strategies adapted to different group situations.

Situational Theory

The situational approach assumes that leaders are made, not born, and that nearly everyone can be an effective leader under the right circumstances. Moreover, **situational theory** explains how leaders can become more effective once they have carefully analyzed themselves, their group, and the circumstances in which they must lead. Rather than describing traits or styles, the situational approach seeks an ideal fit between leaders and leadership jobs.

One of the most influential theories of situational leadership was developed by the researcher Fred Fiedler. Fiedler's **Contingency Model of Leadership Effectiveness** is based on his study of hundreds of groups in numerous work settings.[21] A contingency is something that is dependent upon certain conditions. For example, a leader may not be able to implement a plan of action if members do not like or understand the plan. The contingency model of situational leadership suggests that effective leadership occurs only when there is an ideal match between the leader's style and the group's work situation.

Leadership Style.   Rather than classifying leaders as autocratic or democratic, Fiedler characterizes them as either task-motivated or relationship-motivated. **Task-motivated leaders** want to get the job done; they gain satisfaction from completing a task even if the cost is bad feelings between the leader and group members. Task-motivated leaders may be criticized for being too bossy and too focused on the job rather than on the morale of the group. Sometimes task-motivated leaders take on the jobs of other group members because they're not satisfied with the quality or quantity of work done by others.

Relationship-motivated leaders gain satisfaction from working well with other people even if the cost is neglecting or failing to complete a task. Relationship-motivated leaders may be criticized for paying too much attention to how members feel and for tolerating disruptive members; they may appear inefficient and weak. Sometimes relationship-motivated leaders take on the jobs of other group members because they can't bring themselves to ask their colleagues to do more.

The Situation.   Once you have determined your leadership style, the next step is to analyze the way in which your style matches the group's situation. According to Fiedler, there are three important dimensions to every situation: leader–member relationships, task structure, and power.

Fiedler claims that the most important factor in analyzing a situation is understanding the relationship between the leader and the group. Because **leader–member relations** can be positive, neutral, or negative, they can affect how a leader goes about mobilizing a group toward its goal. Are group members friendly and loyal to the leader and the rest of the group? Are they cooperative and supportive? Do they accept or resist the leader?

The second factor is rating the structure of the task. **Task structure** can range from disorganized and chaotic to highly organized and rule-driven. Are the goals and task clear? Is there an accepted procedure or set of steps for achieving the goal? Are there well-established standards for measuring success?

The third situational factor is the amount of power and control the leader has. Is the source of that power an outside authority, or has the leader earned it from the group? What differences would the use of reward, coercive, legitimate, expert, and/or referent power have on the group?

Matching the Leader and the Situation. Fiedler's research suggests that there are ideal matches between leadership style and the group situation. Task-motivated leaders perform in extremes—such as when the situation is highly controlled or when it is almost out of control. Task-motivated leaders shine when there are good leader–member relationships, a clear task, and a lot of power. They also do well in stressful leadership jobs where there may be poor leader–member relationships, an unclear and unstructured task, and little control or power. Task-motivated leaders do well in extreme situations because their primary motivation is to take charge and get the job done.

Relationship-motivated leaders do well when there is a mix of conditions. They may have a structured task but an uncooperative group of followers. Rather than taking charge and getting the job done at all costs, the relationship-motivated leader uses diplomacy and works with group mem-

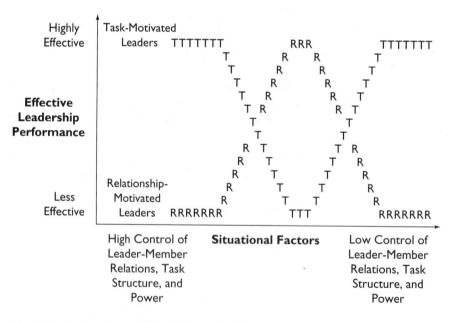

T = Task-Motivated   R = Relationship-Motivated

FIGURE 3.5 Contingency Model of Leader Effectiveness

bers to improve leader–member relationships. If there are good leader–member relations but an unstructured task, the relationship-motivated leader may rely on the resources of the group to develop a plan of action. Whereas a task-motivated leader might find these situations frustrating, a relationship-motivated leader will be quite comfortable.

Implications of Situational Theory.   According to the situational approach, once you know your leadership style and have analyzed the situation in which you must lead, you can begin to predict how successful you will be as a leader. If you are a task-motivated leader, you should feel confident if asked to take on a highly structured or highly unstructured task. If completing the group's task is your major concern and motivation, you should feel confident if asked to lead a group that is unable and unwilling to pursue its goal.

Relationship-motivated leaders have different factors to consider. If there is a moderate degree of structure, a relationship-motivated leader may be more successful. If people issues are your major concern, you should feel confident if asked to lead a group that is able but somewhat unwilling to complete its task.

Unfortunately, you cannot always choose when and where you will lead. You may find yourself assigned or elected to a leadership situation that does not match your leadership style. Rather than trying to change your leadership style, you may find it easier to change the situation you are leading. For example, if leader–member relations are poor, you may decide that your first task is to gain the group's trust and support. You can schedule time to listen to members' problems or take nonmeeting time to get to know key individuals in the group.

If your task is highly unstructured, you can exert your leadership by providing structure or by dividing the task into smaller, easier-to-achieve subunits. On the other hand, you may find yourself in a leadership situation where the task is so highly structured there is almost no need for leadership. The group knows exactly what to do. Rather than allowing the group to become bored, ask for or introduce new and less structured tasks to challenge the group.

Finally, you may be able to modify the amount of power you have. If you are reluctant to use coercive power or if you don't have enough legitimate power, you can earn referent power by demonstrating your leadership ability. If you have a great deal of power and run the risk of intimidating group members, you may want to delegate some of your duties and power.

All the preceding strategies rely on leaders who understand who they are, who recognize the way in which they are motivated to lead, and who have analyzed the group's situation. Rather than wishing you were born with leadership traits or waiting for situations that match your style, the situational approach suggests ways to improve your leadership ability.

Functional Theory

Like the situational approach, the **functional theory** of leadership assumes that people are not born as leaders but learn to function as leaders. Unlike the situational approach, the functional approach focuses on what a leader does rather than who a leader is. Even more significant, the functional approach does not assume that leadership is the sole responsibility of one person—the leader. Instead, it assumes that anyone in a group can and should help the group achieve its goal. There are no rules dictating that only the leader can motivate group members, provide procedural suggestions, or solve group problems. Leadership is a job, not a person. And, according to the functional approach to leadership, any capable group member can assume leadership functions when necessary.

Implications of Functional Theory.   Although the functional approach can shift leadership responsibilities to anyone capable of performing them, doing so does not mean that leadership is unnecessary. Just the opposite may be true. If one participant is better at motivating members while another member excels at keeping the group on track, the group may be better off with both members assuming such leadership functions than if it relies on a single person to assume these important responsibilities.

Another significant implication to the functional approach to leadership is its focus on communication strategies and skills. Rather than relying on a leader's natural traits, styles, or motivation, the functional approach concentrates on what a leader says and does in a group situation. An information-giver, a compromiser, or even a dominator functions by communicating. Given the nature of group discussions, most of these functional leadership behaviors require effective communication skills.

TOOLBOX 3.3   Functional Theory and Participation

Because functional theory maintains that any group member can assume specific leadership tasks, it may be more of a participation theory than a leadership theory. As a theory of participation, functional theory assumes that the behavior of every member is critical to the group's success or failure. The theory divides group members' behaviors into three categories: (1) group task functions such as information giver, evaluator, and energizer; (2) group maintenance functions such as compromiser, tension releaser, and gatekeeper; and (3) self-centered functions such as blocker, dominator, and recognition seeker. An effective leader would assume most task and maintenance roles described by functional theory while minimizing or avoiding self-centered functions. **Chapter 4: Participation in Groups** uses functional theory to describe the most common roles found in groups.

Gender and Leadership

In the early studies of leadership, there was an unwritten but additional prerequisite for becoming a leader: Be a man. Yet there have been and continue to be exceptional women leaders: Clara Barton, Harriet Tubman, Elizabeth Cady Stanton, Susan B. Anthony, Margaret Sanger, Eleanor Roosevelt, Madeleine Albright, and Gloria Steinem; Representatives Shirley Chisholm and Barbara Jordan; Senators Margaret Chase Smith, Diane Feinstein, and Carol Moseley Braun; Attorney General Janet Reno; and Governors Ann Richards and Christine Todd Whitman. Despite the achievements of these individuals, some people still question the ability of women to serve in leadership positions. These doubts are based on long-held prejudices rather than on valid evidence.

In a summary of the research on leadership and gender, Shimanoff and Jenkins conclude that "women are still less likely to be preselected as leaders, and the same leadership behavior is often evaluated more positively when attributed to a male than a female."[22] In other words, even when women talk early and often, are well prepared and always present at meetings, offer valuable ideas, and volunteer for important tasks, a man who has done the same things is more likely to emerge as leader. After examining the research on gender and leadership, Napier and Gershenfeld conclude that "even though male and female leaders may act the same, there is a tendency for women to be perceived more negatively or to have to act differently to gain leadership."[23]

Do male and female leaders differ? According to Julia Wood, dissimilarities may be explained by differences in male-female communication styles:

Leadership . . . is typically linked with masculine styles of communication—assertiveness, independence, competitiveness, confidence. . . . Deference, inclusivity, collaboration, and cooperation, which are prioritized in women's speech communities, are linked with subordinate roles rather than with leadership.[24]

EFFECTIVE leaders select communication strategies that mobilize a group toward achieving shared goals. What might you conclude about the leadership of this group? (Mark Richards/PhotoEdit)

Thus, there is a perception that male leaders are (or are expected to be) more assertive and task oriented, whereas women leaders devote (or are expected to devote) more attention to the social and emotional needs of group members. Because men usually talk more, they may have the advantage of being able to "talk early and often." However, women who do talk may find that their ideas carry less weight than the same ideas expressed by a man.

Deborah Tannen has described the difficulties that women have in leadership positions.[25] If their behavior is similar to that of male leaders, they are perceived as unfeminine. If they act "like a lady," they are viewed as weak or ineffective. One professional woman described this dilemma as follows:

> I was thrilled when my boss evaluated me as "articulate, hard-working, mature in her judgment, and a skillful diplomat." What disturbed me were some of the evaluation comments from those I supervise or work with as colleagues. Although they had a lot of good things to say, a few of them described me as "pushy," "brusque," "impatient," "has a disregard for social niceties," and "hard-driving." What am I supposed to do? My boss thinks I'm energetic and creative while other people see the same behavior as pushy and aggressive.

The preference for male leaders may come down to a fear of or an unwillingness to adjust to different kinds of leaders. Because many people have worked in groups that were led by men, they may feel uncomfortable when leadership shifts to a woman.

Instead of asking whether a female leader is different from a male leader, it is more important to ask whether she is an effective leader. Regardless of gender, effective leaders select strategies that mobilize groups toward achieving shared goals.

Balanced Leadership

The leader performs the most difficult balancing act in a group. Much like a tightrope walker who juggles during a death-defying walk across open space, a group leader must juggle many interests and issues while propelling a group toward its goal. The leader must exert control without stifling creativity. The leader must balance the requirements of the task with the social needs of group members. The leader must resolve conflict without losing the motivation and energy that results from conflict and must encourage participation from quiet members without stifling the enthusiasm and contributions of active members. The effective leader juggles all of these variables while mobilizing a group's resources in pursuit of a common goal that unifies both leaders and followers. The job of a juggling tightrope walker may seem easy compared to balancing all of these leadership tasks.

Group Goal Individual Goals
Task Functions Maintenance Functions
Speaking Listening

FIGURE 3.6 Balanced Leadership

Kevin Freiberg claims that effective "leaders have both the desire and ability to create an environment where the wants and needs of followers can be satisfied. They are particularly adept at using their skills and insight to establish a balance between cooperative common action and the fulfillment of individual goals."[26] Achieving balanced leadership does not depend on developing a particular trait or style but depends rather on a leader's ability to analyze a situation and select leadership strategies that help mobilize a group to achieve its goal.

Summary Study Guide

- A leader mobilizes group members toward a goal shared by the leader and followers. Leadership is a process that requires the ability to make strategic decisions and use communication to mobilize others toward achieving a shared goal.
- Leadership power can be categorized as reward power, coercive power, legitimate power, expert power, and referent power.
- Designated leaders are selected by an outside authority or elected by a group; emergent leaders come from within a group and gradually assume leadership functions.
- Strategies for becoming a leader include talking early and often, knowing more, offering opinions, and volunteering.
- Trait theory attempts to identify individual characteristics and behaviors needed for effective leadership.
- Styles theory describes the strengths and weaknesses of autocratic, democratic, and laissez-faire leaders.

- Situational theory seeks an ideal fit between a leader's style (task or relationship motivated) and three dimensions of the group's work situation (leader–member relations, the task structure, and the leader's power).
- Functional theory focuses on what leaders do rather than on who leaders are; anyone in a group can assume leadership functions.
- Women are less likely to be selected as leaders; the same leadership behavior is often evaluated more positively when attributed to a man than to a woman.

Groupwork *Wanted: A Few Good Leaders*

GOAL   To analyze and discuss different perceptions of effective leadership.

PARTICIPANTS   3–7 members

PROCEDURE

1. Each student should complete *The Least-Preferred Coworker Scale* at the end of this chapter.
2. After everyone has completed the scale, they should form groups based on similar individual results, e.g. relationship-motivated students should join the same groups and task-motivated students should join groups with each other.
3. Each group should then work to write a description of the desired characteristics, skills, and/or duties of a potential leader in the form of a want ad in the employment section of a newspaper. Each advertisement should begin with "WANTED: LEADER The ideal candidate for this job will ..."
4. Each group should post its job description of a leader and have a spokesperson present it to the class.
5. The class should then discuss the following questions:
   - What are the similarities among the want ads?
   - What are the differences among the want ads?
   - Which leadership theories apply to each want ad?
   - In what ways did group members' preferences for relationship motivation or task motivation affect the words they chose to include in each want ad?
   - Who was the leader in each group? Did the group designate a leader or did one emerge?

The Least-Preferred Coworker Scale

Directions   All of us have worked better with some people than with others. Think of the one person in your life with whom you have worked least well, a person who might cause you difficulty in doing a job or completing a task. This person may be someone with whom you have worked recently or someone you have known in the past. This coworker must be the single individual with whom you have had the most difficulty getting a job done, with whom you would least want to work.

On the scale below, describe this person by circling the number that best represents your perception of this person. There are no right or wrong answers. Do not omit any items, and circle a number for each item only once.

Pleasant	8	7	6	5	4	3	2	1	Unpleasant
Friendly	8	7	6	5	4	3	2	1	Unfriendly
Rejecting	1	2	3	4	5	6	7	8	Accepting
Tense	1	2	3	4	5	6	7	8	Relaxed
Distant	1	2	3	4	5	6	7	8	Close
Cold	1	2	3	4	5	6	7	8	Warm
Supportive	8	7	6	5	4	3	2	1	Hostile
Boring	1	2	3	4	5	6	7	8	Interesting
Quarrelsome	1	2	3	4	5	6	7	8	Harmonious
Gloomy	1	2	3	4	5	6	7	8	Cheerful
Open	8	7	6	5	4	3	2	1	Guarded
Backbiting	1	2	3	4	5	6	7	8	Loyal
Untrustworthy	1	2	3	4	5	6	7	8	Trustworthy
Considerate	8	7	6	5	4	3	2	1	Inconsiderate
Nasty	1	2	3	4	5	6	7	8	Nice
Agreeable	8	7	6	5	4	3	2	1	Disagreeable
Insincere	1	2	3	4	5	6	7	8	Sincere
Kind	8	7	6	5	4	3	2	1	Unkind

Scoring

Obtain your Least-Preferred Coworker (LPC) score by adding up the numbers you circled on the preceding scale. Your score should range between 18 and 144.

(continued)

(The Least-Preferred Coworker Scale, *continued*)

Relationship-Motivated Leader. If your score is 73 or above, you derive satisfaction from good relationships with group members. You are most successful when a situation has just enough uncertainty to challenge you: moderate leader-member relations, moderate task structure, and moderate power.

Task-Motivated Leader. If your score is 64 or below, you derive satisfaction from getting things done. You are most successful when a situation has clear guidelines or no guidelines at all: excellent or poor leader-member relations, highly structured or unstructured tasks, and high or low power.

Relationship- and Task-Motivated Leader. If your score is between 65 and 72, you may be flexible enough to function in both leadership styles.

Source: *The Least-Preferred Coworker Scale* reprinted from *Improving Leadership Effectiveness: The Leader Match Concept,* 2nd edition, Fiedler, F. E. & Chemers, M. M. © 1984 John Wiley & Sons, Inc., pp. 17–42. Reprinted by permission of John Wiley & Sons, Inc.

Recommended Readings

Bennis, W. & Nanus, B. (1985). *Leaders: The strategies for taking charge.* New York: Harper & Row.

Dreher, D. (1996). *The tao of personal leadership.* New York: HarperCollins.

Hackman, M. Z. & Johnson, C. E. (1996). *Leadership: A communication perspective* (2nd ed.). Prospect Heights, IL: Waveland.

Notes

1. Cathcart, R. S. & Samovar, L. A. (Eds.), (1992). *Small group communication: A reader* (6th ed.). Dubuque, IA: Wm C. Brown, p. 364.
2. Wills, G. (1994). *Certain trumpets: The call of leaders.* New York: Simon & Schuster, p. 17.
3. Jesuíno, J. C. (1996). Leadership: Micro-macro links. In E. H. White and J. H. Davis (Eds.), *Understanding group behavior, Vol. 2.* Mahwah, NJ: Lawrence Erlbaum, p. 93.
4. Bennis, W. & Nanus, B. (1985). *Leaders: The strategies for taking charge.* New York: HarperPerennial, p. 15.
5. French, J. R. P., Jr. & Raven, B. (1968). The bases of social power. In D. Cartwright & A. Zander (Eds.), *Group dynamics: Research and theory* (3rd ed). New York: Harper & Row, pp. 259–269.
6. Hackman, M. Z. & Johnson, C. E. (1991). *Leadership: A communication perspective.* Prospect Heights, IL: Waveland, p. 77.
7. Hackman & Johnson, p. 79.
8. Heifetz, R. (1997 April). "The work of a modern leader." *Harvard Management Update,* 2, p. 5
9. Lloyd, S. R. (1996). *Leading teams: The skills for success.* West Des Moines, IA: American Media Publishing, p. 13.

10. Ellis, D. G. & Fisher, B. A. (1994). *Small group decision making: Communication and the group process* (4th ed.). New York: McGraw-Hill, p. 202.

11. Hollander, E. P. (1978). *Leadership dynamics: A practical guide to effective relationships.* New York: Macmillan, p. 53.

12. Hackman & Johnson, p. 125.

13. Bonito, J. A. & Hollingshead, A. B. (1997). "Participation in small groups." In B. R. Burleson (Ed.), *Communication Yearbook, 20.* Thousand Oaks, CA: Sage, p. 243.

14. Jesuíno, p. 119.

15. For more on the distinction between leadership and power, see Burns, J. M. (1978). *Leadership.* New York: Harper & Row.

16. Bennis & Nanus, p. 4.

17. Kroeger, O. with Thuesen, J. M. (1992). *Type talk at work: How the 16 personality types determine your success on the job.* New York: Dell, p. 385.

18. Lewin, K., Lippit, R. & White, R. K. (1939). "Patterns of aggressive behaviour in experimentally created social climates." *Journal of Social Psychology, 10,* pp. 271–299.

19. Jesuíno, p. 99.

20. Dressler, A. (1994). *Voyage to the great attractor: Exploring intergalactic space.* New York: Alfred A. Knopf, pp. 193–194.

21. Fiedler, F. E. & Chemers, M. M. (1984). *Improving leadership effectiveness: The leader match concept* (2nd ed.). New York: John Wiley.

22. Shimanoff, S. B. & Jenkins, M. M. (1996). Leadership and gender: Challenging assumptions and recognizing resources. In R. S. Cathcart, L. A. Samovar, and L. D. Henman (Eds.), *Small group communication: Theory and practice* (7th ed). Madison, WI: Brown & Benchmark, p. 327.

23. Napier, R. W. & Gershenfeld, M. K. (1993). *Groups: Theory and experience.* Boston: Houghton Mifflin, p. 371.

24. Wood, J. T. (1994). *Gendered lives: Communication, gender, and culture.* Belmont, CA: Wadsworth, p. 273.

25. Tannen, D. (1994). *Talking from 9 to 5: Women and men in the workplace: Language, sex and power.* New York: Avon.

26. Freiberg, K. L. (1992). Transformation leadership. In R. S. Cathcart & L. A. Samovar (Eds.), *Small group communication: A reader* (6th ed.). Dubuque, IA: Wm. C. Brown, pp. 526–527.

Participation in Groups

Who Wants to Be a Follower?

Without followers, there would be no one to lead. As obvious as this statement is to anyone who has ever worked in a group, followers are much less frequently analyzed than leaders.

> We have thousands of books on leadership, none on followership. I have heard college presidents tell their students that schools are meant to train leaders. I have never heard anyone profess to train followers. The ideal seems to be a world in which everyone is a leader—but who will be left for them to be leading?[1]

In the United States, we place great value on leaders, but rarely do we stop to understand or appreciate followers. Bennis and Biederman maintain that our obsession with leadership has resulted in the mistaken notion that extraordinary achievements are primarily the result of great leaders rather than the collaborative efforts of great groups. They point to the ceiling of the Sistine Chapel as a classic example. Most of us have an image of Michelangelo laboring alone, when in fact thirteen people worked with him.[2]

Interestingly, this admiration and awe of leaders is not shared by all cultures. In some countries, standing out from or above the crowd is considered arrogant. Loyal, hard-working followers are admired. In the United States, however, there often is a negative view of followers. Garry Wills captured this perception in his book *Certain Trumpets: The Call of Leaders*.

> Talk about the nobility of leaders, the need for them, our reliance on them, raises the clear suspicion that followers are *not* so noble, not needed—that there is something demeaning about being a follower. In that view, leaders only rise by sinking others to subordinate roles.[3]

Of course, none of the preceding suspicions about followers has merit in an effective group. In such groups, leaders and followers share a common vision; they develop plans together; they combine their willpower in a concerted effort to achieve a goal.

Rather than being a herd of sheep to be shepherded and led, effective followers are full partners and active participants who help develop a group's vision and course of action. In the best groups, followers have a say about where they are being led. Leaders need good followers who are ready, willing, and able to fulfill their critical roles group participants.

Theories of Participation

In Chapter 3, four different theoretical approaches provided information and advice about effective leadership behavior. There are also theories of participation. By understanding two of these theories—functional theory and personality type theory—we can identify participation strategies that can help a group achieve its goals.

Functional Theory

In 1948, Benne and Sheats published an essay in which they labeled and described the functional roles they had observed in groups.[4] We have modified the original Benne and Sheats list by adding or combining functional behaviors that we have observed in groups, as well as roles identified by other writers and researchers.

The following sections divide twenty-five participant roles into three functional categories: group task roles, group maintenance roles, and self-centered roles.

Group **task functions** affect a group's ability to achieve its goals by focusing on behavior that helps get the job done. Group **maintenance functions** affect how group members get along with each other while pursuing a shared goal. They are concerned with building relationships and keeping the group cohesive and cooperative. **Self-centered functions** describe negative roles in which individual needs are put ahead of the group's goal and other members' needs. In the following section, each functional role is categorized, named, described, and illustrated with a statement that might be heard from a discussant assuming such a role.

Group Task Roles.

1. *Initiator.* Proposes ideas and suggestions; provides direction for the group; gets the group started.
   "Let's begin by trying to look at the problem from the client's point of view."
2. *Information Seeker.* Asks for needed facts and figures; requests explanations and clarification of ideas; makes the group aware of information gaps.
   "How can we decide on a policy for disabled students without knowing more about the new federal laws and regulations?"
3. *Information Giver.* Provides the group with relevant information; researches, organizes, and presents needed information.
   "I checked with our minority affairs officer and she said . . ."
4. *Opinion Seeker.* Asks for others' opinions; tests for group opinions and consensus; tries to discover what others believe or feel about an issue.
   "Lyle, what do you think? Will it work?"
5. *Opinion Giver.* States personal beliefs and interpretations; shares feelings; offers analysis and arguments.
   "I don't agree that radio ads are the answer because they'll use up our entire promotional budget."

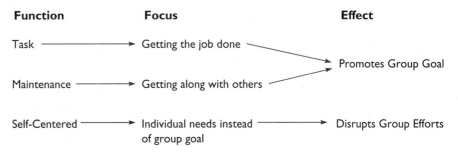

FIGURE 4.1   Functional Theory's Role Categories

6. *Clarifier-Summarizer.* Explains ideas and their consequences; reduces confusion; sums up group progress and conclusions.

"We've been trying to analyze this problem for the last hour. Let me see if I can list the three causes we've identified so far."

7. *Evaluator-Critic.* Assesses ideas, arguments, and suggestions; functions as the group's critical thinker; diagnoses task and procedural problems.

"I think we've forgotten something here. The building figures don't take into account monthly operating costs such as utilities and maintenance."

8. *Energizer.* Motivates group members to do their best; helps create enthusiasm for the task and, if needed, a sense of urgency; serves as the group's "cheerleader."

"This is incredible! We may be the first department to come up with such a unique and workable solution to this problem."

9. *Procedural Technician.* Assists with preparations for meetings including suggesting agenda items, making room arrangements, and providing needed materials and equipment.

"Before our next meeting, let me know whether any of you will need an overhead projector or a flip chart."

10. *Recorder-Secretary.* Keeps and provides accurate written records of a group's major ideas, suggestions, and decisions.

"Maggie, please repeat your two deadline dates so I can get them into the minutes."

Group Maintenance Roles.

1. *Encourager-Supporter.* Praises and agrees with group members; provides recognition and person-to-person encouragement; listens empathetically.

"The information you found has been a big help. Thanks for taking all that time to find it."

2. *Harmonizer.* Helps resolve conflicts; mediates differences among group members; emphasizes teamwork and the importance of everyone getting along.

"I know we're starting to get on each other's nerves, but we're almost done. Let's put aside our differences and finish up."

3. *Compromiser.* Offers suggestions that minimize differences; helps the group reach consensus; searches for solutions acceptable to everyone.

"It looks as though no one is going to agree on this one. Maybe we can improve the old system rather than trying to come up with a brand new way of doing it."

4. *Tension Releaser.* Alleviates tension with friendly humor; breaks the ice and cools hot tempers; monitors tension levels and tries to relax the group.

"Can Karen and I arm wrestle to decide who gets the assignment?"

5. *Gatekeeper.* Monitors participation; encourages quiet members to speak and talkative members to stop speaking; tries to control the flow of communication.

"I think we've heard from everyone except Sophie, and I know she has strong feelings on this issue."

6. *Observer-Interpreter.* Explains what others are trying to say; monitors and interprets feelings and nonverbal communication; expresses group feelings; paraphrases other members.

"I sense that you two are not really disagreeing. Tell me if I'm wrong, but I think that both of you are saying that we should . . ."

7. *Follower.* Supports the group and its members; accepts others' ideas and assignments; serves as an attentive audience member.

"That's fine with me. Just tell me when it's due."

Self-Centered Roles.

1. *Aggressor.* Puts down members to get what he or she wants; is sarcastic toward and critical of others; may take credit for someone else's work or idea.

"It's a good thing I had time to rewrite our report. There were so many mistakes in it, we would have been embarrassed by it."

2. *Blocker.* Stands in the way of progress; presents negative, disagreeable, and uncompromising positions; uses delaying tactics to derail an idea or proposal.

"There's no way I'm signing off on this idea if you insist on putting Gabriel in charge of the project."

3. *Dominator.* Prevents others from participating; asserts authority and tries to manipulate others; interrupts others and monopolizes discussion.

"That's nuts, Wanda. Right off the top of my head I can think of at least four major reasons why we can't do it your way. The first reason is . . ."

4. *Recognition Seeker.* Boasts about personal accomplishments; tries to impress others and become the center of attention; pouts or disrupts the discussion if not getting enough attention.

   "As the only person here to have ever won the company's prestigious top achiever award, I personally suggest that . . . ."

5. *Clown.* Injects inappropriate humor or commentary into the group; seems more interested in goofing off than working; distracts the group.

   "Listen—I've been working on this outrageous impersonation of the boss. I've even got his funny walk down."

6. *Deserter.* Withdraws from the group; appears "above it all" and annoyed or bored with the discussion; remains aloof or stops contributing.

   "I have to leave now. I have to go to a very important meeting."

7. *Confessor.* Seeks emotional support from the group; shares very personal feelings and problems with members; uses the group for emotional support.

   "I had an argument with my boyfriend yesterday. I could really use some advice. Let me start at the beginning."

8. *Special Interest Pleader.* Speaks on behalf of an outside group or a personal interest; tries to influence group members to support nongroup interests.

   "Let's hire my brother-in-law to cater our annual dinner. We'd get better food than the usual rubber chicken."

Depending on your group's goal, the nature of its task, and the attitudes or abilities of other members, you could function in several different roles. If you know the most about the topic being discussed, your primary function might be that of information giver. If two members are locked in a serious disagreement, you might help your group by functioning as a harmonizer. And, if you strongly believe that the group is heading toward a disastrous decision, you might even decide to take on the function of a blocker in order to prevent the group from making a mistake. In the best of all possible groups, all the task and maintenance functions should be available as strategies to mobilize a group toward its goal.

Personality Type Theory

When different personalities join together in pursuit of a common goal, the resulting combination of traits may be harmonious and complementary, or disruptive and chaotic. Understanding personality theories can help a group balance its collection of unique temperaments and talents. Schutz's FIRO theory, discussed in Chapter 2, is an example of a personality theory that explains member motivation and behavior as attempts to satisfy inclusion, control, and affection needs.

In Chapter 3, another personality theory, the Myers-Briggs Type Indicator®, was introduced to explain why some people are described as natural leaders. This personality type theory can also explain why and how certain group members react to specific suggestions and circumstances. In order to appreciate the ways in which personality types can affect the behavior of group members, it is necessary to understand several of the assumptions underlying this theory. Isabel Briggs Myers and her daughter, Katherine Briggs, developed a personality type measure that examines the different ways in which people see and understand the world around them as well as the different ways people reach conclusions and make decisions about what they have seen. Myers-Briggs, as the measure is known, looks at "the very way people *prefer* to use their minds, specifically, the way they perceive and the way they make judgments."[5]

According to Myers-Briggs, all of us have preferences of thought and behavior that can be divided into four categories, with two opposite preferences in each category. As you read about the following categories and traits, ask yourself which preferences best describe the reasons you choose one way of reacting or behaving over another.

Extrovert or Introvert.   These two traits relate to where you like to focus your attention—outward or inward. **Extroverts** are outgoing; they talk more, gesture more, and can become quite enthusiastic during a discussion. Extroverts get their energy by being with people. They enjoy solving problems in groups and like to involve others in projects. In a group setting, extroverts may have a tendency to dominate the discussion without listening to others. At the same time, they can be terrific energizers and contributors. **Introverts** think before they speak. Although they may have a great deal to offer in a group discussion, they can find the experience exhausting. Introverts recharge by being alone; they often prefer to work by themselves rather than in groups.

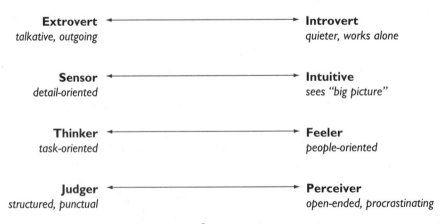

Extrovert
talkative, outgoing

Introvert
quieter, works alone

Sensor
detail-oriented

Intuitive
sees "big picture"

Thinker
task-oriented

Feeler
people-oriented

Judger
structured, punctual

Perceiver
open-ended, procrastinating

FIGURE 4.2 Myers-Briggs Type Indicator® Preferences

Knowing whether you or another group member tends to be an extrovert or an introvert can be valuable. Whereas an extrovert is likely to prefer working on a subcommittee, an introvert may prefer a solo assignment. Because introverts need more time to think before they speak or act, a group may miss out on good ideas and needed analysis if it rushes into solutions proposed by enthusiastic extroverts.

Levasseur reports that misunderstandings between extroverts and introverts are common in groups. "Extroverts complain that introverts don't speak up at the right time in meetings. Introverts criticize extroverts for talking too much and not listening well."[6] Effective groups try to balance the needs of both personality types by accommodating the differences in communication style and tapping the best ideas from all members.

Sensor or Intuitive.   These two traits focus on the way you look at the world around you—whether you see the trees or the forest. **Sensors** focus on details and prefer to concentrate on one task at a time. In groups, they may uncover minor flaws in an idea and request detailed instructions for completing a task. **Intuitives** look for connections and concepts rather than rules and flaws. They like to come up with big ideas but become bored with details.

In a group, sensors and intuitives may see things quite differently. According to Jaffe, sensors focus on regulations, step-by-step explanations, and facts, whereas intuitives focus on outwitting regulations, supplying theoretical explanations, and ignoring details.[7] Conflict between these two types can decrease group productivity.

Groups need both kinds of members in order to function effectively and efficiently. In the example that follows, Larson and LaFasto emphasize the importance of having a balance between the "nuts and bolts types" and those individuals who are capable of being creative and conceptual:

> . . . in the construction business it's important to have the "big picture"
> people who can see the conceptual side of a project and know when major
> changes are necessary. This needs to be balanced, however, by people who
> are at the job site supervising the very detail-oriented portions of the work.
> Both are necessary members of a good project team.[8]

Thinker or Feeler.   These two traits explain how you go about making decisions. **Thinkers** are task-oriented. They take pride in their ability to think objectively and logically. Thinkers often enjoy arguing and making difficult decisions. Like the task-motivated leader, thinkers want to get the job done even if the cost is poor feelings among some group members. **Feelers** are people-oriented. Relationship-motivated leaders are probably feelers who want everyone to get along. Feelers will spend time and effort helping other members.

When thinkers and feelers work together in groups, there is a potential for misunderstanding. Thinkers may appear unemotional and aggressive. Feelers may annoy others by "wasting" time with social chit-chat. However, when thinkers and feelers recognize their differences as decision makers, they can form an unbeatable team. While the thinkers make decisions and move the group forward, feelers make sure the group is working harmoniously.

Judger or Perceiver. The last two traits focus on how you deal with the outer world and its problems. **Judgers** are highly structured and well organized. They plan ahead, follow lengthy "To Do" lists, and like closure. Judgers are very punctual and can become impatient with participants who show up late or waste time. **Perceivers** are less rigid than judgers. Because they like open-endedness, being on time is less important than being flexible and adaptable. Perceivers are risk-takers willing to try new options. They often procrastinate and end up in a frenzy to complete a task on time.

Judgers and perceivers often have difficulty working together. To a judger, a perceiver may appear scatterbrained. To a perceiver, a judger may appear rigid and controlling. Kroeger and Thuesen have described the problems that judgers and perceivers have in the same group. Whereas judgers come prepared to make decisions and solve problems, perceivers wish they "could just leave the room and come back when it's over."[9]

Implications of Participation Theories

Just as it was desirable to have every task and maintenance function assumed by at least one member of a group, the same is true for personality traits. A group without judgers can miss deadlines and fail to achieve its goal. A group without a sensor can overlook important details or critical flaws in a proposal. Although it is tempting to choose members who are just like you, a group will be much better off with representatives of every type. According to Kroeger and Thuesen, in an ideal group "we would have a smattering of Extroverts, Introverts, Sensors, Intuitives, Thinkers, Feelers, Judgers, and Perceivers—and we would put them together in such a way that they would not only understand their differences but could also draw upon them."[10]

Functional and personality theories help us understand and explain how groups work. When you understand that some members are harmonizers while others dominate the discussion, you can take advantage of the maintenance function while trying to minimize the self-centered function. When you understand why extroverted judgers are argumentative whereas introverted feelers are more congenial and agreeable, you can use the strengths of each type to compensate for the weaknesses of the other. Without underlying theories of participation, you will not know why some participant strategies succeed in one situation but fail in another.

Guidelines for Participation

When groups have to share information, motivate members, make decisions, and solve problems, everyone has a stake in the outcome. When a conscientious self-management team hires a new team member, everyone should be involved in the process of reviewing applications and discussing the merits of each candidate. When an experienced convention committee selects a site for an upcoming conference, each member brings unique viewpoints and expertise to the deliberations. In both examples, the qualities that characterize an ideal group member's effective participation can be divided into three categories: readiness, willingness, and an ability to help the group achieve its goal.

Readiness Readiness means being prepared, in advance, for a discussion or group task. Most people would not give a speech or agree to an important interview without, at least, thinking about what they want to say. Why is it, then, that group members show up for meetings with little or no preparation? Group discussants must be well prepared to deal with a host of predictable as well as unpredictable issues and people.

Valuable discussion time and even entire meetings are wasted when group members fail to do their "homework." What is the point of discussing job applicants if some people have not read the applications and resumes? What is the point of discussing possible convention sites if no one knows whether the suggested hotels are available or affordable?

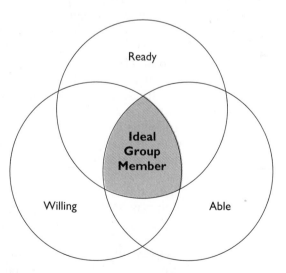

FIGURE 4.3 Ideal Group Member

> **TOOLBOX 4.1** Research and Preparation
>
> As soon as you know the topics and issues that may come up in a discussion, you should begin the preparation process by collecting ideas and information. Unless you are an expert or are well acquainted with all of the possible issues for discussion, you will need to do research. Conducting interviews, reading published materials, and searching electronic databases are avenues for becoming better informed. Attending a meeting equipped with facts, testimony, statistics, definitions, descriptions, and examples can demonstrate that you are ready to serve the needs of your group. The methods and tools for becoming a well-informed group member are described in **Chapter 12: Informed Groups.**

Willingness

Willingness means making a commitment to act and accept responsibility before, during, and after a group discussion. Whereas readiness requires planning, critical thinking, and time, willingness is an attitude, a mental commitment to the group's goal and its members.

Levasseur's *Breakthrough Business Meetings* lists these characteristics of a committed member: willingness to learn from others, to share, to work as a team, to do what needs to be done, to be flexible, to listen, to exercise responsibility, to deal with conflict, to treat others as you want to be treated. Your willingness and level of commitment to a group can differ depending on whether you see your primary role as a follower, an active participant, or both.[11] In other words, commitment comes from a shared sense of ownership and a willingness to do what is needed to achieve a group's goal."[12]

There are groups and circumstances in which willing **followers** are needed to fulfill a group's mission. In addition to energizers and initiators, groups need people who are willing to accept group decisions and carry them out. If you are a good follower, you do what must be done. For example, whereas some committee members may be wined and dined by a hotel seeking convention business, other members must be willing to plan programs, monitor budgets, and prepare publicity.

Regardless of the group or its goal, you should try to balance what you are willing to do with your group's expectations and needs. Sometimes you can make a full commitment to a group as an active participant. At other times, you may not be able to do much more than be a loyal follower.

Ability

Ability refers to the skills or competencies needed to make a significant contribution to your group. Being ready and willing does not guarantee that you will be able to do what is needed in a group. In a group discussion, two kinds of abil-

WHAT would happen if one of these firefighters was not ready, willing, or able to work with the team? What types of communication or technical skills does this group need? (Spencer Grant/Stock Boston)

ities directly affect your performance and productivity—communication skills and technical skills.

Almost every group function described in this chapter requires communication skills. Group members must be able to speak and listen during group discussions. At a more personal level, they need the ability to relate to the feelings and needs of others. Because most of this textbook is devoted to speaking and listening in groups, little more will be said in this section about these essential and critical skills in a group discussion.

Technical skills refer to specialized abilities, knowledge, and talents needed by a group to achieve its goals. Larson and LaFasto describe these skills as "what a team member must know or be able to do well in order to have a reasonable chance of achieving the team's objective."[13] They conclude that the real trick is figuring out which critical skills are needed and what the balance of those skills should be in a group. For example, a team developing new computer programs needs members with very specialized technical skills, including the ability to write code, create graphic images, and write instruction manuals. Well-prepared, highly committed, hard-working groups can come up short simply because they lack members with specific technical skills. "A group of lawyers is not going to do brain surgery, no matter how well they work together."[14]

In Chapter 3, the situational theory of leadership suggests that there are ideal matches between a leader's style and the group situation. Likewise, a member's task responsibilities in the group must be appropriately matched to his or her abilities. In their book *Organizing Genius: The Secrets of Creative Collaboration,* Bennis and Biederman conclude that one of the hallmarks of a great group is that "the right person has the right job."[15] When individual abilities and specific group tasks are properly matched, members are better able to make meaningful contributions toward the group's goal.

Dealing with Difficulties

What do you do if everyone in your group is an introvert—reluctant to speak up and hesitant to make decisions under pressure? How do you deal with a member who is always aggressive and dominating? These questions are obvious concerns for a conscientious group. In this section, we offer some suggestions that can help you deal with difficulties related to group member behavior.

Apathy

Overcoming the problem of member apathy is critical to the success of a group. **Apathy** in groups is the indifference that occurs when members do not find the group or its goal important, interesting, or inspiring. Barnlund and Haiman explain the difficulty of dealing with group apathy as follows:

> One of the most persistent and difficult of all problems that besets groups is that of apathy. To be sure, discussions often suffer from lack of organization, inadequate information, improper leadership, and interpersonal friction, but few of these seem as difficult to diagnose and remedy as that of disinterest on the part of group members. A committee plagued with apathy is about as efficient in discharging its responsibilities as an automobile engine without spark plugs.[16]

Causes.   The reasons for a member or a group exhibiting apathy are many. Sometimes people are assigned or forced into groups whose task appears unimportant or whose methods appear to be a waste of time. If a group assignment is not based on a member's interests or abilities, there may be little reason to become highly involved.

Sometimes members become apathetic when their expectations are not met. If your best ideas are blocked or too much time is taken up with the demands of self-centered recognition seekers, it is easy to become turned off. Finally, some members may avoid involvement for reasons related to personality traits or preferences. An introvert may be overwhelmed by extroverts. An intuitive may give up trying to encourage sensing members to

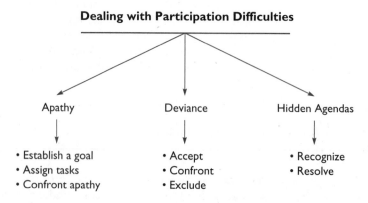

FIGURE 4.4 Participation Difficulties in Group Communication

focus on the "big picture." Other members may experience high levels of speaking anxiety and feel more comfortable taking on an apathetic role rather than an active one.

Cures.   Finding a cure for group or member apathy depends on correctly diagnosing the cause. There are no magic cures for apathy, but there are "treatments" that have the potential to reduce its effects. The key is matching the course of treatment to causes and symptoms of the problem. Treatments include establishing a clear goal, assigning appropriate tasks, and confronting apathy head-on.

Chapter 1 of this textbook emphasizes that the one characteristic most critical to a group's success is whether it has a clear goal—a thorough understanding of its objectives. One way to decrease apathy is to make sure that everyone in your group understands and shares its common goal. Knowing the purpose of the "sport," the responsibilities of the "players," and the "rules of the game" make it much easier and less risky for a participant to join in and "play." Apathy pushes members to the outfield, into the bleachers, and, eventually, out of the ballpark.

Assigning appropriate tasks to group members is a second strategy that can decrease apathy. Often members are unsure of how to contribute to the group's goal. Assigning specific responsibilities and tasks to members can increase commitment to and involvement in the group. Apathetic members are not necessarily uninterested or lazy; they may be bored, intimidated, or frustrated. It is important to help them by finding something they are willing and able to do.

Sometimes there is only one way to deal with apathetic members or an apathetic group—confront apathy head-on. Bring it up and talk about it. For example, asking the group why it seems bogged down or arranging a private meeting with an apathetic member can uncover causes and generate solutions.

Deviant Members

Chapter 2 defines deviant members as participants who choose not to conform to the expectations of the group. In some cases, deviant behavior and attitudes can prevent the group from achieving its common goal.

Before confronting deviant behavior, the group should recognize that there are times and occasions when constructive deviance is needed and valuable. Movies, television shows, and books have championed the holdout juror, the stubbornly honest politician, and the principled but disobedient soldier or crew member. Sometimes there is so much pressure for group members to conform that they need a deviant to shake up the process, to provide critical feedback, and to create doubt about what had been a confident but wrong decision. Taking on a temporary role such as blocker or special interest pleader can serve a group well if it prevents discussants from ignoring important information or making a hasty decision.

While most groups can handle the occasional encounter with a deviant member, constant encounters can be disruptive. Fortunately, several strategies can help a group deal with a destructive deviant. A group can accept, confront, or even exclude the troublesome member.

Accept.　One strategy for dealing with deviants is to accept the deviant behavior. Acceptance is not the same as approval; it involves learning to live with the deviant's behavior. When the deviation is not critical to the group's ultimate success or the deviant's positive contributions far outweigh the inconvenience and annoyance of putting up with the behavior, a group may allow the deviant behavior to continue. For example, a member who is always late for meetings but puts in more than her fair share of work may find her tardy behavior accepted as an unavoidable idiosyncrasy.

Confront.　Another strategy for dealing with deviants is confrontation. Deviant behavior is impossible to accept or ignore when it threatens the group and its members. When a member becomes "impossible," groups may confront the deviant in several ways. At first, members may direct a lot of attention to the deviant in an attempt to reason with the wayward member. They may even talk about him or her during the course of the discussion. "Other than Barry's objections, I think the rest of us are ready to decide." Although such attention can be intimidating and uncomfortable for the nonconforming member, it may not be sufficient to overcome the problem.

Exclude.　When all else fails, a group may exclude the deviant. Exclusion can take several forms. During a discussion, a group can turn away from the deviant, ignore her or his comments, or refuse to make eye contact. Exclusion might mean assigning the deviant to an unimportant, solo task or one that will drive the deviant away. Finally, a group may be able to expel the deviant from the group and be rid of the troublemaker. Being asked to leave a group or being barred from participating is a humiliating experience that all but the most stubborn deviants would prefer to avoid.

Finally, there may be value in discussing the problem with the deviant member outside the group setting. Because there are many reasons why a person exhibits deviant behavior, a frank and open interview between the leader or a trusted member and the deviant may uncover causes as well as cures. Some deviant members may not see their behavior as troublesome and, as a result, do not understand why the group is ignoring, confronting, or excluding them. Taking time to talk with a deviant member in a nonthreatening setting can solve both a personal and a group problem.

Hidden Agendas

Most groups have a public agenda. They know what they want and how they intend to go about achieving their goals. The same is true of individuals within a group. Each member may have private goals and preferred methods

TOOLBOX 4.2 Deviant Behavior in Meetings

Destructive deviation occurs when members resist conformity without re-gard for the best interests of the group and its goals. During formal meet-ings, members can deviate from the norm by becoming a nonparticipant or a loudmouth, by interrupting others, by whispering behind members' backs, and by missing important meetings or always showing up late. Methods of dealing with members who present such difficulties in meetings are dis-cussed in **Chapter 13: Planning and Conducting Meetings.**

for achieving those goals. When a member's private goals conflict with the group's goals, there exists what is called a **hidden agenda.** Hidden agendas represent what people really want, rather than what they say they want. When hidden agendas become more important than a group's public agenda or goal, the result can be group frustration and failure. Hidden agendas dis-rupt the flow of communication. Members with hidden agendas may create diversions in order to achieve their personal goals. Real issues and concerns may be buried while pseudo-issues dominate the discussion. A student re-ported the following incident in which a hidden agenda disrupted a group's deliberations:

> I was on a student government board that decides how college activities funds are distributed to student clubs and intramural teams. About halfway through the process, I became aware that several members were active in intramural sports. By the time I noticed their pro-sports voting pattern, they'd gotten most of what they wanted. You wouldn't believe the bizarre reasons they came up with to cut academic clubs while fully supporting the budgets of athletic teams. What made me mad was that they didn't care about what most students wanted; they only wanted to make sure that their *favorite* teams were funded.

Hidden agendas exist in all groups. The most effective groups deal with hidden agendas by recognizing and trying to resolve them.

Recognize. Recognizing the hidden agendas that are present in most groups is a critical first step in dealing with this difficulty. When group mem-bers refuse to compromise or if group progress is unusually slow, look for hidden agendas. A question such as "What seems to be hanging us up here?" may encourage discussants to reveal some of their private concerns. Recog-nizing the existence of hidden agendas may be sufficient to keep a group moving through its public agenda.

Even when you recognize the existence of hidden agendas, some cannot and should not be shared because they may create an atmosphere of distrust.

Task Functions	Maintenance Functions
Extroverts, Sensors	Introverts, Intuitives
Thinkers, Judgers	Feelers, Perceivers
Hidden Agendas	Group Goals

FIGURE 4.5 Participant Balance

Not many people would want to deal with the following revelation during a group discussion: "The reason I'm against these subcommittee assignments is that I don't want to work with Kenneth, who isn't trustworthy or competent." Recognizing hidden agendas means knowing that some of them can and should be confronted, whereas others cannot and should not be shared with the group.

Resolve.   Groups can resolve some of the problems caused by hidden agendas through early agreement on the group's goal and careful planning of the group's process. Napier and Gershenfeld suggest that discussing hidden agendas during the early planning stages can counteract their blocking power.[17] Initial discussion could include some of the following questions:

- What are the group's public goals?
- Does the leader have any personal concerns or goals?
- Do participants have any personal concerns or goals?
- What outcomes do participants expect?

Discussing these questions openly can be productive if a group recognizes and respects the inevitability and function of hidden agendas. Hidden agendas do not necessarily cause problems or prevent a group from achieving its goal. Understanding them can help explain why members are or are not ready, willing, and able to participate in a group discussion.

Balanced Participation

Participants, just like leaders, have to perform difficult balancing acts in a group. Unlike the tightrope-walking leader whose balancing act is a solo performance, group members are part of a flying trapeze team in which everyone depends on everyone else. Effective group discussion participants balance their own needs and interests with those of the group. Members should understand which functional roles they are likely to assume within a group and whether there is an imbalance in roles. Members should also analyze their personality traits as well as those of others to determine whether there is a difference in the way members see, understand, and make decisions about the world around them.

Balanced participation is not dependent on a standard set of functions or behaviors within a group. Instead, it depends on everyone's readiness, willingness, and ability to analyze a situation, select strategies that maximize group performance, and then contribute to the group's goal.

Summary Study Guide

- Functional theory assumes that all group members can help a group achieve its goal by performing certain task and maintenance functions.
- Group task roles include those of initiator, information seeker, information giver, opinion seeker, opinion giver, clarifier-summarizer, evaluator-critic, energizer, procedural technician, and recorder-secretary.
- Group maintenance roles include those of encourager-supporter, harmonizer, compromiser, tension releaser, gatekeeper, observer-interpreter, and follower.
- Self-centered roles include those of aggressor, blocker, dominator, recognition seeker, clown, deserter, confessor, and special interest pleader.
- The Myers-Briggs Type Indicator® represents a personality type theory that helps explain the ways in which group members see, think, and make decisions about their group, its goals, and the world around them.
- Myers-Briggs divides personalities into four categories with opposite preferences in each category: extrovert or introvert, sensor or intuitive, thinker or feeler, and judger or perceiver.
- Effective participants must be ready, willing, and able to contribute to a group's goal.
- Although there are many causes of individual and group apathy, groups can lessen apathy's effects by establishing clear goals, assigning appropriate tasks, and confronting apathy head-on.
- Although there are occasions when a deviant member is needed and valuable, groups can use several strategies to deal with deviants including accepting, confronting, or excluding such members.
- Hidden agendas occur when a member's hidden goals and methods conflict with the group's goals and methods. Groups can lessen the effects of hidden agendas by recognizing and, if possible, resolving conflicting motives and goals within a group.

Groupwork *Type Talk in Groups*

GOAL   To understand how Myers-Briggs type preferences impact group perceptions and interaction.

PARTICIPANTS   Groups of 4 or 5 members.

PROCEDURE

1. Using the chapter and the descriptive words listed in the following table, group members should select the four types that best describe their own preferences and personality types.
2. Group members should also determine which types best describe the personalities of other group members.
3. Upon completing this step, all members should share their perceptions with the rest of the group, including their own four preferences.
4. Discuss the extent to which member perceptions match one another.
   - To what extent and why is there agreement or disagreement?
   - Is the group missing any of the types?
   - How could the absence of one or more types affect group interaction and productivity?

Types of Preferences

Extrovert. Is outgoing; speaks then thinks; is sociable; likes groups	**Introvert.** Is private; thinks then speaks; is reflective; prefers to work alone
Sensor. Focuses on details; is factual, practical, and realistic; likes facts	**Intuitive.** Focuses on the big picture; is theoretical; gets bored with facts/details
Thinker. Is task-oriented, objective, firm, analytical, and detached	**Feeler.** Is people-oriented, subjective, humane, appreciative, and involved
Judger. Is well-organized, structured, in control, and definite; likes deadlines	**Perceiver.** Is flexible, goes-with-the-flow; dislikes deadlines; is spontaneous

Participation Assessment Instrument

Directions   Use the following items to evaluate the quantity and quality of participation by the individual members of your group. Write a summary assessment in the space provided at the end of the instrument.

1. Contribution to the group's *task functions*. (Provides or asks for information and opinions, initiates discussion, clarifies, summarizes, evaluates, energizes, etc.)

5	4	3	2	1
Excellent		Average		Poor

2. Contribution to the group's *maintenance functions*. (Serves as encourager, harmonizer, compromiser, tension releaser, gatekeeper, standard monitor, observer, follower, etc.)

5	4	3	2	1
Excellent		Average		Poor

3. Contribution to effective and efficient *group process*. (Avoids self-centered roles, follows the agenda, respects and adapts to member traits and differences, etc.)

5	4	3	2	1
Excellent		Average		Poor

4. *Readiness* to contribute. (Being prepared)

5	4	3	2	1
Excellent		Average		Poor

5. *Willingness* to contribute. (Level of commitment to group's goal; willingness to share, listen, adapt, exercise responsibility, etc.)

5	4	3	2	1
Excellent		Average		Poor

6. *Ability* to contribute. (Communication skills and technical skills)

5	4	3	2	1
Excellent		Average		Poor

7. Ability to deal with *difficulties*. (Apathy, deviant members, hidden agendas, etc.)

5	4	3	2	1
Excellent		Average		Poor

8. *Overall Effectiveness*.

5	4	3	2	1
Excellent		Average		Poor

(continued)

(Participation Assessment Instrument, *continued*)

Summary Comments

Recommended Readings

Kroeger, O. with Thuesen, J. M. (1992). *Type talk at work.* New York: Dell.

Larson, C. E. & LaFasto, F. M. J. (1989). *TeamWork: What must go right/What can go wrong.* Newbury Park, CA: Sage.

Levasseur, R. E. (1994). *Breakthrough business meetings: Shared leadership in action.* Holbrook, MA: Bob Adams.

Notes

1. Wills, G. (1994). *Certain trumpets: The call of leaders.* New York: Simon & Schuster, p. 13.
2. Bennis, W. & Biederman, P. W. (1997) *Organizing genius: The secrets of creative collaboration.* Reading, MA: Addison-Wesley, p. 5.
3. Wills, p. 13.
4. Benne, K. D. & Sheats, P. (1948). Functional roles of group members. *Journal of Social Issues,* 4, pp. 41–49.
5. Myers, I. B. with Myers, P. B. (1990). *Gifts differing: Tenth anniversary edition.* Palo Alto, CA: Consulting Psychologists, p. 1.
6. Levasseur, R. E. (1994). *Breakthrough business meetings: Shared leadership in action.* Holbrook, MA: Bob Adams, p. 79.
7. Jaffe, J. M. (1985). Of different minds. *Association Management,* 37, pp. 120–124.
8. Larson, C. E. & LaFasto, F. M. J. (1989). *TeamWork: What must go right/What can go wrong.* Newbury Park, CA: Sage, p. 63.
9. Kroeger, O. & Thuesen, J. M. (1988). *Type talk: Or how to determine your personality type and change your life.* New York: Delacorte.

10. Kroeger & Thuesen, p. 114.
11. Levasseur, pp. 87–88.
12. Billington, J. (1997 January). "The three essentials of an effective team." *Harvard Management Update, 2,* p. 1.
13. Larson & LaFasto, p. 62.
14. Pascarella, P. (1998 April). "Stacked deck." *Across The Board, 35,* p. 48.
15. Bennis and Biederman, p. 210.
16. Barnlund, D. C. & Haiman, C. (1960). *The dynamics of group discussion.* Boston: Houghton Mifflin, p. 208.
17. Napier, R. W. & Gershenfeld, M. K. (1993). *Groups: Theory and experience* (5th ed.). Boston: Houghton Mifflin, p. 194.

Interaction Skills

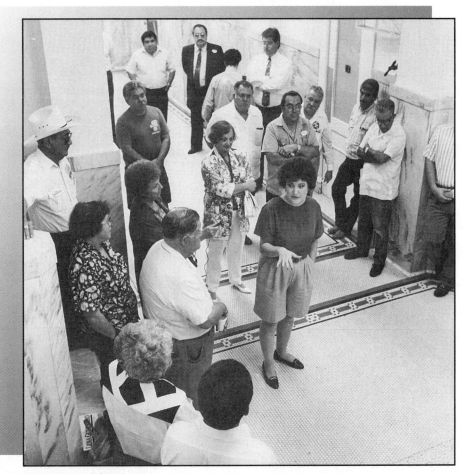

Bob Daemmrich/Stock Boston

Confidence in Groups

You Must Talk

Why is it that some well-informed group members say very little, even when their knowledge is essential to the group's success? Why do some members remain silent even when they strongly disagree with someone else's opinion? One answer to these questions can be found in a single phrase: Lack of confidence.

Regardless of what you know, think, experience, or need, your level of confidence has a direct effect on the amount of talking you do in a group as well as the usefulness of that talk. Members who lack confidence are less likely to share what they know or voice their opinion. Confidence is often the major factor that separates effective group members from those who have difficulty fulfilling their responsibilities.

A member's level of confidence in a group discussion is related to three significant factors: self-concept, oral communication apprehension, and social tensions.

Self-Concept

Self-concept is what you think or believe about yourself and your ability to participate in groups. Without a positive self-concept, it is difficult to become an effective group member. Self-concept is a curious thing. Most of us see ourselves as bright and hard-working team players. At the same time, all of us have occasional doubts. We know people who seem smarter or more interesting than we are. We've seen natural leaders take over groups with assurance. Are these members really superior, or is their confidence a reflection of positive self-concepts? For example, if becoming a leader depends on talking early and often as well as on expressing an opinion in the face of disagreement, members who are sure of themselves are more likely to emerge as leaders. Depending on how good you feel about yourself, you can enter a

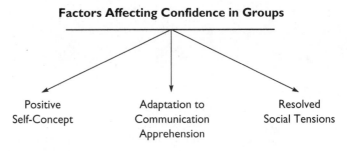

FIGURE 5.1 Factors Affecting Confidence in Groups

group discussion with confidence and confront controversial issues with conviction.

Given the advantages of a positive self-concept, an obvious question arises. Is it possible to improve your self-confidence and, as a result, your self-concept? The answer is yes, depending on how receptive you are to feedback and how well you give helpful feedback to others.

Receiving Feedback

Feedback is the verbal or nonverbal response to communication. Feedback tells us whether our intended message is the message actually received. Everyone in a group discussion reacts in some way to what is said or done. Sometimes that reaction is crystal clear—a group member nods and says, "Yes, that's a good suggestion." At other times, you may have no idea whether other members think a suggestion is good or bad. Most of the time, however, there is some form of feedback that can help you determine the kind of effect you are having on other group members.

According to Napier and Gershenfeld, "In a group honest feedback can increase accuracy, instill a sense of being understood, and promote closeness and a sense of confidence."[1] For example, if feedback indicates that other group members are hesitant to accept your suggestions, you may modify your ideas to adapt to the group's response. Such adaptation can enhance your value to the group and improve your confidence. If, on the other hand, the group looks to you for advice and follows every suggestion you make, your level of confidence may skyrocket.

EFFECTIVE group members are confident group members. How does a member's confidence promote group success? (Rob Lewine/The Stock Market)

As you participate in a group discussion, look for and listen to the ways in which group members react to you. Do they look interested or bored, pleased or displeased? Amazingly, some group members continue to chatter on even though other members have tuned them out.

If you can't see or hear reactions, ask for feedback. There is nothing wrong with asking group members whether they understand or agree with you. A question as simple as "Does this make sense?" or "Is that a frown, Alicia?" can provide you with useful feedback. Not only does such feedback help you adapt to the group, it also lets group members know you are interested in their reactions.

Providing Feedback

The more sensitive a group is to feedback, the better it will understand itself and its members. Just like individual people, groups tend to work more effectively when they get feedback on how they're doing. You can help this process by giving clear feedback to other members. If you don't understand what members are saying, tell them so or ask a direct question. If you like an idea, smile and nod. Just as feedback can help you learn more about yourself, you can help group members become more effective by providing useful feedback.

Giving useful feedback is much more than remembering to nod in agreement or offer praise. If, for example, group members have been side-stepping a tough issue and are complaining about their lack of progress, what would you say? If you said, "well, nobody said this would be easy," your feedback would neither change the situation nor offer hope for improvement. Short suggests that effective feedback identifies your feelings, thoughts, and wants: "I'm a little frustrated with this discussion (feeling), because we seem to be avoiding the real issue (thought). Let's talk about what's really hanging us up (want)."[2] Even though it can be risky to express feedback in this way, the result can increase your credibility and confidence while moving the group forward. The following guidelines can help you provide feedback that facilitates understanding and improves discussion:

Focus on behavior (rather than the person).
Describe the behavior (rather than judge it).
Provide observations (rather than assumptions).
Choose an appropriate time and place.
Give feedback to help the other person (rather than meet your own needs).[3]

Confident group members usually have strong self-concepts and an assurance that they can understand and adapt to feedback from the rest of the group. They also feel more comfortable and willing to express their thoughts, feelings, and wants. Members who lack confidence are often preoccupied with worries about how the group will react to them and their ideas. They rarely provide useful feedback. Members who neglect feedback are neglecting an important and valuable source of information about their own effectiveness.

Communication Apprehension

The anxiety that we sometimes experience when speaking to others is referred to by many names: stage fright, speech anxiety, podium panic, and communication apprehension.

James C. McCroskey and his colleagues have investigated the anxieties people feel when they are asked to speak to others in a variety of settings. The result of this study is a large body of research that has important implications for group effectiveness. McCroskey defines **communication apprehension** as "the fear or anxiety associated with either real or anticipated communication with another person or persons."[4] This definition emphasizes that there are different levels of apprehension, depending on several factors such as the personality of the speaker, the nature of the audience, and the characteristics of the occasion or setting. In other words, a person may have no fears when talking to a friend or colleagues but may experience high levels of anxiety when asked to address a group of strangers in a large auditorium. Talking at a weekly staff meeting may be easy, but defending a department's actions at a meeting of company executives may generate high levels of anxiety.

About 20 percent of the general population experiences very high levels of communication apprehension. When that anxiety is measured in public speaking settings, the numbers go much higher. In fact, several national surveys have discovered that fear of speaking in public is the number one fear among North Americans, way ahead of fear of heights, snakes, financial problems, and even fear of death. However, communication apprehension is not just a fear of public speaking; many people experience fear and anxiety when communicating in groups.

McCroskey and Richmond have declared that "it is not an exaggeration to suggest that CA (Communication Apprehension) may be the single most important factor in predicting communication behavior in a small group."[5] They go on to describe the effects of communication apprehension in several areas including the amount of talk, the content of communication, and the resulting perceptions of other group members.

Quantity of Talk If you are fearful about doing something, you probably will avoid that experience. In groups, anxious members are less likely to talk than confident members. Very often, highly apprehensive members will talk only when called

---

TOOLBOX 5.1 PRCA

At the end of this chapter, there is a self-test called the Personal Report of Communication Apprehension, or PRCA. You might want to complete this questionnaire and follow the scoring instructions before reading the rest of this section. Your PRCA scores, particularly those related to groups and meetings, will help you understand how communication apprehension can affect your participation in small group communication.

upon. When they must speak, they say less or answer questions by agreeing rather than voicing their concerns and opinions. Moreover, members who speak infrequently tend to perceive the group and its processes negatively.[6]

Nonverbal behaviors often reveal a person's level of communication apprehension. Rather than talking, an apprehensive speaker may giggle or smile when asked to discuss a serious issue. Anxious members may repeat a distracting motion such as tapping a pencil or pushing up eyeglasses. Occasionally, highly apprehensive participants talk too much as a way of confronting or overcompensating for their fear. Although such speakers may seem domineering and aggressive, actually they are fearful.

Quality of Talk   If you are fearful about communicating, a lot of your attention and energy will be focused on how you feel rather than on what you say. When highly apprehensive participants are required to talk, their speech is often awkward. Sentences may be loaded with filler phrases such as "you know," "well uh," "like," and "okay." The tone of voice may communicate distress or may be mistaken for disinterest.

Equally significant, apprehensive participants may talk about things that have little to do with the topic being discussed. They are so focused on their internal feelings that they may be unaware of the discussion's direction or focus. There is also a tendency for apprehensive speakers to avoid disagreement or conflict. They may go along with the majority whether they agree or not. Expressing disagreement is too risky. Someone might challenge their position or, even worse, ask them to explain or justify their disagreement. For a highly apprehensive group member, it's much easier to become a silent member of the majority.

Perception of Others   As a result of talking less, apprehensive participants are viewed as less confident, less assertive, and even less responsible. Furthermore, group members who speak more are often better liked than those who speak infrequently.[7] Chapter 3 indicated that leadership is often granted to members who talk early and often and who volunteer ideas and extra effort. Rarely will a reluctant communicator be seen as a potential leader.

As real as communication apprehension is, it is not an insurmountable obstacle. Highly apprehensive speakers do not wear signs declaring their lack of confidence. Neither are they less intelligent, less hard working, or less competent than their more confident colleagues. In fact, participants who experience very little communication apprehension may exhibit many of the same characteristics as high apprehensives. One such participant put it this way:

> Sometimes I choose to remain silent if I don't know much about the topic or if the issue being discussed is something I don't care about. Sometimes I'm quiet because I don't want to be an active participant. You see, I'm often selected to chair subcommittees or complete an extra task just because

I'm so vocal. If I'm quiet, I can avoid the extra work. There are even times when I don't express my opinion because I know better than to challenge a strong group member during a meeting, particularly if I'm more likely to succeed in a private, one-on-one conversation.

There are two interesting points to be noted in the preceding comments. The first is the fact that a low apprehensive may exhibit the same behavior as a high apprehensive. The second point is that the group member chooses to be quiet as part of her strategy, rather than as a response to anxiety. A more apprehensive speaker can make these same choices.

Whether your score on the Personal Report of Communication Apprehension at the end of this chapter is high or low, there are ways you can help everyone in a group improve her or his level of communication confidence. First, it is important to understand that it is impossible to predict what is going to happen in a group solely on the basis of members' communication apprehension scores. Although someone is anxious, she or he may still speak or express an opinion. On the other hand, the fact that someone is a confident speaker doesn't necessarily mean that this person is the group's natural leader. Don't stereotype group members on the basis of their feelings about communicating. Categorizing members as fearful or fearless will not help your group become more productive.

Coping with Communication Apprehension

By learning to deal with communication apprehension, all group members can become more confident and competent as they balance talking with listening. Methods of coping with communication apprehension are separated into two categories: guidelines for high apprehensives and those for low apprehensives.

Guidelines for High Apprehensives

If your PRCA score classifies you as an apprehensive speaker or if you believe your level of anxiety associated with talking in groups is unusually high, the following four strategies may help you reduce your level of fear:

- Realize you are not alone.
- Read and talk about it.
- Be well prepared.
- Learn communication skills.

You Are Not Alone.   Everyone has experienced communication apprehension in certain settings. According to McCroskey and Richmond, "almost 95 percent of the population reports being scared about communicating with a person or group at some point in their lives."[8] If you dread the thought of communicating in a group or public setting, you are joined by thousands of people who feel the same way. Such feelings are normal. As you listen to other group members, don't assume that it is easy for them to talk. Several of them probably experience the same level of fear and anxiety that you do.

Read and Talk about It. If you were experiencing a personal problem, there would be nothing unusual about reading a self-help book or asking a friend or family member for advice or assistance. The same is true about communicating. Letting a trusted member of your group know how difficult it is for you to enter the discussion can give you a helpful ally. Not only can such an ally help you get a word in when you have something to say, you may also discover that your friend is just as nervous as you are. If you want the advice of experts, the books listed as recommended reading at the end of this chapter can help you understand and deal with communication apprehension.

Be Well Prepared. Although you cannot totally eliminate communication apprehension, you can and should be well prepared for every group discussion. Being prepared can reduce anxieties about participating. Many successful participants who also experience high levels of communication apprehension spend extra time making sure that they have prepared themselves for the topics scheduled for discussion. Well-prepared members know more about the topic and have a clear idea of the positions they support. As a result, they are more confident when asked to participate. Being well prepared will not completely eliminate anxiety, but it can reduce a member's fear that he or she will be at a loss for relevant ideas and information when asked to contribute to the group discussion. Chapter 12 provides guidance on how to gather and use research for a group discussion.

Learn Communication Skills. If you were trying to improve your tennis game, you would try to improve specific skills—your serve, your return, or your backhand shot. The same is true about communicating in groups. There are specific and learnable communication skills that can help you improve your ability to participate in groups. These skills are described throughout this textbook. Learning skills related to becoming more sensitive to feedback, following a group's agenda, or serving as an effective group leader and follower can give you the tools you need to succeed in a group discussion. Improving communication skills will not erase communication apprehension, but it can reduce your level of anxiety. So, instead of telling yourself "I can't participate, I'm not a skilled communicator," try telling yourself "I'm learning."[9]

Guidelines for Low Apprehensives If your PRCA score classifies you as a low apprehensive speaker, you may be able to help group members whose anxieties jeopardize their ability to participate in a group discussion. The following three strategies may reduce other members' level of communication apprehension:

- Be supportive.
- Include anxious members.
- Stop talking.

Be Supportive.   Members who experience very little communication anxiety should be patient with and supportive of those who lack confidence. For those who are fearless in groups, it is fairly easy to interrupt a speaker or make a point in a strong and confident voice. Such interruptions may devastate a reluctant group member who is struggling to participate but is overlooked by more aggressive members. Without support and encouragement, "even seasoned team members may never develop the confidence required to make their views known."[10]

Include Anxious Members.   Patience and understanding alone may not be enough to encourage a member too frightened to join in a discussion. Members who experience low levels of communication apprehension should try to include their nervous colleagues. Quiet members often have important information and good ideas. Encouraging anxious members to speak up contributes to the group's overall success.[11] There are, however, both effective and counterproductive ways to include someone. Confronting a reluctant speaker with a direct request such as "Why in the world do you disagree with the rest of us?" is not very helpful. Asking a question that you know the apprehensive person is able to answer or taking turns in speaking are much more likely ways to include all members.

Stop Talking.   Finally, the most obvious thing you can do to help those who have difficulty participating is to stop talking. If you know that other members have difficulty entering the discussion or interrupting someone who is speaking, try to curb your own comments so that others have a chance to contribute.

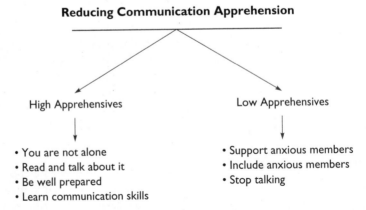

Reducing Communication Apprehension

High Apprehensives

- You are not alone
- Read and talk about it
- Be well prepared
- Learn communication skills

Low Apprehensives

- Support anxious members
- Include anxious members
- Stop talking

FIGURE 5.2 Reducing Communication Apprehension

It is helpful to keep a careful eye on less-than-confident participants. Often you will see members take in a breath as though they want to speak only to be stifled by your continued comments or by the comments of others. When that happens, conclude your remarks and turn to the person who was trying to contribute in order to give that person an opportunity to speak.

Social Tensions

Although communication apprehension is an important factor in predicting behavior, it cannot totally explain why a group is confident or anxious. The social tension in a group also has a major influence on the amount and quality of talk in a group discussion. Not only can individual group members experience anxieties, but groups as a whole can experience tension. Ernest G. Bormann describes two types of group tension: primary tension and secondary tension.[12] Rather than examine how individual anxieties affect group behavior, Bormann observed the ways in which newly formed groups exhibit a unique but predictable set of behaviors. Understanding the causes and consequences of a group's social tension can help a group become more efficient and effective.

Primary Tension

When you join a group and attend its first meeting, you don't know what to expect. Will everyone get along and work hard? Will you make a good first impression? Will this be a positive experience or a nightmare? Most people enter a new group with caution. Bormann describes **primary tension** as the social unease and inhibitions that accompany the getting-acquainted stage in a new group. At a group's first meeting, several signs can indicate whether primary tension is affecting group behavior.

Because most new group members want to create a good first impression, they tend to be overly polite with one another. Members don't interrupt each other; there may be long, awkward pauses between comments. When members do speak, they often speak softly and avoid expressing strong opinions. Although laughter may occur, it is often strained, inappropriate, or awkward. When the group starts its discussion, the topic may be small talk about sports, the weather, or a recent news event.

Not surprisingly, primary tension and communication apprehension are related. Much like a highly apprehensive person, a group experiencing primary tension may talk less, provide little in the way of content, and be perceived as ineffective. Before a group can work efficiently and effectively, primary tension must be reduced. Usually, as members feel more comfortable with each other, initial tension decreases. In some groups, primary tension lasts only a few minutes. In less fortunate groups, primary tension may continue for months. Extreme politeness, hushed speech, and strained laughter can become irritating. That situation, in addition to lack of progress, can

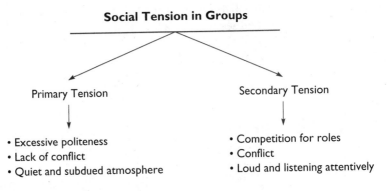

FIGURE 5.3 Social Tension in Groups

increase the number of absences. The group may fail to become a cohesive and productive team.

In many groups, primary tension will disappear quickly and naturally as group members gain confidence and become better acquainted. In other groups, direct intervention is needed to relieve this early form of tension. Recognizing and discussing primary tension is one way of breaking its cycle. A perceptive leader or participant can purposely exhibit behavior that counteracts primary tension such as talking in a strong voice, looking involved and energized, sticking to the group's topic, and expressing an opinion.

Usually, with each group meeting, the amount of primary tension decreases. For better or worse, first impressions have been made. If, however, primary tension remains, a group can stall and never get anywhere. On the other hand, if primary tension is resolved, a group may then move on to a very different kind of social tension.

Secondary Tension

Once a group overcomes primary tension, it tries to get down to business. As soon as the group engages in this process, though, a different kind of tension can develop. The most confident members now begin to compete for social acceptance and leadership. They openly disagree on issues of substance. It is still too early in the group's existence to predict the outcome of such competition. The frustrations and personality conflicts experienced by group members as they compete for social acceptance and achievement within a group are the source of what Bormann calls **secondary tension.**

Whereas primary tension arises from lack of confidence, secondary tension emerges when members have gained enough confidence to become assertive and even aggressive as they pursue positions of power and influence. In periods of secondary tension, personality conflicts can result from disagreements over issues, conflicts in values, and an inability to deal with disruptive members. Regardless of the causes, a group cannot hope to achieve its goals if secondary tension is not controlled. The signs of secondary tension

> **TOOLBOX 5.2** Group Development and Tension
>
> Primary and secondary tension resemble the first two stages of group development. During the initial forming or orientation phase, group members are cautious; they hold back and don't commit themselves to specific positions or proposals. During the storming or conflict phase of group development, controversy and conflict are common. Members begin competing for leadership positions. **Chapter 2: Group Formation and Development** discusses the phases of group development in detail.

are almost the direct opposite of those of primary tension. There is a high level of energy and agitation. The group is noisier, more dynamic, and physically active. Members speak in louder voices, interrupting and overlapping one another so that two or three people may be speaking at the same time. Members sit up straight, lean forward, or squirm in their seats. Everyone is watching and listening intently.

As with primary tension, secondary tension is a natural occurrence and must be resolved if a group is to become effective. Members of successful groups develop ways to handle this phase in a group's development. Often, one or two members will joke about the tension within the group. The resulting laughter is likely to ease the stress of secondary tension. Sometimes individual members will work outside the group setting to discuss the personal difficulties and anxieties of group members. It can be difficult, and even painful, to deal with secondary tension. However, if a group fails to resolve human relations problems, it will not become an effective work group.

Most groups experience some form of primary and secondary tension. In fact, a little bit of tension is advantageous. It can motivate a group toward action and increase a group's sensitivity to feedback. Ellis and Fisher summarize the impact of social tensions on a group by writing that "the successful and socially healthy group is not characterized by an absence of social tension, but by successful management of social tension."[13]

Balancing Confidence and Tension

Group effectiveness and member confidence are inseparable. Balancing the quantity and quality of participation in a group discussion means understanding how confidence affects group interaction. Group leaders as well as members should try to balance the amount of talk in a group by providing opportunities for quiet members while restraining members who may dominate a discussion.

Receptive to Feedback
High Communication Apprehension
Primary Tension

Provides Feedback
Low Communication Apprehension
Secondary Tensions

FIGURE 5.4 Member and Group Confidence

When the confidence of individual team members is combined with a successful resolution to primary and secondary tension, the outcome is a strong feeling of team confidence among group members. The group, as a whole, becomes more sure of itself, its goals, and the ability of members to achieve those goals. Larson and LaFasto have concluded that this kind of confidence "translates into the ability of a team to be self-correcting in its capacity to adjust to unexpected adversity and emergent challenges."[14] In other words, a confident group is highly adaptive and welcomes challenge.

A group's ability to achieve its goals is directly related to finding the right balance between tension and confidence. Whereas a certain level of tension can motivate a group to resolve differences and move forward, too much tension can preoccupy a group with personal anxieties and role conflicts. On the other hand, whereas the right amount of confidence can give a group energy and determination, too much confidence can make a group arrogant and insensitive. An effective group tries to balance tension and confidence; it seeks ways to strengthen each member's self-concept in order to strengthen the group as a whole.

Summary Study Guide

- A person's self-concept as well as his or her level of oral communication apprehension significantly affects member confidence.
- Adapting to and giving feedback are critical communication skills because they help members understand and modify the effect they are having on the rest of the group.
- Communication apprehension is the fear and anxiety associated with either real or anticipated communication with another person or persons.
- A person's level of communication apprehension affects the quantity and quality of talk and the resulting perceptions of other group members.

- Coping with communication apprehension requires the self-understanding and effort of low apprehensive members as well as remedial action by high apprehensive members.
- Most groups experience both primary and secondary tension during the early stages of the group's development.
- Productive groups are characterized by successful management of social tension.

Groupwork *Sorting the Symptoms*

GOAL   To summarize and understand the symptoms of communication apprehension.

PARTICIPANTS   Groups of 5–7 members.

PROCEDURE

1. Make a list of the symptoms of communication apprehension (increased heart rate, excessive perspiration, filler phrases such as "you know" and "o.k.") that *you* experience when speaking to a group or giving a public presentation.
2. Create a master list of symptoms by combining the lists of all group members.
3. Identify the symptoms that are more likely to occur during a group discussion.
4. Discuss the following questions:
    - How can the type of group or topic of discussion affect the number and severity of symptoms?
    - Which symptoms can or cannot be seen or heard by other group members?
    - What is the relationship, if any, between the number and type of symptoms and a person's PRCA score for groups, meetings, interpersonal communication, and public speaking?
    - How can you alleviate some of the causes and symptoms of communication apprehension in groups?

ASSESSMENT

Personal Report of Communication Apprehension (PRCA-24)

Directions This instrument is composed of twenty-four statements concerning feelings about communication with other people. Please indicate the degree to which each statement applies to you by marking whether you (1) strongly agree, (2) agree, (3) are undecided, (4) disagree, or (5) strongly disagree. Work quickly; record your first impression.

_____ 1. I dislike participating in group discussions.

_____ 2. Generally, I am comfortable while participating in group discussions.

_____ 3. I am tense and nervous while participating in group discussions.

_____ 4. I like to get involved in group discussions.

_____ 5. Engaging in a group discussion with new people makes me tense and nervous.

_____ 6. I am calm and relaxed while participating in a group discussion.

_____ 7. Generally, I am nervous when I have to participate in a meeting.

_____ 8. Usually I am calm and relaxed while participating in a meeting.

_____ 9. I am very calm and relaxed when I am called upon to express an opinion at a meeting.

_____ 10. I am afraid to express myself at meetings.

_____ 11. Communicating at meetings usually makes me feel uncomfortable.

_____ 12. I am very relaxed when answering questions at a meeting.

_____ 13. While participating in a conversation with a new acquaintance, I feel very nervous.

_____ 14. I have no fear of speaking up in conversations.

_____ 15. Ordinarily I am very tense and nervous in conversations.

_____ 16. Ordinarily I am very calm and relaxed in conversations.

_____ 17. While conversing with a new acquaintance, I feel very relaxed.

_____ 18. I'm afraid to speak up in conversations.

_____ 19. I have no fear of giving a speech.

_____ 20. Certain parts of my body feel very tense and rigid while I am giving a speech.

_____ 21. I feel relaxed while giving a speech.

_____ 22. My thoughts become confused and jumbled when I am giving a speech.

_____ 23. I face the prospect of giving a speech with confidence.

_____ 24. While giving a speech, I get so nervous I forget facts I really know.

Scoring

The PRCA permits computation of one total score and four subscores. The subscores are related to communication apprehension in each of four common communication contexts: group discussions, meetings, interpersonal conversations, and public speaking. To compute your scores, merely add or subtract your scores for each item as indicated below.

Subscores	Scoring Formula
Group Discussion	18 + scores for items 2, 4, and 6; − scores for items 1, 3, and 5.
Meetings	18 + scores for items 8, 9, and 12; − scores for items 7, 10, and 11.
Interpersonal Conversation	18 + scores for items 14, 16, and 17; − scores for items 13, 15, and 18.
Public Speaking	18 + scores for items 19, 21, and 23; − scores for items 20, 22, and 24.

To obtain your total score for the PRCA, simply add your four subscores together. Your score should range between 24 and 120. If your score is below 24 or above 120, you have made a mistake in computing the score. Scores on the four contexts (groups, meetings, interpersonal conversations, and public speaking) can range from a low of 6 to a high of 30. Any score above 18 indicates some degree of apprehension. If your score is above 18 for the public speaking context, you are like the overwhelming majority of Americans.

Norms for PRCA-24:

	MEAN	STANDARD DEVIATION
Total Score	65.5	15.3
Group	15.4	4.8
Meetings	16.4	4.8
Interpersonal	14.5	4.2
Public Speaking	19.3	5.1

Source: *PRCA-24* reprinted with permission from the author from: James C. McCroskey (1993). *An introduction to rhetorical communication,* 6th ed. Englewood Cliffs, N.J.: Prentice Hall, Inc. p. 37.

Recommended Readings

Dwyer, K. K. (1998). *Conquer your speech fright*. Forth Worth, TX: Harcourt Brace.

McCroskey, J. C. & Richmond, V. (1995). *Communication: Apprehension, avoidance, and effectiveness* (4th ed.). Scottsdale, AZ: Gorsuch, Scarisbrick.

Motley, M. T. (1997). *Overcoming your fear of public speaking: A proven method*. Boston, MA: Houghton Mifflin Company.

Notes

1. Napier, R. W. & Gershenfeld, M. K. (1993). *Groups: Theory and experience* (5th ed.). Boston: Houghton Mifflin, p. 32.
2. Short, R. (1991). *A special kind of leadership: The key to learning organizations*. Seattle, WA: The Leadership Group, pp. 17 & 26.
3. Lloyd, S. R. (1996). *Leading teams: The skills for success*. West Des Moines, IA: American Media, p. 57.
4. McCroskey, J. C. & Richmond, V. (1995). *Communication: Apprehension, avoidance, and effectiveness* (4th ed.). Scottsdale, AZ: Gorsuch, Scarisbrick, p. 32.
5. McCroskey, J. C. & Richmond, V. (1992). Communication apprehension and small group communication. In R. S. Cathcart & L. A. Samovar (Eds.). *Small group communication: A reader* (6th ed.). Dubuque, IA: Wm. C. Brown, p. 368.
6. Bonito, J. A. & Hollingshead, A. B. (1997). Participation in small groups. In B. R. Burleson (Ed.), *Communication Yearbook, 20*. Thousand Oaks, CA: Sage, p. 245.
7. Bonito & Hollingshead, p. 245.
8. McCroskey & Richmond, p. 46.
9. Dreher, D. (1996). *The tao of personal leadership*. New York: HarperCollins, p. 75.
10. Crowe, M. (1996 November). "Why the members of your group won't speak up, and what you can do about it." *Harvard Management Update, 1*, p. 8.
11. Bonito and Hollingshead, p. 249.
12. Bormann, E. G. (1990). *Small group communication: Theory and practice* (3rd ed.). New York: Harper & Row.
13. Ellis, D. G. & Fisher, B. A. (1994). *Small group decision making: Communication and the group process* (4th ed.). New York: McGraw-Hill, pp. 43–44.
14. Larson, C. E. & LaFasto, F. M. J. (1989). *TeamWork: What must go right/What can go wrong*. Newbury Park, CA: Sage, p. 71.

Listening in Groups

Speaking and Listening

We cannot overestimate the importance of effective listening in groups as well as the consequences of poor listening. As Michael Nichols has written, "When we're with someone who doesn't listen, we shut down. When we're with someone who's . . . a good listener . . . we perk up and come alive."[1] Would you prefer to work with someone who listens attentively or someone who interrupts you, completes other members' sentences for them, and concentrates on the next thing he or she is going to say? Bonnie Jacobson, author of *If Only You Would Listen,* believes that "the main skill required to build an effective work team is keeping your mouth shut and giving your team members the chance to give you their point of view."[2]

At first, listening may appear to be as easy and natural as breathing. After all, everyone listens. In fact, just the opposite may be closer to the truth. Although most of us can *hear,* we often fail to *listen* to what others have to say. Hearing and listening are not the same. Hearing requires only physical ability; listening, however, requires thinking ability. In some groups, a member who is hearing-impaired may be a better listener than someone who can hear the faintest sound. The International Listening Association defines **listening** as "the process of receiving, constructing meaning from, and responding to spoken and/or nonverbal messages."[3]

The Need for Effective Listening

Listening is our number one communication activity. Although percentages vary from study to study, Figure 6.1 summarizes how most people divide their daily communication time.

One study of college students found that listening occupies more than half of their communicating time.[4] In the corporate world, where it has been estimated that managers spend the equivalent of two out of every five working days in meetings, executives may devote over 60 percent of their workday listening to others.[5]

Communication Activity	Percentages
Listening	40–70%
Speaking	20–35%
Reading	10–20%
Writing	5–15%

FIGURE 6.1   Percent of Time Spent Communicating

EFFECTIVE listening involves appropriate verbal and nonverbal behaviors. What nonverbal behaviors do these group members exhibit that suggest they are listening effectively? (Gale Zucker/Stock Boston)

Numerous studies have pointed to the importance of listening in education, law, health care, customer service, journalism, counseling, and business management.[6]   Unfortunately, most of us have had little or no listening instruction. The need for such training was demonstrated in a survey of the five hundred largest U.S. corporations, in which 59 percent of the respondents reported that they provide listening training for their employees.[7]

Listening is more difficult in groups than in almost any other situation.   There are multiple speakers, multiple perspectives, and multiple goals. In groups, you are expected to listen and, at the same time, be able to respond, on the spot, to unexpected news, unusual ideas, and conflicting points of view. Instead of concentrating on what one person says and does, an effective group listener must pay attention to the reactions of everyone in the group. In a group discussion, a short daydream, a side conversation, or thoughts about a personal problem can result in missed information, misinterpreted instructions, and inappropriate reactions. Complicating matters is the fact that the social pressure to listen in groups is not as strong as it would be in a conversation with just one other person. If one group member doesn't listen or respond, others usually will. Thus, group members may be poor listeners because they count on others to listen for them.[8]

On the whole, most of us are not very good listeners. Several studies have reported that immediately after listening to a short talk, most of us cannot accurately report 50 percent of what was said. Without training, we listen at only 25 percent efficiency.[9] And, of that 25 percent, most of what we remember is a distorted or inaccurate recollection.[10]

The vast majority of your time in groups will be spent listening. Even during a simple half-hour meeting of five people, it is unlikely that any member will talk more than a total of ten minutes—unless that person wants to be accused of monopolizing the discussion. Unfortunately, many of us place more emphasis on the roles and responsibilities of group members who talk rather than those who listen. Kelly has claimed that "this unbalanced emphasis, especially as it actually affects persons in real discussions, could be an important cause of the problems that speaking is supposed to cure. . . ."[11] In other words, if you are only concerned about what you are going to say in a group discussion, you can't give full attention to what is being said by others.

Types of Listening

Listening is a complex behavior. Researchers have identified several types of listening, each requiring the ability to hear and see reactions, but different enough to call upon unique listening skills. Within groups, the most important types of listening are comprehensive, empathic, critical, and appreciative listening.

Comprehensive Listening

Comprehensive listening in a group discussion requires an answer to the following question: What do group members mean? **Comprehensive listening** focuses on accurately understanding the meaning of group members' spoken and nonverbal messages.

Two basic steps are involved in this fundamental type of listening. The first is making sure you accurately hear what a member is saying while paying attention to nonverbal cues such as facial expressions, gestures, posture, and vocal quality. The second step in comprehensive listening is making sure that a group member's meaning and your interpretation are similar. Make sure you accurately understand what the person means. Can you identify the main ideas as well as the arguments or evidence used to support a conclusion?

Comprehensive listening is such a vital skill that there is little point in mastering other types of listening until you are sure you understand what other group members have said. After all, if you don't understand what a person means, you can't be expected to respond in a reasonable way. For example, an after-class discussion might begin as follows: "Let's have a party on the last day of class," says Geneva. A comprehensive listener may wonder whether Geneva means (1) we should have a party instead of an exam, (2) we should ask the instructor whether we can have a party, or (3) we should have a party after class. Misinterpreting the meaning of Geneva's comment could result in an inappropriate response.

Empathic Listening

Empathic listening in a group discussion requires an answer to the following question: How do group members feel? **Empathic listening** goes beyond understanding what a person means; it focuses on understanding and identifying with a member's situation, feelings, or motives. Can you see the situation through the other member's eyes? Put another way, how would you feel in a similar situation?

By not listening for feelings, you may overlook the most important part of a message. Even if you understand every word a person says, you can still miss the anger, enthusiasm, or frustration in a group member's voice. An empathic listener doesn't have to agree with or feel the same as other group members but does have to try to understand the type and intensity of feelings that those members are experiencing. For example, the after-class discussion might continue as follows: "A class party would be a waste of time," exclaims Kim. An empathic listener may wonder whether Kim means (1) she has more important things to do during exam week, (2) she doesn't think the class or the instructor deserves a party, or (3) she doesn't want to be obligated to attend such a party.

Critical Listening

Critical listening asks this question: What's my opinion? **Critical listening** focuses on analyzing and forming appropriate opinions about the content of a message. It requires critical thinking and careful analysis. Once you understand and empathize with group members, you may ask yourself whether you think they are right or wrong, logical or illogical. Good critical listeners understand why they accept or reject another member's ideas and suggestions.

Russell makes the following proposal: "Suppose we chip in and give Professor Hawkins a gift at the party?" A critical listener might think (1) the instructor could misinterpret the gift, (2) some class members won't want to make a contribution, or (3) there isn't enough time to collect money and buy an appropriate gift.

TOOLBOX 6.1 Listening, Argumentation, and Conflict

Effective listening skills are needed in order to judge the validity of an argument and the factors that separate credible sources from biased sources. Effective critical listeners are better equipped to assess the strength and merit of another person's ideas and opinions. Listening is also one of the most important tools needed to understand and resolve conflict in groups. When emotions are high, it is difficult to listen comprehensively and empathically. **Chapter 10: Argumentation in Groups** focuses on the principles and techniques needed to analyze and evaluate the arguments made by group members. **Chapter 8: Conflict and Cohesion in Groups** focuses on methods for understanding and resolving different types of conflict in groups.

Appreciative Listening

Appreciative listening answers this question: Do I like or value what another member has said? **Appreciative listening** applies to the way group members think and speak—the way they choose and use words; their ability to inject appropriate humor, argue persuasively, or demonstrate understanding. For example, if a group is struggling with the wording of a recommendation, appreciative listening can help identify the statement that best captures and eloquently expresses the central idea and spirit of the proposal. When we are

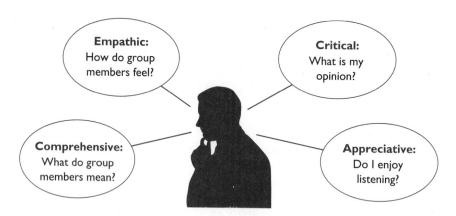

FIGURE 6.2 Types of Listening

pleased to hear a member find the right words to calm a frustrated member or energize an apathetic group, we are listening appreciatively. Appreciative listening skills help us enjoy and acknowledge good talk in groups.

"Well," suggests Paul, "why not buy a thank-you card, ask class members to sign it, and present it to Mr. Hawkins at the party?" An appreciative listener might think (1) Paul always comes up with the best ideas, (2) a well-selected card may be able to express our appreciation better than we could, or (3) I will thank Paul for making a suggestion that doesn't obligate anyone to contribute to or attend the party.

Group Roles and Listening

No one is a perfect listener. Certainly, it is unreasonable to expect that every group member will be an ideal comprehensive, empathic, critical, and appreciative listener. Fortunately, the group situation provides a way of balancing the strengths and weaknesses of listeners within a group. One way to assess and improve the listening behavior of a group as a whole is to understand the relationship between listening abilities and member roles.

Task Roles and Listening

Members who assume important task roles are often good comprehensive and critical listeners. Elaborator-clarifiers and orienter-summarizers use comprehensive listening to accurately reexplain the ideas of others and summarize group conclusions. Evaluator-critics are usually effective critical listeners who assess ideas and suggestions as well as the validity of arguments. An ef-

---

TOOLBOX 6.2 Group Roles

Group members often assume task, maintenance, and self-centered roles. For example, task roles include functions such as initiator, information seeker and giver, opinion seeker and giver, clarifier-summarizer, evaluator-critic, energizer, procedural technician, and recorder-secretary. Maintenance roles include encourager, supporter, harmonizer, compromiser, tension releaser, gatekeeper, observer-interpreter, and follower. Self-centered roles are exemplified by the aggressor, blocker, recognition seeker, clown, deserter, confessor, and special interest pleader. **Chapter 4: Participation in Groups** describes and provides examples of all three types of group roles.

---

fective recorder-secretary, however, must be a comprehensive rather than a critical listener when taking minutes. If several group members effectively assume most of the traditional task roles, the group, as a whole, is likely to be good at comprehensive and critical listening.

Maintenance Roles and Listening

Maintenance roles affect how well a group gets along. They focus on building relationships and maintaining a friendly atmosphere. Members who assume important maintenance roles are often good empathic and appreciative listeners. Encourager-supporters and observer-interpreters use comprehensive, empathic, and appreciative listening to explain how others feel as well as what others are trying to say. Harmonizers and tension releasers are often empathic listeners who understand when and how to resolve conflicts, mediate differences, and relax the group. If several group members effectively assume most maintenance roles, the group, as a whole, is likely to be good at empathic and appreciative listening.

Self-Centered Roles and Listening

Self-centered roles occur when members put their own needs ahead of the group's goal and other members' needs. Members who assume self-centered roles may be excellent or poor listeners. Aggressors and dominators may be critical listeners who eagerly expose the weaknesses in members' comments in order to get their own way. Blockers may be good listeners who purposely ignore what they hear or poor listeners who are incapable of comprehending or appreciating the comments of others. The recognition seeker, confessor, and special interest pleader may be so preoccupied with their own needs, they are unable to listen to anyone else in the group.

Leadership Functions and Listening

Good leaders are good listeners. They know when to use comprehensive, empathic, critical, or appreciative listening. Effective leaders are also proactive listeners. They don't wait to clear up misunderstandings; they try to make sure that every group member comprehends what is being said. They don't wait for misunderstandings to escalate into arguments; they intervene at the slightest hint of hostility.

The proactive leader tries to find out what members think and feel by asking them, rather than guessing what is on their minds. Leaders who are good listeners do not fake attention, pretend to comprehend, or ignore members. Instead, they work as hard as they can to better understand what members are saying and how those comments affect the group and its goals. In studying the characteristics of effective groups and their leaders, Larson and LaFasto share the comments of a successful aerospace leader: "The worst failing is a team leader who's a nonlistener. A guy who doesn't listen to his people—and that doesn't mean listening to them and doing whatever the hell he wants to do—can make a lot of mistakes."[12]

Group Listening Skills

Two major listening principles balance the need for comprehensive and critical listening with the need for empathic and appreciative listening. The two principles are (1) use your extra thought speed and (2) apply the golden listening rule. Once these principles are understood and employed as overriding listening standards, group members can begin to work on specific listening skills.

Use Your Extra Thought Speed

Most people talk at about 125–150 words per minute. According to Ralph Nichols, there is good evidence that if thought were measured in words per minute, most of us could think at three to four times the rate at which we speak.[13] Thus, we have about four hundred extra words of spare thinking time during every minute a person talks to us.

Thought speed is the speed (words per minute) at which most people can think compared to the speed at which they can speak. Ralph Nichols asks the obvious question: "What do we do with our excess thinking time while someone is speaking?"[14] Poor listeners use their extra thought speed to daydream, engage in side conversations, take unnecessary notes, or plan how to confront the speaker. Good listeners use their extra thought speed productively when they

- Identify and summarize main ideas
- Pay extra attention to nonverbal behavior

- Analyze arguments
- Assess the relevance of a speaker's comments.

Effective group members don't waste their extra thought speed—they use it to enhance comprehensive and critical listening.

Apply the Golden Listening Rule

The **golden listening rule** is easy to remember: Listen to others as you would have them listen to you. Unfortunately, this rule can be difficult to follow. It asks you to suspend your own needs in order to listen to someone else's. Michael Nichols counsels, "Let go of what's on your mind long enough to hear what's on the other person's."[15]

Napier and Gershenfeld emphasize how important it is to suspend your own needs when listening to others. They maintain that "a critical factor in any problem-solving group is the willingness and ability of group members to listen. People are so busy selling their own ideas, proving themselves, and reacting to personality rather than words that it is a wonder we hear as much as we do."[16] The principle that protects group members from such selfishness is the golden listening rule.

Listening Strategies

Although using your extra thought speed and applying the golden listening rule are critical listening goals, how to achieve them may not be obvious. The following six strategies can improve your listening ability and help apply the two basic principles of effective listening:

- Overcome distractions.
- Listen for main ideas.
- "Listen" to nonverbal behavior.
- Paraphrase.
- Listen before you leap.
- Help the group listen.

Overcome Distractions.   Distractions can take many forms in a group discussion.[17] Loud and annoying noises, uncomfortable room temperature and seating, frequent interruptions, or distracting decor and outside activities are environmental distractions. Distractions also can be caused by members, such as someone talking too softly, too rapidly, or too slowly; someone speaking in a monotone or with an unfamiliar accent; or someone's unusual mannerisms or appearance. It is difficult to listen when someone is fidgeting, doodling, tapping a pencil, or openly reading or writing something unrelated to the discussion.

When a distraction is environmental, you are well within your rights to get up and shut the door, open the window, or turn on more lights. When another member's behavior is distracting, you can try to minimize or stop the disruption. If members speak too softly, have side conversations, or use visual aids that are too small, a conscientious listener will ask a member to speak up, request that side conversations be postponed, or move closer to a visual aid.

Listen for Main Ideas. Good listeners can identify a speaker's central idea. They can tell the difference between facts and opinions, between arguments and evidence. Poor listeners tend to listen and only remember isolated facts.

Admittedly, the fault for this problem may rest, in part, with the speaker. If someone is not clear or keeps talking long after the point is made, members may lose track and drift off. Good listeners who sense such problems may interrupt such a speaker and ask "Could you help me out here and try to summarize your point in a couple of sentences?" Such an interruption is not rude when it is the only way to focus the group on important issues. Good listeners try to cut through facts and irrelevant comments in order to identify the most important main ideas.

"Listen" to Nonverbal Behavior. Speakers don't always put everything that's important to them into words. Very often you can understand a speaker's meaning by observing nonverbal behavior. A change in vocal tone or volume may be another way of saying "Listen up—this is very important." A person's sustained eye contact may be a way of saying "I'm talking to you!" Facial expressions can reveal whether a thought is painful, joyous, exciting, serious, or boring. Even gestures can be used to express a level of excitement that words cannot convey.

It is, however, easy to misinterpret nonverbal behavior. Effective listeners verbally confirm their interpretation of someone's nonverbal communication. A question as simple as "Do your nods indicate a yes vote?" can make sure that everyone is on the same nonverbal wavelength. If, as nonverbal research indicates, more than half of a speaker's meaning is conveyed nonverbally,[18] we are missing a lot of important information if we fail to "listen" to nonverbal behavior. Even Freud suggested that "he that has eyes to see and ears to

---

TOOLBOX 6.3 Listening and Nonverbal Communication

Correctly interpreting nonverbal responses can tell a listener as much or more than spoken words. At the same time, the nonverbal reactions of listeners (head nods, smiles, frowns, eye contact, and gestures) can affect the quality, quantity, and content of a speaker's message. Even the nonverbal setting of a group discussion can communicate a wealth of meaning about the status, power, and respect given to speakers and listeners. A significant portion of **Chapter 7: Verbal and Nonverbal Communication in Groups** focuses on nonverbal communication in groups.

hear may convince himself that no mortal can keep a secret. If his lips are silent, he chatters with his fingertips; betrayal oozes out of him at every pore."[19] No wonder it is difficult for most people to conceal what they mean and feel in a face-to-face group discussion.

Paraphrase. **Paraphrasing** is the ability to restate what people say in a way that indicates you have understood what they mean. Paraphrasing is a form of feedback—a listening check that asks, "Am I right—is this what you mean?" Too often we jump to conclusions and incorrectly assume we know what a speaker means and feels.

Paraphrasing is not repeating what a person says; it requires finding new words to describe what you have heard. In addition to this restatement of the speaker's message, a paraphrase usually includes a request for confirmation. Paraphrasing can be used for many purposes:

To clarify meaning: "When you said you were not going to ask Richard, did you mean you want me to do it?"
To ensure understanding: "I know you said it's okay with you, but I sense you're not happy with the group's decision—am I way off?"
To summarize a discussion: "What everyone seems to be saying is that we don't think it's the best time to change this procedure, right?"

Notice that each example represents a restatement and a request for confirmation. The speaker can then confirm listener perceptions. Effective paraphrasing requires us to use our extra thought speed to produce a statement that follows the golden listening rule.

There is an added advantage to paraphrasing group members' statements. Jacobson has written, "One of the best things about listening, at least when we're in small groups, is that we can find out how well we're doing." Such "reality checks" are most important when dealing with emotional issues. Emotions, writes Jacobson, "tend to make a person less articulate. You'll hear the sputtering of disjointed words and phrases. So it's up to you to do even more to make sure you're getting the person's real message."[20] Paraphrasing can help ensure that everyone in the group understands what is said.

Listen before You Leap. One of the most often quoted pieces of listening advice to come from Ralph Nichols' writings is "we must always withhold evaluation until our comprehension is complete."[21] This phrase counsels listeners to make sure they understand a speaker before responding.

Sometimes when we become angry, friends may tell us to "count to ten" before reacting. The same caution is good advice when we listen. Counting to ten, however, implies more than withholding evaluation until comprehension is complete. You may comprehend a speaker perfectly but be infuriated or offended by what you hear. If an insensitive leader asks that "one of you girls take minutes," it may take a count to 20 to collect your thoughts before responding in a professional manner to this sexist comment. If a group member tells an offensive joke, you may have a double reaction—anger at the speaker and disappointment with those who laughed. Listening before you leap gives you time to adjust your reaction in a way that will help rather than disrupt a group discussion.

Help the Group Listen.   In the most effective groups, members help each other listen. The most effective listeners may become the group's translators—explaining what other group members mean and interpreting participant responses. One way to help a group listen is to do periodic group listening checks that ask for a confirmation of comprehension. By asking "What is everyone's understanding of . . . ?" or "Am I right in saying that all of us agree to . . . ?" you are making sure that everyone is understanding and responding to the same message.

You also can help a group listen when group members disagree or argue. When members' emotions are stirred up, their thoughts may be devoted to responding to the opposition rather than to applying the golden listening rule. You can help a group resolve such conflicts by summarizing different positions in accurate and neutral terms.

Try to keep good listening habits at the forefront of the group's attention. Remind members how important it is for everyone to improve their listening behavior. Such reminders can have powerful consequences. In fact, some experts claim that 50 percent of our potential improvement in listening can come simply from realizing we have poor listening habits and are capable of listening much better.[22] As important as listening is to group success, the realization that everyone can become a better listener is well worth remembering.

Taking Notes in Groups

If most of us only listen at 25 percent efficiency, why not take notes during a discussion? Why not write down important ideas and facts? Taking notes makes a great deal of sense but only if it is done with caution and skill.

The inclination to take notes is understandable. After all, that's what we do in a classroom when an instructor lectures. If, however, you are like most listeners, only one-fourth of what is said will end up in your notes. Even if it were possible to copy down every word uttered in a group discussion, your notes would be missing the nonverbal clues that often tell you more about what a person means and feels. And if you spend all of your time taking notes, when will you put aside your pen and participate? Ralph Nichols summarized the dilemma of balancing note-taking and listening when he concluded that "there is some evidence to indicate that the volume of notes taken and their value to the taker are inversely related."[23] Thus, the challenge for a group discussion participant is this: How do I obtain brief, meaningful records of a group discussion? Several methods can help, depending upon your needs and role in the group.

If a member is assigned to take minutes, you can rely on the official record of the meeting. But here too there are potential problems. What if the secretary is a poor listener? What if you need the notes immediately and can't wait for the official minutes to be distributed and approved? Suppose you need personalized meeting notes that record your assignments and important information? In that case, minutes may not be enough.

Flexibility is the key to taking useful and personalized meeting notes. Good listeners adjust their note-taking system to a group's agenda or impose a note-taking pattern on a disorganized discussion. In some cases, margin notes on an agenda may be sufficient to highlight important information and actions. If you attend a lot of meetings, you may find it useful to use a brief form that records important details and provides space for critical information and action. The form shown in Figure 6.3 is an example of the way in which vital information and actions can be recorded.

Meeting Notes

Group: Goal/Topic:

Date and Time: Place:

Members Attending:

Members Absent:

Vital Information

1.

2.

3.

Decisions Reached

1.

2.

3.

Personal To-Do List   Date Due

1.

2.

3.

Date/Time/Place of Next Meeting:

FIGURE 6.3 Sample Form for Meeting Notes

Self-Listening in Groups

As important as it is to listen to other members of your group, it is just as important to listen to yourself. If you can monitor and understand the effects of what you and others say, you can become a more effective group member. Two strategies can enhance your ability to listen to yourself. The first is to translate feedback into useful information about the way you speak and listen, so you can answer questions such as these:

> Do members listen to me, or do I seem to be talking to a blank wall?
> Do members seem to understand what I am saying, or are there frequent questions or confusion following my remarks?
> Do I feel my voice rising and my heart racing when I address a controversial issue or argumentative member?

Robbins and Finley suggest that when listening to yourself "whatever you have to say needs only to pass the simple test of teamwork: Are you saying something that is germane to the team as a whole—to its objectives, to its overriding vision, to the tasks it has set out for itself? . . . If not, fix your message so that it is direct, relevant, and respectful of others."[24]

A second way to listen to yourself is to become aware of your internal thought process. This strategy recognizes that, in a group discussion, what you *want* to say may not be what you *should* say. In order to illustrate the usefulness of this strategy, consider the following hypothetical situation:

> A human resources consultant has been assigned to work with a well-established committee charged with planning an advanced job training program for a group of employees. Right from the start the committee chairperson and the consultant do not hit it off. The situation has become so bad that the committee is paralyzed. Nothing gets done as everyone spends valuable meeting time watching the chairperson and consultant fight over every issue on the group's agenda.

If you were a member of this group, what would you say or do to help resolve such a problem? A lot depends on how well you listen to others and to yourself, how efficiently you use your extra thought speed, and how fairly you apply the golden listening rule. The following seven questions may help you assess your internal thought process:

1. *What do I want to say?* "I wish you two would stop acting like babies. We're sick and tired of your bickering."
2. *What are the consequences of saying what I want to say?* Both of them will become angry or hurt, and what is left of group morale and cohesiveness could fall apart.

3. *Have I listened comprehensively?* What is each side trying to say? Is the chair saying that the consultant has no right to impose her will on the group? Is the consultant saying that the chair doesn't respect her as an expert?
4. *Have I listened critically?* Is either side right or wrong? Both the chair and the consultant have legitimate complaints, but their arguments are becoming personal rather than substantive.
5. *Have I listened empathically?* How would I feel if someone treated me this way? I'd probably be just as angry.
6. *Have I listened appreciatively?* Do the chair and consultant have positive contributions to make? The chair should be commended for how well he has led our group. The consultant should be thanked for sharing useful resources and helping us understand the scope of our assignment.
7. So, *what* should *I say?* I should speak on behalf of the group and tell the chair and consultant how much we value both of them but that the group, as a whole, is distressed by the conflict between them. I should ask whether there is something we can do to resolve the problem.

Taking the time to ask a series of listening questions can help you develop an appropriate and useful response. Analyzing your own thought process lets you employ different types of listening to come up with a useful response that can help resolve a group problem.

Adapting to Different Listeners

Just as there are differences among members' backgrounds, perceptions, and values, there are differences in the way people listen. Fortunately, a group provides a setting in which different listening abilities and styles can be an asset rather than a liability. If you have difficulty analyzing an argument, there may be someone else in the group who can be relied upon to serve as a critical listener. If you know that several members only pay attention to the words they hear rather than observing the nonverbal behavior that accompanies those words, you may appoint yourself the group's empathic listener.

Listening behavior may also differ between male and female members. Tannen suggests that men are more likely to listen to the content of what is said, whereas women focus on the relationships among speakers.[25] In other words, men tend to focus on comprehensive and critical listening, whereas women are more likely to be empathic and appreciative listeners. If "males tend to hear the facts while females are more aware of the mood of the communication,"[26] a group is fortunate to have both kinds of listeners contributing to the group process.

Differences in personalities also may affect the way members listen. The Myers-Briggs Type Indicator® predicts that introverts will be better listeners than extroverts, who are more eager to speak. Judgmental members may be highly critical listeners, whereas perceivers take time to comprehend what they hear without leaping to immediate conclusions.[27]

In addition to gender and personality type distinctions, cultural differences can influence the ways in which group members listen and respond to each other. One study concludes that international students perceive U.S. students to be less willing and less patient as listeners than they perceive listeners in African, Asian, South American, or European cultures.[28] One way to explain such differences in perceived listening behavior is offered by Lustig and Koester, who explain that English is a speaker-responsible language in which the speaker structures the message and relies primarily upon words to provide meaning. In Japanese, however, which is a listener-responsible language, speakers indirectly indicate what they want the listener to know. The listener must rely on nonverbal communication and an understanding of the relationship between the speaker and listener to interpret meaning.[29] Thus, an English-speaking listener may feel as though a Japanese speaker is leaving out important information; the Japanese listener, however, may think that the English speaker is overexplaining or talking down to him or her. Such misunderstanding and perceived discourtesy are the result of speaking and listening differences rather than of substantive disagreement. Adapting your listening style to diverse group members can be a complicated and challenging task when gender, personality types, and cultural differences are taken into account.

Balanced Listening

Groups lose their balance when too many members want to talk rather than listen. If members fail to listen comprehensively, critically, empathically, and appreciatively, a group will soon lose its ability to work together. In a well-balanced group, members spend more time listening than speaking; they try to balance their own needs with those of listeners. In fact, there may be no more difficult task in a group discussion than suspending your own needs and desire to talk in order to listen to what someone else has to say. In 1961, Ralph Nichols contrasted the hard work of listening with faked attention:

> Listening is hard work. It is characterized by faster heart action, quicker circulation of the blood, a small rise in bodily temperature. The over-relaxed listener is merely appearing to tune-in and then feeling conscience-free to pursue any of a thousand mental tangents. . . . For selfish reasons alone, one of the best investments we can make is to give each speaker our conscious attention.[30]

Speaker Interests   Listener Needs
Extra Thought Speed   The Golden Listening Rule
Group Listening   Self Listening

FIGURE 6.4   Listening

Balancing our own interests with an interest in others is the key to listening. A generation after Ralph Nichols drew that conclusion, Michael Nichols repeated his call when he wrote that "perhaps if we started listening to one another we could move toward greater balance in ourselves and in our relationships."[31]

Summary Study Guide

- Effective listening in groups requires understanding and reacting appropriately to what you hear and see in a group discussion.
- Listening is our number one communication activity.
- Most people cannot accurately report 50 percent of what they hear after listening to a short talk; without training, most people listen at just 25 percent efficiency.
- There are four important types of listening essential for effective small group communication—comprehensive, critical, empathic, and appreciative listening.
- Members who excel in task and maintenance roles are often skilled comprehensive, critical, empathic, and/or appreciative listeners. Members who assume self-centered roles may be either poor listeners or excellent listeners who take advantage of member weaknesses.
- Two major listening principles are (1) use your extra thought speed and (2) apply the golden listening rule.
- The following six strategies can improve listening within a group discussion: (1) overcome distractions, (2) listen for main ideas, (3) "listen" to nonverbal behavior, (4) paraphrase, (5) listen before you leap, and (6) help the group listen.
- Taking brief, meaningful notes during meetings can improve your ability to follow and remember what was said.

- Self-listening helps you monitor and understand the effects of what you say during a group discussion.
- Differences in listening skills, gender, personality types, and culture can affect and enhance a group's ability to listen.

Groupwork *Listening Triads*

GOAL   To give group members an opportunity to understand their listening strengths and weaknesses.

PARTICIPANTS   Groups of three members.

PROCEDURE

1. Before beginning the exercise, all group members should complete the *Group Listening* assessment instrument included in this chapter.
2. There are three rounds in the Listening Triads exercise. Each round includes three tasks:
   - The **speaker** selects and explains two or three items from the instrument that best describe his or her listening strengths and/or weaknesses.
   - The **listener** listens and may ask questions to help the speaker explain why certain skills are strengths or weaknesses. The **listener** summarizes the speaker's main ideas.
   - The **observer** observes the listener and provides feedback about the listener's listening behavior and summary.
3. Triads have five minutes for each round of listening. After each round is completed, the group should discuss the listening behavior of the **listener.**
4. At the end of three rounds, the group should discuss what they learned or observed from the exercise.
   - What general observations can we make about our listening behavior?
   - How easy or difficult was the exercise for the listener?
   - How can we improve our listening behavior?

Group Listening

Directions Respond to each of the following assessment criteria and questions by describing your listening behavior and the listening behavior of a group in which you are an active member.

1. **Types of Listening**
   Use the letters of the following answers to fill in the blanks in this section.
   A. Comprehensive Listening
   B. Critical Listening
   C. Empathic Listening
   D. Appreciative Listening

   _____ My listening strength(s)

   _____ My listening weakness(es)

   _____ My group's listening strength(s)

   _____ My group's listening weakness(es)

   Are you or your group missing one or more types of listening?

2. **Listening Principles**
   Use the letters of the following answers to fill in the blanks in this section.
   A. Use extra thought speed to advantage
   B. Apply the golden listening rule

   _____ My listening strength(s)

   _____ My listening weakness(es)

   _____ My group's listening strength(s)

   _____ My group's listening weakness(es)

   Are you or your group not applying one or both of these principles?

3. **Listening Strategies**
   Use the letters of the following answers to fill in the blanks in this section.
   A. Overcome Distractions
   B. Listen for Main Ideas
   C. "Listen" to Nonverbal Behavior
   D. Paraphrase
   E. Listen Before You Leap
   F. Help the Group Listen

   _____ My listening strength(s)

   _____ My listening weakness(es)

(continued)

(Group Listening, *continued*)

———— My group's listening strength(s)

———— My group's listening weakness(es)

Are you or your group not employing one or more of these strategies?

4. **Self-Listening**

Use the letters of the following answers to fill in the blanks in this section.

A. Translate Feedback

B. Monitor Your Internal Thought Process

———— My listening strength(s)

———— My listening weakness(es)

———— My group's listening strength(s)

———— My group's listening weakness(es)

Are you or members of your group not listening to yourselves?

5. **Assessment and Conclusions**

Given your assessment of the preceding listening strategies and skills, list three ways in which you could improve your listening behavior and three ways in which your group could improve its listening.

To improve my own listening behavior, I should . . .

1.

2.

3.

To improve our group's listening behavior, we should . . .

1.

2.

3.

Recommended Readings

Burley-Allen, M. (1995). *Listening: The forgotten skill* (2nd ed.). New York: John Wiley & Sons.

Nichols, M. P. (1995). *The lost art of listening*. New York: Guilford.

Wolvin, A. D. & Coakley, C. G. (1996). *Listening* (5th ed.). Madison, WI: Brown & Benchmark.

Notes

1. Nichols, M. P. (1995). *The lost art of listening*. New York: Guilford, p. 36.
2. Stauffer, D. (1998 July). "Yo, listen up: A brief hearing on the most neglected communication skill." *Harvard Management Update*, 3, p. 10.

3. The International Listening Association's definition is based on a study in which a content analysis was performed on 50 definitions of listening. See P. Emmert (1996 Spring). "President's perspective." *ILA Listening Post, 56,* pp. 2–3.

4. Barker, L. L., Edwards, R., Gaines, C., Gladney, K. & Holley, F. (1980). An investigation of proportional time spent in various communication activities by college students. *Journal of applied communication research, 8,* pp. 101–109.

5. Wolvin, A. D. & Coakley, C. G. (1996). *Listening* (5th ed.). Madison, WI: Brown & Benchmark, p. 15.

6. Purdy, M. (1997). "What is listening?" In M. Purdy & D. Borisoff (Eds.). *Listening in everyday life: A personal and professional approach* (2nd ed.). Lanham, MD: University Press, pp. 1–20.

7. Wolvin & Coakley, p. 38.

8. Johnson, P. M. & Watson, K. W. (1997). "Managing interpersonal and team conflict: Listening strategies." In M. Purdy & D. Borisoff (Eds.). *Listening in everyday life: A personal and professional approach* (2nd ed.). Lanham, MD: University Press, pp. 121–137.

9. Nichols, R. G. (September 1987). Listening is a 10-part skill. *Nation's Business, 75,* p. 40.

10. Benoit, S. S. & Lee, J. W. (1986). Listening: It can be taught. *Journal of Education for Business, 63,* 229–232.

11. Kelly, C. M. (1974). Empathetic listening. In R. S. Cathcart & L. A. Samovar (Eds.), *Small group communication: A reader* (2nd ed.). Dubuque, IA: Wm. C. Brown, p. 340.

12. Larson, C. E. & LaFasto, F. M. J. (1989). *TeamWork: What must go right/What can go wrong.* Newbury Park, CA: Sage, p. 90.

13. Nichols, R. G. (1987), p. 40.

14. Nichols, R. G. (1987), p. 40.

15. Nichols, M. P., p. 42.

16. Napier, R. W. & Gershenfeld, M. K. (1993). *Groups: Theory and experience* (5th ed.). Boston: Houghton Mifflin, p. 358.

17. Burley-Allen, M. (1995). *Listening: The forgotten skill* (2nd ed.). New York: John Wiley, pp. 68–70.

18. See Knapp, M. L. & Hall, J. A. (1992). *Nonverbal communication in human interaction* (3rd ed.). Fort Worth, TX: Holt, Rinehart, & Winston, pp. 28–29.

19. As cited in Knapp, M. L. & Hall, J. A. (1992). *Nonverbal communication in human interaction* (3rd ed.). Fort Worth, TX: Holt, Rinehart, & Winston, p. 391.

20. Stauffer, p. 11.

21. Nichols, R. G. (1961). Do we know how to listen? Practical helps in a modern age. *Speech Teacher, 10,* p. 121.

22. Stauffer, p. 11.

23. Nichols, R. G. (1987), p. 40.

24. Robbins, H. & Finley, M. (1995). *Why teams don't work: What went wrong and how to make it right.* Princeton, NJ: Peterson's/Pacesetter Books, p. 124.

25. Tannen, D. (1990). *You just don't understand: Women and men in conversation.* New York: William Morrow, pp. 149–151.

26. Booth-Butterfield, M. (1984). She hears . . . he hears: What they hear and why. *Personnel Journal, 44,* p. 39.

27. See chapter 4 for a discussion of the Myers-Briggs Type Indicator®. Also see Myers, I. B. with Myers, P. B. (1990). *Gifts differing: Tenth anniversary edition.* Palo

Alto, CA: Consulting Psychologists; Kroeger, O. with Thuesen, J. M. (1992). *Type talk at work*. New York: Dell.

28. Wolvin & Coakley, p. 125.
29. Lustig & Koester, p. 220.
30. Nichols, R. G. (1961), p. 122.
31. Nichols, M. P., p. 57.

Verbal and Nonverbal Communication in Groups

Two Essential Tools

Verbal and nonverbal communication are the most powerful tools you possess in any group setting. The verbal component of communication focuses on how we use the words in our language. Communication may be "face to face, fax to fax, over the phone, or through electronic mail, but regardless of the channel used, groups do their work through language."[1] Without spoken and written language you cannot have a group discussion; you cannot follow an agenda, take minutes, read a report, or effectively interact with other group members.

The other essential communication tool, nonverbal communication, is just as important as language. Without the nonverbal component, it would be difficult to interpret the meaning of spoken language. The tone of voice, directness of eye contact, and physical proximity of group members can reveal as much or more about their thoughts and feelings as the words they speak.

Principles of Language

Within a group discussion, your ability to use language helps determine the extent to which you successfully convey your ideas and influence the actions of other members. We begin by introducing two basic principles of language that address the relationship between words and meaning.

Connotation and Denotation

When communicating in small groups, you will encounter different meanings for and reactions to words depending on the type of group, its goal, its history of interaction, and the background and experience of members. The multiple meanings of words can be further understood by examining two major types of meaning: denotative and connotative.

Denotation refers to the objective, dictionary-based meaning of a word. However, words usually have more than one definition. For example, the *minutes* taken in a meeting are not the same as the *minutes* it may take to get a meeting started. **Connotation** refers to the personal feeling connected to the meaning of a word. S. I. Hayakawa refers to connotation as "the aura of feelings, pleasant or unpleasant, that surround practically all words."[2] We evaluate the extent to which we like or dislike the thing or idea the word represents.

Connotation, rather than denotation, is more likely to influence how we respond to words. For example, the denotative meaning or dictionary definition of a *meeting* is "an assembly or gathering of people, as for a business, so-

> **TOOLBOX 7.1** Using Listening to Clarify Language
>
> Many listening strategies focus on clarifying the meaning of words. Comprehensive, empathic, critical, and appreciative listening depend on an essential first step—making sure that you accurately understand what a person means. Because you can think much faster than a person can speak, use your extra thought speed to make sure that you accurately interpret the meaning of words. When good listeners are in doubt about their interpretation of words, they ask questions or paraphrase a speaker's comments to ensure that they have understood what a person means. **Chapter 6: Listening in Groups** suggests several listening principles and strategies that can enhance your ability to understand the meaning of the words spoken in a group discussion.

cial, or religious purpose." However, the word *meeting* can connote hours of wasted time to some members or the best way to solve a complex problem to others. When the word *meeting* comes to mean a dreaded event at which unpleasant people argue over trivial issues, you are letting the word influence your feelings about the event it symbolizes.

Levels of Meaning

All of us have different experiences and backgrounds. As a result, we develop different connotative meanings for many of the words we use to describe those experiences and events. One way of minimizing the misinterpretation of such words is understanding that there are different levels of meaning in our language, or as some scholars put it, different **levels of abstraction.** Some words are highly abstract. An **abstract word** refers to an idea or concept that cannot be observed or touched. Words such as *fairness* and *freedom* may not have the same meaning for everyone. Sole reliance on abstract words increases the chances of misunderstanding. The more abstract your language is, the more likely group members may interpret your meaning other than the way you intended. **Concrete words** refer to specific things that can be perceived by our senses. They narrow the number of possible meanings and decrease the likelihood of bypassing.

Try to avoid using overly abstract words when engaged in group discussion. Use words that refer directly to observable objects, people, or behavior. For example, stating that "Greg's behavior was disruptive" could imply many things. Did he yell at a group member, use profanity, refuse to participate, or insist that his ideas were superior? Stating that "Greg arrived fifteen minutes late to the meeting" is more descriptive. Clarifying what you mean by using concrete words prevents inaccurate inferences and misunderstandings.

Team Talk

Communication is the medium through which groups work. Much like fish out of water, a group cannot survive without language. Donnellon has labeled this essential ingredient **team talk**—the nature of language that group members use as they work together. Not only does team talk enable group members to share information and express opinions, analysis of team talk "reveals where the team is coming from and where it is headed. More importantly, talk is a tool for changing a team's destination" and achieving success.[3] Our interpretation of Donnellon's theory is this: Team talk is the means we use to achieve group goals, the stimulus we use to build group relationships, and the evidence we use to assess group work.

Donnellon urges group members to listen for words, sentences, and patterns of speech that are used repetitively during discussions and meetings. By listening to each other talk and analyzing the way such language fits into six categories of team talk, it is possible for a group to differentiate between communication that will foster or inhibit success. Such an analysis also can help a group improve the way it communicates. Figure 7.1 illustrates the dimensions of team talk and provides examples of successful and unsuccessful language use.

Implications of Team Talk

Once a group analyzes the nature of team talk, it can take steps to modify the ways in which members talk to one another. The following suggestions can help produce a stronger and more cooperative group:

- Use the pronouns "we," "us," and "our" when referring to the group and its work.
- Express shared rather than individual needs: "We need to . . ." rather than "I want . . ."
- If you are in a position of power, let others interrupt you or change the subject.
- If you are in a position of power, refrain from talking and interrupting more than others and asking more questions than others.
- Speak in a specific and active voice ("I haven't finished the report due next week.") rather than an abstract and passive voice ("The task hasn't been completed.")
- Ask group members to address you by your first name or nickname.
- Encourage group members to express disagreement and listen patiently to dissenters.
- Ask more "what if" questions and make fewer "we can't do it" statements.

Team Talk Dimensions	Successful Examples	Unsuccessful Examples
1. Identification. Members use plural pronouns rather than singular ones when talking about the group and its work.	"Let's keep working on this until we're ready for lunch."	"I don't think you should quit until you've finished."
2. Interdependence. Members use language that acknowledges shared needs, solicits opinions, and expresses the need for cooperation.	"If we can develop a plan, our work will be much easier to schedule. What do you think?"	"We can develop this plan without input from the group. I'll tell the boss that Fred and I will do it on our own."
3. Power Differentiation. Members talk to one another on equal terms.	"Sorry. My other meeting ran overtime. Is there a way I can catch up?" "Fred, could you tell me more about that? Thanks."	"Stop and tell me what's happened so far." "I don't like this—if you can't do it, we'll have to assign this to someone else."
4. Social Distance. Members use casual language, nicknames, slang. Members express empathy, liking, and avoid titles.	"What's up, Doc?" "Fred, try to find out where Bob stands on this." "Hey guys!"	"Let us review our progress thus far." "Mr. Nunez, contact Dr. Ford after the meeting." "Ladies and gentlemen . . . ."
5. Conflict Management Techniques. Members express interest in solving problems, use a non-threatening tone & nonjudgmental language. Members paraphrase others.	"What do you need to know from us to do this?" "Could we back up and look at this from a different angle?"	"How many of you think that Fred is right?" "We're not getting anywhere so I'll take it up with Dr. Ford after the meeting."
6. Negotiation Process. Members ask "what if" questions, propose objective criteria for solutions, and summarize areas of agreement.	"What if we wrote up a justification for the cost?" "Does this meet our standard?" "What else could persuade us to do this?"	"We've always done it this way." "Why? Because I just don't like it, that's why."

FIGURE 7.1   The Dimensions of Team Talk[4]

- When in doubt, paraphrase what someone else has said to ensure understanding.

If, as Donnellon claims, "language creates thoughts, feelings, and behavior in team members which affect the way the team uses power, manages conflict, and negotiates,"[5] language must be viewed as more than the medium through which groups work. Language is the most critical tool we have to shape the future and success of a group.

Language Difficulties

In addition to analyzing your teamtalk, many misunderstandings in group discussions can be avoided by overcoming other language-based barriers to communication. Among the most common language difficulties are bypassing, sexist language, and jargon.

Bypassing   When group members have different meanings for the same words and phrases, they risk engaging in a process known as **bypassing,** a form of miscommunication that occurs when people "miss each other with their meanings."[6] An entire group discussion can be compromised if there are differences in the interpretation of a single word or phrase. Note the problems created by the following example of bypassing:

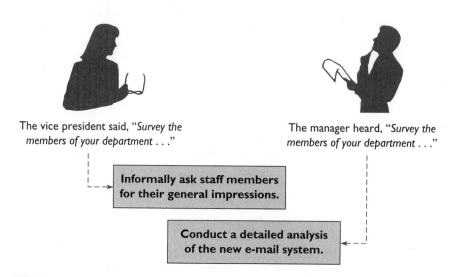

The vice president said, "*Survey the members of your department . . .*"

The manager heard, "*Survey the members of your department . . .*"

Informally ask staff members for their general impressions.

Conduct a detailed analysis of the new e-mail system.

FIGURE 7.2   Bypassing

At a routine staff meeting, a vice president asks her managers to "survey the members of your department to find out whether they are satisfied with the new e-mail system." During the following week, the vice president receives a copy of a memo from one manager requesting that everyone in his department fill out a two-page questionnaire about the e-mail system. The vice president telephones the manager and asks, "What's this question-naire all about?" The manager replies, "I thought you said I have to survey everyone in my department."

What the vice president had in mind was for the manager to informally ask staff members for their initial impressions rather than a detailed analysis of the new system. Although the manager heard the vice president's words, the communicators "missed" one another's meaning.

Haney maintains that "communicators who habitually look for meanings in the people using words, rather than in the words themselves, are much less prone to bypass or to be bypassed."[7] In other words, it's not what words mean but what speakers mean when they use words.

Sexist Language

Sexist language employs terminology that demeans, inappropriately excludes, or stereotypes people on the basis of gender. Using sexist language in a group may alienate and offend male and female members. Referring to women as "girls" implies that women are childlike and not capable of adult thought and responsibilities. Refer to female group members as "girls" only if you also refer to male members as "boys." Recognizing your own gender-based biases is the first step to preventing sexist and stereotyped language.

Using the word or suffix *man* implies a male human being. Even when used to represent all people, the word is likely to bring to mind a male. Instead, use words that refer to both men and women. Avoid words that specify the gender of individuals in particular roles or occupations. Consider the following alternatives:

Sexist	*Nonsexist Alternatives*
Chairman	Chair or Chairperson
Foreman	Supervisor
Newsman	Reporter or Journalist
Policeman	Police Officer

Jargon

Jargon is the specialized or technical language of a profession. William Lutz points out that groups use jargon as "verbal shorthand that allows members to communicate with each other clearly, efficiently, and quickly."[8] In some groups, the ability to use jargon properly is a sign of team membership. In other groups, jargon can make ideas difficult to understand and may be used to conceal the truth. Members unfamiliar with a group's jargon are easily intimidated and frustrated. Consider the following statement made by the leader of a computer company's newly formed self-management team:

> We can become the best team here. In no time, we'll consider the OS/2 Red Books light reading. By the time we get up and running, we'll be able to re-configure firewalls in our sleep and write device drivers faster than the vendor can overnight the device.[9]

If terms like *Red Books, firewalls,* and *device drivers* are not familiar to all members of the group, language has created a barrier between those who know the jargon and those who don't.

Some people use jargon to impress others with their specialized knowledge. Such tactics usually fail to inform others and often result in misunderstandings and resentment. Use jargon only when you are sure that all the members of your group will understand it and that it's absolutely necessary. If some of the jargon or technical terms of a field are important, take the time to explain those words to new members.

Adapting to Language Differences

It is likely that many of the groups you belong to include male and female members from different cultures and backgrounds. Gender and culture influence how we learn and use language. Although there is nothing right or wrong in the different ways that people use language, such differences can create misunderstandings among group members.

Language and Gender

Deborah Tannen compares the differences between male and female communication to that of different cultures. She writes that "communication between men and women can be like cross-cultural communication, prey to a clash of conversational styles. Instead of different dialects, it has been said they speak different genderlects."[10]

Tannen maintains that men and women use language quite differently. Women tend to use communication to maintain relationships and cooperate with others. Many women speak tentatively. Their speech is more likely to contain qualifiers and tag questions. A qualifier conveys uncertainty through words such as "maybe" and "perhaps." Tag questions are questions connected to a statement. For instance, "It may be time to move on to our next point, don't you think so?" is a statement made tentatively with a tag question. This tentative style does not necessarily represent a lack of confidence. Instead it can be viewed as a cooperative approach that encourages others to respond.

In general, men tend to use communication to assert their ideas and compete with others. Men are less likely to express themselves tentatively. Male speech is generally characterized as direct and forceful. One style of communication is not better than another. They are simply different. Effective group members use elements from both male and female approaches to language.

Language and Culture

For most groups, a single language is the medium of interaction even though members from different backgrounds, generations, and geographic areas may speak the same language quite differently. Variations in vocabulary, pronunciation, syntax, and style that distinguish speakers from different ethnic groups, geographic areas, and social classes are referred to as **dialects.** Dialects are distinct from the commonly accepted form of a particular language. In the United States, there are southern dialects, New England dialects, Brooklyn dialects, and a whole range of foreign accents. Approximately 80 to 90 percent of all African Americans use a distinct dialect at least some of the time.[11]

No one dialect is superior to another. However, General American speech is the most commonly accepted dialect in the United States. "A majority of outstanding educators and social and civic leaders use General American (as well as) prominent newscasters, commentators, and talk show hosts."[12] General American speech is the dialect spoken by as much as 60 percent of the U.S. population.

If, however, you enjoy *pizzer* and *beah* instead of pizza and beer, you may be from Massachusetts. If you say "*Ah nevah go theyuh,*" you could be from Alabama or parts of Texas. Unfortunately, studies repeatedly find that "accented speech and dialects provoke stereotyped reactions in listeners, so that the speakers are usually perceived as having less status, prestige, and overall competence."[13] The implications of such research are clear: Group members who do not use General American speech in business and academic settings may be viewed as less articulate or less competent.

THE full meaning of messages is found in both the spoken word and nonverbal behavior. What might you conclude about this group based on nonverbal communication? (Bob Daemmrich/Stock Boston)

Because dialects have the potential to influence the perceptions of group members, speakers may engage in codeswitching as a way to avoid negative stereotypes related to language. **Codeswitching** refers to the ability to change from the dialect of one's own cultural setting and adopt the language of the majority in particular situations. In other words, the dialect you speak at home may not be the best way to communicate in a business meeting. In reviewing the research on dialects, Dodd concludes "that: (1) people judge others by their speech, (2) upward mobility and social aspirations influence whether people change their speech to the accepted norms, (3) general American speech is most accepted by the majority of the American culture, and (4) people should be aware of these prejudices and attempt to look beyond the surface."[14] In the context of small group communication, we should try to understand, respect, and adapt to the dialects we hear.

Importance of Nonverbal Communication

Not all of your ideas are communicated with words. Much of your communication is nonverbal. **Nonverbal communication** refers to the behavioral elements of messages other than the actual words spoken. Your appearance, posture, and facial expressions send messages. Using and interpreting nonverbal behavior is critical to effective communication in groups.

Research has suggested that over half of all meaning is derived from nonverbal behavior.[15] Regardless of the exact percentage, it is undeniable that people base their understanding of what you mean not only on what you say but on how you say it. Unfortunately, we often put more thought into choosing the best words rather than into the most appropriate behavior for conveying an idea.

Despite all that has been written about nonverbal communication, we share Fisher and Adams' concern that it is difficult to draw conclusions about nonverbal behavior: "Researchers know very little about it. Unfortunately, people think they know much more than they actually do."[16] Thus, we urge caution when interpreting the meaning and uses of nonverbal communication in groups.

Individual Nonverbal Behavior

A group member's nonverbal behavior assumes many forms in a discussion. Group members send messages through their personal appearance as well as through facial, vocal, and physical expression. When all of these nonverbal elements are combined, they add enormous complexity and subtlety to group interaction.

Personal Appearance

How you look can affect how other group members interpret what you say and do. The physical appearance of group members is particularly important during the initial phase of group development. When group members meet for the first time, they know very little about each other beyond what they see. Physical appearance is influential in forming first impressions. Members may be stereotyped on the basis of appearance alone. For better or worse, attractive members tend to be perceived as friendly and more credible than those considered less attractive. Older members may be viewed as more knowledgeable and experienced than younger members. Men may seem more assertive than women.

Even the clothes you wear send messages to other group members. Peter Anderson maintains that "effective small group members should view clothes and hair styles as an important silent statement made to the group. Dress that is appropriate is perhaps most important."[17] Thus, casual attire is more acceptable in informal groups, whereas a professional appearance is expected in business settings and important group presentations. Your appearance should communicate that you respect the group and take its work seriously.

Facial Expression

The face is capable of expressing more varied emotions than any other part of the body. The facial expressions of group members let you know if they are interested in, agree with, or understand what you have said. Generally, women tend to be more facially expressive while men are more likely to limit the amount of emotion they reveal. Good listening requires that you look at a speaker in order to comprehend the full message.

Of all your facial features, your eyes are the most revealing. Generally, North Americans perceive eye contact as an indicator of attitude. Lack of eye contact is frequently perceived as signifying rudeness, indifference, nervousness, or dishonesty. However, perceptions of eye contact are culturally based. According to Chen and Starosta, "direct eye contact is a taboo or an insult in many Asian cultures. Cambodians consider direct eye contact as an invasion of one's privacy."[18]

Eye contact influences interaction in small groups. A seating arrangement that allows group members to face each other and establish eye contact helps maintain interaction. Eye contact also tells others when you want to speak. Returning eye contact to a group leader indicates that you are ready to respond, whereas avoiding eye contact is perceived as an attempt to avoid interaction.

Vocal Expression

Vocal expression is the way you say a word rather than the word itself. Some of the most important vocal characteristics are pitch, volume, rate, and word stress. Variations in these elements can result in different messages. For example, a group may find it difficult or unpleasant to listen to a member with a very high pitched or a monotone voice. A loud voice can convey anger, excitement, or dominance. Group members speaking quietly may signal that the information is confidential. Your volume should be adjusted to the group setting and type of activity. Rate refers to the speed at which words are spoken. A group may be bored by or stop listening to a member who speaks too slowly. A speaking rate that is too fast makes it difficult to understand the message.

When pitch, volume, and rate are combined, they can be used to vary the stress you give to a word or phrase. **Word stress** refers to the "degree of prominence given to a syllable within a word or a word within a phrase or sentence."[19] Notice the differences in meaning as you stress the italicized words in the following three sentences: Is *that* the report you want me to read? Is that the report you want *me* to read? Is that the report you want me to *read?* Although the same words are used in all three sentences, the meaning of each question is quite different.

Physical Expression The study of body movement and physical expression is referred to as **kinesics.** Gestures are one of the most animated forms of kinesics. They can emphasize or stress parts of a message, reveal discomfort with the group situation, or convey a message without the use of words. For example, Jeff points to his watch to let the chairperson know that time is running short. At the end of a discussion, a thumbs-up gesture from several group members signals that everyone is satisfied with the group's progress.

Even your posture can convey moods and emotions. For example, slouching back in your chair may be perceived as lack of interest or dislike for the group. On the other hand, sitting upright and leaning forward communicates interest and is a sign of attentive listening.

One of the most potent forms of physical expression is touch. Touch can convey a wide range of meanings. In small groups, touch is typically used to express encouragement, support, or happiness. Anderson points out that "touch in a small group may establish greater teamwork, solidarity, or sharing."[20] Some group members, however, are more comfortable with touch than others. At one end of a continuum are touch avoiders; at the other end are touch approachers. Misunderstandings can occur between these two kinds of people. Approachers may view avoiders as cold and unfriendly. However, avoiders may perceive approachers as invasive and too forward.

The Nonverbal Environment

Nonverbal communication extends beyond the behavior of individual members; it also includes the group's environment. Three important aspects of a group's nonverbal environment are the arrangement of space, perceptions of personal space, and perceptions and use of time.

Arrangement of Space The way members are seated in relation to each other significantly affects group interaction. Arrangements that physically separate members make group interaction difficult. For example, the traditional classroom arrangement of rows facing the teacher promotes interaction between the students and teacher but does not encourage communication among the students. Arrangements that bring people closer together and permit direct eye contact among all members promote group interaction. Group members arranged in a circle or around a table can more easily interact with each other.

According to Judee Burgoon, our choice of seating position has a direct effect on interaction and influence.[21] She notes that a number of studies have demonstrated that group members prefer corner-to-corner or side-by-side seating for cooperative activities. Such an arrangement allows them to be close enough to share materials. Members who anticipate competition or disagreement often choose seats across from each other.

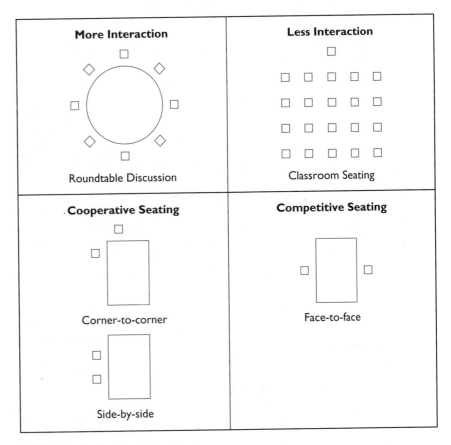

FIGURE 7.3 Seating Arrangements

Leadership and group dominance often can be determined by seating positions. Group leaders are more likely to choose or be assigned a seat at the head of a table. Knapp and Hall further note that task-oriented leaders are attracted to the head of a table while the middle position at the side of a table attracts more socially-oriented leaders—members who are more concerned about group relationships and encouraging everyone to participate.[22] These two locations place the leader in a position to see and be seen by everyone in the group. Choosing one of these centrally located positions also makes it easier for a member to gain speaking opportunities.

Even the arrangement of a room or shape of a conference table sends a message to group members. A long rectangular table gives a group's leader a special place of prominence at its head. A round table allows all members to sit in equally important positions. The Paris peace talks that helped end the war in Vietnam were bogged down for eight months until delegates from South Vietnam, the National Liberation Front, and the United States agreed to a round table as the setting for negotiation. When the leaders of Bosnia, Croatia, and Serbia met at Wright-Patterson Air Force Base in Ohio, the United States made sure that each party had equal seating space around a modest but perfectly round table. The arrangement of space is not a trivial matter when the success of a group is so consequential.

Perceptions of Personal Space

Groups and their members may function quite differently depending on how they perceive the space and people around them. The study of how we perceive and use personal space is referred to as **proxemics**. Within groups, two important proxemic variables are territoriality and interpersonal space.

Territoriality. **Territoriality** is the sense of personal ownership that is attached to a particular space. For instance, most classroom students sit in the same place every day. If you have ever walked into a classroom to find another person in *your* seat, you may have felt that your territory or space was violated. Ownership of space is often designated by objects acting as markers of territory. Placing a coat or books on a chair lets others know that a space is taken. As a group develops, members often establish their individual territory. They may sit in the same place near the same people during every meeting. Individuals who fail to respect the territory of others are violating an important group norm.

Interpersonal Space. **Interpersonal space** can be thought of as an invisible, psychological "bubble" surrounding each person that "expands or contracts according to our needs and the situation."[23] Anthropologist Edward T. Hall identifies four zones of interaction used by most North Americans.[24]

- Intimate Distance: touching to eighteen inches
- Personal Distance: eighteen inches to four feet

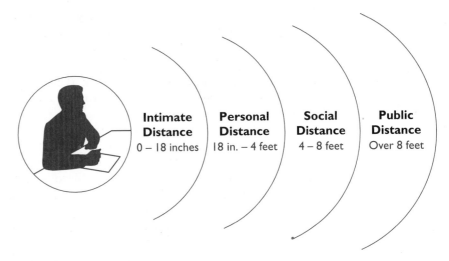

FIGURE 7.4 Zones of Personal Space

- Social Distance: four to eight feet
- Public Distance: eight or more feet

Intimate distance ranges from touching to approximately eighteen inches apart. Close friends, some family members, and lovers are normally permitted to come this close. Peter Anderson notes that "at such close distances group members will feel inhibited from interacting and will make an attempt to restore their personal space bubble by moving back even if that means leaving the group."[25]

Personal distance ranges from about eighteen inches to four feet apart. The typical distance is an arm's length away. This zone is used for conversations with friends and acquaintances. Most well-established groups interact with each other at this distance. Members feel close enough to engage in discussion but far enough away to feel comfortable.

Social distance encompasses a range of four to eight feet apart. We usually interact with new acquaintances and strangers in this zone. Groups in which members use the outer limits of this zone will find it difficult to maintain interaction.

Public distance extends beyond eight feet. Lectures and speeches are usually presented using this distance. Small groups are unlikely to use this zone unless making a presentation to a larger audience.

Perceptions and Use of Time

Group members may perceive and use time quite differently. Two distinct approaches to time are referred to as monochronic and polychronic. The **monochronic** approach divides time into precise units that can be scheduled. In a monochronic time system, time is scheduled, managed, and arranged—one thing at a time.[26] Groups with a monochronic orientation set deadlines and focus on completing activities on schedule. Northern European and North American cultures tend to be monochronic. These cultures often describe time as a commodity that is saved, spent, wasted, and lost. The phrase "time is money" is typical of this approach. For example, among monochronic members, being late for a group meeting or missing a deadline may be perceived as rude and irresponsible.

A **polychronic** approach to time allows many things to be done at once. The completion of tasks is left up to individual members. Group interaction and roles are considered more important than adhering to deadlines. Mediterranean, Latin American, and Middle Eastern cultures tend to be more polychronic. In these cultures, appointments are not considered as important and are frequently broken.

While perceptions of time vary according to culture, individuals within a given culture will also approach time differently. Although most North Americans are monochronic, some individuals may be more polychronic. In effective groups, members often share a common approach to time or understand the differences in members' perceptions and use of time. If your group is monochronic, it would be wise to arrive to meetings on time and complete work by the established deadlines. If your group is polychronic, meetings probably start late, and the discussion may run overtime. Understanding and adjusting to group members' perceptions of time can help avoid misunderstandings.

Nonverbal Communication and Culture

When we interact with group members from different cultural backgrounds, interpreting their nonverbal behavior may be as difficult as translating an unfamiliar foreign language. The multiple meanings of nonverbal communication in other cultures can be illustrated by focusing on two elements: personal space and eye contact. The earlier summary of Hall's research on personal space indicates that most Latin Americans, Arabs, and Greeks require less distance between people than do North Americans. In fact, in several Middle Eastern countries, being close enough to breathe on another person is considered proper.[27] Cultural differences also are evident when measuring the amount and directness of eye contact. If, for example, a white teacher reprimands a young black male, the student may respond by looking downward rather than looking at the teacher. In some cases, the student's response may anger the teacher and be interpreted as inattention or defiance. Yet, intercultural researchers report that "members of certain segments of black culture reportedly cast their eyes downward as a sign of respect; in white cultures, however, members expect direct eye contact as a sign of listening and showing respect for authority."[28]

As accurate as this research about personal space and eye contact may be, there is a danger of stereotyping people from different backgrounds and cultures on the basis of their nonverbal behavior. Latino, Arab, and Greek group members may not require less personal space than a North American requires. Young black males may look directly at a white teacher with respect. When interpreting nonverbal behavior, try to understand, respect, and adapt to individual differences rather than assuming that all people from all cultures behave alike.

If you are unsure about the appropriate way to respond nonverbally, ask. Too often, we find out about the nonverbal rules of another culture only after we have broken them.

Creating a Communication Climate

Our use of and reaction to language and nonverbal communication establishes a unique group atmosphere or climate. Specifically, a group's **climate** is the degree to which members feel comfortable interacting. In some groups the climate is warm and supportive. Members like and trust each other as they work toward a common goal. In chillier group climates, defensiveness and tension pollute the atmosphere. Members may feel threatened by and suspicious of one another.

Jack Gibb has described six pairs of communication behavior that influence whether a group's climate is defensive or supportive.[29] When the group climate is defensive, members devote attention to defending themselves and defeating perceived opponents. Synergy occurs only when a group functions in a supportive climate.

Defensive Climates	Supportive Climates
• Evaluation	• Description
• Control	• Problem Orientation
• Strategy	• Spontaneity
• Neutrality	• Empathy
• Superiority	• Equality
• Certainty	• Provisionalism

FIGURE 7.5   Group Communication Climates

Evaluation versus Description

Which of the following statements would you prefer to hear from a member of your group: "That's the dumbest idea you've ever come up with" or "I'd like to think we could do that, but I have some concerns"? The first statement evaluates the person and the idea, whereas the second begins a description of the speaker's reservations. Statements and behavior that evaluate or judge others elicit defensiveness. Even nonverbal behavior such as laughter or groans can be as evaluative as the sharpest verbal criticism. Description includes neutral requests for information and statements that do not attack other people's opinions or actions. Although groups cannot and should not completely eliminate evaluative communication, highly judgmental remarks aimed at particular individuals should be avoided.

One of the best ways to move from evaluation to description is to substitute specific "I" statements for critical "you" statements. Beginning a statement with "You disappoint me when . . ." can promote defensiveness. "You" implies blame. "I" clarifies what you think and feel, while "you" can make a person feel criticized. "I am disappointed that your portion of the report isn't complete" acknowledges that you are responsible for your own thoughts and feelings while describing the situation you find troublesome.

Control versus Problem Orientation

Problem orientation implies that members are highly committed to the group and its goal. Control implies that some members are more interested in power and their own personal goals. For example, the overly aggressive salesperson or telephone solicitor is trying to separate you from your money rather than understanding and finding the solution that best meets your needs. If you think that someone is trying to manipulate or control you, you are likely to resist. Approaching communication from the perspective of problem orientation results in a message that indicates you are not trying to control or impose a predetermined solution upon the group.

Strategy versus Spontaneity

Strategic communication suggests that hidden agendas are operating within the group. Members suspect that their ideas are not being listened to fairly. Spontaneous communication implies the use of honest and open responses. How would you feel if, after what appears to be sincere and spontaneous discussion, someone in your group says, "I just happen to have a proposal that George and I put together—it's written and ready to sign off on." Suspicion and defensiveness would be a natural reaction to such a strategic move by two group members.

Neutrality versus Empathy

Neutral behaviors are impersonal and fail to express concern for another person's emotional needs. Empathic communication conveys an understanding of members' feelings. When your words and nonverbal behavior communicate a lack of concern or understanding, resentment and defensiveness can result. If you are explaining why you have not met a deadline and group members sit stone-faced, they may be telling you that your personal problems are of no interest to them. If group members nod their heads and look concerned when you describe the difficulties you have encountered, their understanding and sympathy have created a much more supportive group climate.

Superiority versus Equality

A meeting may be the worst place to show off and brag about your accomplishments and status. If your communication style and comments suggest that you are better than other members, your suggestions may be met with hostility and defensiveness. Arranging a meeting room so that some members have more prominent seats or better chairs than other members suggests that not all members are created equal. Conveying a willingness to cooperate with group members implies an attitude of equality. When all members are viewed equally, then loyalty, respect, and effort can be expected from everyone.

Certainty versus Provisionalism

Members who insist they are always right and focus on winning arguments produce a climate of certainty. As a result, other group members are inclined to make greater efforts to defend their own ideas. An attitude of provisionalism suggests a willingness to modify one's own attitudes and behaviors as a result of group feedback. If you are certain, you are less likely to listen to other members and less likely to alter your opinion. If you can be flexible and focus on achieving the group's goal, there is a greater likelihood that the group's performance and outcome will be successful.

Balancing Language and Nonverbal Behavior

There is an inseparable relationship between language and nonverbal communication. When verbal and nonverbal behavior repeat and complement one another, communication is enhanced. When verbal and nonverbal messages contradict each other, the group can become confused and defensive. If members put too much emphasis on the meanings of words, bypassing is more likely to occur.

In a supportive group climate, members are more likely to feel comfortable and confident. By avoiding statements and actions that are highly evaluative, controlling, strategic, neutral, superior, and certain, a group is more likely to succeed in working together toward the achievement of a shared goal.

Groups must achieve a balance of language with nonverbal behavior in order to maximize the effectiveness of both forms of communication. Although language and nonverbal behavior are powerful tools, they will only

Language   Nonverbal Behavior
Gender Differences   Cultural Differences
Supportive Climate   Defensive Climate

Verbal
and Nonverbal
Communication

FIGURE 7.6 Verbal and Nonverbal Communication

be as effective as the member who uses them. As Schrage observes, "Most people can speak a language fluently, but it takes care, craftsmanship, and sincerity to speak in a way that consistently evokes empathy, understanding, and commitment."[30]

Summary Study Guide

- Because meaning depends on individual interpretation, words can have many meanings.
- Team talk is the means used to achieve group goals, the stimulus to build group relationships, and the evidence used to assess group work.
- Avoiding bypassing, seeking gender-neutral terms, and minimizing jargon can improve group communication.
- Women tend to use a more tentative language style, while men's language tends to be more direct and to the point.
- General American speech is the most commonly accepted form of language in the United States. If you have the ability to use more than one dialect, codeswitch in appropriate situations.
- Nonverbal communication conveys as much or more meaning as do words.
- Personal appearance influences how group members perceive you and your messages.
- The face expresses more emotions than any other part of the body. Eye contact significantly influences group interaction.
- Vocal characteristics include pitch, volume, rate, and word stress.
- Physical expression includes gestures, posture, and touch.
- Group seating arrangements can promote or discourage communication. Leaders tend to choose centrally located positions.

- Territoriality refers to a sense of ownership of a particular space.
- Interpersonal space consists of four zones of interaction: intimate, personal, social, and public.
- Perception and use of time vary across cultures. Time orientation can be monochronic or polychronic.
- Take time to observe, interpret, and adapt to the nonverbal behavior in your group, particularly when members represent different ethnic groups and cultures.
- Groups characterized by evaluation, control, strategy, neutrality, superiority, and certainty foster defensive climates. Description, problem orientation, spontaneity, empathy, equality, and provisionalism characterize supportive climates.

Groupwork *Context, Context, Context*

GOAL   To demonstrate the extent to which the meaning of language and nonverbal behavior are dependent on social climate and group circumstances.

PARTICIPANTS   Groups of at least three members.

PROCEDURE

1. Each group creates a situation in which the following sentence is uttered: "I don't think that's right." The group must:
   - Decide what sentence came before and after "I don't think that's right."
   - Decide upon the physical setting and situation confronting the group in which a member would say, "I don't think that's right."
2. Each group creates and presents a "scene" for the class in which three different group members are assigned to "act" the three sentences they have developed and placed in a specific context.
3. After all the groups have "performed" their scene, the class should discuss the following questions:
   - How did the context or situation change the meaning of "I don't think that's right?"
   - How did the nonverbal behavior and setting differ in each scene?
   - How could each group's "I don't think that's right" be paraphrased into a different sentence?
   - Which component communicated the most information about the meaning of the scene—the words, the nonverbal behavior, or the situation?

ASSESSMENT

Auditing Team Talk

Directions   Circle the term that best describes the extent to which the members of your group engage in productive team talk.

When your group communicates . . .

Do members use plural pronouns rather than singular ones?	Very Often	Sometimes	Rarely
Do members use language that acknowledges shared needs?	Very Often	Sometimes	Rarely
Do members solicit opinions and express the need for cooperation?	Very Often	Sometimes	Rarely
Do members talk to one another on equal terms?	Very Often	Sometimes	Rarely
Do members use casual language, nicknames, slang?	Very Often	Sometimes	Rarely
Do members express empathy and liking?	Very Often	Sometimes	Rarely
Do members express interest in solving problems?	Very Often	Sometimes	Rarely
Do members use a nonthreatening tone and nonjudgmental language?	Very Often	Sometimes	Rarely
Do members paraphrase each other?	Very Often	Sometimes	Rarely
Do members ask "what if" questions?	Very Often	Sometimes	Rarely
Do members propose objective criteria for solutions?	Very Often	Sometimes	Rarely
Do members summarize areas of agreement?	Very Often	Sometimes	Rarely

Scoring

Analyze your group's team talk by looking at the number of times you circled *Very Often, Sometimes,* and *Rarely*. The more times you circled *Very Often,* the more likely it is that your group engages in productive team talk. The more times you circled *Rarely,* the more likely it is that team talk inhibits group progress and success. To get a more accurate assessment of team talk for your entire group, everyone should complete the questionnaire and share their responses. Is there a consistent response to each question? If there are significant disagreements on several questions, the members of your group may benefit from a discussion about the nature of their team talk.

Recommended Readings

Donnellon, A. (1996). *Team talk: The power of language in team dynamics.* Boston, MA: Harvard Business School Press.

Hall, E. T. (1982). *The hidden dimension.* New York: Doubleday.

Knapp, M. L. & Hall, J. A. (1997). *Nonverbal communication in human interaction* (4th ed.). Fort Worth, TX: Harcourt Brace.

Notes

1. Donnellon, A. (1996). *Team talk: The power of language in team dynamics*. Boston, MA: Harvard Business School Press, p. 6.
2. Hayakawa, S. I. & Hayakawa, A. R. (1990). *Language and thought in action* (5th ed.). San Diego, CA: Harcourt Brace Jovanovich, p. 43.
3. Donnellon, p. 25.
4. Based on Donnellon, pp. 31–33.
5. Donnellon, p. 25.
6. Haney, W. V. (1992). *Communication and interpersonal relations: Text and cases* (6th ed.). Homewood, IL: Irwin, p. 269.
7. Haney, p. 290.
8. Lutz, W. (1990). *Doublespeak*. New York: HarperPerennial, p. 3.
9. Based on an excerpt from *Wired* (July 1995), p. 94.
10. Tannen, D. (1990). *You just don't understand: Women and men in conversation*. New York: William Morrow, p. 42.
11. Weber, S. N. (1995). The need to be: The sociocultural significance of black language. In K. S. Verderber, *Voices: A selection of multicultural readings*. Belmont, CA: Wadsworth, p. 30.
12. Mayer, L. V. (1996). *Fundamentals of voice and diction* (11th ed.). Madison, WI: Brown & Benchmark, p. 8.
13. Lustig, M. W. & Koester, J. (1996). *Intercultural competencies: Interpersonal communication across cultures* (2nd ed.). New York: HarperCollins, p. 180.
14. Dodd, C. H. (1995). *Dynamics of intercultural communication* (4th ed.). Madison, WI: Brown & Benchmark, p. 151.
15. See Hickson, M. L. & Stacks, D. W. (1993). *Nonverbal communication: Studies and applications* (3rd ed.). Dubuque, IA: Brown & Benchmark, p. 4; Mehrabian, A. (1981). *Silent messages: Implicit communication of emotions and attitudes* (2nd ed.). Belmont, CA: Wadsworth, p. 77; Birdwhistell, R. L. (1970). *Kinesics & context: Essays on body motion*. Philadelphia: University of Pennsylvania, p. 158.
16. Fisher, B. A. & Adams, K. L. (1994). *Interpersonal communication: Pragmatics of human relationships* (2nd ed.). New York: McGraw-Hill, p. 153.
17. Anderson, P. A. (1992). Nonverbal communication in the small group. In R. S. Cathcart & L. A. Samovar (Eds.), *Small group communication: A reader* (6th ed.). Dubuque, IA: Wm. C. Brown, p. 273.
18. Chen, G. M. & Starosta, W. J. (1998). *Fundamentals of intercultural communication*. Boston, MA: Allyn & Bacon, p. 91.
19. Mayer, p. 228.
20. Anderson, p. 267.
21. Burgoon, J. K. (1996). Spatial relationships in small groups. In R. S. Cathcart, L. A. Samovar, & L. D. Henman (Eds.), *Small group communication: Theory and practice* (7th ed). Madison, WI: Brown & Benchmark, p. 249.
22. Knapp, M. L. & Hall, J. A. (1997). *Nonverbal communication in human interaction* (4th Ed.). Fort Worth, TX: Harcourt Brace, p. 177.
23. Burgoon, p. 242.
24. Hall, E. T. (1982). *The hidden dimension*. New York: Doubleday.
25. Anderson, p. 269.
26. Lustig & Koester, p. 209.
27. Dodd, pp. 166 and 167.
28. Dodd, p. 160.

29. Gibb, J. R. (1974). Defensive communication. In R. S. Cathcart & L. A. Samovar (Eds.), *Small group communication: A reader.* Dubuque, IA: Wm. C. Brown, pp. 327–333.

30. Schrage, M. (1995). *No more teams! Mastering the dynamics of creative collaboration.* New York: Currency Doubleday, p. 66.

Conflict and Cohesion in Groups

Conflict in Groups

Conflict is unavoidable in an effective group. Rarely do conscientious members work in groups for any length of time without expressing differences and disagreeing. Yet, despite the inevitability of conflict, many of us go out of our way to avoid or suppress it. One of the myths about effective groups is "that they are characterized by chumminess. Many effective teams look more like battlegrounds, it turns out. . . . Teams with vastly competent members embrace conflict as the price of synergy and set good idea against good idea to arrive at the best idea."[1]

The word *conflict* is frequently associated with quarreling, fighting, anger, and hostility. While these elements may be present in a group situation, conflict does not have to involve the expression of negative emotions. We define **conflict** as the disagreement and disharmony that occurs in groups when differences are expressed regarding ideas, methods, and/or members. This definition emphasizes that conflict only occurs when differences are expressed. Hocker and Wilmot are adamant about this point: "It is impossible to have conflict without either verbal or nonverbal communication behavior, or both."[2] When treated as an expression of legitimate differences, conflict "can be used as the spur to find the wider solution, the solution that will meet the mutual interest of the parties involved in it."[3]

The definition also indicates that conflict occurs when group members express differences about ideas, methods, and group members. Putnam has classified these three sources of conflict as substantive, procedural, and affective.[4]

Substantive Conflict

Substantive conflict is disagreement over members' ideas and group issues. For example, when members of a student government council argue whether or not student activities fees should be raised, their conflict is substantive. Such conflict is directly related to working toward the group's goal of serving students' cocurricular needs.

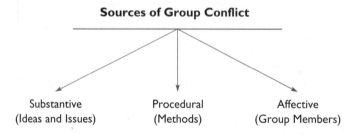

Sources of Group Conflict

Substantive	Procedural	Affective
(Ideas and Issues)	(Methods)	(Group Members)

FIGURE 8.1 Sources of Group Conflict

Procedural Conflict

Procedural conflict is disagreement among group members about the methods or process the group should follow in its attempt to accomplish a goal. Whereas some group members may want to begin a discussion by suggesting solutions to a problem, others may want to start by gathering and discussing information. Some members may believe that a decision should be made by secret ballot, while others may want a show of hands.

Affective Conflict

Affective conflict centers around the personalities, communication styles, and emotions of group members. Its causes are numerous. Affective conflict may occur when a member does not feel valued or is threatened by the group. Affective conflict also occurs when members believe that their ideas are not judged fairly or when group members are struggling for power. Affective conflict is more difficult to resolve because it involves people's feelings and the way members relate to one another.

Frequently when disagreement occurs in groups, both substantive and affective types of conflict are present. For example, Dee believes student fees should be raised in order to fund more campus activities. Charles disagrees and suggests that the existing funds should be used more efficiently rather than placing a larger financial burden on students. At this point in the discussion, the conflict is substantive; it is focused on issues. However, when responding to Dee, Charles rolls his eyes and states that "only a political fool believes that higher fees are the answer to the problem." Not only does Dee disagree with Charles on the issues, but she is also angered by his comment. Now the conflict is not just substantive; it has become affective as well.

Constructive and Destructive Conflict

Conflict itself is neither good nor bad. However, the way in which a group deals with conflict can be constructive or destructive. Katzenbach and Smith observe the following:

> Seldom do we see a group of individuals forge their unique experiences, perspectives, values, and expectations into a *common* purpose . . . without encountering significant conflict. And the most challenging risks associated with conflict relate to making it constructive for the team instead of simply enduring it.[5]

Destructive conflict results when groups engage in behaviors that create hostility and prevent achievement of the group's goal. The consequences of destructive group conflict are significant. The quality of group decision making deteriorates when members are inflexible, avoid conflict, or are not open

Constructive Conflict	Destructive Conflict
• Focus on Issues	• Personal Attacks
• Respect for Others	• Insults
• Supportiveness	• Defensiveness
• Flexibility	• Inflexibility
• Cooperation	• Competition
• Commitment to Conflict Management	• Avoidance of Conflict

FIGURE 8.2 Constructive and Destructive Conflict

to other points of view. Destructive conflict has the potential to permanently disable a group.

Constructive conflict results when group members express disagreement in a way that values everyone's contributions and promotes the group's goal. The table shown in Figure 8.2 characterizes the differences between destructive and constructive conflict. Constructive group conflict has many positive outcomes. Issues and people are better understood through an open exchange. The quality of decision making improves as opposing viewpoints and concerns are discussed. Expressing differences constructively can make a group discussion more interesting and promote participation.

Conflict Styles

There are many ways of identifying and classifying different styles of conflict. One of the most preferred methods suggests that individuals are predisposed to using one of the following five conflict styles: avoidance, accommodation, competition, compromise, and collaboration.[6] These five styles can be further understood by examining the extent to which a group member's approach to conflict is focused on achieving personal goals and/or the group's goal. Members who are motivated to achieve their own goals tend to choose more competitive approaches. Cooperative members are usually more concerned with achieving the group's goals. Figure 8.3 illustrates the relationship of each conflict style to a group member's motivation.

Avoidance When members are unable or unwilling to accomplish their own goals or contribute to achieving the group's goal, they may adopt the **avoidance conflict style.** Group members using this style may change the subject, avoid bringing up a controversial issue, and even deny that a conflict exists. Avoid-

FIGURE 8.3   Conflict Styles

ing conflict in groups is usually counterproductive because it fails to address a problem and can increase group tensions. Furthermore, ignoring or avoiding conflict does not make it go away.

However, in some circumstances, avoidance of conflict can be an effective approach, specifically when

- the issue is not that important to you.
- you need to take time to collect your thoughts or control your emotions.
- other group members are effectively addressing the same concerns.

Accommodation   Group members using the **accommodating conflict style** give in to other members at the expense of their own goals. A genuine desire to get along with other group members is often the motivation of accommodators. Such members believe that giving in to others serves the needs of the group even when the group could benefit from further discussion. A group member who always approaches conflict by accommodating others may ultimately be perceived as less powerful and have less influence in group decision making.

Accommodating during conflict can be an appropriate approach when

- the issue is very important to others but not very important to you.
- it is more important to preserve group harmony than to resolve the current issue.
- you realize you are wrong or have changed your mind.
- you are unlikely to succeed in persuading the group to adopt your position.

Competition   The **competitive conflict style** occurs when group members are more concerned with their own goals rather than with meeting the needs of the group. Competitive members want to win; they argue that their ideas are superior to the alternatives suggested by others. When used inappropriately, the competitive style may be characterized by hostility, ridicule, and personal attacks against group members. Approaching conflict competitively tends to reduce group members to winners and losers. Ultimately, this may damage the relationships among group members.

In certain group situations, however, the competitive approach may be the most appropriate style. Approach conflict competitively when

- you have strong beliefs about an important issue.
- the group must act immediately on an urgent issue or emergency situation.
- the consequences of the group's decision may be very serious or harmful.
- you believe the group may be acting unethically or illegally.

Compromise   The **compromising conflict style** is a "middle ground" approach that involves conceding some goals in order to achieve others. When group members compromise, each member is willing to suffer some losses in exchange for gaining something else. Group members who approach conflict through compromise argue that it is a fair method of resolving problems since everyone loses equally. However, groups that begin compromising before attempting other methods of conflict resolution often fail to think of more creative, synergistic options for solving a problem. Steven Covey summarizes this point by drawing a distinction between compromise and synergy. "Compromise," he observes, "is the proposition that $1 + 1 = 1.5$. Synergy is the proposition that $1 + 1 = 3$."[7]

The compromise approach should be used when the group has been unable to find a more constructive solution. Groups should consider compromising when

- other methods of resolving the conflict will not be effective.
- the members have reached an impasse and are no longer progressing toward a reasonable solution.
- the group does not have enough time to explore more creative solutions.

Collaboration   The **collaborative conflict style** searches for new solutions that will achieve both the individual goals of group members and the goals of the group. Instead of arguing over whose solutions are superior, the collaborative group

IN many group situations—like this rope-pulling contest—a competitive conflict style is appropriate. When is competition not appropriate for resolving group conflict? (© Jean-Claude Lejeune/Stock Boston)

looks for new and creative solutions that satisfy everyone in the group. Collaboration focuses on problem solving through a team effort rather than arguing over whose ideas are better. Collaboration seeks synergy.

There are, however, two important drawbacks to the collaborative approach. First, collaboration requires a lot of the group's time and energy. Some issues may not be important enough to justify such creative effort and extra time. Second, in order for collaboration to be successful, all group members must fully participate. Avoiders and accommodators can prevent a group from engaging in true collaboration.

Groups should approach conflict resolution collaboratively when

- they want to find a solution that will satisfy all group members.
- new and creative ideas are needed.
- a commitment to the final decision is needed from each group member.
- the group has enough time to commit to creative problem solving.

Choosing a Conflict Style

While individuals may be predisposed to a particular style, effective group members choose the conflict style that is most appropriate for a particular group in a particular situation. As situations change, so may the group's conflict style. For instance, a member may initially avoid the conflict, then compete to have a particular idea accepted, and ultimately engage in collaboration to seek a creative solution.

Folger, Poole, and Stutman suggest that when selecting a conflict style, you should consider the following questions:

How important is the issue to you?
How important is the issue to other members?
How important is it to maintain positive relationships within the group?
How much time does the group have to address the issue?
How fully do group members trust each other?[8]

Answers to these questions can suggest whether a particular conflict style is appropriate or inappropriate in a particular situation. For instance, if group members are not trusting of one another, the compromising style would be less appropriate. If the issue is very important and the group has plenty of time to discuss it, collaboration should be explored. There is no single conflict style that will be effective in all group situations. The skilled member balances a variety of considerations and chooses an appropriate style.

Approaches to Conflict Management

Groups can choose from a variety of conflict management methods. Careful analysis of the conflict should determine which approach best suits the situation and the group. Effective group members are flexible and able to use a variety of approaches to resolving conflict. The methods described in this section range from individual approaches to the intervention of a third-party mediator.

The 4Rs Method

In order to choose the most appropriate conflict management method, you should make sure you understand your group's conflict. We suggest using the 4Rs method for analyzing the conflict in a particular situation. The four steps of the method are accompanied by these relevant questions:

- **Reasons.** What are the reasons for or causes of the conflict? Are the causes associated with expressed differences about issues, methods, and/or members? Do other concerned members agree with your assessment of the reasons for conflict?
- **Reactions.** How are group members reacting to one another? Are the reactions constructive or destructive in nature? Can member reactions be modified into more constructive behavior?
- **Results.** What are the consequences of the group's current approach to the conflict? Is the conflict serious enough to jeopardize the group's goal and member morale?
- **Resolution.** What are the available methods for resolving the conflict? Which method best matches the nature of the group and its conflict?

Analyzing the group's conflict before taking action will result in a better resolution because it is based on an understanding of the nature of the disagreement. The 4Rs method provides a way of thinking about conflict and selecting an appropriate approach to conflict management.

Managing Anger

During the course of a conflict, members may become angry because their needs are not being met or because they believe they are being treated unfairly. The way in which group members express anger can determine whether conflict is destructive or constructive. Whereas unrestrained expres-

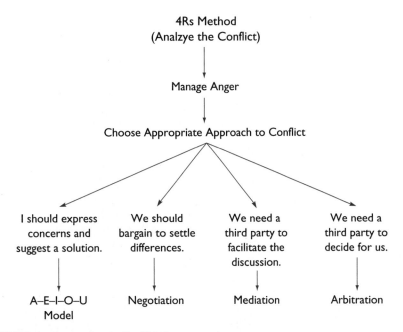

FIGURE 8.4   Approaches to Conflict Management

sions of anger often generate hostility and anger in others, suppressed anger can lead to resentment.[9] The key to dealing with anger is taming it so that it can be harnessed and used to manage and resolve conflict.

If you decide to express your anger, follow these guidelines:

- Determine whether your anger should be expressed to the group at this place and time.
- Make a statement that describes your anger and its source. Be descriptive rather than evaluative, spontaneous rather than strategic, and provisional rather than certain. Use "I" statements to describe your feelings and concerns.
- Allow other group members to express their anger. Apply the golden listening rule: Listen to others as you would have them listen to you.
- Discuss the source of the anger and possible solutions. Focus on issues and try to maintain a supportive group climate.
- Insist upon appropriate expressions of anger and conflict throughout the process. There should be no name calling or accusations.

The A-E-I-O-U Model

In order to resolve conflict, a group must fully understand member concerns. If members do not understand the problem, they cannot effectively find solutions. Wisinski's A-E-I-O-U Model is a way to clearly communicate concerns and suggest alternative actions.[10] The steps in the A-E-I-O-U Model are as follows:

> **A**—Assume the other members mean well.
> **E**—Express your feelings.
> **I**—Identify what you would like to happen.
> **O**—Outcomes you expect are made clear.
> **U**—Understanding on a mutual basis is achieved.

The first step, *A*, requires a belief that other group members are willing to cooperate. Such a belief could be expressed as follows: "I know that all of us want this project to succeed."

The second step, *E*, identifies your feelings associated with a specific behavior or action. "But, I'm really worried because it seems as though we're not putting in the work that's needed." Expressing your feelings and describing behavior helps the group interpret your reaction to the situation.

The third step, *I*, requires that you not only express your concerns but also identify what you want to happen. "I would like to be assured that all of you are as concerned about the success of this project as I am and that you have been thinking about how we can make sure the work gets done on time." The group can now focus its discussion on solving the problem.

The fourth step, *O*, directs you to inform members of the potential outcomes of their behavior. "I sincerely believe that if we don't work late for the next couple of days, we will not be prepared to make an effective group presentation next week."

The final step, *U*, recognizes that your group may need to discuss your suggestions. "Could we try staying late for the next few days to get ahead of the game? What do you think?" A group will frequently reject an initial suggestion but then go on to develop a more satisfactory solution. The final step requires that all group members understand and agree to a solution. When all the steps in the A-E-I-O-U Model are combined, they become the essential ingredients in creating a constructive approach to conflict management.

Negotiation

Negotiation is a process of bargaining in order to settle differences or reach solutions. Normally, negotiation takes the form of compromise, with group members conceding some issues in order to achieve agreement on other points. Group members are more willing to bargain if they believe they will be no worse off and might even be better off by the end of the negotiation process.

Fisher, Ury, and Patton suggest that conflict can be resolved through a process of "principled negotiation."[11] The four principles are as follows:

- Separate the people from the problem.
- Focus on group interests, not positions.
- Generate a variety of possible solutions for mutual gain.
- Insist on objective criteria for choosing a solution.

> **TOOLBOX 8.1**   Brainstorming and Criteria
>
> Brainstorming is a process for generating as many ideas as possible. In simplified terms, brainstorming can be described as "all input, no put down." During a brainstorming session, group members are encouraged to generate as many ideas and solutions as possible. Only after the group has spent time generating a wide range of solutions does the group evaluate each idea by using an agreed-upon set of criteria. These criteria should focus on the feasibility and mutual gain to be derived from each solution. **Chapter 9: Decision Making in Groups** discusses the guidelines for brainstorming and ways to establish decision-making criteria.

Fisher and his colleagues contend that effective negotiation requires "a working relationship where trust, understanding, respect, and friendship are built up over time."[12] When the focus is on defending positions, the result is winners and losers. By focusing on group interests, the entire group wins. Effective groups brainstorm alternatives and establish criteria with which to evaluate and choose a solution to their problem. Objective and agreed-upon criteria assure that no individual group member has an unfair advantage during negotiation.

The atmosphere is more competitive, partisan, and political in negotiation than it would be if the climate were suitable for collaboration. Wood notes that "because it allows members to pursue personal interests while acknowledging those of others, negotiation constrains communication to respect a delicate balance between individualism and interdependence."[13]

Clearly, group members must balance a variety of needs during negotiation.[14] They must be willing to cooperate with others while attempting to meet as many of their own needs as possible. They must openly communicate what they are willing to concede yet not sacrifice more than necessary. Finally, members must balance the need to gain their own short-term goals against the benefits of mutually desirable long-term conflict resolution.

Mediation   During the last two decades, a process called mediation has become an alternative tool for resolving disputes. **Mediation** has been described as "facilitated negotiation [that] employs the services of impartial third parties only for the purpose of guiding, coaching, and encouraging the disputants through negotiation to successful resolution and agreement."[15]

Groups can use the principles and methods of mediation when conflicts have the potential to become barriers to group progress. Mediation is an appropriate approach to conflict resolution when the group members are unable to resolve the conflict by themselves and when everyone concerned is willing to participate in the process and abide by the final settlement. If group members cannot agree to these terms, then mediation is not an option.

Once a group has decided to use mediation, there are two basic ingredients that must be included: an impartial mediator and a well-planned mediation session.

The Mediator. The first step in the mediation process is choosing an impartial mediator who is not involved in the conflict. If a conflict involves all members of the group, a mediator from outside the group should be chosen. The group leader or another group member should be considered as a mediator only if he or she is not involved in the conflict.

The mediator does not take sides in the dispute. Keltner notes that "the mediator makes no decisions for the parties, has no authority to direct or control the action of the parties, and only work effectively when both parties are willing to use the process."[16] During the process of conflict resolution, the mediator monitors the honesty and accuracy of the information discussed, helps group members accurately interpret each other's messages, and allows members to make concessions without appearing weak or defeated.[17]

The Session. Based on McKinney, Kimsey, and Fuller's recommendations on how to lead disputants through a mediation session, the following four-step process can be used to guide a group or its members through mediation.[18]

Step 1: Introduce the Process. The mediator creates a supportive climate in which group members can reach an agreement to settle their conflict. The mediator also explains the process and the rules for interaction. Usually, mediators will emphasize that name calling, profanity, or interruptions will not be tolerated.

Step 2: Define the Conflict. During this phase, each group member is given time to describe the conflict from her or his perspective. Members are allowed to "tell their story" and share their feelings without interruption or criticism. The mediator will summarize each person's story and ask for further explanations if they are needed to understand the dispute.

Step 3: Solve the Problem. During the third phase, the mediator tries to move members "away from hostile independent attitudes and toward an attitude of cooperative interaction."[19] The mediator tries to guide group members toward possible solutions. The solving phase is complete "when all issues, all points in dispute, have been discussed and an acceptable resolution is achieved."[20]

Step 4: Implement the Agreement. Upon agreeing to a resolution of the conflict, the group should discuss how the agreement will be implemented. In most mediation sessions, the agreement is put in writing. Details should specify conditions, responsibilities, deadlines, and criteria for judging effectiveness. In some groups, an oral agreement may be sufficient to end the dispute. If an entire group is involved in a mediation session, Tjosvold and van

> **TOOLBOX 8.2** Decision Making and Problem Solving
>
> Many of the techniques for group problem solving and decision making can be used to manage conflict and resolve disagreements. For example, brainstorming can be used in a mediation session when disputants are having difficulty finding ways to solve their problem. When group members are reluctant to express differences, the nominal group technique can provide a way in which written suggestions substitute for verbal interaction. By using a detailed standard agenda or parliamentary procedure, groups can focus on substantive conflict while reducing affective and procedural conflict. Chapter 9 describes several decision-making and problem-solving methods. Chapter 15 reviews the principles and rules of parliamentary procedure.

de Vliert recommend that the mediator take time to lead a discussion on ways the group can resolve future conflict.[21]

Arbitration Groups often resort to mediation when all other methods of resolving a conflict have failed. If mediation does not work, a group may seek arbitration. **Arbitration,** like mediation, involves a third party. However, after considering all sides, the arbitrator decides how to resolve the conflict. The arbitrator may choose one person's solution or may develop a solution the group has not yet considered. Whatever the final decision, group members are obligated to accept and implement the solution, no matter what they think about the decision.

When turning to an arbitrator to make a decision, group members "have acknowledged that their own decision-making powers are insufficient to resolve the dispute. Their function, therefore, is to present their side of the case as fully and as capably as possible so that fairness and justice can prevail."[22] Despite the hope for a just outcome, professional arbitrators understand that their decisions may not satisfy or please everyone in a group. Yet, for groups that cannot resolve conflicts or solve problems on their own or with the help of a mediator, arbitration may be the only way to make a needed decision.

Group Cohesion

Resolving conflict in groups does not guarantee success, nor does it ensure that group members will work together in pursuit of a common goal. Working in groups also requires cohesiveness. **Cohesion** is the mutual attraction that holds the members of a group together. Groups that are cohesive feel committed and unified; members develop a sense of teamwork and pride in the group.

Shaw identifies five characteristics of cohesive groups.[23] First, the more cohesive a group, the more the members interact with one another. Cohesive groups develop supportive communication climates in which members feel comfortable expressing their thoughts and feelings. Second, the interaction in a cohesive group tends to be more friendly and cooperative than in less cohesive groups. Members of a cohesive group make positive statements to others about the group and its members. Third, cohesive groups exert greater influence over members and foster a desire to conform to the group's expectations. In some highly cohesive groups, members may unquestioningly support each other's suggestions. Fourth, cohesive groups achieve their goals more effectively by being more creative and productive in approaching their work. (There is, however, some evidence that extremely cohesive groups may focus too much attention on the social aspects of the group and become less productive.) Fifth, members are more satisfied in cohesive groups. They believe their personal goals and the group's goals are successfully achieved.

Enhancing Cohesion

Cohesive groups are happier and get more work done. Clearly, your group wants to strive for cohesion. Based on Bormann and Bormann, we suggest four general strategies for developing group cohesion.[24]

Establish a Group Identity and Traditions. Begin by referring to the group with terms such as "we" and "our" instead of "I" and "my." The language that members use to refer to the group can influence the way they perceive their connection to it. Some groups create more obvious signs of identity such as a group name, logo, or motto. As members continue to work and interact with one another, the group begins to develop its own history. Many groups develop rituals and ceremonies to reinforce traditions.

Emphasize Teamwork. The members of cohesive groups believe that their contributions are essential to the success of the group. Group members feel responsibility for and take pride in the work they do as well as the work of other members. They frequently make statements that stress the importance of everyone's role. Rather than the individual members taking personal credit for success, a cohesive group will emphasize the group's accomplishments.

Recognize and Reward Contributions. Frequently, group members become so involved in their own work that they neglect to praise others for their contributions. In addition, members are often quick to criticize mistakes and poor work. While constructive criticism is important, members must feel that their efforts are appreciated. Cohesive groups establish a climate in which praise is encouraged. Many groups reward individual efforts and initiative. Celebration dinners, letters of appreciation, certificates, and gifts are all ways in which some groups reward themselves.

Respect Group Members.   When strong interpersonal relationships are developed in groups, members become more sensitive to each other's needs. Groups that require members to do their part of the work without regard for individual concerns will develop little cohesion. Treating members with respect, showing concern for their personal needs, and appreciating diversity will promote a feeling of acceptance.

Groupthink

Groupthink is a term that describes the deterioration of group effectiveness that results from in-group pressure.[25] Highly cohesive groups are at greater risk of succumbing to groupthink. Bennis, Parikh, and Lessem suggest that "perhaps the most damaging disease to a group's health is over-conformity, always the result of group pressure."[26]

Symptoms of Groupthink.   Irving Janis, a professor at Yale University, developed the theory of groupthink after recognizing patterns in what he termed policy-making fiascoes. He suggests that groupthink was a significant factor in several major policy decisions, including the Bay of Pigs invasion, the escalation of both the Korean and Vietnam wars, the attack on Pearl Harbor, and the Watergate burglary and cover-up.[27] After analyzing many of these policy decisions, Janis identified eight symptoms of groupthink. The table shown in Figure 8.5 illustrates the symptoms and expressions of groupthink.

Groupthink Symptoms	Expressions of Groupthink
Invulnerability: Is overly confident; willing to take big risks.	"We're right. We've done this many times, and nothing's gone wrong."
Rationalization: Makes excuses; discounts warnings.	"What does Lewis know? He's been here only three weeks."
Morality: Ignores ethical and moral consequences.	"Sometimes the end justifies the means."
Stereotyping Outsiders: Considers opposition too weak and stupid to make real trouble.	"Let's not worry about the subcommittee—they can't even get their own act together."
Self-Censorship: Doubts his or her own reservations; unwilling to disagree or dissent.	"I guess there's no harm in going along with the group—I'm the only one who disagrees."
Pressure on Dissent: Pressures members to agree.	"Why are you trying to hold this up? You'll ruin the project."
Illusion of Unanimity: Believes everyone agrees.	"Hearing no objections, the motion passes."
Mindguarding: Shields members from adverse information or opposition.	"Rhea wanted to come to this meeting, but I told her that wasn't necessary."

FIGURE 8.5   Groupthink

Moorhead, Ference, and Neck have identified groupthink as a significant cause of the *Challenger* disaster.[28] When NASA officials ignored negative data and critics, refused to seek or listen to outside expert opinion, and failed to examine all alternatives, they became classic victims of groupthink.

Dealing with Groupthink.   The best way to deal with groupthink is to prevent it from happening in the first place. The following list provides practical ways to minimize the potential of groupthink.[29] Choose the methods that are most appropriate for your group.

- Ask each member to serve in the role of critical evaluator.
- If possible, have more than one group work on the same problem independently.
- Discuss the group's progress with someone outside the group. Report the feedback to the entire group.
- Periodically invite an expert to join your meeting and encourage constructive criticism.
- Discuss the potential negative consequences of any decision or action.
- Follow a formal decision-making procedure that encourages expression of disagreement and evaluation of ideas.
- Ask questions, offer reasons for positions, and demand justifications from others.
- Before finalizing the decision, give members a second chance to express doubts.

In the short term, groupthink decisions are easier. The group finishes early and doesn't have to deal with conflict. However, the decision is often poor and sometimes results in harm. Spending the time and energy to work through differences will result in better decisions without sacrificing group cohesiveness.

Adapting to Differences

Conflict becomes more complex when group members are diverse; differences in cultural perspectives may result in more disagreements among members. Deutsch points out that cultural differences may result in misunderstandings, prejudices, and unintentionally offensive behavior.[30] A group's failure to effectively manage conflict among culturally diverse members can have serious consequences. Companies that fail to understand, respect, and adapt to differences are likely to have more strikes and lawsuits,

FIGURE 8.6 Conflict Management

low morale among workers, less productivity, and a higher turnover of employees.[31]

The cultural values of individual members will greatly influence the degree to which they are comfortable with conflict and the way conflict is resolved. For instance, U.S. and Japanese cultures differ significantly in their approach to negotiation.[32] Americans tend to approach negotiation as competitive, time pressured, emphasizing knowledge, and seeking contractual agreements. In contrast, the Japanese tend to view negotiation as collaborative, time consuming, based on seniority, and resulting in mutual understanding rather than detailed agreements.

Cultures also differ in their willingness to engage in open conflict. Members from cultures that value conformity are less likely to express disagreement than those from cultures that place a higher value on individualism. Whereas Japanese, German, Mexican, and Brazilian cultures value group conformity, Swedish and French cultures are generally more comfortable expressing differences.[33]

Groups must also be sensitive to how gender differences influence conflict. In general, men tend to approach conflict more competitively. Women tend to search for a collaborative resolution. When engaging in conflict, male group members are more likely to focus on the content of the conflict or substantive issues. Female members are more likely to be concerned with relational issues or affective conflict.[34] Men and women can learn from each other's perspectives as they work through a group's conflict. Finally, it is important to note the gender differences summarized here are only generalizations. Both men and women can and do use both competitive and collaborative approaches to conflict.

Groups that successfully manage conflict with a sensitivity to cultural and gender differences can increase their members' commitment to the group. Bennis, Parikh, and Lessem remind us that "if people's interests were always identical, life would stagnate. Diversity is the most essential feature of life."[35]

Balancing Conflict and Cohesion

Hocker and Wilmot refer to the management of conflict as "a delicate balancing act, like that of a tightrope walker, or a rock climber who must find just the right handholds or fall to sure death."[36] The group must balance the need to express differences with the need to achieve group consensus. Individual thought must be encouraged, yet collective group goals need to be achieved.

A group that lacks cohesion is less creative, productive, and satisfied. Extremely cohesive groups, however, risk engaging in groupthink. Yet, fear of groupthink should not discourage efforts to promote cohesion. Groups that are characterized by too much or poorly managed conflict do not develop cohesion. However, groups that place too much emphasis on cohesion while avoiding conflict will often make bad decisions. Groups that engage in constructive conflict are able to successfully balance conflict and cohesion.

Summary Study Guide

- Conflict occurs when group members express differences about ideas, methods, and/or members.
- The three types of conflict are substantive (focuses on ideas), procedural (focuses on group process), and affective (focuses on personalities, communication styles, and emotions of group members).
- Destructive conflict is characterized by hostility directed toward other group members. Constructive conflict values members and promotes the group's goal.
- The five major conflict management styles are avoidance, accommodation, competition, compromise, and collaboration.
- Before reacting, analyze conflict using the 4**R**s method—consider the reasons, reactions, and results of conflict along with approaches to resolution.
- When group members feel angry, they should determine whether expressing their anger will help the group achieve its goals.
- The A-E-I-O-U Model of conflict resolution is a technique for expressing your concerns and proposing alternatives in a supportive and constructive manner.
- The steps to principled negotiation include focusing on issues and group interests while generating solutions and establishing objective criteria.
- Groups can use the principles and methods of third-party mediation when conflicts have the potential to become a destructive force and barrier to group progress.

- Cohesive groups are highly interactive and cooperative; they are more likely to achieve their goals and satisfy member needs.
- Groups can promote cohesion by establishing a group identity and tradition, stressing teamwork, recognizing and rewarding contributions, and respecting individual members' needs.
- Groupthink occurs when a group fails to sufficiently evaluate its decisions in order to achieve a consensus. Highly cohesive groups are at greater risk of becoming victims of groupthink.
- Groups can better adapt to cultural and gender differences when engaging in conflict by treating all members equally and focusing on shared goals.

Groupwork *Win as Much as You Can*

GOAL   To demonstrate the merit of competitive and cooperative models of conflict styles within the context of small group communication.

PARTICIPANTS   One or more groups of eight divided into four dyads (two-person subgroups).

PROCEDURE*

1. There are ten rounds in this exercise. During each round you and your partner will have to choose an "X" or a "Y." The "payoff" for each round is determined by the choices of all the dyads in your eight-person group.
2. There are three key rules:
   - Do not confer with other members of your group unless you are told to do so.
   - Each dyad must agree upon a single choice for each round.
   - Make sure that other members of your group do not know your dyad's choice until you are told to reveal it.
3. Confer with your partner on every round. Before rounds 5, 8, and 10, you can confer with the other pairs in your group.

Payoff Chart

4	Xs:	Lose	$1.00 each
3	Xs:	Win	$1.00 each
1	Y:	Lose	$3.00 each
2	Xs:	Win	$2.00 each
2	Ys:	Lose	$2.00 each
1	X:	Win	$3.00 each
3	Ys:	Lose	$1.00 each
4	Ys:	Win	$1.00 each

*The textbook's *Instructor's Manual* explains how to conduct this GroupWork exercise.

Tally Sheet

Round	Time Allowed	Confer with	Choice	$ Won	$ Lost	Balance
1	2 min.	partner				
2	1 min.	partner				
3	1 min.	partner				
4	1 min.	partner				
5*	3 min. +1 min.	group partner				
6	1 min.	partner				
7	1 min.	partner				
8**	3 min. +1 min.	group partner				
9	1 min.	partner				
10***	3 min. +1 min.	group partner				

*Payoff is multiplied by 3
**Payoff is multiplied by 5
***Payoff is multiplied by 10

Source: Based on Gellerman, W. (1970). Win as much as you can. In J. W. Pfeiffer & J. E. Jones (Eds.), *A handbook of structured experiences for human relations training, Vol. 2.* La Jolla, CA: University Associates (1974), pp. 66–69.

A S S E S S M E N T

Ross-DeWine Conflict Management Message Style Instrument

Directions Below you will find messages which have been delivered by persons in conflict situations. Consider each message separately and decide how closely this message resembles the ones that you have used in conflict settings. The language may not be exactly the same as yours, but consider the messages in terms of similarity to your messages in conflict. There are no right or wrong answers, nor are these messages designed to trick you. Answer in terms of responses you make, not what you think you should say. Give each message a 1–5 rating on the answer sheet provided according to the following scale. Mark one answer only.

In conflict situations, I

1	2	3	4	5
never say things like this	rarely say things like this	sometimes say things like this	often say things like this	usually say things like this

_____ 1. "Can't you see how foolish you're being with that thinking?"

_____ 2. "How can I make you feel happy again?"

_____ 3. "I'm really bothered by some things that are happening here; can we talk about these?"

_____ 4. "I really don't have any more to say on this . . . (silence)."

_____ 5. "What possible solutions can we come up with?"

_____ 6. "I'm really sorry that your feelings are hurt—maybe you're right."

_____ 7. "Let's talk this thing out and see how we can deal with this hassle."

_____ 8. "Shut up! You are wrong! I don't want to hear any more of what you have to say."

_____ 9. "It is your fault if I fail at this, and don't you ever expect any help from me when you're on the spot."

_____ 10. "You can't do (say) that to me—it's either my way or forget it."

_____ 11. "Let's try finding an answer that will give us both some of what we want."

_____ 12. "This is something we have to work out; we're always arguing about it."

(continued)

(Ross-DeWine Conflict Management Message Style Instrument, *continued*)

_____ 13. "Whatever makes you feel happiest is OK by me."

_____ 14. "Let's just leave well enough alone."

_____ 15. "That's OK . . . it wasn't important anyway. . . . You feeling OK now?"

_____ 16. "If you're not going to cooperate, I'll just go to someone who will."

_____ 17. "I think we need to try to understand the problem."

_____ 18. "You might as well accept my decision; you can't do anything about it anyway."

Scoring Instructions

By each item number, list the rating (from 1–5) you gave that item. When you have entered all ratings, add total ratings for each column. Enter the resulting score in the space provided.

SELF Items	ISSUE Items	OTHER Items
1. _____	3. _____	2. _____
8. _____	5. _____	4. _____
9. _____	7. _____	6. _____
10. _____	11. _____	13. _____
16. _____	12. _____	14. _____
18. _____	17. _____	15. _____

Your Total Score	_____	_____	_____
Average Score	(13.17)	(24.26)	(21.00)

The items comprising the SELF focus deal with one's personal interests in the conflict situation. These messages suggest that one's primary concern is in resolving the conflict so that a person's personal view of the conflict is accepted by the other. This is a "win" approach to conflict resolution.

The items comprising the ISSUE focus deal with an emphasis on both parties dealing with the problem. These message statements suggest an overriding concern with the content of the conflict rather than the personal relationship.

The items comprising the OTHER focus deal with neither the conflict issues nor personal interests, but emphasize maintaining the relationship at a cost of resolving the conflict. These statements suggest that one would rather ignore the problem to maintain a good relationship with the other person.

All of us may use one of these styles in different settings and under different circumstances. People do tend to have a predominant style which is evidenced by the kinds of messages sent during conflict situations. The intent of this instrument is to cause individuals to focus on what they are communicating in the messages they send during conflict and to make sure that what they are saying is what they intended to say.

The averages are an indication of scores one might expect to receive. Scores that are higher or lower than these means indicate a higher or lower use of this message style than would normally be expected.

Source: DeWine, S. (1994). *The consultant's craft: Improving organizational communication.* New York: St. Martin's, pp. 268–272; Ross, R. G. & DeWine, S. (1988). Communication messages in conflict: A message-focused instrument to assess conflict management styles. *Management Communication Quarterly, 1,* pp. 389–413.

Recommended Readings

Folger, J. P., Poole, M. S., & Stutman, R. K. (1997). *Working through conflict: Strategies for relationships, groups and organizations* (3rd ed.). New York: Longman.

Hocker, J. L. & Wilmot, W. W. (1995). *Interpersonal conflict* (4th ed.). Dubuque, IA: Brown & Benchmark.

Janis, I. L. (1982). *Groupthink: Psychological studies of policy decisions and fiascoes* (2nd ed.). Boston, MA: Houghton Mifflin.

Notes

1. Billington, J. (1997 January). "The three essentials of an effective team." *Harvard Management Update, 2,* p. 3.
2. Hocker, J. L. & Wilmot, W. W. (1995). *Interpersonal conflict* (4th ed). Madison, WI: Brown & Benchmark, p. 23.
3. Bennis, W., Parikh, J., & Lessem, R. (1994). *Beyond leadership: Balancing economics, ethics and ecology.* Cambridge, MA: Blackwell Business, p. 140.
4. Putnam, L. L. (1986). Conflict in group decision-making. In R. Y. Hirokawa & M. S. Poole (Eds.), *Communication and group decision-making.* Beverly Hills, CA: Sage, pp. 175–196.
5. Katzenbach, J. R. & Smith, D. K. (1993). *The wisdom of teams: Creating the high performance organization.* New York: HarperBusiness, p. 110.
6. See Thomas, K. W. & Kilmann, K. W. (1977). Developing a forced-choice measure of conflict-handling behavior: The MODE instrument. *Educational and Psychological Measurement, 37,* pp. 390–395; Hocker & Wilmot, pp. 95–136.
7. Billington, p. 3.
8. Folger, J. P., Poole, M. S., & Stutman, R. K. (1997). *Working through conflict: Strategies for relationships, groups, and organizations* (3rd ed.). New York: Longman, pp. 199–200.
9. Hocker & Wilmot, pp. 176–177.
10. Wisinski, J. (1993). *Resolving conflicts on the job.* New York: American Management Association, pp. 27–31.

11. Fisher, R., Ury, W. & Patton, B. (1991). *Getting to yes: Negotiating agreement without giving in.* Boston, MA: Houghton Mifflin, p. 15.
12. Fisher et al., p. 19.
13. Wood, J. T. (1992). Alternative methods of group decision making. In R. S. Cathcart & L. A. Samovar (Eds.), *Small group communication: A reader* (6th ed.). Dubuque, IA: Wm. C. Brown, p. 159.
14. Rubin, J. Z. (1992). Negotiation: An introduction to some issues and themes. In Cathcart, R. S. & Samovar, L. A. (Eds.), *Small group communication: A reader* (6th ed.). Dubuque, IA: Wm. C. Brown, pp. 415–423.
15. Kimsey, W. D., Fuller, R. M., & McKinney, B. C. (n.d.) *Mediation and conflict management: General mediation manual.* Harrisonburg, VA: James Madison University Center for Mediation, p. 21; also see Keltner, J. W. (1994). *The management of struggle: Elements of dispute resolution through negotiation, mediation, and arbitration.* Cresskill, NJ: Hampton Press, pp. 101–149.
16. Keltner, J. W. (1994). *The management of struggle: Elements of dispute resolution through negotiation, mediation, and arbitration.* Cresskill, NJ: Hampton, p. 102.
17. Pavitt, C. & Curtis, E. (1994). *Small group discussion: A theoretical approach* (2nd ed.). Scottsdale, AZ: Gorsuch, Scarisbrick, pp. 129–130.
18. McKinney, B. C., Kimsey, W. D. & Fuller, R. M. (1995). *Mediator communication competencies: Interpersonal communication and alternative dispute resolution* (4th ed.). Edina, MN: Burgess, pp. 67–98.
19. McKinney et al., p. 78.
20. McKinney et al., p. 82.
21. Tjosvold, D. & van de Vliert, E. (1994). Applying cooperative and competitive conflict to mediation. *Mediation Quarterly, 11,* pp. 303–311.
22. Keltner, p. 168.
23. Shaw, M. E. (1992). Group composition and group cohesiveness. In Cathcart, R. S., & Samovar L. A. (Eds.), *Small group communication: A reader* (6th ed.). Dubuque, IA: Wm. C. Brown, pp. 214–220.
24. Bormann, E. G. & Bormann, N. C. (1988). *Effective small group communication* (4th ed.). Edina, MN: Burgess Publishing, pp. 74–76.
25. Janis, I. L. (1982). *Groupthink: Psychological studies of policy decisions and fiascoes* (2nd ed.). Boston, MA: Houghton Mifflin, p. 9.
26. Bennis et al., p. 128.
27. Janis, pp. 174–175.
28. Moorhead, G., Ference, R. & Neck, C. P. (1996). Group decision fiascoes continue: Space shuttle *Challenger* and a groupthink framework. In R. S. Cathcart, L. A. Samovar & L. D. Henman (Eds.), *Small group communication: Theory and practice* (7th ed.). Madison, WI: Brown & Benchmark, pp. 161–170. For a different perspective, see Vaughan, D. (1996). *The Challenger launch decision: Risk technology, culture, and deviance at NASA.* Chicago: University of Chicago.
29. See Janis, I. L. (1982). *Groupthink: Psychological studies of policy decisions and fiascoes* (2nd ed). Boston, MA: Houghton Mifflin; Cline, R. J. W. (1994). Groupthink and the Watergate cover-up: The illusion of unanimity. In L. R. Frey (Ed.), *Group communication in context: Studies of natural groups.* Hillsdale, NJ: Lawrence Erlbaum, pp. 199–223; 3M Meeting Management Team (1994). *Mastering meetings: Discovering the hidden potential of effective business meetings.* New York: McGraw-Hill, p. 58.

30. Deutsch, M. (1991). Subjective features of conflict resolution: Psychological, social, and cultural influences. In R. Vayrynen (Ed.), *New directions in conflict theory: Conflict resolutions and conflict transformation*. London: Sage, pp. 26–56.

31. Murphy, B. O. (1995). Promoting dialogue in culturally diverse workplace environments. In L. R. Frey (Ed.), *Innovation in group facilitation: Applications in natural settings*. Cresskill, NJ: Hampton, pp. 77–93.

32. Deutsch, p. 37.

33. Lustig, M. W. & Cassotta, L. L. (1996). Comparing group communication across cultures: Leadership, conformity, and discussion processes. In R. S. Cathcart, L. A. Samovar, & L. D. Henman (Eds.), *Small group communication: Theory and practice* (7th ed.). Madison, WI: Brown & Benchmark, pp. 316–326.

34. Hocker & Wilmot, p. 196.

35. Bennis et al., p. 140.

36. Hocker & Wilmot, p. 11.

P A R T   **T H R E E**

*A*chieving Group Goals

Alan Carey/The Image Works

Decision Making in Groups

Group Decision Making

Many group decisions are predictable and fairly easy to make—when to meet again, what to include in a monthly report, whom to assign to a routine task. Other group decisions are much more complex and difficult—what the group's common goal is, whom to hire or fire, where to hold a convention, how to solve a serious problem. As difficult as it can be to make a personal decision, these challenges are multiplied in groups. On the other hand, while the road may be paved with obstacles, the goal reached through effective group decision making can be more satisfying and worthwhile than a decision made by individuals working alone.

Decision Making and Problem Solving

Although the terms *decision making* and *problem solving* are often used interchangeably, it is important to clarify the meaning of these commonly used terms. **Decision making** refers to the "passing of judgment on an issue under consideration" and "the act of reaching a conclusion or making up one's mind."[1] In a group setting, decision making results in a position, opinion, judgment, or action. Most groups make decisions, but not all groups are asked to solve problems. For example, hiring committees, juries, and families make decisions. Which applicant is best? Is the accused guilty? Whom should we invite to the wedding? Such decisions do not arise from problems. They do, however, require careful consideration before reaching a conclusion. Peter Drucker put it simply when he wrote, "A decision is a judgment. It is a choice between alternatives."[2]

Problem solving is a complex, decision-making *process* in which groups analyze a problem and develop a plan of action for solving or reducing the problem's harmful effects. For example, if student enrollment has significantly declined, a college faces a serious problem that must be analyzed and dealt with if the institution hopes to survive. Problem solving usually requires a group to make many decisions. Because the group's task and options may not be clear or well defined, the group will have to come up with several alternatives and possible solutions. Fortunately, there are decision-making and problem-solving procedures that can help a group "make up its mind."

Costs and Benefits of Group Decision Making

All groups engage in some form of decision making and problem solving. How they go about these tasks can determine whether a group achieves its goals or whether it falls short. Napier and Gershenfeld maintain that "unless well designed, a group effort at problem solving can be a colossal waste of time, money, and effort."[3] Instead of building team spirit and group morale, ineffective decision making can overwhelm and destroy a group. Such devastating effects occur for several reasons. If two or three members dominate meetings or inhibit the participation of others, decision making

185

DECISION making and problem solving are the focus of many community group meetings. What happens when such groups don't use procedures? (Lawrence Migdale/Photo Researchers, Inc.)

and problem solving become difficult and frustrating. Even in the best of circumstances, decisions made by a group take longer and can run the risk of causing conflict and hard feelings among members.

Despite these disadvantages, there are many reasons to trust the decision-making ability of a group. Sheer numbers enable a group to generate more ideas than a single member working alone. Even more important is the fact that, given a complex problem, a group is better equipped to find rational and workable solutions. As a rule, decision making in groups can generate more ideas and information, test and validate more arguments, and produce better decisions and solutions to complex problems.[4]

However, several conditions must be met to ensure that a group achieves its decision-making goals. The rest of this chapter focuses on ways to maximize the advantages of group decision making while minimizing the disadvantages.

Decision-Making Methods

There are many ways for groups to make decisions. Groups can let the majority have its way, try to find a decision or solution that everyone can live with, or leave the final decision to someone else. In group discussions, these decision-making methods translate into voting, consensus seeking, and letting a leader or outside authority make the decision. Each approach has strengths and should be selected to match the needs and purpose of a group and its task.

Voting Voting is the most obvious and easiest way to make a group decision. When a quick decision is needed, there is nothing more efficient and decisive. Sometimes, though, voting may not be the best way to make important deci-

Decision Making	Problem Solving
A Judgment:	*A Process:*
The Group Chooses an Alternative	*The Group Develops a Plan*
• Guilty or not guilty.	• Analyze the problem.
• Hire or fire.	• Develop options.
• Spend or save.	• Debate pros and cons.
Asks Who, What, Where, and When	• Select and implement solution. *Asks Why and How*
• Whom should we invite?	• Why doesn't our promotional campaign attract students?
• What should we discuss?	• How should we publicize the college's new programs?
• Where should we meet?	
• When should we meet?	

FIGURE 9.1 Decision Making and Problem Solving

sions. When a vote is taken, some members win, but others lose. A **majority vote** requires that more than half the members vote in favor of a proposal.

If a group is making a major decision, there may not be enough support if only 51 percent of the members vote in favor of the project. The 49 percent who lose may resent working on a project they dislike. In order to avoid such problems, some groups use a two-thirds vote rather than majority rule. In a **two-thirds vote,** at least twice as many group members vote for a proposal as against it. A two-thirds vote assures a group that a significant number of members support the decision.

Voting works best when

- a group is pressed for time.
- the issue is not highly controversial.
- a group is too large to use any other decision-making method.
- there is no other way to break a deadlock.
- a group's constitution or rules require voting on certain issues and proposals.

Consensus Seeking

Because voting has built-in disadvantages, many groups rely on consensus to make decisions. **Consensus** is reached when all group members agree to support a group decision. Julia Wood describes a consensus decision as one "that all members have a part in shaping and that all find at least minimally acceptable as a means of accomplishing some mutual goal."[5] Consensus does not work for all groups. Imagine how difficult it would be to achieve consensus if a leader had so much power that group members were unwilling to express their honest opinions. Consider how difficult it would be to reach consensus among pro-life and pro-choice or pro-gun control and anti-gun control members trying to reach a unified group decision about abortion or gun control.

Listen carefully to other members and consider their information and points of view.

• Try to be logical rather than emotional.

• Don't be stubborn and argue only for your own position.

Don't change your mind in order to avoid conflict or reach a quick decision.

• Don't give in, especially if you have a crucial piece of information to share.

• Don't agree to a decision or solution you can't possibly support.

Avoid "easy" ways of reaching a decision.

• Avoid techniques such as flipping a coin, letting the majority rule, or trading one decision for another.

If there is a deadlock, work hard to find the next best alternative that is acceptable to everyone.

• Make sure that members not only agree but also will be committed to the final decision.

Get everyone involved in the discussion.

• The quietest member may have a key piece of information or a brilliant suggestion that can help the group make a better decision.

Welcome differences of opinion.

• Disagreement is natural and can expose a group to a wide range of information and opinions.

FIGURE 9.2   Consensus Guidelines

When reached, consensus can unite and energize a group. Not only does consensus provide a way of avoiding a disruptive win/lose vote, but it also can present a united front to outsiders. The guidelines shown in Figure 9.2 should be used to seek consensus.

Authority Rule   Sometimes a single person or someone outside the group will make the final decision. When **authority rule** is used, groups may be asked to gather information for and recommend decisions to another person or larger group. For example, an association's nominating committee considers potential candidates and recommends a slate of officers to the association. A hiring committee may screen dozens of job applications and submit a top-three list to the person or persons making the hiring decision.

Unfortunately, authority rule can have detrimental effects on a conscientious group. If a leader or outside authority ignores or reverses group recommendations, members may become demoralized, resentful, and unproductive on future assignments. Even within a group, a strong leader or authority figure may use a group and its members to give the appearance of collaborative decision making. The group thus becomes a "rubber stamp" and surrenders its will to authority rule.

Understanding the Discussion Question

Regardless of which decision-making method a group chooses, there is an immediate judgment that must be made: What is our decision-making goal? In some group settings, the decision-making goal or question has been dictated by an outside group or authority. Yet, even when the group does not create the discussion question, it has an obligation to examine that question and determine whether the group is capable of answering it. To assist in this process, it is useful to look at four different kinds of discussion questions: questions of fact, conjecture, value, and policy.

Questions of Fact

A **question of fact** asks whether something is true or false, whether an event did or did not happen, whether something was caused by this or that. Did the college's enrollment decrease last year? The answer is either yes or no. However, a question such as "What was the decrease in enrollment?" can require a more detailed answer with possible subquestions about the enrollment of different ethnic groups or the status of part-time and full-time students. When a group confronts a question of fact, it must consider the best information it can find and subject that information to close scrutiny.

Questions of Conjecture

A **question of conjecture** asks whether something will or will not happen. Unlike a question of fact, only the future holds the answer to this type of question. Instead of focusing on reality, the group must consider possibilities. Waiting until the future happens can be too late to make a good decision or solve a problem. In asking a question of conjecture, the group does its best to predict what the future will bring. Will enrollment increase next semester? Will the Board of Trustees raise tuition next year? Who will be the next student government president? Gouran notes that "although the decision in a question of conjecture is speculative, it should be based as much as possible on fact and expert opinion, on information that can help decision makers establish probabilities."[6] Questions of conjecture are not answered with wild guesses; answers are developed by group members who have gathered and analyzed the best information available.

Questions of Value

A **question of value** asks whether something is worthwhile—is it good or bad, right or wrong, moral or immoral, best, average, or worst? Questions of value can be difficult to discuss because the answer depends on the attitudes, beliefs, and values of group members. In many cases, the answer to a question of value may be "It depends." Are community colleges a better place to begin higher education than a prestigious university? The answer to this question depends on a student's financial situation, professional goals, academic achievement record, work and family situation, and beliefs about the quality of an education at each type of institution.

Questions of Policy

A **question of policy** asks whether a particular course of action should be taken to solve a problem. Many groups focus on questions of policy. How can we improve student services? Which candidate should we support as president of the student government association? What plan, if any, should be enacted to ensure that our school system maintains a culturally diverse teaching staff?

Combining All Four

Questions of fact, conjecture value, and policy are not isolated inquiries. Within a group discussion, all four types of questions may require consideration. For example, if your family were trying to decide how to plan a summer vacation while saving money for a new car, you might start with questions of fact and conjecture. "How much do we usually spend on a summer vacation?" "How much money will we need for a new car?" Then the discussion would move to questions of value. "How much do we value the time and place where our family vacations?" "How important is it that we buy a new car this year?" Finally, you conclude with a question of policy. "How can we take a summer vacation and save money for a new car?" Thus, when trying to determine the most suitable course of action, a group usually deals with all four types of questions. A policy decision that does not consider the facts of the situation or the attitudes, beliefs, and values of members may be headed for a poor decision about an important policy question.

The Need for Procedures

Even if everyone understands why group decision making is valuable and appreciates the different ways in which a group makes up its mind, there is no guarantee the group will make good decisions. What is needed are clear procedures that specify how a group should organize and carry out the decision-making process. Marshall Scott Poole has called procedures "the heart of group work [and] the most powerful tools we have to improve the conduct of meetings."[7] Even a simple procedure such as creating and following a short agenda enhances meeting productivity. Time and effort spent on using a well-planned procedure can reap the following benefits:

- **Balanced Participation.** Procedures can minimize the impact of a powerful leader or member by making it difficult for a few talkative or high-status members to dominate a group's discussion.

- **Conflict Resolution.** Procedures often incorporate guidelines for managing conflict, resolving disagreements, and building consensus.
- **Organization.** Procedures require members to follow a clear organizational pattern and focus on the same thing at the same time. Procedures also ensure that major discussion items are not missed or ignored.
- **Group Empowerment.** Procedures provide a group with a sense of control. "This happens when members know they have followed a procedure well, managed conflict successfully, given all members an equal opportunity to participate, and as a result have made a good decision."[8]

There are, however, many different types of procedures. There are complex, theory-based, problem-solving models designed to tackle the overall problem facing a group. There are also decision-making methods and tools designed for subgoals of the problem-solving process such as idea generation and solution implementation. The next few sections of this chapter describe how these different types of procedures can and should be used to improve decision making and problem solving.

As a way of understanding the common traits and differences among these models, methods, and tools, we have provided an extended example to illustrate how these procedures can be applied:

Fallingstar State College

For three consecutive years Fallingstar State College has experienced declining enrollment and no increase in funding from the state. In order to balance the budget, the board of trustees has had to raise tuition every year. There are no prospects for more state funding in the near future. Even with significant tuition increases, there has been a drop in overall college revenue. The college's planning council, composed of representative vice presidents, deans, faculty members, staff employees, and students, has been charged with answering the following question: Given severe budget constraints, what should the college do to continue providing high-quality instruction and student services?

Although this example does not offer many details, it can demonstrate the ways in which a group can use several of the most common procedures to solve problems and make decisions.

Problem-Solving Models

While there are several problem-solving models, there is no "best" model or magic formula that ensures effective problem solving in every group. As groups gain experience as decision makers and as they successfully solve problems, they learn that some procedures work better than others and some

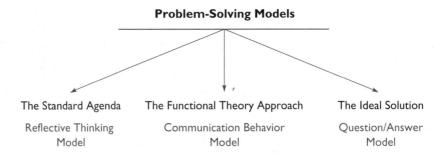

FIGURE 9.3 Problem-Solving Models

need modification to suit group needs. In short, there are no hard-and-fast rules for problem solving. There are, however, well-accepted guidelines to help groups through this complex process.

The Standard Agenda

The founding father of problem-solving procedures is a U.S. philosopher and educator named John Dewey. In 1910 Dewey wrote a book entitled *How We Think* in which he described a set of practical steps that a rational person should follow when solving a problem.[9] These guidelines have come to be known as Dewey's reflective thinking process.

Dewey's ideas have been adapted to the process of solving problems in groups. The reflective thinking process begins with a focus on the problem itself and then moves on to a systematic consideration of possible solutions. We offer one approach to this process—The Standard Agenda—developed by Julia Wood, Gerald Phillips, and Douglas Pedersen.[10] With slight modifications, the basic steps in **The Standard Agenda** are summarized in Figure 9.4.

Task Clarification. The goal of this initial phase is to make sure that everyone understands the group's assignment. According to Wood and her colleagues, "each member must understand what the group is to do, why it is important to do it, what its business is, what its output is to look like, who is to get it, to what purpose it will be put,"[11] and what the deadline is for completing the entire task. For example, Fallingstar State College's planning council could dedicate the beginning of its first meeting to making sure that everyone is aware of the time frame in which to work and the need to produce a written set of recommendations. During this phase group members can ask questions about their roles and responsibilities in the problem-solving process.

Problem Identification. Overlooking this second step can send a group in the wrong direction. In the case of Fallingstar State College, there may be several different ways to define the college's problem. Is the problem declining enrollment? Some discussants may consider this situation an advantage rather than a disadvantage, because having fewer students can result in smaller classes, more individualized instruction, less chaos at registration, and easier parking. Is the problem a lack of money? Although lack of money seems to be a universal problem, an inefficiently run college could find it has enough money if it enhances productivity and becomes more businesslike.

The group's problem should be worded as an agreed-upon question. Whether it is a question of fact, conjecture, value, or policy determines the way the discussion will be focused. The question "What should the college do to continue providing high-quality instruction and student services?" is a question of policy that can only be answered by also considering questions of fact, value, and conjecture.

Fact Finding and Problem Analysis.   During the third step—fact finding and problem analysis—group members have several obligations that are reflected in the following questions of fact and value. What are the facts of the situation? What additional information or expert opinion do we need? How serious or widespread is the problem? What are the causes of the problem? What prevents or inhibits us from solving the problem? These questions require investigations of facts, conclusions about causes and effects, and value judgments about the seriousness of the problem.

Fallingstar State College's planning council could look at the rate of enrollment decline and future enrollment projections, the anticipated budgets for future years, the efficiency of existing services, the projected impact of inflation, salary increases, maintenance costs, and the likely causes of declining enrollment. It could take months to investigate such questions, and even then, there may not be clear answers to all of them. Failure to search for such answers, however, is much more hazardous than ignoring them.

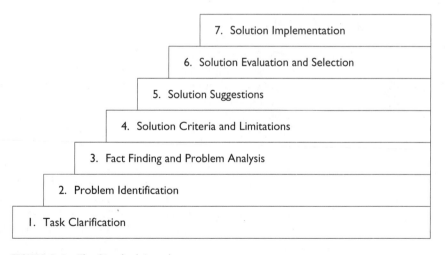

FIGURE 9.4   The Standard Agenda

Rothwell offers a word of caution about this phase of The Standard Agenda. "Although analyzing the problem is important and should be undertaken before exploring potential solutions, bogging down by analyzing the problem too much can also thwart effective decision making. **Analysis paralysis** prevents a group from ever getting on with business and making a decision."[12] In other words, a college planning council could collect dozens of reports and identify ten possible causes of declining enrollment but still be unable to verify or settle on the most important reasons. Rather than spending months arguing about the issue or giving up on finding the correct answer, a group may have to move on and begin its search for solutions.

Solution Criteria and Limitations.   **Solution criteria** are standards that should be met for an ideal resolution of a problem. The development of realistic criteria should also include an understanding of solution limitations that can be financial, institutional, practical, political, and legal in scope. For a college planning council, criteria could include the cost of potential solutions, the goal of ensuring that all subgroups—administrators, faculty, staff, and students—accept the solution, a commitment to using fair and open procedures to assess existing programs, and considerations of the political and legal consequences of proposed actions.

Solution Suggestions.   At this point in a group's deliberations, some solutions are probably apparent. Even so, the group should concentrate on suggesting as many solutions as possible without criticizing them. Later in this chapter, a technique called brainstorming will be described as an appropriate method for generating suggestions. Having spent time understanding the task, identifying the problem, analyzing its consequences and causes, and establishing criteria, members should be able to offer numerous solutions.

Suggestions from the college's planning council could include a wide range of options: raising tuition, embarking on a new promotional campaign, seeking additional grants and corporate donations, forgoing raises, freezing promotions, requiring additional teaching by faculty, increasing class size, reducing the number of administrators and staff, eliminating expensive programs and services, lobbying the state for more funds, and charging students fees for special services. The list could double or triple depending on the creativity and resourcefulness of the group.

Solution Evaluation and Selection.   This stage of The Standard Agenda may be the most difficult and controversial. Here, group members discuss the pros and cons of each suggestion in light of their agreed-upon criteria for a solution. Questions of conjecture arise as the group considers the possible consequences of each suggestion. Discussion may become heated, and disagreements may grow fierce. In some groups, members may be so tired or frustrated by the time they get to this phase there is a tendency to jump to conclusions. If the group has been conscientious in analyzing the problem and establishing criteria for solutions, however, some solutions will be rejected quickly while others will swiftly rise to the top of the list.

The college's planning council may hear students arguing against increased tuition and fees whereas faculty are predicting a decline in instructional quality if they are required to teach more courses or larger classes. Administrators and staff may cringe at freezing salaries, whereas faculty may support reductions in administrative staff. In this phase, a group should remember its solution criteria and use them to evaluate the strengths and weaknesses of each suggested solution. At the end of this stage, a group should identify the solutions it wishes to endorse and implement.

Solution Implementation.   Having now made a difficult decision, a group faces one more challenge. How should the decision be implemented? Who should be charged with this responsibility? How will the group explain the wisdom or practicality of its decision to others? For all the time a group spends trying to solve a problem, it may take even more time to organize the task of implementing the solution. If a planning council wants a new promotional campaign to attract students, the campaign must be well planned and affordable in order to achieve its goal. If a college wants to enhance its fund-raising efforts, a group or office must be given the authority and resources to seek such funds. Brilliant solutions can fail if no one takes responsibility or has the authority to implement a group's decision.

The Functional Theory Approach

During the 1980s and 1990s, Randy Hirokawa and Dennis Gouran theorized that a set of "critical functions" can explain and predict how well a group will make decisions and solve problems.[13] Unlike The Standard Agenda Model, functional theory claims that "communication is the instrument by which members or groups, with varying degrees of success, reach decisions and generate solutions to problems."[13] Effective performance of communication functions is considered more important than the order in which functions are performed. (Hirokawa cautions, however, that if groups stray too far from an agenda, the quality of the group decision may suffer.)

As is the case with many theorists, Gouran and Hirokawa's ongoing research has expanded the scope of functional theory. They now hold that certain conditions explain the likelihood of a group's making good decisions and selecting appropriate solutions to a problem. We have grouped these conditions into three categories: (1) Appropriate preparation, (2) Appropriate procedures, and (3) Appropriate precautions.

Preparation.   Before a group engages in specific problem-solving tasks, it is important that the group is well prepared for the process. Gouran and

Hirokawa believe that there are four prerequisites for effective decision making and problem solving. The group must

- Make clear their interest in arriving at the best possible decision
- Identify the resources necessary for making such a decision
- Recognize possible obstacles to be confronted
- Specify the procedures to be followed.[14]

These prerequisites ensure that the group is ready, willing, and able to tackle the issue. The first task—participant interest and energy—is not sufficient to ensure success. Group members also must make sure they have identified the sources of information they will need, the limits or constraints on their ability to make a decision, and the appropriate decision-making or problem-solving procedure.

Procedures.   Once a group is ready, willing, and able to tackle an issue, an additional set of functional tasks is needed. Gouran and Hirokawa contend that in order for groups to satisfy fundamental task requirements they must

- Show correct understanding of the issue to be resolved
- Determine the minimal characteristics of any alternative
- Identify a relevant and realistic set of alternatives
- Carefully examine the alternatives in relationship to each previously agreed-upon minimum characteristic
- Select the alternative that analysis reveals to be most likely to have the desired outcome.[15]

These tasks have always been the heart of functional theory. Addressing each one is critical if a group hopes to make an effective decision or solve a problem.

1. *Understanding the Issues.* This function combines the second and third steps in The Standard Agenda—problem identification and analysis. Hirokawa cautions that "breakdowns in analysis at this point are likely to carry over and adversely affect other aspects of the process."[16] Two related errors can occur in this phase. The first error is a failure to recognize or accurately define the problem. The second is a failure to identify the causes of the problem. If, in the case of Fallingstar State College, the planning council mistakenly decides that decreased enrollment is caused by higher tuition, it may have ignored other factors such as competition from other colleges, the state of the economy and its effect on students' ability to find jobs, or even a public perception that the college does not offer high-quality instruction. If the college decides to hold the line on tuition but eliminate popular programs, the problem could be made worse.

2. *Determining Criteria.* Once a group believes it understands the nature and causes of a problem, it needs to establish criteria or standards for a solution. In many groups, this process is governed by specific goals or unspoken objectives. For example, a college's planning council may want to develop a plan that saves money for the college without affecting or jeopardizing anyone's job. Given such a goal, options such as reducing the number of administrators, increasing the number of teaching hours, or freezing salaries and promotion could be out of the question. In the end, such limitations could hamper the planning council's ability to solve its budgetary problem. On the other hand, when underlying goals and values match potential solutions, the final decision will be better. For example, if everyone on the planning council agrees that employee sacrifices are inevitable, the road has been cleared for a wider range of possible actions.

3. *Identifying Possible Solutions.* With an understanding of the problem and, in some cases, a set of goals or standards against which to measure suggested actions, a group will suggest possible solutions. This third function is similar to the solution suggestions step in The Standard Agenda.

4. *Reviewing Pros and Cons of Each Solution.* The fourth function is the group's ability to analyze and discuss the positive and negative aspects of suggested solutions. Breakdowns at this stage of the discussion process can have serious consequences. Hirokawa points out that because it is impossible to examine *all* the positive and negative aspects of every proposed solution, a group "tends to focus on the more important or obvious positive and negative attributes of certain attractive choices."[17] As a result, the group may overestimate a solution's strengths and fail to recognize its weaknesses.

5. *Selecting the Alternative.* At this point in the process, a group should be prepared to make a decision or decide on an appropriate action to solve a problem. If a group has completed the prerequisite preparation tasks and followed the appropriate procedures, selection can and should occur. Although there may be more than one good decision or solution, the group should feel confident that their choice will be appropriate and effective.

Precautions. Although it may seem as though all of the important decision-making tasks are completed, Gouran and Hirokawa urge groups to engage in two more functions that help ensure the quality of a decision or solution. They recommend that a group must become aware of and overcome any constraints that prevent effective decision making and problem solving. They also recommend that members review the entire process the group used to come to a decision and, if necessary, reconsider judgements reached (even to the point of starting over).

As we have indicated in previous chapters, there are many factors—member needs, styles, and confidence, listening ability, verbal and nonverbal variables, the potential for conflict—that can enhance or reduce group effectiveness. When these factors are not taken into consideration, they can become negative influences on the performance of a group. If there isn't enough available information, time is limited, the issue is complex, or member relations are strained, decision-making and problem-solving efforts may be compromised or even sabotaged. As difficult as it can be to recognize these constraints, it is critical for group members to assess the extent to which any of these factors affect the decision-making process. Gouran and Hirokawa warn that "left unchecked (these constraints) will exert an unhealthy influence on a group's performance of its task."[18]

Finally, once a group has reached a decision or agreed on a solution to a problem, time should be taken to review the entire process and, if necessary, reconsider a decision. Our own experience is that at the very end of the decision-making process, group members can experience an uneasiness. Something is not right. Reviewing the functional tasks from the very beginning and taking time to think about the potential constraints that could have influenced the group can be time well spent. It takes a brave participant to suggest that something is not right with the final product. Perhaps there has been a trace of groupthink, perhaps an early assumption was based on erroneous information, perhaps the decision failed to take into account the criteria established by the group, perhaps a strong group member had too much influence. Once a group implements its decision, it can be difficult to undo the consequences.

Functional theory has several qualities that distinguish it from The Standard Agenda Model. The first is that the competent performance of each of the functions is more important than performing the functions in exact order. A second difference is that the functional approach recognizes that group goals and unspoken assumptions can affect the choice of solutions. Finally, this approach emphasizes the group's ability to recognize and realistically understand both the pros and cons when considering a solution, as well as the constraints that can undermine decision making. It is not enough for a group to follow a list of steps; it must also be well informed, realistic, and highly motivated if it hopes to solve a problem through group communication.

The Ideal-Solution Model

The **ideal-solution model** is a problem-solving procedure that takes into account the different viewpoints of individuals and factions within a group. The process is designed to give group members a chance to hear and understand the opinions and needs of others. The ideal-solution method asks the following questions:[19]

1. Do all members agree on the nature of the problem?

2. What would be the ideal solution from the point of view of everyone involved in the discussion?
3. What conditions could be changed so that the ideal solution could be achieved?
4. Of all the discussed solutions, which one best approximates the ideal solution?

For example, at Fallingstar State College, the planning council agrees that declining enrollment has caused a serious financial crisis. At this point, the group would listen to ideal solutions from different members. A vice president might suggest efficiency moves, such as increasing class size. A dean might suggest the development of a new curriculum that would attract more students. The administrator in charge of marketing might suggest an ambitious promotional campaign. A student might suggest an organized protest at the state capital in support of more funding. In an ideal-solution model, the group would have to consider every proposed solution and decide the extent to which each suggestion could or should be incorporated into an ideal solution.

Decision-Making Methods and Tools

As was the case with problem-solving models, there are dozens of decision-making methods and tools. Again, there is no "best" technique. There are, however, recommended procedures for making the decision-making process more efficient and effective.

Brainstorming

In 1953 Alex Osborn introduced the concept of brainstorming in his book *Applied Imagination*.[20] **Brainstorming** is a technique for generating as many ideas as possible in a short period of time. When a group is asked to suggest

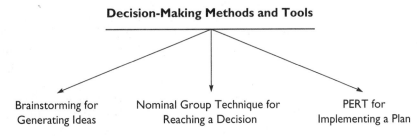

Decision-Making Methods and Tools

Brainstorming for Generating Ideas

Nominal Group Technique for Reaching a Decision

PERT for Implementing a Plan

FIGURE 9.5 Decision-Making Methods and Tools

Brainstorming Rules

The more the better

Suggest as many ideas as you can. Quantity is more important than quality.

Be creative

Free your imagination. Wild and crazy ideas are welcome.

Never criticize

Never analyze, oppose, praise, or laugh at another member's ideas. Do not discuss, defend, clarify, or comment upon your own suggestions. Evaluation occurs only after the brainstorming session is over.

Hitchhike

Build on or modify ideas presented by others. Someone else's wild ideas can trigger a creative suggestion.

Combine and extend

Combine two or more ideas into a new idea.

FIGURE 9.6 Brainstorming Rules

the causes of or solutions to a problem, brainstorming can be used to increase the number and creativity of suggestions. The guidelines shown in Figure 9.6 explain the rules and nature of brainstorming.

The 3M Meeting Management Team offers the following explanation of how and why brainstorming works:

> Brainstorming is governed by two key principles: (1) deferring judgment improves the quality of participants' input, and (2) quantity of ideas breeds quality. . . . The idea that quantity breeds quality is based on the notion that the first ideas we come up with are usually the most obvious, and that truly creative ideas will come only after we have gotten the obvious suggestions out.[21]

Before beginning a brainstorming session, two prerequisites can help a group get the most out of the process. First, someone should be assigned to record the ideas and suggestions generated by the group. Second, the group should take a few minutes to think about possible ideas and suggestions *before* the brainstorming session begins. In the case of Fallingstar State College, the council could brainstorm a list of untapped sources of grant funds and donations. Members could brainstorm ways in which the college could become more efficient by using existing funds. What is critical in any brainstorming session is that everyone follow the same basic principle of "all input, no put down" in order to encourage the generation of innovative ideas.

Although brainstorming is often used in groups, a lot depends on the nature of the group and the character of its members. If a group is self-conscious and sensitive to implied criticism, brainstorming can flop. If a group is comfortable with such a freewheeling process, brainstorming can enhance creativity and produce numerous ideas and suggestions.

Nominal Group Technique

Nominal Group Technique, also known as NGT, was developed by Andre L. Delbecq and Andrew H. Van de Ven as a way of maximizing participation in problem-solving and program-planning groups while minimizing some of the interpersonal problems associated with group interaction.[22] The term *nominal* means "existing in name only." Thus, a nominal group is a collection of people who, at first, work individually rather than collectively. NGT combines aspects of silent voting with limited discussion to help a group build consensus and arrive at a decision.[23]

There are two separate phases in a nominal group technique session: a fact-finding phase and an evaluation phase. During the first phase, seven to ten individuals sit around a table in full view of each other. The fact-finding phase includes these four steps:

1. Each member writes his or her ideas on a separate piece of paper.
2. At the end of five to ten minutes, a structured sharing of ideas takes place. Each member, in turn, presents one idea from his or her private list.
3. A recorder writes each idea on a flip chart in full view of other members. There is still no discussion at this point—only the recording of member ideas.
4. Round-robin listing continues until all members indicate they have no further ideas to share.[24]

Returning to the case of the college planning council, members could use the nominal group technique to generate a list of possible causes of declining enrollment or a list of possible solutions to the budgetary shortfall. The listing of ideas in an NGT session is different from brainstorming because items are generated by individuals working alone rather than emerging from group interaction.

During the second, evaluative phase of a nominal group technique session, the group discusses each recorded idea and then votes to create a rank order of items as follows:

1. Discussion is structured so that each idea receives attention before independent voting.
2. Members are asked to clarify or state support or nonsupport of each idea listed on the flip chart.
3. Independent voting then takes place. Each member privately, in writing, selects priorities by rank-ordering (or rating) each idea.
4. The group decision is the mathematically pooled outcome of the individual votes.[25]

Nominal group technique can be used in a variety of group settings, particularly when individual judgments and expertise are valued. NGT can be used to rank job applicants, to select a campaign slogan, to determine which of many possible solutions receives the most support, to establish budget priorities, to reach agreement on the causes of a problem, and to make a final decision. The highly structured NGT process guarantees equal participation

PERT Guidelines	Example
1. Determine the final step; what will the solution look like?	The college will launch a major promotional campaign in January to attract students for the fall semester.
2. List the events that must occur before the final goal is realized.	The college will develop new college-wide brochures, radio ads, training for recruiters, and special publicity.
3. List these steps chronologically.	(1) The college's PR office will develop a promotional plan; (2) PR staff members and deans will hold preliminary meetings to discuss brochure design and copy, (3) . . . etc.
4. If necessary, develop a chart that tracks the process and all the steps in it.	A chart that details the campaign's goals, overlapping tasks, persons responsible, and deadlines will be created and distributed.
5. Generate a list of all activities, resources, and materials needed to accomplish each step.	The PR office will develop a list of needed activities, resources, and materials with an accompanying budget for submission to the planning council.
6. Estimate the time needed to accomplish each step, then add all the estimates together.	Each activity will be assigned a realistic time for completion (e.g., photography = 5 days; brochure design = 2 weeks; brochure printing = 3 weeks).
7. Compare the total time estimate with deadlines, and correct as necessary.	During the printing of the college-wide brochure, the recruiters can attend orientation and training sessions.
8. Determine which members hall be responsible for each step.	The college will designate an office or person responsible for each activity along with the dates on which the tasks must be completed.

FIGURE 9.7 PERT Guidelines

during the idea generation phase and also provides opportunities for discussion and critical evaluation in the second phase. NGT can also be useful when dealing with a sensitive or controversial topic on which contrary opinions and a myriad of details could paralyze the discussion.[26]

An NGT session requires a great deal of time and a skilled moderator to make the session work efficiently and effectively. Given its highly structured format, NGT makes it difficult to adjust or modify suggested items and may frustrate group members who prefer more spontaneous interaction. At the same time, NGT can curb members who dominate or block the ideas and comments of others. Because it begins with individual ideas, all members are able to see their suggestions discussed by the entire group.

PERT

PERT, which stands for Program Evaluation and Review Technique, is a tool for planning and coordinating the many steps needed to carry out a solution or plan of action. PERT is a decision-making tool that requires a group to decide how, when, and under what conditions and authority a plan should be implemented.

The underlying question in PERT is: Where do you want to go and how are you going to get there? PERT helps chart the journey that leads a group to its goal. In practice, PERT can be quite complicated. In Figure 9.7, Seibold's summary of PERT guidelines has been illustrated with examples from the college planning council problem.[27]

Ellis and Fisher emphasize the need for PERT in their discussion of groups that "meet, discuss, and come up with solutions but never put them into practice."[28] PERT may be just what such groups need to ensure that solutions or plans are implemented.

Creative Problem Solving

In their book, *Organizing Genius: The Secrets of Creative Collaboration*, Bennis and Biederman claim that curiosity and creativity fuel all *great* groups. This quality "allows them to both identify significant problems and find creative, boundary-bursting solutions rather than simplistic ones."[29] Moreover, effective group leaders understand the near-magical quality that creativity can inject into the group process. When, for example, Walt "Disney asked his artists to push the envelope of animation, he told them 'If you can dream it, you can do it.' He believed that, and, as a result, they did too."[30]

Encouraging and rewarding creativity can be as important to problem solving as following any of the procedures described in this chapter. It is creativity and "thinking outside the box" that facilitates breakthrough decisions and solutions. For example, one of us once chaired a meeting in which the injection of creativity broke through a problem-solving log jam:

> I was chairing a meeting of graphic artists, copy writers, and public relations staff members at the college. Our assignment was to write and design a commemorative booklet for the college's 40th anniversary. On the conference table sat a dozen such booklets from other colleges. The group had reviewed all the samples and come up with a list of common features. The problem was this: We had limited funds to print the booklet and had to find a way to confine ourselves to 24 pages. At one point in the meeting, the group became bogged down trying to decide which elected officials should be invited to send letters of congratulations. Very quickly, it became evident that these letters could fill the entire booklet with no space left for other material. Maybe we should ask them to limit the number of words in their letters? Maybe we should print the booklet on less expensive paper in order to add more pages? Frustration grew to the point where an uncomfortable silence settled over the group. At this point I interjected with two questions: Why do we need letters from elected officials? and If you hadn't

seen any of these model booklets, what would you write and design to commemorate our anniversary? The response was immediate and energizing: You mean we can come up with something new and different? My answer: yes. The result: A new sense of excitement and eagerness permeated the group. The "model" booklets were swept off the table. Highly creative, out-of-the-box alternatives materialized.

The Creative Process

Isaksen describes creative thinking as the process "in which one makes and communicates meaningful new connections by devising unusual new possibilities."[31] Although it is impossible to describe the creative process in precise terms (it wouldn't be all that creative if we could), we can outline the basic stages of the creative thinking process in groups. Generally, there are four stages:

Investigation. Group members gather information and attempt to understand the nature and causes of the problem.

Imagination. Free thinking is encouraged; mental roadblocks are removed or temporarily suppressed. Many ideas, some of them quite unusual, are generated and discussed.

Incubation. A period of time occurs during which imaginative ideas are allowed to percolate and recombine in new ways. The group may take a break or focus their attention on another topic or issue during the incubation stage.

Insight. The "Aha" moment when a new approach or solution emerges. Group members recognize the breakthrough moment and may build upon or improve the idea.

Many group members enjoy the fun that comes with the creative problem-solving process. In fact, laughter may play a large part in the last three stages.[32] As a result, it may appear as though a group is not serious about solving a problem or reaching a decision. Because the incubation stage is usually a prerequisite for the "Aha" moment of insight, it may look as though the group has abandoned its task. As a result, creative problem solving is often squelched or sacrificed in the interest of following a detailed agenda or rigid procedure. For group leaders and members with strong control needs, members engaged in creative problem solving may appear to be spending too much energy on a good time rather than dealing with the problem. Despite these concerns, there is good evidence that creative thinking in groups is well worth the time and laughter. Firestein found that groups trained in creative problem solving participated more, criticized ideas less, supported ideas more, exhibited humor, and produced more ideas.[33]

Creative Methods

Given the benefits of creative problem solving, we recommend four methods for enhancing group creativity: (1) Control judgment, (2) Encourage innovation, (3) Ask *what if?* and (4) Use metaphors.

Control Judgment. Almost nothing inhibits group creativity as much as negative responses to new ideas. "That won't work." "We've tried that." "That's too bizarre." Apply the rules of brainstorming to generating creative ideas. Alex Osborn, the father of brainstorming has compared "the idea and evaluation phases of brainstorming to the gas and brake pedals of a car. Using them at the same time makes both less effective. Separating the acts of creating and evaluating ideas yields better results in both areas."[34] Remember that a bizarre idea generated in a brainstorming session can evolve into a creative solution. "Keeping the process open and avoiding premature closure are crucially important. Because creative work is exploratory in nature, it deserves suspension of belief in the early stages."[35]

Encourage Innovation. Towe maintains that there are four sources of action that guide us through each workday.[36] These same sources of action can apply to the way groups approach problem solving.

Inertia. We've done it before.
Instruction. Someone showed us how to do it.
Imitation. We've seen how it's done.
Innovation. We have developed a new way to do it.

Think of how these sources of action could apply to the group that was trying to design the commemorative booklet for their college's 40th anniversary. Until their creativity was released, they were bogged down in inertia, instruction, and imitation. Encouraging a group to be innovative, to think outside the box, to be more imaginative may be all that is needed to spark and harness a group's creative power.

Ask *What If?* One of the reasons groups are often reluctant to think creatively is that they have preconceived notions about what can and can't be done. Although there are real constraints in almost all problem-solving situations, there is no harm in removing those restraints for a discussion that asks *What if?* John Kao, the Academic Director of the Managing Innovation program at Stanford University, suggests that there are two types of knowledge. The first is raw knowledge consisting of facts, information, and data. The second type of knowledge is insight, or the "Aha!" It is "a response to the *what ifs* and *if only we coulds*."[37] Kao points out that it is "creativity that enables the transformation of one form of knowledge to the next."[38]

Here are some questions the commemorative booklet committee could have asked: What if we had a million dollars to design and print the commemorative booklet; what would we do? What if the "booklet" were a videotape rather than a publication? What if we had 100 pages to work with? What if we could hire a famous author to write the copy—what would the booklet "say?" No one even suggests that groups consider one more "what if" scenario: What if we do nothing.[39] In other words, what are the consequences, if any, if we don't produce a commemorative booklet? Our own experience in working with groups is that a million-dollar idea can often be implemented with a few thousand dollars. An award-winning design can be created by an artist inspired by video imagery. Rousing words can be crafted by a talented copywriter.

Use Metaphors. Towe contends that the answers to many problems already exist. It's just that they are hiding in other areas of our lives.[40] These hiding places can be found in common metaphors. Why? Because metaphors can help group members explain, understand, guide, and direct their creative thinking in ways they would not have thought of otherwise.[41] For example, the metaphor of an emergency room has been used to redesign the registration process at some colleges. Students who don't need any help can register on line or over the telephone. Those who need help are met by a kind of "triage nurse," a college counselor who can answer simple questions, direct them to a clerk for processing, or send them to a private room where they can receive "intensive care" from a "specialist" counselor.

Try thinking of the ways in which the following metaphors could be used: a problem-solving group and a beehive; student success in college and a horse race; developing a public speech and planting a healthy tree. In her book, *Secrets of Successful Speakers*, Lilly Walters takes the familiar concept of growing a tree and compares it to unfamiliar things she wants to teach her readers about public speaking. She discusses selecting the seed—deciding what you want to achieve in your speech; finding fertile soil—choosing and understanding the audience; and pruning the deadwood—editing the speech.[42] The beauty of metaphors is that they force group members to look at a problem in new and creative ways.

Despite our enthusiasm for creative problem solving, there is a difference between creativity and creative problem solving. A highly creative group may not be a highly productive group. Let's face it: A free-wheeling creative meeting can be a lot more fun than routine work. Once a group releases its creative energies, it may be reluctant to return to a standard agenda or nominal group technique to refine a solution. In such a case, a group must work out an internal balance between creative discussions and productive research, analysis, and action.[43] Kao compares balancing creativity and group process to tending the flames of a fire. "The spark needs air, breathing room, and freedom to ignite. But let the air blow too freely, and the spark will go out. Close all the doors and windows, and you will stifle it."[44]

Match the Tool to the Task

All the decision-making and problem-solving procedures described and listed in this chapter have unique strengths and weaknesses. Research has been unable to identify one method as group-proof or significantly better

> **TOOLBOX 9.1**   Agendas and Parliamentary Procedure
>
> Two important decision-making tools—using a meeting agenda and parliamentary procedure—can help groups balance participation, manage conflict, and make effective decisions. A meeting agenda is an outline of the items to be discussed and the tasks to be accomplished at a meeting. Parliamentary procedure is a set of formal rules used to determine the will of the majority in a way that ensures fair and orderly discussion and debate. Both of these procedures can help a group achieve its common goal in a manner that is efficient, well organized, civil, and empowering. Because Chapter 14 and Chapter 15 provide detailed information about these two procedures, they are not discussed in this chapter.

than another. An effective group matches the appropriate decision-making tool with the group and its task. Whereas The Standard Agenda provides a detailed blueprint for a group embarking on a complex problem-solving assignment, brainstorming may be all a group needs to generate a list of possible speakers for a college's commencement. Whereas the NGT can provide a group with a systematic way of identifying and analyzing the causes of or solutions to a problem, PERT may be the best way to ensure that a solution is implemented effectively.

A mismatch between the procedural tool and the group task can waste time, frustrate members, and produce disastrous decisions. Not all procedures are appropriate for all groups. Procedures such as brainstorming and NGT work best with small groups, whereas parliamentary procedure may be more effective with larger groups. Decision making and problem solving are complex processes. The best way to go about either task is to ensure that the group's goal and the needs of individual members match the selection of methods and procedures.

Decision-Making Realities

Although procedures may be the most powerful tool available to improve the conduct of meetings, there are other factors that affect the outcome of every decision and problem a group confronts. Scheerhorn, Geist, and Teboul put it in even simpler terms: "Decision making in the real world is often messy. . . ."[45] We would be remiss if we did not acknowledge that even the best of groups can be led astray when politics, preexisting preferences, and power infiltrate the group process.

Politics   In organizational settings, almost all decisions have a political component. Regardless of the decision-making procedure being used, many group members come to meetings with hidden agendas and political interests. Some members may never voice their real reasons for opposing a proposed solution, whereas others may withhold valuable information as a way of influencing the outcome of a discussion.

The motives for such actions often are political. A person who wants to get ahead may be reluctant to oppose an idea loved by the boss. A member who knows why a plan won't work may remain silent in order to make sure that the person responsible for implementing the plan fails. Although most conscientious group members do not engage in such deceptive behavior, it would be naive to proceed as though all members care equally about achieving the group's common goal. Meetings can become a political arena in which individuals and special-interest groups are dedicated to meeting their own private needs. Fortunately, the use of clear procedures can minimize the influence of such members.

Preexisting   An intelligent group member is rarely a blank slate who walks into a meeting
Preferences   uninformed and unconcerned about the topic or issue to be discussed. When a decision must be made, most of us know how we might decide. We may even have ideas about who should be in charge, how the task should be done, and when it should be completed. It would be a mistake to ignore the fact that many group members have preexisting preferences about what a group should do.[46]

Fortunately, open discussion and the use of procedures makes sure that these preferences are dealt with logically and fairly. For example, the functional approach to problem solving acknowledges that groups do not always discuss issues in a predetermined order. In fact, there may be nothing wrong with members coming to a meeting with proposed solutions as long as the group engages such members in a discussion of the pros and cons of their position and makes sure that the group understands the nature and causes of the problem. As much as we may wish that everyone would follow the order of steps in The Standard Agenda, that is rarely the case. The use of procedures can ensure that all those steps are at least considered before a group makes its final decision.

Power   The power of individual group members can have a significant effect on the outcome of any meeting. It is no secret that powerful people influence group decisions. They affect how and whether other members participate, whose ideas and suggestions are given serious consideration, and which solutions are chosen. Hirokawa and Pace warn that "influential members [can] convince the group to accept invalid facts and assumptions, introduce poor ideas

TOOLBOX 9.2 Power in Groups

In most groups, power can be measured by the ability of members to mobilize a group toward its goal. Despite the potential for abuse of power, most groups appreciate a member or leader who has the power to make things happen. Power in groups can vary depending on whether a member has reward, coercive, legitimate, expert, or referent power. Someone with referent power may be the member best suited to help a group select and use an appropriate decision-making procedure. A member with coercive power has the potential to intimidate members at a time when creative problem solving and responsible decision making are most needed. **Chapter 3: Leadership in Groups** discusses how these five types of power affect group members and group outcomes.

and suggestions, lead the group to misinterpret information presented to them, or lead the group off on tangents and irrelevant discussion."[47] In short, one powerful but misguided member can be responsible for the poor quality of a group's decision. Lucky is the group in which powerful members are rational, helpful, and encouraging. Under such circumstances, group decisions are likely to be of high quality.

One of the major advantages of using an established decision-making procedure is that it can protect a group from the debilitating effects of politics, preexisting preferences, and powerful members. Procedures make clear the rules of engagement. Anyone violating such rules or failing to meet assigned responsibilities may justly face isolation and criticism. Rare is a group that escapes the effects of politics, preexisting preferences, and power. Yet, every group can rest more secure when appropriate procedures are used to guide it toward its common goal.

Balanced Decision Making

When group decision making works efficiently and effectively, it offers both social and task rewards to group members. Poole identifies balancing independence and groupwork as one of the keys to using meeting procedures effectively. His conclusion emphasizes how important such balance is to a group making an important decision or solving a significant problem.

Time and Energy
Creativity
Individual Needs

Effective Decisions
Structured Procedures
Group Goals

FIGURE 9.8 Group Decision Making

To be effective, a group must maintain a golden mean, a balance between independent thinking and structured, coordinated work. Too much independence may shatter group cohesion and encourage members to sacrifice group goals to their individual needs.... Too much synchronous, structured work ... is likely to regiment group thinking and stifle novel ideas.[48]

How, then, can groups balance such extreme requirements? The answer is procedures. Procedures provide explicit instructions that let members know when they can work alone and when they must work together. Procedures also tell a group how much effort must be spent gathering and analyzing information, generating ideas, offering suggestions, and arguing for or against proposals. When procedures are used wisely and well, they maximize creative thinking and, at the same time, encourage coordination of efforts. In such a balanced climate, a group is more likely to be creative, productive, and satisfied.

*S*ummary *Study Guide*

- Decision making requires a group to make a judgment or choose an alternative. Problem solving is a complex decision-making process in which groups analyze a harmful situation and decide on a plan to solve or reduce the effects of the problem.
- Whereas inefficient and unskilled decision making can waste time, money, and effort, effective group decision making generates more ideas and produces better solutions than can individuals working alone.
- There are three different ways in which a group can make a final decision, each of which has strengths and weaknesses: voting, consensus seeking, and authority rule.
- A consensus decision is one that all members have a part in shaping and that all find at least minimally acceptable as a means of accomplishing mutual goals.

- There are four basic kinds of discussion questions: questions of fact (what is true?); questions of conjecture (what if?); questions of value (what is worthwhile?); and questions of policy (what should be done?).
- The benefits of using decision-making procedures include balanced participation, conflict resolution, better organization, and group empowerment.
- The standard agenda includes the following steps: task clarification, problem identification, fact finding and problem analysis, solution criteria and limitations, solution suggestions, solution evaluation and selection, and solution implementation.
- The functional theory approach identifies critical communication behaviors that are instrumental in group decision making and problem solving. These behaviors focus on the group's level of preparation, the selection of appropriate procedures, and the consideration of precautions.
- The ideal-solution format takes into account and accommodates different points of view within a group.
- Brainstorming asks group members to generate as many ideas as possible in a short period of time without criticism or analysis.
- Nominal Group Technique (NGT) is a two-phase group process in which individual members engage in fact finding and idea generation followed by an analytical discussion and decision making.
- PERT (Program Evaluation and Review Technique) is a tool for planning and coordinating the many steps needed to carry out a solution or plan of action.
- Creative problem solving in groups includes four stages: Investigation, the gathering of information about the problem; Imagination, generating unusual, out-of-the-box ideas; Incubation, a time in which ideas percolate and recombine in new ways; and Insight, the breakthrough moment when a new approach or solution emerges.
- Even in the best of groups, decision making can be compromised if politics, preexisting preferences, and power infiltrate the group process.

Groupwork *Lost on the Moon*[49]

GOAL   To demonstrate the advantages and disadvantages of group problem solving.

PARTICIPANTS   Groups of 5–7 members.

PROCEDURE

1. Each group member should complete the individual work sheet without help from or discussion with other group members.

2. After everyone has completed the individual work sheet, group members should share their answers and agree upon a group listing of items—one ranking for each of the fifteen items that best satisfies *all* group members.
3. Groups should be encouraged to use the guidelines for seeking consensus when discussing and making their decisions.
4. After all groups have reached consensus, the correct answers should be distributed to score the work sheets. Individual and group scores should be compared and discussed.*

Lost on the Moon Work Sheet

DIRECTIONS   You are a member of a space crew originally scheduled to rendezvous with a mother ship on the lighted surface of the moon. Because of mechanical difficulties, however, your ship crash-landed on a lighted spot some two hundred miles from the rendezvous point. During landing, much of the equipment aboard was damaged and, since survival depends on reaching the mother ship, the most critical items available must be chosen for the two-hundred-mile trip. Below are listed the fifteen items left intact and undamaged after landing. Your task is to rank them in terms of their importance to your crew in allowing them to reach the rendezvous point. Place the number 1 by the most important item, the number 2 by the second most important, and so on, through number 15, the least important.

_____ Box of matches

_____ Food concentrates

_____ Fifty feet of nylon rope

_____ Parachute silk

_____ Solar-powered portable heating unit

_____ Two .45-caliber pistols

_____ One case of dehydrated milk

_____ Two 100-pound tanks of oxygen

_____ Stellar map (of the moon's constellations)

_____ Self-inflated life raft

_____ Magnetic compass

_____ Five gallons of water

_____ Signal flares

_____ First-aid kit containing injection needles

_____ Solar-powered FM receiver-transmitter

*The textbook's *Instructor's Manual* explains how to conduct and score this GroupWork exercise.

Reprinted with Permission from *Psychology Today Magazine,* Copyright © 1971 (Sussex Publishers, Inc.).

Decision-Making Competencies

Directions This instrument represents a modified version of an assessment tool designed to evaluate the performance of individual group members who participate in task-oriented, decision-making discussions.[50] There are five competencies related to accomplishing the group's task and three competencies dealing with conflict, climate, and interaction. Rate individual members on each item as well as the group as a whole in order to assess how well an observed group solves problems and makes important decisions.

	SUPERIOR	SATIS-FACTORY	UNSATIS-FACTORY
1. Defines/analyzes problem. Appropriately defines and analyzes the problem that confronts the group.			
2. Identifies criteria. Appropriately participates in the establishment of the group goal and identifies criteria for assessing the quality of the group outcome.			
3. Generates solutions. Appropriately identifies the solutions or alternatives identified by group members.			
4. Evaluates solutions. Appropriately evaluates the solutions or alternatives identified by group members.			
5. Maintains task focus. Appropriately helps the group stay on the task, issue, or agenda item the group is discussing.			
6. Manages conflict. Appropriately manages disagreements and conflict.			
7. Maintains climate. Appropriately provides supportive comments to other group members.			
8. Manages interaction. Helps manage interaction and appropriately invites others to participate.			

Recommended Readings

Higgins, J. M. (1994) "101 creative problem solving techniques: The handbook for new ideas for business:" *The New Management*. Winter Park, FL.

Howard, V. A. & Barton, J. H. (1992). *Thinking together: Making meetings work*. New York: William Morrow.

3M Meeting Management Team with J. Drew. (1994). *Mastering meetings: Discovering the hidden potential of effective business meetings*. New York: McGraw-Hill.

Notes

1. *The American Heritage Dictionary* (3rd ed.). (1992). Boston: Houghton Mifflin, p. 484.
2. Drucker, P. R. (1967). *The effective executive*. New York: HarperBusiness, p. 143.
3. Napier, R. W. & Gershenfeld, M. K. (1993). *Groups: Theory and experience* (5th ed.). Boston: Houghton Mifflin, pp. 329–330.
4. See Pavitt, C. & Curtis, E. (1994). *Small group discussion: A theoretical approach* (2nd ed.). Scottsdale, AZ: Gorsuch, Scarisbrick, pp. 25–52; Cathcart, R. S., Samovar, L. A. & Henman, L. D. (1996). *Small group communication: Theory and practice* (7th ed.). Madison, WI: Brown & Benchmark, pp. 102–103; Ellis, D. G. & Fisher, B. A. (1994). *Small group decision making: Communication and the group process* (4th ed.). New York: McGraw-Hill, pp. 17–18.
5. Wood, J. T. (1992). Alternative methods of group decision making. In R. S. Cathcart & L. A. Samovar (Eds.), *Small group communication: A reader* (6th ed.). Dubuque, IA: Wm. C. Brown, p. 159.
6. Gouran, D. S. (1997). "Effective versus ineffective group decision making." In L. R. Frey & J. K. Barge (Eds.). *Managing group life: Communicating in decision-making groups*. Boston: Houghton Mifflin, p. 139.
7. Poole, M. S. (1990). Procedures for managing meetings: Social and technological innovation. In R. A. Swanson & B. O. Knapp (Eds.), *Innovative meeting management*. Austin: 3M Meeting Management Institute, pp. 54–55.
8. Pavitt, C. & Curtis, E. (1994). *Small group discussion: A theoretical approach* (2nd ed.). Scottsdale, AZ: Gorsuch, Scarisbrick, p. 432.
9. Dewey, J. (1910). *How we think*. Boston: Heath.
10. Wood, J. T., Phillips, G. M. & Pedersen, D. J. (1986). *Group discussion: A practical guide to participation and leadership* (2nd ed.). New York: Harper & Row.
11. Wood et al., p. 58.
12. Rothwell, J. D. (1995). *In mixed company: Small group communication* (2nd ed.). Fort Worth, TX: Harcourt Brace, p. 196.
13. See Hirokawa, R. Y. & Pace, R. (1983). A descriptive investigation of the possible communication-based reasons for effective and ineffective group decision making. *Communication Monographs*, 50, pp. 363–379; Hirokawa, R. Y. & Scheerhorn, D. (1986). Communication and faulty group decision-making. In R. Y. Hirokawa & M. S. Poole (Eds.), *Communication and group decision-making*. Beverly Hills, CA: Sage, pp. 63–80; Hirokawa, R. Y. (May 24, 1993). *Avoiding camels: Lessons learned in the facilitation of high- quality group decision making through effective discussion*. The Van Zelst Lecture in Communication delivered at the School of Speech, Northwestern University, Evanston, IL; Gouran, D. S. & Hirokawa, R. Y. (1996). Functional theory and communication in decision-making and problem-solving groups. In R. Y. Hirokawa & M. S. Poole (Eds), *Communication and group decision making* (2nd ed). Thousand Oaks, CA.

14. Gouran & Hirokawa, p. 76.

15. Gouran & Hirokawa, pp. 76–77.

16. Hirokawa, 1993, p. 11.

17. Hirokawa, 1993, p. 10.

18. Gouran & Hirokawa, p. 68.

19. Goldberg, A. A. & Larson, C. E. (1975). *Group communication: Discussion processes and applications.* Englewood Cliffs, NJ: Prentice-Hall, p. 149.

20. Osborn, A. F. (1957). *Applied Imagination* (rev. ed.). New York: Scribner.

21. 3M Meeting Management Team with J. Drew. (1994). *Mastering meetings: Discovering the hidden potential of effective business meetings.* New York: McGraw-Hill, p. 59.

22. Delbecq, A. L., Van de Ven, A. H. & Gustafson, D. H. (1975). *Group techniques for program planning.* Glenview, IL: Scott, Foresman. •

23. Kelly, P. K. (1994). *Team decision-making techniques.* Irvine, CA: Richard Chang Associates, p. 29.

24. Delbecq et al., p. 8.

25. Delbecq et al., p. 8.

26. Kelly, p. 29

27. Seibold, D. R. (1992). Making meetings more successful: Plans, formats, and procedures for group problem solving. In R. S. Cathcart & L. A. Samovar (Eds.), *Small group communication: A reader* (6th ed.). Dubuque, IA: Wm. C. Brown, p. 187.

28. Ellis, D. G. & Fisher, B. A. (1994). *Small group decision making: Communication and the group process* (4th ed.). New York: McGraw-Hill, p. 149.

29. Bennis, W. & Biederman, P. W. (1997). *Organizing genius: The secrets of creative collaboration.* Reading, MA: Addison-Wesley, p. 17.

30. Bennis & Biederman, p. 20.

31. Isakesen, S. G. (1988). "Human factors for innovative problem solving." In R. L. Kuhn (Ed.), *Handbook for creative and innovative managers.* New York: McGraw-Hill, pp. 139–146.

32. Rawlinson, J. G. (1981). *Creative thinking and brainstorming.* New York: John Wiley, p. 28.

33. Firestein, R. L. (1990). "Effects of creative problem-solving training on communication behaviors in small groups." *Small Group Research,* 21, pp. 507–521.

34. Towe, L. (1996). *Why didn't I think of that? Creativity in the workplace.* West Des Moines, IA: American Media, p. 19.

35. Kao, J. (1997). *Jamming: The art and discipline of business creativity.* New York: HarperBusiness, p. 87.

36. Towe, p. 14.

37. Kao, p. 8.

38. Kao, p. 8.

39. Noone, D. J. (1998). *Creative problem solving* (2nd Ed). New York: Barron's, p. 60.

40. Towe, p. 77.

41. Noone, p. 93.

42. Walters, L. (1993). *Secrets of successful speakers: How you can motivate, captivate, and persuade.* New York: McGraw-Hill.

43. Carr, C. (1996). *Team leader's problem solver.* Englewood Cliffs, NY: Prentice Hall, p. 230.

44. Kao, p. 17.

45. Scheerhorn, D., Geist, P. & Teboul, J. B. (1994). Beyond decision making in decision-making groups: Implications for the study of group communication. In L. R. Frey (Ed.), *Group communication in context: Studies of natural groups.* Hillsdale, NJ: Lawrence Erlbaum, p. 256.

46. Pavitt, C. (1993). Does communication matter in social influence during small group discussion? Give positions. *Communication Studies, 44,* pp. 216–227.

47. Hirokawa & Pace, p. 379.

48. Poole, pp. 73–74.

49. Based on Hall, J. (November 1971). Decisions, decisions, decisions. *Psychology Today, 5,* pp. 51–54, 86, 88.

50. Based on Beebe, S. A., Barge, J. K. & McCormick, C. (1994). The competent group communicator. *Proceedings of the 1994 Summer Conference on Assessing College Student Competency in Speech Communication.* Annandale, VA: Speech Communication Association, pp. 353–369.

Argumentation in Groups

Why Argue?

One of the advantages of working in groups is that members can share and discuss a variety of ideas and opinions. At the same time, a group must be able to agree on a particular position or action if it hopes to progress toward its goal. In order to balance the value and consequences of opinion giving, group members must be able to advance their own viewpoints and discuss the views of others. Successful groups encourage independent thinking and the exploration of ideas to discover the best solution. "This search for a common solution is often the result of a continuous exchange of arguments and counterarguments among participants."[1] In other words, group members must be able to argue.

Brashers, Adkins, and Meyers claim that "central to group discussion . . . is the process of argumentation."[2] Whether a group meets to share information or reach a decision, members should be able to advance and evaluate different ideas, information, and opinions.

Arguments and Argumentation

We often think of an argument as a disagreement or hostile confrontation between two people. An **argument** is simply a claim supported by evidence or reasons for accepting it. An argument is more than an opinion: "The Hispanic Heritage Club should be given more funds next year." An argument is an idea or opinion *supported* by evidence and reasoning: "The Hispanic Heritage Club should be given more funds next year because it has doubled in size and cannot provide the same number or quality of programs without an increase in funding." When viewed this way, an argument does not have to involve conflict or even disagreement.

Argumentation is the way group members advocate their own positions, examine competing ideas, and influence other members. The following example illustrates a situation in which argumentation is an important group function:

> A college's Student Finance Board is made up of elected students who are responsible for distributing funds to campus clubs and organizations. The board meets throughout the academic year to consider funding requests. Clubs usually request more money than is available. Board members evaluate all requests and argue about the significance of each club's activities and the reasonableness of its funding request. Finally, the board decides how the funds should be distributed and submits those recommendations to the vice president for Student Services.

In such a decision-making group, members must read funding requests and listen to oral presentations by club members who argue that their organization should receive increased funding. Then board members share their own positions and, in many cases, find it necessary to argue for or against pro-

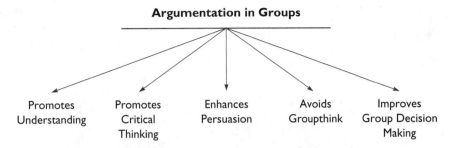

FIGURE 10.1 Argumentation in Groups

posed funding levels. After a period of discussion and argumentation, the group makes its final decision—even though it knows that some club officers and advisors will argue that the decision was unfair or unjust.

The Value of Argumentation in Groups

Effective argumentation helps a group understand and analyze ideas, influence members, make informed and critical decisions, and achieve its goal. Thus, argumentation is a significant factor in how group communication influences decision making.

Promotes Understanding.   Through the process of argumentation, you may discover that not all members reason in the same way—some members may seek group goals, others may seek personal goals. Some may argue logically, others emotionally. For example, as a member of the Student Finance Board, Charles argues in favor of funding the Philosophy Club because he is a club member. Karen supports the funding request because the club sponsored a successful forum last semester. Although both members support the same position, they do so for different reasons. Understanding how other group members reason and feel about individual issues can help you adapt your arguments to their perspectives.

Promotes Critical Thinking.   Effective argumentation helps group members analyze issues and critically examine ideas. When you present your position on an issue, you may be challenged to justify that position to the rest of the group. Your explanations will require strong evidence or sound reasons to support your conclusions. The process of argumentation often causes us to rethink our own positions and beliefs. Thus, the evaluation of arguments in groups encourages group members to think critically and flexibly. Kuhn maintains that "it is in argument that we are likely to find the most significant way in which higher order thinking and reasoning figure in the lives of most people. . . . Hence, argumentative thinking lies at the heart of what we should be concerned about in examining how, and how well, people think."[3]

THESE group members are discussing a proposed community policing program. What might happen if their arguments are not well organized and supported with evidence? (McLaughlin/The Image Works)

Enhances Persuasion. Persuasion is communication that influences the beliefs or actions of others. Argumentation is a specific means of persuasion.[4] As group members are exposed to different arguments, they can decide which ones are better supported and make more sense. Group members who are skilled at argumentation are often the most influential and persuasive.

Avoids Groupthink. Groupthink occurs when, in an effort to discourage conflict and maintain group cohesion, a group makes flawed decisions. Makau emphasizes that "unlike groups that engage in groupthink, groups trained to employ cooperative argumentation are able to form constructive forms of cohesion."[5] Constructive argumentation encourages critical examination of opposing ideas without impairing group cohesion. As Chapter 8 explains, groupthink can be avoided when members ask questions, offer reasons for positions, and demand justifications from others.

Improves Group Decision Making. Dominic Infante claims that "the quality of decision making and problem solving in groups is enhanced by argument."[6] As a group considers alternate ideas, argumentation helps members examine the consequences of a potential action before making a final decision. Errors in reasoning are exposed, and weaknesses in evidence are uncovered. Beatrice Schultz notes that "studies show that a diversity of points of view can be conducive to effective problem solving, and that a willingness to disagree has meant an increase in the range of alternatives considered in making a decision."[7]

Argumentation in groups can also improve decision making because, unlike one-on-one argumentation, several group members may work together to develop the same argument. In this "tag team" situation, group members build upon the argument presented by one member by providing additional evidence or reasons to support a particular position. The result is a single comprehensive argument constructed cooperatively within the group.

Although there is strong evidence that argumentation can improve decision making,[8] such conclusions are based on an underlying assumption that group members know how to develop and use arguments that will help achieve a group's goal. If argumentation is to be a constructive process, group members must know how to develop valid arguments and how to engage in cooperative argumentation with other group members.

*A*rgumentativeness

In Chapter 5 the concept of communication apprehension explained why some group members lack confidence in their ability to interact in a group. Similarly, researchers have suggested that individuals vary in how comfortable they feel about engaging in argumentation. This characteristic is referred to as argumentativeness. Dominic Infante and Andrew Rancer define **argumentativeness** as the willingness to argue controversial issues with others.[9] Argumentativeness is a constructive trait because it does not necessarily promote hostility or personal attacks. The argumentative person focuses on a discussion of the issues rather than attacking personalities.

Argumentativeness and Group Decision Making

An individual's level of argumentativeness provides some insight into how a group member will approach a discussion. Group members with lower levels of argumentativeness generally avoid conflict. These individuals are often viewed as not only nonconfrontational but also unskilled in argumentation. Because they are unwilling to engage in argumentation during group discussions, they have less influence in group decision making.

Group members who are highly argumentative welcome constructive conflict. They enjoy the intellectual challenge of an argument and show genuine interest in the discussion. Highly argumentative members confidently defend their own positions and challenge the arguments of others. Groups usually view the most argumentative members as dynamic and skillful arguers with high levels of credibility and influence. Argumentative members are frequently chosen as group leaders. On the other hand, they are less likely to be persuaded by others' arguments and may be perceived as inflexible and overly talkative.

TOOLBOX 10.1   How Argumentative Are You?

At the end of this chapter, there is a self-test called the Argumentativeness Scale. The questionnaire will help you identify your own level of argumentativeness. You might want to complete the questionnaire and calculate your results before continuing this chapter. Your score will help you understand how comfortable you are arguing in groups.

Argumentative members are very influential in group decision making. Kazoleas and Kay confirm that argumentative group members create more arguments on both sides of a position.[10] When the number of choices a group can consider is thus expanded, the group is less likely to come to a biased decision or succumb to groupthink.

Learning to Be Argumentative

You can learn to argue. Sanders, Wiseman, and Gass report that "students trained in argumentation were better able to identify logically weak arguments than those who had not received such instruction."[11] By practicing the skills in this chapter, you should become better able to argue your ideas and analyze the arguments of other group members. Learning to argue can make you more influential in group decision making.

It is important to know how to achieve a balanced level of argumentativeness. Arguing too little diminishes your influence. On the other hand, members who are *extremely* argumentative can be the least influential in group decision making. You should know when it is important to argue an issue and when to acknowledge that someone else has made a good point.

The Structure of an Argument

Before you can build strong arguments or refute the arguments of others, it is helpful to understand the components of a complete argument. Stephen Toulmin, an English philosopher, developed a model representing the structure of an argument. The **Toulmin Model** consists of the following components: claim, data, warrant, backing, reservation, and qualifier.[12]

Components of the Toulmin Model

The **claim** is the conclusion or position you are advocating. The **data** constitute the evidence you use to support your claim. For example, the statement "My group will do well on our class project" is a claim. The data for this claim might be the fact that during the first meeting, all group members said they would work hard on the project. Data answer a challenger's questions: "What makes you say that?" or "What do you have to go on?"

The third component of the model is the warrant. The **warrant** explains why the data support the claim. For example, the warrant might say that when group members are willing to work hard, a successful outcome is usually the result. Rather than asking "What do you have to go on?" the warrant wants to know "How did you get there?" The relationship among these three components of the Toulmin Model is illustrated in Figure 10.2.

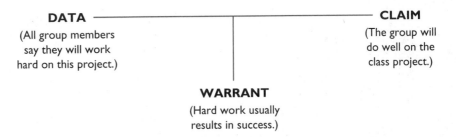

FIGURE 10.2   Basic "T" of the Toulmin Model

The preceding argument would sound like this: "All group members said they would work hard. Because hard work usually results in success, the group will do well on the class project." The combined data, claim, and warrant make up the "basic T" of the Toulmin Model.

Beyond the "basic T," there are three additional components: backing, reservation, and qualifier. The **backing** provides support for the argument's warrant. In the preceding example, backing for the warrant might be the fact that the group that worked the hardest on the last assignment received the best grade.

Not all claims are true all the time. The **reservation** is the component of the Toulmin Model that recognizes exceptions to an argument or indications that a claim may not be true under certain circumstances. The group members at the first meeting said they would work hard. If, however, they do not attend important meetings, the group is unlikely to do well.

The final component of the model is the qualifier. The **qualifier** states the degree to which the claim appears to be true. Qualifiers are usually words or phrases such as *likely, possibly, certainly, unlikely,* or *probably.* A claim with a qualifier might be "The group will *probably* do well on the class project." The way that the entire argument would look is shown in Figure 10.3.

Applying the Toulmin Model

The Toulmin Model is a way to diagram and evaluate arguments. It is not necessary to state each component of the argument when advancing your position. In fact, often only the claim is stated. However, understanding the model lets you know what questions to ask about an argument. If only the claim is stated, then you may ask what evidence or data support that claim. If the warrant is questionable, you may ask what backing exists to support it. Recognizing that situations may alter the certainty of your claim helps you advocate more reasonable positions. When developing your own arguments, the Toulmin Model can help you test the strength of an argument. Analyzing someone else's argument by using the model helps reveal the strengths and weaknesses of a position.

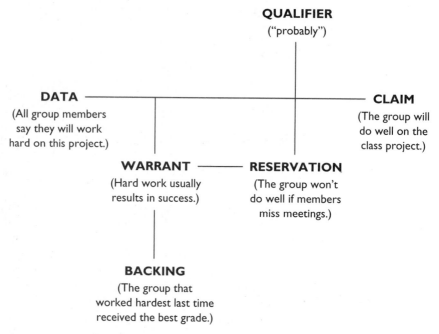

FIGURE 10.3 The Toulmin Model of an Argument

*P*resenting Your Arguments

If your ideas are to be taken seriously by your group, your arguments must be well presented. Infante suggests that arguers follow a four-step procedure for presenting arguments: state your claim, present evidence, provide reasons, and summarize.[13] The process is illustrated in Figure 10.4.

It is not always necessary to complete every step of the process when you present an argument. Often the evidence is sufficiently clear and does not require additional reasons for supporting the claim. If your argument is very brief, a summary may not be necessary. However, you should be prepared to complete all the steps if group members want further justification for your arguments.

State the
Claim

The first step in the presentation of an argument is the clear statement of your claim. Chapter 9 identified three types of discussion questions—fact, value, and policy. Discussion questions help a group focus on its problem-solving

```
CLAIM  ──────▶  EVIDENCE  ──────▶  REASONS  ──────▶  SUMMARY
```

FIGURE 10.4   Procedure for Presenting Arguments

or decision-making goal. Claims for arguments can be divided into the same three categories. However, when arguing, group members rarely state their claims in the form of questions. A claim tells the group your position on a particular issue.

Arguments involving a **claim of fact** attempt to prove the existence of things, occurrence of events, classification of things or events, or cause of an event. For example, "Sex education in schools promotes teenage promiscuity" is a claim of fact. Whether this claim is true or not depends on further analysis of the data and warrant. **Claims of value** evaluate the quality or worth of things or suggest that certain values are more important than others. "My instructor is the best professor at the college" is a claim that places a value on someone. Arguments involving claims of value can be very difficult to resolve, because each group member brings individual opinions and beliefs to the discussion. **Claims of policy** are arguments that recommend a certain course of action. "Our company should develop guidelines for dealing with inquiries from the press and electronic media" is an example of a claim of policy.

Support the Claim with Evidence

The fact that a claim is stated does not mean it is true. For the group to be convinced, you must support your claim with evidence. In the Toulmin Model, this means supplying the group with the relevant data.

TOOLBOX 10.2   Using and Evaluating Evidence

Claims should be supported with strong and valid evidence. The most common types of evidence are facts, testimony, statistics, definitions, descriptions, and examples. The group must continuously evaluate the quality of the evidence used to support arguments. There are several general questions the group should ask. Is the evidence relevant? Is the source of the evidence credible? How recent is the evidence? Does the evidence contain all the facts? Is it consistent with other evidence? Are the statistics reliable? Is there enough evidence? **Chapter 12: Informed Groups** explains how to locate information and evaluate evidence.

Provide Reasons for the Claim

Sometimes it is not clear to others why a particular piece of evidence proves your claim. Reasons are needed to demonstrate the link between your evidence and your claim. In the Toulmin Model, this link is the warrant and the backing—statements that explain why the evidence is sufficient to prove the claim.

A prosecutor might argue that one of the reasons a jury should convict a murder suspect is that he lied about knowing the victim. At first, it may not be clear why evidence of lying is linked to being a murderer. The prosecutor might then provide the argument's warrant by stating that unlike guilty people, the innocent have nothing to hide. Evidence of lying may weaken the defendant's claim of innocence.

Summarize Your Argument

A good summary restates the original claim and summarizes the evidence supporting it. Be brief. Do not repeat all your evidence and reasons. When the presentation of the claim and evidence has been brief and clear, the summary can be omitted. However, lengthy and complicated arguments often need to be summarized to ensure that all members understand your argument.

Refuting Arguments

Wilbanks and Church define **refutation** as the "act of proving an argument either erroneous or false, or both."[14] Refutation is used to question, minimize, and deny the validity or strength of someone else's argument. It is important that group members be willing and able to refute claims that are unsupported or untrue. A group that is not willing to evaluate arguments risks the perils of groupthink. These six guidelines can help you refute another member's argument:

- Listen to the argument.
- State the claim you oppose.
- Overview your objections.
- Assess the evidence.
- Assess the reasoning.
- Summarize your refutation.

Listen to the Argument

First, listen for comprehension. You must fully understand an argument before you can effectively respond to it. Ask questions and take notes. Once you have comprehended the meaning of an argument, you can shift to critical listening. What type of claim is being made? Is evidence supplied to support the claim? How well do the data support the claim? Is the claim qualified in any way? Analyzing the argument as you listen will help you formulate a response.

*State the
Claim You
Oppose*
There may have been a number of arguments made by different group members. Don't try to respond to all of them. When you are ready, state the claim that you are opposing. Clearly stating the opposing claim gives you an opportunity to make sure that you understand the argument. You may think the claim was "employees are stealing supplies from the company." Instead, the claim was that "the company should identify ways to use supplies more efficiently." If you have misunderstood a claim, other group members can clarify their arguments for you.

*Overview Your
Objections*
Provide a brief overview of your objections or concerns. Letting the group know the general direction of your arguments is particularly important when your refutation will be lengthy or complicated, such as, "I don't believe we should raise funds for a carnival for three reasons: the high cost, the unpredictable weather, and the undesirable location." With a general idea of the reasons for your refutation, group members will be better prepared to listen to and understand your objections and concerns.

*Assess the
Evidence*
When refuting a claim you may be able to show that the evidence is faulty. One way is to present contradictory evidence. For example, if a group member contends that the college's tuition is high, you may present evidence from a survey showing that the college's tuition is one of the lowest in the state. You can also question the quality of the person's evidence. For example, an outdated statistic or a quotation by a discredited source can be reason enough to reject an arguer's evidence. Proving that the evidence is of poor quality does not mean the claim is untrue, but it does show that the claim has potential weaknesses.

*Assess the
Reasoning*
Assess reasoning by identifying fallacies. A **fallacy** is an argument based on false or invalid reasoning. It is not always necessary to identify the fallacy by name, particularly if group members are not familiar with the different types of fallacies. It is much more important to clearly explain why the reasoning in the argument is flawed. The following list describes some of the most common fallacies of argument:

- *Ad Hominem.* In Latin this phrase means "to the person." An *ad hominem* argument makes irrelevant attacks against a person's character rather than responding to the argument. Responding to a claim that women in the military should be able to serve in combat situations with "You're just saying that because you're a woman" attacks the person rather than the real argument.
- *Appeal to Authority.* Expert opinion is often used to support arguments. However, when the supposed expert has no relevant expertise on the

issues being discussed, the fallacy of appeal to authority occurs. The argument that "According to a talk show host, most men cheat on their wives" commits this fallacy. Unless the talk show host has expert credentials on issues of fidelity and marriage, the argument is vulnerable.

- *Appeal to Popularity.* An argument of this nature claims that an action is acceptable or excusable because many people are doing it. During the Los Angeles riots following the Rodney King trial, some people justified the looting of neighborhood stores by claiming that everyone else was doing it. Just because a lot of people engage in an action does not make it right. Instead, it may mean that a lot of people are wrong.
- *Appeal to Tradition.* Claiming that people should continue a certain course of action because they have always done so in the past is an appeal to tradition, as illustrated in the argument that "the group must meet on Monday afternoons because that is when the group has always met." Just because a course of action has been followed for a long period of time does not mean it is the superior choice.
- *Faulty Analogy.* Claiming that two things are similar when they differ on relevant characteristics is a faulty analogy. During Operation Desert Storm, many critics claimed that the United States was involving itself in another Vietnam. However, the argument was frequently refuted by pointing out the critical differences between these two encounters. Faulty analogies are often referred to as the comparison of "apples and oranges." Both are fruits, but beyond that they are very different.
- *Faulty Cause.* Claiming that a particular event is the cause of another event before ruling out other possible causes is a faulty cause fallacy. The claim that "Increases in tuition have caused enrollment to decline" may overlook other explanations, such as the possibility that a decline in enrollment can be attributed to fewer eligible high school graduates.
- *Hasty Generalization.* An argument flawed by a hasty generalization uses too few examples or experiences to support its conclusion. This fallacy argues that if it is true for some, it must be true for all. "A Volvo is an unreliable car, because I once owned one that was always breaking down" is a hasty generalization. The experience of a single car owner does not prove that all cars produced by that manufacturer are unreliable.

Summarize Your Refutation

The final step in refuting a group member's argument is to summarize your response. If your refutation has been lengthy or complex, it is helpful to restate the major points of your response. It is not necessary to review all your arguments in detail, because doing so wastes valuable group discussion time. If your refutation has been short and to the point, it may not be necessary to summarize your argument.

Fallacy	Description
Ad Hominem	Attacks the person rather than the argument made by that person.
Appeal to Authority	Relies on biased or unqualified expert opinion to support a claim.
Appeal to Popularity	Justifies an action because many others do the same thing or share the same opinion. "Everyone's doing it."
Appeal to Tradition	Resists changes to traditional behavior and opinions. "We have always done it this way."
Faulty Analogy	Compares two items that are not similar or comparable. "Comparing apples and oranges."
Faulty Cause	Claims that an effect is caused by something that has little or no relationship to the effect.
Hasty Generalization	Uses isolated or too few examples to draw a conclusion.

FIGURE 10.5   Fallacies of Argument

Ethical Arguments

Regardless of how well discussants present persuasive arguments, group members should strive to be ethical arguers. Rybacki and Rybacki have identified four ethical responsibilities of arguers: the research responsibility, common good responsibility, reasoning responsibility, and social code responsibility.[15]

The research responsibility expects group members to come to the discussion informed and prepared to discuss the issues. Information must be used honestly. To fulfill this responsibility, follow these guidelines:

- Do not distort information.
- Do not suppress important information.
- Never fabricate or make up information.
- Reveal the sources of your information so others can evaluate them.

The common good responsibility requires that ethical arguers look beyond their own needs and consider the circumstances of others. Members should be committed to achieving the group goal rather than merely winning an argument. The following two principles are important for preserving the common good responsibility:

- Consider the interests of those affected by the decision.
- Promote the group's goal as more important than winning an argument.

The reasoning responsibility requires members to avoid presenting faulty arguments. Understanding the structure of an argument, methods of building a persuasive argument, and ways to recognize fallacies will help you fulfill this ethical responsibility, as will following these rules:

- Do not misrepresent the views of others.
- Use sound reasoning supported by evidence.
- Avoid making arguments containing fallacies.

The final ethical consideration is the social code responsibility. This requires that group members promote an open and supportive climate for argumentation. Follow these guidelines for fulfilling the social code responsibility:

- Treat other group members as equals.
- Give everyone the opportunity to respond to an argument, including those who disagree.
- Do not insult or attack the character of a group member.
- Give the group an opportunity to review the evidence.
- Respect established group norms.

Adapting to Argumentative Styles

Research suggests that men and women argue differently. There also are argumentative differences among people from different cultures. These differences appear to be a function of how we learn to argue and what values we believe are important. Effective group members recognize and try to adapt to others' ways of arguing.

Gender Differences

According to sociolinguist Deborah Tannen, men and women approach argument differently.[16] Men tend to be competitive arguers; women, on the other hand, are more likely to seek consensus within a group. Men tend to be more direct, open, and logical in their argumentation. Women are often indirect and are both logical and emotional. However, women are just as likely as men to support their arguments with evidence.[17] Men tend to view issues as only two-sided, or pro and con. Women are more likely to search out many different perspectives on a subject.

Of course, many women enjoy a direct and competitive debate. And when women make up the majority of group members, they may feel more comfortable voicing their objections.[18] While the research provides generalizations, there are always exceptions. At the same time, it is useful to recognize that men and women may come to a group with different argumentation styles. Groups should create an environment in which everybody feels comfortable arguing.

Cultural Differences

Approaches to argumentation are often influenced by members' cultures. Cultural perspectives can influence the level of argumentativeness, the values that form the basis for arguments, and approaches to evidence and reasoning. Some cultures are not as argumentative as others. For example, Asians and Asian Americans are generally less comfortable engaging in an argument. Asians may go to great lengths to preserve the harmony of a group, preferring to avoid an argument because it could jeopardize that harmony.[19] It is important, however, not to overgeneralize about the characteristics of any culture. There are significant differences among Asian cultures. For instance, in some Indian subcultures, argumentation is encouraged.

Culture also may dictate who should argue. Many cultures give enormous respect to the elderly. In these cultures, a young person arguing with someone older is viewed as disrespectful. Among several American Indian and African cultures, the elderly are viewed as wiser and more knowledgeable. The young are taught that the views of the elderly are to be accepted rather than challenged.

One of the most significant cultural differences in argumentation is the way people use evidence to support a claim. According to Lustig and Koester,

> There are no universally accepted standards about what constitutes evidence. . . . The European American culture prefers physical evidence and eyewitness testimony, and members of that culture see "facts" as the supreme kind of evidence . . . [whereas] in certain portions of Chinese culture . . . physical evidence is discounted because no connection is seen between . . . the physical world and human actions. . . . In certain African cultures, the words of a witness would be discounted and even totally disregarded because the people believe that if you speak up about seeing something, you must have a particular agenda in mind; in other words, no one is regarded as objective.[20]

Given such different perspectives about the value of evidence, the data used to support a claim in one culture may seem irrational in another.

Balanced Argumentation

Effective arguers balance their own needs to win an argument with the needs of the group to solve a problem or make a decision. Argumentation in groups should be cooperative rather than competitive.

Josina Makau defines **cooperative argumentation** as "a process of reasoned interaction on a controversial topic intended to help participants and audiences make the best assessments or decisions in any given situation."[21] Cooperative arguers focus on the group's shared goal of solving a problem or making the best decision. They recognize that the group is better informed through an open exchange of ideas. Although cooperative arguers

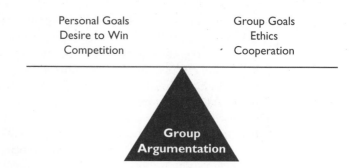

Personal Goals	Group Goals
Desire to Win	Ethics
Competition	Cooperation

FIGURE 10.6 Group Argumentation

want to win arguments, they do not want to do so at the expense of the group goal.

Certainly you should present your best arguments in the hopes of persuading others. However, keep in mind that winning is not as important as helping the group make the best possible decision, which may not happen to include your ideas. Effective arguers are willing to share their views at the risk of losing the argument. Cooperative group members adhere to ethical guidelines and recognize that the arguments of all group members are potentially valid and should receive a fair hearing. "Balancing the tension between the need to agree and disagree, to challenge and reach convergence, to ask questions and make statements, is the central paradox of effective argument in decision-making groups."[22]

Summary Study Guide

- An argument is a conclusion supported by evidence or reasons for accepting it. Argumentation is the way group members advance their own positions and influence other members.
- Argumentation promotes understanding and evaluation of issues and different perspectives, enhances critical thinking and persuasion, helps avoid groupthink, and aids decision making.
- Argumentativeness is a constructive trait describing a person's willingness to engage in argumentation.
- The Toulmin Model represents the structure of an argument and a way to diagram and evaluate arguments. The components of the model are claim, data, warrant, backing, rebuttal, and qualifier.
- When presenting an argument, state the claim, prove it with evidence, provide reasons, and summarize your main points.

- Claims for arguments are divided into three categories—fact, value, and policy.
- Refutation is the act of proving another's argument erroneous or false. When refuting arguments, follow these five steps: listen, state the claim, overview your objections, refute the evidence and/or reasoning, and summarize your refutation.
- A fallacy is an error in reasoning. Some of the most common fallacies are: *ad hominem*, appeal to authority, appeal to popularity, appeal to tradition, faulty analogy, faulty cause, and hasty generalization.
- Group members must be ethical arguers. The ethical considerations of arguers include the research responsibility, reasoning responsibility, common good responsibility, and social code responsibility.
- The influence of gender and culture accounts for some differences in argumentative styles. Men tend to be more competitive, whereas women tend to be more cooperative. Culture will influence the level of argumentativeness, and approaches to evidence and reasoning.

Groupwork *Divide and Debate*

GOAL   To practice argumentation skills in a group setting.

PARTICIPANTS   Groups of 5–7 members.

PROCEDURE

1. Approximately half the members of each group (the pro side) should be assigned to present arguments in support of the following claim: "It is better to work in groups than it is to work individually." The other half of the group (the con side) is to oppose the claim.
2. Group members may consult the textbook for evidence in support of their arguments.
3. Groups are to adhere to the following format for discussion:

Pro Side	4 minutes
Con Side	4 minutes
Pro Side	2 minutes
Con Side	4 minutes
Pro Side	2 minutes

4. Remember to follow the guidelines discussed in this chapter for presenting and refuting arguments.
5. All members of the group should be encouraged to participate.

A S S E S S M E N T

Argumentativeness Scale

Directions   This questionnaire contains statements about arguing controversial issues. Indicate how often each statement is true for you personally by placing the appropriate number in the blank. Use the following ratings to respond to each statement:

1 = almost never true
2 = rarely true
3 = occasionally true
4 = often true
5 = almost always true

_____   1. While in an argument I worry that the person I am arguing with will form a negative impression of me.

_____   2. Arguing over controversial issues improves my intelligence.

_____   3. I enjoy avoiding arguments.

_____   4. I am energetic and enthusiastic when I argue.

_____   5. Once I finish an argument, I promise myself that I will not get into another.

_____   6. Arguing with a person creates more problems for me than it solves.

_____   7. I have a pleasant, good feeling when I win a point in an argument.

_____   8. When I finish arguing with someone, I feel nervous and upset.

_____   9. I enjoy a good argument over a controversial issue.

_____ 10. I get an unpleasant feeling when I realize I am about to get into an argument.

Recommended Readings

Infante, D. A. (1988). *Arguing constructively.* Prospect Heights, IL: Waveland.
Makau, J. M. (1990). *Reasoning and communication: Thinking critically about arguments.* Belmont, CA: Wadsworth.
Toulmin, S. (1958). *The uses of argument.* London: Cambridge University.

Notes

1. Bui, T. X., Bodart, F. & Ma, P. (1997/1998 Winter). "ARBAS: A formal language to support argumentation in network-based organizations." *Journal of Management Information Systems, 14,* p. 223.

_____ 11. I enjoy defending my point of view on an issue.

_____ 12. I am happy when I keep an argument from happening.

_____ 13. I do not like to miss the opportunity to argue a controversial issue.

_____ 14. I prefer being with people who rarely disagree with me.

_____ 15. I consider an argument an exciting intellectual exchange.

_____ 16. I find myself unable to think of effective points during an argument.

_____ 17. I feel refreshed after an argument on a controversial issue.

_____ 18. I have the ability to do well in an argument.

_____ 19. I try to avoid getting into arguments.

_____ 20. I feel excitement when I expect that a conversation I am in is leading to an argument.

Scoring Instructions

1. Add your scores on items: 2, 4, 7, 9, 11, 13, 15, 17, 18, 20.
2. Add 60 to the sum obtained in step 1.
3. Add your scores on items: 1, 3, 5, 6, 8, 10, 12, 14, 16, 19.
4. To compute your argumentativeness score, subtract the total obtained in step 3 from the total obtained in step 2.

Interpretation

73–100 = High in Argumentativeness
56–72 = Moderate in Argumentativeness
20–55 = Low in Argumentativeness

Argumentativeness Scale reprinted with permission from the authors, Dominic A. Infante and Andrew Rancer.

2. Brashers, D. E., Adkins, M., & Meyers, R. E. (1994). Argumentation and computer-mediated group decision making. In L. R. Frey (Ed.), _Group communication in context: Studies of natural groups_. Hillsdale, NJ: Lawrence Erlbaum, p. 264.

3. Kuhn, D. (1992). Thinking as argument. _Harvard Educational Review, 62,_ pp. 156–157.

4. Govier, T. (1992). _A practical study of argument_ (3rd ed.). Belmont, CA: Wadsworth, p. 3.

5. Makau, J. M. (1990). _Reasoning and communication: Thinking critically about arguments_. Belmont, CA: Wadsworth, p. 54.

6. Infante, D. A. (1988). *Arguing constructively.* Prospect Heights, IL: Waveland, p. 9.

7. Schultz, B. (1982). Argumentativeness: Its effect in group decision-making and its role in leadership perception. *Communication Quarterly, 30,* p. 369.

8. See Ketrow, S. M. & Schultz, B. (1993). Using argumentative functions to improve decision quality in the small group. In R. E. McKerrow (Ed.), *Argument and the postmodern challenge: Proceedings of the eighth SCA/AFA conference on argumentation.* Annandale, VA: Speech Communication Association, pp. 218–225.

9. Infante, D. A. & Rancer, A. S. (1982). A conceptualization and measure of argumentativeness. *Journal of Personality Assessment, 46,* pp. 72–80.

10. Kazoleas, D. & Kay, B. (November, 1994). *Are argumentatives really more argumentative?: The behavior of argumentatives in group deliberations over controversial issues.* Paper presented at the meeting of the Speech Communication Association, New Orleans, LA.

11. Sanders, J. A., Wiseman, R. L., & Gass, R. H. (1994). Does teaching argumentation facilitate critical thinking? *Communication Reports, 7,* p. 28.

12. Toulmin, S. (1958). *The uses of argument.* London: Cambridge University.

13. Infante, p. 57.

14. Wilbanks, C. & Church, R. T. (1991). *Values and policies in controversy: An introduction to argumentation and debate* (2nd ed.). Dubuque, IA: Kendall/Hunt, p. 159.

15. Rybacki, K. C. & Rybacki, D. J. (1991). *Advocacy and opposition: An introduction to argumentation* (2nd ed.). Englewood Cliffs, NJ: Prentice Hall.

16. Tannen, D. (1990). *You just don't understand: Women and men in conversation.* New York: William Morrow.

17. Meyers, R. A., Brashers, D. E., Winston, L. & Grob, L. (1997). "Sex differences and group argument: A theoretical framework and empirical investigation." *Communication Studies, 48,* p. 33.

18. Meyers, *et al.,* p. 35.

19. Porter, R. E. & Samovar, L. A. (1996). Communication in the multicultural group. In R. S. Cathcart, L. A. Samovar, & L. D. Henman (Eds.), *Small group communication: Theory and practice* (7th ed.). Madison, WI: Brown & Benchmark, p. 311.

20. Lustig, M. W. & Koester, J. (1996). *Intercultural competence: Interpersonal communication across cultures* (2nd ed.). New York: HarperCollins, p. 223.

21. Makau, p. 49.

22. Meyers, *et al.,* p. 35.

Making Presentations in Groups

Presentations in Groups

The spontaneous, give-and-take nature of a group discussion enhances a group's ability to share information and solve problems. There are, however, circumstances in which groups may set aside time for less spontaneous and more structured forms of communication. Individual members or a selected spokesperson may be asked or required to make an oral presentation. The following three scenarios illustrate how such presentations become part of the group process:

- *Debating the Tuition Proposal.* The student government association at Fallingstar State College has been asked to discuss the college's proposal to increase tuition by 10 percent. In order to ensure that everyone has an equal chance to speak at the meeting, student representatives are limited to three-minute statements.
- *Opposing the Tuition Proposal.* The student government association selects a spokesperson to make an oral presentation opposing the proposed tuition increase at the monthly meeting of Fallingstar State College's board of trustees.
- *Appealing for State Funding.* The president of Fallingstar State College asks the student government association's spokesperson to be part of a group presentation to the state legislature's appropriations committee in which a team of administrators, faculty, staff, and students will be given forty-five minutes to present a request for increased state funding.

During the course of any group discussion or meeting, an oral presentation may be required by one or more group members. In other situations, a group member may be asked to make an oral presentation to an outside group or audience. In such situations, the reputation and quality of a group may be judged by how well its members succeed as speakers. As Leech put it, re-

---

TOOLBOX 11.1 Fear of Speaking

The number one fear of most North Americans is the fear of speaking in front of groups. Regardless of the setting of an oral presentation, there are several guidelines that can help a nervous speaker manage and survive the effects of "stage fright." Included among these guidelines are (1) realize you are not alone; (2) read and talk about it; (3) be well prepared; and (4) learn communication skills. In this chapter, we focus on how to make sure you are well prepared as well as how to practice and deliver an effective oral presentation. **Chapter 5: Confidence in Groups** discusses additional ways of coping with communication apprehension.

gardless of the setting, "a presentation is your opportunity to shine or to blow it. I have seen careers take quantum jumps as a result of good performance in presentations and receive severe setbacks for poor communication."[1] Whether it is within a group, on behalf of a group, or by an entire group, an **oral presentation** occurs when a member is given the opportunity to speak, uninterrupted, to a group of people.

This chapter offers specific guidelines that can help you prepare and present a successful oral presentation that is adapted to the needs and characteristics of a group and its goals. These guidelines also can be used in the event that you or your group has to make a presentation to an outside audience.

Oral Presentation Guidelines

Most experienced speakers do not follow a strict set of rules. Instead, they use a set of guidelines to direct them through critical decision-making steps. Based on a model developed by Engleberg, the guidelines shown in Figure 11.1 represent essential decision-making points and questions that should be addressed when developing an oral presentation.[2]

Purpose The first and most important step in developing a successful oral presentation is identifying your purpose. Purpose is not the same as topic. Purpose determines what you want your listeners to know, think, believe, or do as a result of your presentation. For example, the discussion topic for the student government association at Fallingstar State College is the proposed tuition increase. A student speaker's purpose, however, may be to support or oppose

Order	Guideline	Key Question
1	Purpose	What is the goal of your oral presentation?
2	People	How will you adapt to the members of your audience?
3	Place	How will you adapt to the occasion and setting of your presentation?
4	Preparation	What ideas and information should you include?
5	Planning	How will you organize and support your ideas?
6	Personal Credibility	How can you enhance your believability and perceived competence?
7	Performance	How should you practice and deliver your presentation?

FIGURE 11.1 Oral Presentation Guidelines

the increase. In a group discussion, the general topic of an oral presentation is usually predetermined by the group and its agenda. Thus, when a student rises to speak for or against higher tuition, everyone is well aware of the topic but may be unable to predict the speaker's position or arguments. Having a clear purpose does not necessarily mean you will achieve it. Without a purpose, though, little can be accomplished and much can be lost.

People

If the first and most important guideline in developing an oral presentation is identifying your purpose, the next most important is to analyze and adapt to your listeners—the people who are members of your group or an outside audience. This process begins by finding answers to these two questions: What are their characteristics? What are their opinions?

Characteristics. Two characteristics to consider when analyzing a group of listeners are demographic traits and individual attributes. **Demographic traits** include age, gender, race, ethnicity, religion, and marital status. If you have been working in a group for a long time, it will be easy to catalog the demographic traits of its members. Before a new or large audience, the task is more difficult. Take a good look at your listeners to note visible demographic traits such as age, gender, and race. At the same time, assume that there is more diversity than similarity among audience members.

Within a group, **individual attributes** take into account the distinctive features of group members such as job title and status, special interests, relationships with other members, and length of group membership. Demographic traits and individual attributes can affect how group members react to you and your message. For example, students who support themselves on limited incomes may oppose a tuition increase more strongly than students whose parents pay their tuition and can afford the increase.

EFFECTIVE speakers adapt their presentations to the characteristics of audience members. What might a speaker consider when adapting to this audience? (Bob Daemmrich/The Image Works)

Opinions. There can be as many opinions in an audience as there are members. Some members will agree with you before you begin your oral presentation, whereas others will disagree no matter what you say. Some listeners will have no opinion about an issue and be quite willing to accept a reasonable point of view or proposal. Try to predict who or how many listeners will agree, disagree, or be undecided.

If most of your listeners agree with you, are undecided, or have no opinion, your oral presentation should focus on introducing new information or summarizing the most important ideas and arguments. When people share the same opinions and goals, an oral presentation should update listeners who are in need of information and motivate them to work as a united team. For example, if student government members are universally opposed to a tuition increase, a speaker could focus on motivating that audience to take political action.

If audience members disagree with you, make sure that you have set realistic goals. Asking students to storm the president's office may get the administration's attention but may be too radical for most students to support. A second strategy is to work at getting audience members to listen to you. You can't do that by telling them that you're right and they're wrong. You can't change their minds if they won't listen. Instead, try to find **common ground.** Find a belief or value that you share with those who disagree. Emphasizing the ideas, feelings, history, and hopes that people share can help you overcome resistance. For example, if a student speaker tells the board of trustees that the student government wants to help them find a solution to the financial crisis, the board may be more willing to listen to student concerns about the proposed tuition increase. Finally, when you address a controversial issue, make sure you support your arguments with fair and reasonable evidence. If your arguments and evidence are weak, your opponents are likely to use those weaknesses against you.

Place   Deciding how to adapt to the occasion and setting of an oral presentation requires more than taking a quick look at the seating arrangements for a meeting. Ask questions about *where* and *when* you will be speaking.

Where?   Where will you deliver your oral presentation—in a large conference room, an auditorium, a classroom? What are the seating arrangements? Are there any distracting sights or sounds? Can the lighting be changed? Will

---

TOOLBOX 11.2   Influencing Group Members

Understanding how to develop and defend an argument is a valuable skill when presenting an oral presentation or answering group questions. By clearly stating the claim of your argument, supporting your claim with evidence, providing valid reasons for your position, and summarizing your conclusion, you are more likely to have your ideas and opinions taken seriously by others. **Chapter 10: Argumentation in Groups** examines the role and uses of argumentation as a means of achieving group and individual goals.

> **TOOLBOX 11.3** Information as Supporting Material
>
> Different types of information (facts, testimony, statistics, definitions, descriptions, and examples) can be used as supporting material for an oral presentation. In choosing a specific type of information as supporting material, make sure that it is appropriate for your audience and advances your purpose. For example, whereas facts and statistics can be useful to compare tuition rates at different colleges, testimony and examples of the personal hardships that students will face if tuition is increased can be highly persuasive. **Chapter 12: Informed Groups** focuses on how to search for and select information that can be used as supporting material for an oral presentation.

you need a microphone? Will special equipment be needed for presentation aids? Once you have answered such questions, the next step is figuring out how to adapt to where you will be delivering your presentation. For example, a request for a microphone would be in order if a student government spokesperson learns that several hundred students plan to attend the board of trustees meeting.

When?   Will you be speaking in the morning or afternoon? Are you scheduled to speak for five minutes, twenty minutes, an hour? What comes before or after your presentation—other presentations, lunch, a question-and-answer session? The answers to questions about timing may require you to make major adjustments to your oral presentation. If you are given a time limit for your presentation, the limit should be respected. Whether you are scheduled for five minutes or one hour, never add more than 5 percent to your allotted time. Even better, aim for 5 percent less. Most people lose patience with someone who speaks too long.

Preparation   As soon as you know you have to make an oral presentation, start collecting ideas and information. Gathering materials can be as simple as spending a few hours thinking about the purpose of your presentation or as complicated and time-consuming as spending days doing research on the Internet and in the library. Regardless of the topic or your purpose, try to research multiple sources and include more than one type of information in your oral presentation.

Planning   Planning a speech requires organizing your ideas and supporting material in a way that will help you achieve your purpose. Ask yourself whether there is a natural structure or framework for your message. What common ideas have appeared in most of your materials? What information seems most interesting, important, and relevant to the purpose of your presentation?

Organizational Pattern	*Example*
Reason Giving	Three reasons why we should increase the dues are . . .
Time Arrangement	The college's hiring steps must be complied with in the following order . . .
Space Arrangement	The following membership increases occurred in the east, south, west, and central regions . . .
Problem–Solution	This research method avoids the problems we encountered last time . . .
Causes and Effects	Here's what could happen if we fail to increase our dues . . .
Stories and Examples	I've contacted four community associations in this county and here's what I found . . .
Compare–Contrast	Let's take a look at the two research methods we considered . . .

FIGURE 11.2 Organizational Pattern

Organizational Patterns.   Fortunately, there are many patterns of organization that can help you put your ideas and information in order. Figure 11.2 summarizes some common patterns.

Regardless of whether you choose one of the patterns shown in the figure or invent a different organizational structure better suited to your needs, you should always focus on your purpose. Consider whether a pattern lends itself to achieving the purpose of your oral presentation. If it does, you can move on to connecting your supporting material to the organizational pattern you have chosen.

Outlining Your Presentation.   Outlines for an oral presentation start with a few basic building blocks. A simple model outline can be used to organize almost any kind of oral presentation.

I. Introduction
II. Central Idea or Purpose
   (Preview of Main Points)
III. Body of Presentation
   A. Main Point #1
      1. Supporting Material
      2. Supporting Material
   B. Main Point #2
      1. Supporting Material
      2. Supporting Material
   C. Main Point #3
      1. Supporting Material
      2. Supporting Material
IV. Conclusion

Naturally, every outline will differ depending on the number of main points and the amount and type of supporting material you use. Once you have outlined your presentation, the major sections should be filled in with more specific ideas and supporting material.

The introduction of an oral presentation should be used to gain audience attention and interest. An effective beginning should direct the audience's attention toward you and your message. An interesting example, statistic, quotation, or story at the beginning of a presentation can "warm up" your audience and prepare them for your message.

The "central idea or purpose" section of an oral presentation lets you explain your basic purpose and provides an opportunity to preview the main points of your presentation. This section should be brief, no more than a few sentences. It just reveals your purpose and, in some cases, the organizational plan you will use in the body of the presentation.

The heart of your oral presentation is the "body" section. Here you add your supporting material to each main point. No matter how many main points there are, each should be justified or backed up with at least one type of supporting material. If you can use several different types, your presentation will be more interesting and impressive.

The end of a presentation should have a strong and well-planned conclusion. An effective conclusion can help listeners remember the most important parts of your message. A quick summary, a brief story, a memorable quotation, or a challenge to the group can leave a strong final impression.

Figure 11.3 represents the organizational structure and notes that could be used for a presentation by a student spokesperson to Fallingstar State College's board of trustees.

Personal Credibility

In an oral presentation, your personal credibility depends on how well the audience can identify with you and your message. No matter how much you know about the subject or how sincere you are about your purpose, it is your audience's opinion that determines whether you are perceived as qualified and believable. Hart, Friedrich, and Brooks define a speaker's **personal credibility** as "an audience's perceptions of the speaker (independent of the speaker's intent or purpose) which vary over time and lead the audience to accept or reject the attitude, belief, and/or action the speaker proposes."[3] This guideline may sound simple—improve your credibility and the audience will believe you—but it depends on many factors. Two important factors that have been isolated by researchers are competence and character.

Competence describes whether you know what you are talking about and can effectively communicate that content to your audience.[4] If you are not a recognized expert on a subject, you must demonstrate that you are well prepared. There is nothing wrong with letting your group or audience members know how much time and effort you have put into researching the topic or with sharing your surprise at discovering new ideas and information. In

---

SAMPLE PRESENTATION OUTLINE

Hold the Line on Tuition

I.   Introduction

Story: Student who had to choose between buying shoes for her children and paying tuition for her nursing courses.

II. Central Idea or Purpose

Because a tuition increase will have a devastating effect on many students, we ask you to search for other ways to manage the college's financial crisis.

III. Body of Presentation

   A. Another tuition increase will prevent students from continuing or completing their college education on schedule.

       1. More students are becoming part-time rather than full-time students. (College statistics)

       2. Students are taking longer to complete their college degrees. (College statistics)

       3. Students are sacrificing important needs to pay their tuition bills.
           (Quotations and examples from college newspaper)

   B. There are better ways to manage the college's financial crisis.

       1. Consolidate areas and reduce the number of administrators and support staff.
           (Comparison college of same size that has less staff)

       2. Seek more state and grant funding.
           (Statistics from national publication comparing funding levels and grants at similar types of colleges)

       3. Re-evaluate cost and need for activities and services such as athletic teams, the off-campus homecoming and scholarship balls, intersession courses, and full staffing during summer sessions. (Examples)

IV. Conclusion
     Money is a terrible thing to waste when students' hearts and minds are at stake. Let's work together to guarantee that all of our students become proud and grateful alumni.

FIGURE 11.3   Sample Presentation Outline

both cases, you would be demonstrating that you have worked hard to become a qualified and competent speaker.

Character raises questions about your goodwill and honesty. Are you trustworthy and sincere? Do you put the group's goal above your own? Sprague and Stuart ask a third question: "Do you make a special effort to be fair in presenting evidence, acknowledging limitations of your data and opinions, and conceding those parts of your opponent's case that have validity?"[5] If audiences and group members don't trust you, it won't matter what you say.

Performance

By the time you start asking questions about delivery, you should know what you want to say and have given some thought to how you want to say it. Zarefsky writes that "*how* you say something affects *what* is really being said, and it certainly affects what is heard and understood. Good delivery will help the audience to listen, understand, remember, and act on the speech."[6]

Forms of Delivery. In many group and public audience settings, you will be asked to speak **impromptu**—a form of delivery without advance preparation or practice. For example, a board of trustees member may ask a student spokesperson a question after an oral presentation. The student must respond impromptu. Being well informed and anticipating such requests is the best way to be prepared for impromptu speaking.

When you do have advance notice, you will be more effective if you speak extemporaneously. In **extemporaneous** speaking, you have time to prepare but do not write out and read your presentation word for word. Instead you should use an outline of key words or a brief set of notes for guidance. Try to avoid reading your presentation. Even though it may be well written and well read, such delivery is too formal for many settings. Moreover, reading from a script prevents you from observing listener reactions and modifying your presentation as a result of those reactions.

Vocal and Physical Delivery. The key to a successful performance is practice. Waiting until you begin your presentation is much too late to make delivery decisions. Moreover, the only way to accurately predict the length of your presentation is to practice out loud and time it. The place to work on how you sound and look is during rehearsal sessions.

Vocal characteristics such as volume, rate, pitch, articulation, and pronunciation can be controlled and practiced. Rehearse your presentation in a voice loud enough to be heard but without shouting. Even in a small group setting, an oral presentation requires a bit more volume than you would use in a normal conversation. It is also advisable to monitor the rate at which you speak. Many listeners have difficulty following someone who speaks at a rate that exceeds 180 words per minute. The most tolerable and useful all-purpose rate is 140–180 words per minute.[7]

Sometimes speakers are difficult to understand because their articulation is not clear. Poor articulation is often described as sloppy speech or mumbling. Generally, it helps to speak a little slower and a little louder, and to open your mouth a little wider than usual. Similar problems can occur when words are mispronounced. Because it can be embarrassing to mispronounce a word or a person's name, look up the words in a dictionary or ask someone how to pronounce them correctly.

The single most important physical characteristic in an oral presentation is eye contact. Look directly at the individual members of your audience, eye-to-eye. Holcombe and Stein contend that even before a large audience "the only kind of eye contact that successfully establishes the feeling of connection with members of the audience is a reasonably long, in-focus look at specific individuals."[8]

There is more to body movement than thinking about how you sit in a chair or stand before a group. Your gestures, appearance, and actions can add to or detract from your presentation. If you are well prepared and have practiced, your gestures and movements should be natural. At the same time, try to avoid distracting gestures such as pushing up eyeglasses, tapping the table with a pencil, and pulling on a strand of hair. Such annoying movements can draw attention away from the content of your presentation.

Presentation Aids.   **Presentation aids** are supplementary audio and/or visual materials that help an audience understand and remember what is said in a discussion or oral presentation. Effective presentation aids can make a dull topic interesting, a complex idea understandable, and a long presentation endurable. In fact, "for many people, well-designed visuals are the hallmark of a professional presentation."[9] Studies sponsored by the 3M corporation found that group "presenters who use visual aids are perceived as better prepared, more professional, more highly credible, and more interesting than those who do not."[10] At first, these findings may be difficult to believe. Can something as simple as an overhead transparency make that much difference? The answer is yes.

Presentation aids can take many forms: handouts, posters, flip charts, overhead transparencies, computer-generated slides, and videos. The following list of dos and don'ts can help you avoid some of the common pitfalls that speakers encounter when using presentation aids.

- *Explain the Point.* A presentation aid does not speak for itself. You may need to explain why you have chosen it and what it means.
- *Wait Until It's Time.* Prepare listeners for a presentation aid so they will want to see it. Give them enough time to look at it so that they don't mind turning their attention back to you.
- *Don't Talk to Your Aid.* You control the presentation aid; it shouldn't control you. Talk directly to the people in your audience, not to the poster, flip chart, or slide.

- *Be Prepared to Do Without.* Presentation aids can be lost or damaged; equipment can malfunction. Have a backup plan. Be prepared to make your presentation without your aids.

Above and beyond these dos and don'ts, there is one more piece of advice that should not be ignored—practice, practice, practice. Not only can practice improve your overall performance, it can alert you to problems with your presentation aids. For example, we once watched a consultant put almost everything in her talk on transparencies. As soon as she projected something onto the screen, she would turn around and point out the numbers that she thought were important. Unfortunately she stood right between the screen and the projector so that most of the information was projected onto her back. If she had practiced in front of others before making the presentation, the problem could have been avoided.

Technology and Presentation Aids

Only a dozen years ago, a hand-drawn poster would have been an acceptable presentation aid in most situations. This is no longer the case. The availability of presentation software has increased audience expectations and made it possible for speakers to create more professional-looking presentation aids. You are probably familiar with some presentation software. Among the more popular products are Microsoft PowerPoint, Adobe Persuasion, Correll's Presentation, and Astound's Astound! **Presentation software** is used to create slides that can be displayed on an overhead projector, a computer monitor, or directly from a computer onto a screen. Most presentation software packages also contain features for printing a speaker's notes and handouts.

The first question you should ask yourself is whether you even need a slide to make a particular point. Sometimes a message can be communicated more effectively through words alone. As the use of presentation software has become more popular, many listeners complain that even the simplest presentations have become dull displays of unnecessary slides that waste everyone's time. Although we cannot provide comprehensive instruction on how to use presentation software, we can urge you to follow some basic design principles regardless of the software you use. Figure 11.4 provides five guidelines for designing computer-based presentation aids.

Restraint Presentation software offers such a dazzling array of graphics, fonts, colors, and other visual elements that the first inclination is to use them all. Resist the

Presentation Software Design Guidelines

| Exercise restraint | Choose readable typefaces | Use appropriate templates and graphics | Don't overuse multimedia effects | Avoid copyright violations |

FIGURE 11.4   Presentation Software Design Guidelines

temptation. More often than not, a simple slide will be much more effective than a complex one.

We offer two recommendations that can help you decide how much is "just right" for a presentation using computer-generated slides: (1) Make only one point on each slide and (2) Follow the 6-by-6 rule. Each slide should make only one point, and the title of the slide should state that point. Everything else on the slide should support the main point. It takes less time to present two well-structured slides than to load up one slide with a muddled message.[11] In addition, aim for no more than six lines of text with six words per line. This rule of thumb allows your slide to contain the main heading and several bullet points below without bloating into information overload.[12] These recommendations also make excellent guidelines for other types of presentation aids, including hand-drawn posters and flip charts.

Please remember that an aid is only an aid; slides are not a presentation. They are not meant to be a script, read word for word. Ringle recommends balancing "tersity" and diversity. By tersity, he means making slides compact and concise while using them to add variety and interest. Finding this balance depends on understanding the value of presentation aids and the pitfalls to avoid when adding technical "sizzle" to your presentation.[13]

Type   After deciding what you want to put on a slide, you will need to select a typeface or font. "Users of presentation software have instant access to a veritable candy store of typefaces with tempting names like Arial, Calypso, Gold Rush, and Circus."[14] Again, exercise restraint. Too many typefaces looks amateurish. As a general rule, never use more than two different fonts on a single slide. As much as you may be tempted, avoid the fancy, but difficult-to-read, fonts. You are better off choosing common typefaces such as Helvetica, Arial, or Times Roman.

The size of type is as important as the selection of font. The best way to determine if your type is large enough is to prepare a few sample slides and project them in the room where your group will be meeting. Generally, you should try to avoid type that is smaller than 24 points. If you find that you have more text then will fit on a slide, don't reduce the size of the type. This is an indication that you are trying to put too much text on one slide. Textual slides should contain just a few key words. Reducing the size of the type to include more text not only makes for a poor visual aid, but also makes it less legible.

Templates and Graphics

On a slide-by-slide basis, use a consistent style and background. From within your presentation software, you can select any of several dozen backgrounds or templates. Here too, it is important to exercise restraint. In most cases, it is better to choose a modest background that will spruce up your slide but not compete with your words, charts, or graphics.

In choosing graphics, the first question you must ask yourself is whether group members really need to see the picture you want to use. If, for example, you are making a presentation about a new medical device, it may be useful to show the actual device or a picture of the device. On the other hand, including a picture of a doctor during the presentation would probably not be useful. A picture of a doctor does not help explain the medical device.

Artwork that doesn't have a specific purpose can get in the way of your presentation. Presentation software often comes with numerous clip-art images that you may be tempted to use. Resist the temptation to use graphic elements just because you can. More often than not, clip-art graphics get in the way of messages when the graphic is not the reason for displaying the slide.

Multimedia

Today's **multimedia** technology allows you to use words, charts, graphics, sounds, and animation in a single presentation. It is possible to create presentation aids so dazzling that group members remember more about the slides than about you or your message. While there are times when animation or sound may enhance understanding, these multimedia components are frequently no more than window dressing. They can be extraneous items that get in the way of the message rather than increase understanding. The last thing you want is for your group to leave a presentation wondering how you got the Tyrannosaurus rex to eat the pie chart instead of discussing the data that was represented in the pie chart.

Multimedia is often misused by presenters. Some multimedia effects are so overused that they are becoming cliches. Beginning a presentation with the theme from *Rocky* or *2001: A Space Odyssey* is not only unnecessary, but tired. If you decide to include multimedia effects in a presentation, you should be able to articulate a reason for doing so other than "it's neat." Ringle warns that the fine line between "adding enough to spice up the presentation" and "overpowering" your listeners is often trampled by enthusiastic presenters.[15] Multimedia presentations may be fun to put together, but they must be well designed, well rehearsed, and well presented.

Ethical Considerations

Technology not only makes it easier to create professional-looking presentation aids, it also makes it easier to appropriate the creative work of others into a presentation. When the creation of visual or audio images is a person's livelihood, the uncompensated use of such images raises ethical questions. Such unfair use may even be a violation of federal copyright laws. A discussion of whether a particular use of an image is illegal is far beyond the scope of this book; however, you should be aware of the legal and ethical implications of using unlicensed images.

A whole industry has developed to provide clip-art and clip-audio to computer users. A user who purchases these packages has the right to make copies of the images and use them in presentations. Likewise, the visual and audio images that are included with presentation software can be used in your presentations. On the other hand, if you create a computer image by scanning the image from another source or you obtain the image from the Internet, your conscience and your knowledge of copyright law must act as your guide.

Group Presentations

So far, this chapter has emphasized the ways in which oral presentation guidelines can be applied to small groups and to external audiences. If, however, you are asked to make a presentation as a member of a public group or as part of a team presentation, there are special factors to consider.

Public Group Presentations

Chapter 1 describes four different types of public groups: panel discussions, symposia, forums, and governance groups. In all these settings, group members speak to a public audience.

In addition to following the oral presentation guidelines described in this chapter, you should go one step further. Make sure you have considered the unique requirements of a presentation by a public group for a public audience. As a member of a public group, you have a responsibility to yourself, your group, and your audience.

When you are participating in a public group, remember that you are "on stage" all the time—even when you are not speaking. If you look bored while another member is speaking, the audience may wonder whether that speaker has anything worth sharing. Holcombe and Stein maintain that during a public group presentation, an attentive audience will notice other group members' "gestures, facial expression, and posture. They deliberately look for unspoken disagreements or conflicts."[16] For example, if a member of Fallingstar State College's board of trustees rolls his eyes every time another board member speaks in support of student concerns, the audience will receive a mixed message about the board's commitment to serving student needs. Try to look at and support the other members of your group when they speak and hope that they will do the same for you.

Team Presentations

When a solitary group member prepares an oral presentation, dozens of decisions must be made. When an entire group is charged with preparing a presentation, the task becomes enormously complex. Unlike a panel discussion, symposium, forum, or governance group, a team presentation is not, necessarily, designed for a general audience; its goal is to inform and influence a very special audience. A **team presentation** is a well-coordinated, persuasive presentation by a cohesive group of speakers who are trying to influence an audience of key decision makers. Team presentations are common in nonprofit agencies and international corporations. They are seen in marketing presentations, contract competitions, and organizational requests for funding.

- A professional football team seeking backing for a new stadium brings a well-rehearsed group of executives and players to a public meeting at which they explain how the stadium will enhance the economic development and prestige of the community without adversely affecting the surrounding neighborhoods.
- Companies making the "shortlist" of businesses considered for a lucrative government contract are asked to make team presentations to the officials who will award the final contract.
- In a presentation to the state legislature's appropriations committee, a state college's board chairperson, college president, academic vice president, and student representative are given a total of forty-five minutes to justify their request for more state funding.

Team presentations are used to decide whether a group or company is competent enough to perform a task or take on a major responsibility. Team presentations are also used to present a united front when organizations are seeking support and endorsements. Thomas Leech describes how significant a team presentation can be:

> Team presentations are important; the stakes are often high. There generally has to be a significant reason to gather a diverse, highly paid, and often influential group together to hear a team of presenters. And whether the presentation involves the company president or a junior designer, the presenting team has to put forth a great deal of time and money in getting ready, reflecting the importance an organization places on team presentations.[17]

A team presentation is not a collection of individual speeches; it is a team product. Although a symposium is a coordinated presentation, symposium speakers do not necessarily present a unified front or have a strategic goal as their purpose. In many ways, the team presentation is the ultimate group challenge because it requires efficient and effective decision making as well as coordinated performance. Groups that work well in the conference room may fall apart in the spotlight of a team presentation.

Fortunately, the oral presentation guidelines described in this chapter can direct a group through the critical decision-making steps needed to develop an effective team presentation. Much like a single speaker, a team should (1) determine the team presentation's overall purpose or theme; (2) adapt the presentation to a specific group of decision makers; (3) adjust to the place where the team presentation will be delivered; (4) prepare and share appropriate supporting materials; (5) plan the introduction, organization, and conclusion to each team member's presentation as well as to the entire team's presentation; (6) enhance the team's credibility by demonstrating its expertise and trustworthiness; and (7) practice until the team's performance approaches perfection. In addition to these guidelines, a team must make sure that everyone, including management, knows what the team is going to do and that every detail has been considered.

Team presentations require a great deal of time, effort, and money to prepare and present. The payoffs, however, are high. Leech reports that in 1992, the Department of Energy awarded a $2.2 billion contract for environmental cleanup to a team headed by Fluor Corporation, following team presentations by several companies. Assistant Energy Secretary Leo P. Duff said Fluor made the best impression. "All the firms had capabilities, but how the team works as a team in the oral presentations is a key determining factor."[18] The awarding of a $2.2 billion contract should convert anyone who doubts the value of effective team presentations.

Questions and Answers

Once you or your team has completed a well-prepared presentation, you may not be finished; group or audience members may have questions or comments. The key to making a question-and-answer session a positive experience for everyone is to be prepared to answer a variety of questions and to know what to do when you don't have an answer.

If there is a single rule, it is this: answer the question. One way to practice for a question-and-answer session is to follow these guidelines:

- *Be brief.* Respond to questions with no more than three sentences.
- *Be honest.* If you don't know the answer to a question, admit it. Don't change the subject. The audience will know if you are avoiding the issue.

- *Be specific.* Provide appropriate information. Have some ready-made remarks including interesting statistics, stories, examples, and quotations that you can use in your answers.

If you run into difficult or hostile questions, remember that just because one listener disagrees with you doesn't mean that everyone is against you. If you encounter an antagonistic question, remember the listening guideline "Listen before you leap." Take your time before answering and do not strike back in anger. Try to paraphrase the question to make sure you understand what the person is asking. If you are prepared and ready for questions, you should have little difficulty dealing with the unexpected.

*B*alanced Oral Presentations

"Having the floor" in a group discussion is not the same as "being on stage" for a public presentation. When preparing and delivering an oral presentation, a group member must adapt to the needs and expectations of the audience. In an oral presentation, listeners may expect to hear accurate information but not a long-winded technical report; that can be done in writing. In an oral presentation, listeners may want to understand every word but not be exposed to a dramatic performance; that should be done on the stage. Finally, an audience may expect to hear a well-developed argument but not an impassioned plea; that should be done in court.

The guidelines outlined in this chapter cannot produce a successful oral presentation—only *you* can. Yet regardless of whether you are talking to a group of friends or the state legislature, you should try to make informed decisions about purpose, people, place, preparation, planning, personal credi-

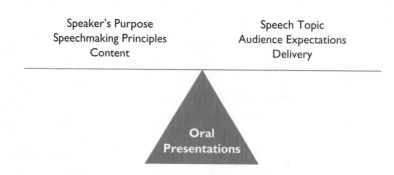

FIGURE 11.5 Oral Presentations

bility, and performance. Understanding and balancing these factors will guide you toward an effective and impressive oral presentation.

Summary Study Guide

- In certain situations, group members may be asked or required to give an oral presentation within a group, on behalf of a group, or as part of a team presentation.
- The seven critical decision-making guidelines in the presentation process are (1) purpose, (2) people, (3) place, (4) preparation, (5) planning, (6) personal credibility, and (7) performance.
- The first and most important step in developing a successful oral presentation is determining what you want your listeners to know, think, believe, or do as a result of your presentation.
- Audience analysis requires adapting to listener characteristics and opinions.
- Adapting to the place where you will be speaking involves asking questions about where and when you will deliver your presentation.
- Commonly used patterns of organization for an oral presentation are reason giving, time arrangement, space arrangement, problem–solution, causes and effects, stories and examples, and compare–contrast.
- An effective oral presentation should have an interesting introduction, a statement of purpose, a well-organized body, and a memorable conclusion.
- Two major factors that enhance a speaker's credibility are competence and character.
- The elements of delivery that can be practiced and controlled are use of notes, vocal characteristics, eye contact, and body movement.
- When using presentation aids to enhance your oral presentation, talk to your audience rather than to the aids, explain the aids at the appropriate time, and be prepared to present without them.
- When using computer software to develop presentation aids, exercise restraint in the selection of typefaces, templates, graphics, and multimedia effects.
- When delivering an oral presentation as a member of a public group, remember that you are "on stage" at all times.
- Developing and delivering an effective team presentation requires a rigorous approach to all phases of the speechmaking process.
- You can prepare for listener questions in advance. During a question-and-answer session you should answer questions as directly and clearly as possible.

Groupwork *A Practice Speech*

GOAL   To practice delivery skills by providing experience in impromptu, extemporaneous, manuscript, and memorized speaking.

PARTICIPANTS   All members of the class.

PROCEDURE

1. Each student should prepare a short oral presentation in which four forms of delivery are used as follows:
   - Memorized. Recite 30 seconds of something memorized—a poem, the Pledge of Allegiance, song lyrics, etc.
   - Manuscript. Read 60 seconds of any piece of prose—a book, a newspaper or magazine article, etc.
   - Extemporaneous. Spend 60 seconds talking to the audience about a personal experience or opinion—what hobbies you have, what you think about a campus or political issue, etc.
   - Impromptu. After completing these presentations, someone in the audience should ask a question. Answer the question in 30 seconds or less.
2. Assess each speaker's performance, and answer the following questions about all of the oral presentations:
   Which forms of delivery
   - were the most natural?
   - had the most eye contact?
   - were the most interesting to look at?
   - were the easiest to listen to?

ASSESSMENT

Oral Presentation Rating Scale

Directions   Use the following presentation guidelines to assess how well a group member, group spokesperson, or team makes an oral presentation to the group or a public audience. Identify the speaker's strengths as well as suggestions for improvement.

PRESENTATION GUIDELINES	SUPERIOR	SATIS-FACTORY	UNSATIS-FACTORY
Purpose: Sets clear and reasonable goal.			
People: Adapts to listeners.			
Place: Adapts to occasion and setting.			
Preparation: Uses a variety of effective supporting material.			
Planning: Uses clear organization; effective introduction and conclusion; clear language.			
Personal credibility: Demonstrates competence and character.			
Performance: Uses voice, body, and presentation aids effectively.			

Comments
Strengths of Oral Presentation:

Suggestions for Improvement:

Recommended Readings

Leech, R. (1993). *How to prepare, stage, and deliver winning presentations.* New York: American Management Association.

Ringle, W. J. (1998). *TechEdge: Using computers to present and persuade.* Boston: Allyn and Bacon.

Sprague, J. & Stuart, D. (1996). *The speaker's handbook* (4th ed.). Fort Worth, TX: Harcourt Brace.

Notes

1. Leech, R. (1993). *How to prepare, stage, and deliver winning presentations.* New York: American Management Association, p. 7.
2. Engleberg, I. N. (1994). *The principles of public presentation.* New York: Harper-Collins, pp. 36–41.
3. Hart, R. P., Friedrich, G. W. & Brooks, W. D. (1975). *Public communication.* New York: Harper & Row, p. 90.
4. Sprague, J. & Stuart, D. (1996). *The speaker's handbook* (4th ed.). Fort Worth, TX: Harcourt Brace, p. 256.
5. Sprague & Stuart, p. 257.
6. Zarefsky, D. (1996). *Public speaking: Strategies for success.* Boston: Allyn and Bacon, p. 334.
7. Mayer, L. V. (1996). *Fundamentals of voice and articulation* (11th ed.). Madison, WI: Brown & Benchmark, pp. 231–232.
8. Holcombe, M. W. & Stein, J. K. (1983). *Presentations for decision makers: Strategies for structuring and delivering your ideas.* Belmont, CA: Wadsworth, p. 169.
9. Holcombe & Stein, p. 73.
10. 3M Meeting Management Team with J. Drew. (1994). *Mastering meetings: Discovering the hidden potential of effective business meetings.* New York: McGraw-Hill, p. 140.
11. Guidelines for preparing briefings [on-line]. (1996). This document is available at *http://www.rand.org/publications/electronic/*.
12. Ringle, W. J. (1998). *TechEdge: Using computers to present and persuade.* Boston: Allyn and Bacon, p. 125.
13. Ringle, pp. 125 and 135.
14. Hinkin, S. (1994 August). "Designing standardized templates: First you choose it, but how do you get them to use it?" *Presentations, 8,* p. 34.
15. Ringle, p. 132.
16. Holcombe & Stein, p. 178.
17. Leech, p. 278.
18. Leech, p. 288.

*I*nformed Groups

Becoming a Well-Informed Group

Well-informed groups are more likely to succeed. Researchers investigating why some groups succeed while others fail emphasize that the amount and accuracy of information available to a group is a critical factor in predicting its success. Hirokawa concludes that "the ability of a group to gather and retain a wide range of information is the single most important determinant of high-quality decision making."[1] In looking at organizational groups, Goodall maintains that "the presence or absence of information needed to accomplish a task is a consistent problem. . . . If the information is available, it may not be readily accessible; if it is not available, then the task is delayed until the necessary information can be found."[2]

The key to becoming a well-informed group lies in the ability of members to do **research**—the search for, collection, and analysis of information needed to achieve a group's goal. When a group lacks information, responsible decision making and problem solving become difficult. For example, a group charged with developing a sexual harassment policy for a college campus must be well informed in order to develop a fair and effective policy. Group members must search for applicable definitions of sexual harassment. They must collect and review the policies of other colleges and understand their legal implications. They should test possible policies against case studies and documented court cases. None of these tasks can be accomplished without accurate and relevant information.

During an initial meeting, a group should discuss how it is going to become better informed. The following steps should help your group get started:

- Assess present knowledge.
- Identify areas needing research.
- Assign research responsibilities.
- Determine how to share the information.
- Set deadlines.

Assess Present Knowledge

Before members begin looking for information on their own, they should determine what the group already knows about the topic. Members might want to brainstorm the facts that are known, the documents they have, the kinds of personal expertise represented among group members, and any other piece of information or resource already possessed by the group.

Identify Areas Needing Research

Group members should carefully examine the issues to be discussed in order to determine the kind of information they need to make informed decisions. The group could also brainstorm a list of subtopics that need to be supported with additional information. For example, although a college committee may

> **TOOLBOX 12.1**   Brainstorming
>
> Brainstorming helps groups generate a maximum number of ideas in a short period of time. Brainstorming can also help a group inventory its current knowledge about an issue. In such a session, group members would share the information they already have on an issue or topic, regardless of its source or validity. After identifying what a group already knows, members can then spend their time finding additional information as well as analyzing the value of the information they already have. **Chapter 9: Decision Making in Groups** includes guidelines for conducting a brainstorming session.

have a national newspaper's definition of sexual harassment, they may decide that sample definitions from other colleges would help them understand the special circumstances in higher education. The group should create a list of the topic areas that the members agree should be researched.

Assign Research Responsibilities

A group's research effort is unlikely to be effective unless members know and fulfill their individual research responsibilities. Everyone should be assigned a specific research task. For example, in a sexual harassment discussion, Jo researches definitions of sexual harassment, TaMara finds out what policy the state university recently adopted, and David meets with the college attorney to discuss the institution's liability. According to Booth, Colomb, and Williams, "No matter how the group divides the [research] work, it needs good management skills, because the greatest danger is lack of coordination. Whether you parcel out tasks or parts, you should spend time talking about what you are doing and being utterly clear about who is supposed to do what."[3]

In addition to completing their own research assignments, all members should become as well informed as possible about the group's overall topic. For example, what if Jo doesn't show up at the next meeting, or TaMara fails to contact the state university? The group should always be prepared to discuss an issue even if some members fail to fulfill their research obligations.

Determine How to Share the Information

In his analysis of what distinguishes great groups from ordinary ones, Warren Bennis concluded that "sharing information is essential to a Great Group."[4] Bennis offers the PARC group as an example of the importance of shared information. During the development of the personal computer, members of the Palo Alto Research Center attended mandatory weekly meetings in which members shared information and achievements. These "bits and pieces" of information provided the members with insights into and inspirations for their own research.[5] The result was the development of technology that has revolutionized the way we work and live.

Unfortunately, many groups do a poor job of keeping each other informed.[6] Members often fail to share information because it doesn't support their personal position on an issue or for fear that others will respond negatively.[7] However, Propp points out that sharing information allows a group to develop a more complete understanding of a problem. "Although individuals may only have partial or biased information, bringing a group of individuals together may serve a corrective function that allows the group to piece their information together to create a less biased characterization of the situation."[8]

So, in addition to gathering research individually, members must share what they know with each other. Group members should decide how to organize the information in order to present it to the rest of the group. The group may decide that each member should come prepared to brief the group. The group also might decide that the information should be summarized in a brief report or in handouts. The best way to share information with a group depends on the needs of the group and the nature of the information. What is important is that all group members know how and when they are expected to share their researched information.

Set Deadlines

Groups should establish clear deadlines for gathering and sharing information. The group leader might want to check with individual members as the deadline approaches to assess the group's progress and motivate lagging members. At some point the group must complete the research process so information can be shared. Without deadlines, it will be difficult for the group to progress toward its goal.

Note Your Sources

Before you begin research on any topic, make sure you have a clear system for noting the sources and content of the information you find. It is important to take accurate and complete notes as you gather information. In addition to summarizing the main ideas from each source, specific facts and opinions should be noted. Use quotation marks when you are recording an author's exact words. Write down the author's name and qualifications, title of the book or magazine, title of the article, date of publication, and exact page numbers. Even when your information is found on the Internet, carefully note "where and when you got it, not only the sender and date, but also the electronic source—a discussion or news list, a commercial database."[9] Include enough details so that someone else can easily locate that information source.

Definition: Sexual Harassment

Sexual harassment. Unwanted or offensive sexual advances or sexually derogatory or discriminatory remarks made by an employer to an employee.

Source: Copyright © 1996 by Houghton Mifflin Company. Reproduced by permission from *The American Heritage Dictionary of the English Language*, Third Edition.

FIGURE 12.1   Sample Index Card

Index cards can be helpful when recording and organizing research. Each card should contain only one piece of information and its source, and the index cards should be separated by subtopics. A computer subdirectory can serve a similar function with separate files for different subtopics. Organizing information helps you quickly find what you need during a group discussion.

Primary and Secondary Sources

There are two types of information sources: primary and secondary. A **primary source** is the document, testimony, or publication in which the information first appears. An article in a scientific journal reporting the results of an author's experiment is an example of a primary source. **Secondary sources** report, repeat, or summarize information from one or more other sources. A magazine article that refers to several behavioral studies on disciplining children is a secondary source. The article probably uses information from primary sources and other secondary sources.

One type of source is not necessarily better than another. Booth, Colomb, and Williams contend that "one *good* source is worth more than a score of mediocre ones, and one *accurate* summary of a good source is sometimes worth more than the source itself."[10] However, each time information is reported, it is subject to reinterpretation and even misinterpretation. The further information is removed from its primary source, the more likely it is that inaccuracies have been introduced.

Sources of Information

Once you know your research responsibilities, your search can begin. The type of information you need and its source will depend on the nature of the group and its topic. A group of managers making decisions regarding the

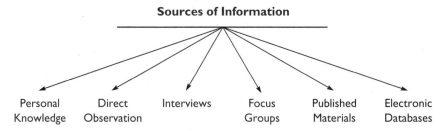

FIGURE 12.2 Sources of Information

company's hiring procedures may need to look for information in the company's own records. Students preparing for a class discussion on teen pregnancy will probably rely on information found in books and magazines. A committee developing a college's sexual harassment policy would have to use multiple sources of information to reach a high-quality decision.

When you begin a search for information, consider the following sources: personal knowledge, direct observation, interviews, focus groups, published materials, and electronic databases.

Personal Knowledge and Direct Observation

Just as a group assesses its current knowledge, you need to assess your personal knowledge about the group's topic and your research assignment. Personal knowledge is your own experience or expertise related to a specific topic or issue. Take an inventory of your personal knowledge by writing down what you already know; you may discover that it is more than you think. Make sure that your personal knowledge is based on facts and not merely on your opinions or inferences.

Personal knowledge can be generated by direct observation—gathering information by watching, listening, or experiencing a set of circumstances that are relevant to the group's topic. A campus committee responsible for addressing the problem of a long and unpleasant registration process might consider using direct observation. For example, members might go through the registration process noting how long each step takes and whether students are treated politely. Personal knowledge and direct observation are often the initial phase of the research process.

Interviews

Some information may be so current or specialized that it is not readily available in print. When you need such information or want insight from a particular expert, an interview may be appropriate. An **interview** is a method of gathering information from a conversation with people who have expertise or experience related to the group's topic. A group researching the issue of sexual harassment might assign a group member to interview the college's attorney or a local researcher who has published an article on the topic. A good interview follows these steps:

- Make an appointment.
- Prepare in advance.
- Arrive on time.
- Be professional.
- End the interview appropriately.

Make an Appointment.   Never drop in unannounced. Most people want and need an opportunity to prepare for an interview. When scheduling an appointment, the purpose and subject of your interview should be made clear. The person to be interviewed will then have an opportunity to properly prepare for your questions. This procedure also applies to interviews conducted over the telephone.

Prepare in Advance.   According to Booth, Colomb, and Williams, ". . . you should remember one similarity between learning from people and learning from books: the more you sort out what you know from what you want to know, the more efficiently you will find what you need."[11] Prior to the interview, you should already have gathered information from other sources. With that information, develop questions to ask during the interview. Ask only questions the person is qualified to answer and stay focused on gathering information and opinions.

Arrive on Time.   Never be late. Remember that the other person is doing you a favor by granting an interview. If she or he has to wait for you to arrive, you have created a negative impression before the interview starts.

Be Professional.   Begin by reminding the other person of the purpose of the interview. Ask whether the person is willing to be quoted. If statements are made "off the record," the desire for confidentiality should be respected. Ask your prepared questions and any necessary follow-up questions. Good interviewers take detailed notes and listen carefully. If you intend to tape-record the interview, permission to do so should be requested first. Conduct yourself in a polite and professional manner, even if you strongly disagree with the other person.

End the Interview Appropriately.   If the interview is scheduled to last one hour, make sure you are finished by then. Do not expect others to take additional time from their work. Finally, remember to thank the person at the end of the interview or later in writing.

Focus Groups

Focus group interviews are an exploratory research technique that uses a group of carefully selected people to examine a specific research question. During a focus group, a trained moderator guides group interaction in order to probe participants' thinking and feelings about the object of discussion. Comments are recorded, summarized, and subsequently analyzed.[12]

RESPONSIBLE decision making and problem solving rely on well-informed group members. What are the potential consequences to a group that lacks sufficient information? (Kenneth Gabrielsen/The Liaison Agency)

In marketing, focus groups are used to test new products, evaluate commercials, and assess consumer opinions. In politics, focus groups are used to assess a candidate's image, test survey questions, interpret poll results, and predict voter behavior. For example, a college could use focus groups composed of prospective and current students to evaluate the usefulness and appeal of publications such as the college catalog, class schedule, and program brochures.

Effective focus groups are difficult to organize, conduct, and interpret. Hours of attention must be devoted to choosing the ideal participants, developing a strategic agenda of research questions, and ensuring that the moderator has the skills and background needed to secure valid answers. Even more difficult is the process of analyzing the results. There is "a temptation to use the raw data results as the basis for final decision making. Focus group research . . . should not be substituted for more significant and substantive quantitative research."[13] In other words, don't rely on the results of one or two focus groups to make an important decision. Used properly, however, focus groups are an effective way of using groups to help researchers understand and solve problems.

Published Materials

The following forms of published information are available to most groups. Members should consider which kinds of published materials are most likely to contain the information they need.

Books. Books are an excellent source of information. They provide in-depth information; however, they can become dated very quickly. Locate books using the on-line or card catalog in your public or college library. Librarians can provide easy-to-follow directions for both.

General Reference Works. General reference works include almanacs, atlases, bibliographies, dictionaries, encyclopedias, quotation books, and specialized handbooks. Reference works are particularly useful for checking facts. Examples are *The World Almanac, Rand McNally New International Atlas, Statistical Abstract of the United States,* and *The Encyclopaedia Britannica.* Like other books within a library, general reference works are listed in the on-line or card catalog. If you are unsure what type of reference work might be helpful, a librarian can often recommend some useful sources.

Periodicals and Newspapers.   Periodicals include magazines, professional journals, and newspapers that are published daily, weekly, monthly, or on some other periodic basis. Articles in periodicals are found by looking up your topic in an index. The most common index is the *Reader's Guide to Periodical Literature*, which includes most of the major magazines in this country. Other indexes, more specialized in their focus, include the *Business Periodicals Index, Education Index, Humanities Index,* and *Social Sciences Index.* These indexes are relatively simple to use. Many are available electronically through on-line computer searches or CD-ROM databases.

Many major newspapers have their own index of articles. The two most common are *The New York Times Index* and *The Wall Street Journal Index.* The *Bell & Howell Newspaper Indexes* contains references for several major U.S. newspapers. *Ethnic News Watch* is an on-line index to newspapers and newsletters that serve the interests of various ethnic groups. Unless the newspaper is very recent, it will probably be on microfilm, microfiche, or CD-ROM. A librarian can show you how to use each.

Government Documents.   The Freedom of Information Act (FOIA) of 1966 requires the fullest possible disclosure of federal information to the public. "Sunshine laws" have since been passed that provide the public access to state and local government records.

To locate information from a government hearing on the group's topic, refer to the *Congressional Index Service.* The *Congressional Record Index* references all speeches and debates on the floor of the U.S. Congress. The *United States Government Publications Monthly Catalog* indexes documents published by all federal government agencies. At first, researching government documents can be intimidating and difficult. However, there is a wealth of information to be found in these documents.

Internal Documents.   Some of the information your group needs might be available not from the library but contained within your college's, organization's, or business's internal documents. **Internal documents** include policies, procedures, manuals, reports, and memos that are specific to the operations of a particular organization or company and not intended for use by the general public. Remember, your group may not be the first to have dealt with an issue. Earlier groups may have produced reports and other documents that provide valuable information. Be cautious; some documents are developed for internal use only.

Electronic Databases   Electronic searches can generally be conducted in two ways, through CD-ROMs or on-line. CD-ROMs look like music CDs but serve to retrieve data. Many of the indexes mentioned earlier are available on CD-ROM. An electronic index contains all the same information as indexes in print. However, electronic indexes often include abstracts, or summaries, of articles. Many

Source	Advantages	Disadvantages
Books	• Detailed information • Cited sources	• Can quickly become outdated • Often relied upon as only source
Newspapers	• Up-to-date • Current events • Local interests	• Quality varies • Short deadlines can result in inaccuracies • May have biased perspectives
Magazines	• Fairly current • Perceived as credible	• Can oversimplify complex issues • May be entertaining but not newsworthy • May have biased perspectives
Journals	• Detailed information • Expert authors • Cited sources • Reviewed by other experts prior to publication	• Contains complex reading • Is more difficult to locate • Can become outdated

(Based upon Pfau, M., Thomas, D. A., & Ulrich, W. (1987). *Debate and argument: A systems approach to advocacy.* Glenview, IL: Scott, Foresman.)

FIGURE 12.3   Advantages and Disadvantages of Common Sources of Published Information

libraries now have computer terminals for CD-ROM databases, such as *Infotrak* and *ProQuest,* that include many indexes in one system. These allow you to type topic words into the computer instead of looking up your topic in several books of indexes. The computer then will list all the articles on your topic contained in the system.

On-line searches, on the other hand, involve accessing information from databases on other computers. There are a number of on-line search services, such as *DIALOG, Lexis/Nexis,* and *Dow Jones News Retrieval,* that provide specialized on-line information. Other, more general on-line services, like *CompuServe, America On-Line, Microsoft Network,* and *Prodigy,* also offer access to information databases. Thousands of databases are currently available online. Many on-line searches can be done from a personal computer or through a service provided by your library.

A growing source of information is the Internet. A vast amount of information has become available via the Internet, and most of it is accessible at no charge. However, while the Internet provides access to a tremendous amount of information, there is no guarantee that it is accurate. Unlike most traditional information sources, not all information on the Internet is scrutinized by editors, journalists, or experts in a field. Remember that anyone can post almost any information, true or not, on the Internet. The following guidelines can help you determine the reliability of the information on a website.[14]

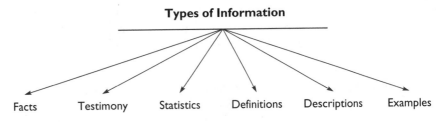

FIGURE 12.4 Types of Information

Is the individual or organization posting the information qualified and unbiased?
Does the site refer to other sites or sources?
Can the information be verified by other sources?
Does the site include a recent date for revisions?

In addition to not always being accurate, the Internet is not a complete source of information. While you may find the title, you are unlikely to find the entire text of a book you need on the Internet. The entire text of many newspaper, magazine, and journal articles is not available. While many government documents are available via the Internet, many are not. "Remember, the Internet does not contain the sum of all knowledge. You may still need to hit the library."[15]

Types of Information

Now that you have gathered your sources, you must decide what type of information to collect for your group. Information takes many forms, including facts, testimony, statistics, definitions, descriptions, and examples.

Facts   A **fact** is a verifiable observation, experience, or event known to be true.

> EXAMPLE: In 1876, Colonel Henry M. Robert used the British Parliament's procedures and Thomas Jefferson's code of rules as sources for *Robert's Rules of Order*.

It is important that groups make a clear distinction between facts and opinions. An **opinion** is a conclusion regarding the meaning or implications of facts. For example, some group members may be of the opinion that *Robert's Rules of Order* is outdated and makes a meeting more complicated than necessary, whereas other group members believe that parliamentary procedure is time-tested and ensures fair and objective decision making. Unlike opinions, facts can usually be proved true or false. Group members should not mistake their opinions for facts.

Testimony

Testimony refers to statements that express an authority's judgment or interpretation of facts.

EXAMPLE: Dr. Marshall Scott Poole, professor of speech communication at the University of Minnesota, has described structured group procedures as "the heart of group work . . . the most powerful tools we have to improve the conduct of meetings." **Primary Source:** Poole, M. S. (1991). Procedures for managing meetings: Social and technological innovation. In R. A. Swanson & B. O. Knapp (Eds.), *Innovative meeting management.* Austin, TX: 3M Meeting Management Institute, pp. 54 & 55.

While authorities may base their opinions on fact, different authorities often reach different conclusions using the same facts and research. Look for testimony from various experts rather than relying too heavily on testimony that represents only one perspective.

Statistics

Information presented in a numerical form is the basis for **statistics.** Statistics take various forms, including averages, percentages, rates, rankings, etc.

EXAMPLE: A 1989 study conducted by the Annenberg School of Communications at the University of Southern California concluded that nearly "two-thirds (66%) of meetings in corporate America are held to reconcile a conflict (29%); reach a group judgement or decision (26%); or solve a problem (11%)." **Secondary Source:** 3M Meeting Management Team with J. Drew (1994). *Mastering meetings.* New York: McGraw-Hill, p. 4.

As group members collect statistical information, they must evaluate it carefully. The source and form of a statistic can result in different interpretations of the same numbers. For example, at first glance, the preceding statistics may appear to conclude that two-thirds of meetings are held to reconcile conflicts. Instead, the Annenberg School's statistics reveal that two-thirds of corporate meetings are held to accomplish one of three goals: to resolve conflict, make a decision, or solve a problem. Misinterpreting statistical information can jeopardize group effectiveness and success.

Definitions

Definitions clarify the meaning of a word, phrase, or concept. A definition can be as simple as explaining what you mean by a word or as complex as an encyclopedia or unabridged dictionary definition.

EXAMPLE: "There is a profound difference between management and leadership, and both are important. 'To manage' means 'to bring about, to accomplish, to have charge of or responsibility for, to conduct.' 'Leading' is 'influencing, guiding in direction, course, action, opinion.'"
Primary Source: Bennis, W., & Nanus, B. (1985). *Leaders: The strategies for taking charge.* New York: HarperPerennial, p. 21.

During an initial meeting, the group should determine what definitions are needed. For example, a group dealing with sexual harassment policies should gather several definitions of sexual harassment. Groups negotiating legal contracts must carefully define terms before an understanding can be reached between the parties.

Descriptions

Descriptions help to create a mental image of a person, event, place, or object. Descriptions are often more detailed than are definitions. Causes, effects, historical contexts, characteristics, and operations can all be included in a description.

EXAMPLE: "The authoritarian leader maintains strict control over followers by directly regulating policy procedures, and behavior. . . . Many authoritarian leaders believe that followers would not function effectively without direct supervision. The authoritarian leader generally feels that people left to complete work on their own will be unproductive."
Primary Source: Hackman, M. Z. & Johnson, C. E. (1991). *Leadership: A communication perspective.* Prospect Heights, IL: Waveland, p. 22.

Many groups need descriptive information in order to make decisions or solve problems. A group planning a conference will want descriptions of proposed sites. A group trying to understand the motives of an authoritarian leader may benefit from a description of that leadership style.

Examples

An **example** refers to a specific case or instance. Examples can be as brief as one word or as complicated as lengthy stories.

EXAMPLE: "It is not unusual for highly effective members on creative teams—the IBM PC team, McDonald's Chicken McNugget team, the Boeing 747 airplane project—to find themselves working on weekends and during the evening, and to be thinking about the problem at all times."
Primary Source: Larson, C. E. & LaFasto, F. M. (1989). *Team-Work: What must go right/what can go wrong.* Newbury Park, CA: Sage, p. 68.

It is important to remember that one or two examples may not represent an entire category, situation, or group of people. If examples are to be used as evidence to support an argument, the group needs as many examples as possible representing similar situations and results.

Evaluating Information

All the information you gather will not necessarily be reliable or relevant. The group must continuously evaluate the quality of the evidence by asking the five general questions shown in Figure 12.5.

Source Qualifications Is the source of the information credible? You should know your sources. Referring to the opinion of "an expert" is insufficient. Without knowing whose opinions are being considered, the group has no way of evaluating the credibility of the information. Ask what the basis is for the source's expertise. Is the source biased in any way? Is the source reporting facts or expressing opinions? What evidence does the source use to support claims? Answers to these questions help a group determine the credibility of its sources of information. After all, even though the sensational and often bizarre *National Enquirer* may be fun reading, *The Wall Street Journal* is more likely to contain information from credible sources.

Recency Everything changes over time. Generally, the most recent information is best. For instance, groups dealing with national economic policies must be able to rely on the most recent economic data available on issues such as inflation and employment. Groups that make decisions having legal implications must be informed of the most recent laws and court decisions.

Consistency Facts or conclusions that are contrary to the rest of the information the group has collected should be carefully evaluated. A group examining the problem of polluted rivers from a local factory would be irresponsible if its decision were

---

How Valid Is Your Information

- Is the source of the information credible?
- How recent is the information?
- Is it consistent with other information?
- Are the statistics reliable?
- Has the group gathered enough information?

FIGURE 12.5 How Valid Is Your Information?

based on just one study that found no contamination when five other studies reported clear evidence of pollution. However, inconsistency does not necessarily mean the information is inaccurate. That piece of information may be more up-to-date or more accurate for a number of reasons. Inconsistency should simply prompt a group to examine information more critically before accepting it.

Statistical Validity

Determining the validity of statistics generally requires answers to three questions. First, what is the source of the statistic? Knowing who or what organization collected information may alert a group to biases in the data. For example, a tobacco company reporting the result of a study that found no relationship between cigarette smoking and cancer rates should be treated with skepticism.

Second, are the statistics accurate? Often statistics are generated as a result of surveying or observing people. Studies that include too few people or participants who are not representative of the entire population may be considered invalid. For example, one study examined the effects of diet on breast cancer by studying only men.[16] Clearly, the exclusion of women from the study makes any results or conclusions suspect.

Third, how are the statistics reported? Frequently statistics use terms such as means, modes, medians, and percentages to report results. The way in which the source chooses to report the statistic can conceal or distort the information. For example, group members who have been told that customer complaints have increased 100 percent over the past year may believe they have a serious issue to address. Upon closer examination of the statistic, though, they may discover that last year only two customers complained and that this year four complaints were reported. The problem no longer appears as serious.

Quantity

The final question members should ask themselves is whether the group has gathered enough information. After careful review, the group should identify any additional areas that need to be researched. The group's effort to gather information continues until the group is knowledgeable enough to solve a problem or make a decision. Of course, groups should ensure that information is gathered in a timely fashion. Ultimately the group must shift its focus from information gathering to using the information to make decisions.

Using Information Effectively

Hirokawa and Scheerhorn emphasize that because "a group's information base is directly or indirectly tied to all phases of the decision-making process, . . . any errors occurring within the base are likely to contribute to faulty decision making."[17] Here are several factors that can create a flawed information base for group decision making:

- Groups reject useful information.
- Groups accept invalid information.
- Groups gather too little information.
- Groups gather too much information.[18]

When group members have preconceived notions about the nature of a problem or which decision is best, they may reject information that does not support their conclusions. In addition, information that reinforces members' beliefs may be accepted even if it is inaccurate. The result is that the group fails to fully understand an issue or consider other options. Overlooking useful information or accepting inaccurate information will produce poor decisions.

Groups can also suffer from information underload or overload.[19] **Information underload** occurs when a group does not have enough information to effectively make a decision. Information underload usually happens when research responsibilities are not clear or the group lacks open communication. Clearly defining research assignments encourages members to provide relevant information to the group. However, unless the group has established an open climate of communication, that information may never be shared with the group. **Information overload** occurs when a group receives too much information or information that is too complex for the group to understand. When groups gather too much information, valuable time is spent determining what is relevant and what is not.

Balancing Information Quality and Quantity

Groups should strive to locate as much relevant information about the group's topic as possible. However, members should not mistake quantity for quality. Having a lot of information does not make you well informed if it

Quantity	Quality
Personal Knowledge	Researched Information
Types of Information	Tests of Information

Informed Groups

FIGURE 12.6 Informed Groups

isn't the right information. Throughout the research process, members should evaluate evidence in order to choose the most relevant information.

Establishing clear research deadlines lets members know when they must be prepared to present information to the group. At some point the group must stop researching and start making decisions. Members must carefully evaluate the group's purpose and time limitations when searching for a balance between too little and too much information.

Summary Study Guide

- Informed group members gather, record, and are prepared to discuss pertinent information related to a group's topic of discussion.
- A group should initially assess its present knowledge, identify areas needing further research, assign members specific research responsibilities, determine how the information will be shared with the group, and set clear deadlines.
- Take accurate and complete notes as you gather information.
- Information is found in two types of sources, primary and secondary. Good secondary sources refer to their primary sources.
- Personal knowledge is your personal experience or expertise that relates to the group topic. Direct observation generates information by observing or experiencing a set of circumstances that are relevant to the group's topic.
- A good interview is scheduled in advance, carefully prepared for, begun on time, conducted in a professional manner, and ended on time.
- Focus group interviews are an exploratory research tool that uses a carefully selected group of people to discuss a specific research question.
- Useful information may be found in published materials, including books, general reference works, periodicals, newspapers, government documents, and an organization's internal documents.
- Electronic databases can be searched on CD-ROMs or on-line. On-line information must be carefully evaluated.
- Common types of information include facts, testimony, statistics, definitions, descriptions, and examples.
- Five general questions a group should ask when evaluating information are as follows: Is the source credible? Is the information recent? Is it consistent? Are the statistics reliable? Does the group have enough information?
- A flawed information base results when groups reject useful information, accept invalid information, gather too little information, or gather too much information.

Groupwork *Research Scavenger Hunt*

GOAL   To practice group research techniques.

PARTICIPANTS   Groups of 5–7 members.

PROCEDURE

1. Each group and its members are given the Research Scavenger Hunt Questions.
2. Groups have ten minutes to develop an action plan for answering all questions on the list.
3. Groups have thirty minutes to collect as many answers as they can and return to the classroom by the deadline. (The instructor may change the time limit depending on available class time.)
4. Upon returning to the classroom, groups have five minutes to compile their answers onto a single group answer sheet.
5. The class should discuss any difficulties encountered during the research scavenger hunt.

Research Scavenger Hunt Questions

1. Locate an article in a magazine or newspaper about conducting effective business meetings.
   Article Title:
   Title of Magazine or Newspaper:
2. What is the population of Texas?
   Population:
   Source:
3. Locate the title of a book about AIDS in your library's on-line or card catalog.
   Title of Book:
   Call Number:
4. Who is the current U.S. Secretary of Education?
   Name:
   Source:
5. How long has your college's current president served in that office?
   Answer:
   Source:
6. In what year did the U.S. Supreme Court hand down its decision in *Miranda* v. *Arizona*?
   Year:
   Source:

7. On what date was the charter of the United Nations approved?
   Date:
   Source:
8. What Shakespearean character said "All the world's a stage"? What was the play?
   Character:
   Play:

Information Checklist

Directions Use the following checklists to assess the quality and quantity of information you search for, collect, and analyze during the research process.

Gathering Information:

Consider the following ways of gathering information.

_____ 1. Inventory personal knowledge.

_____ 2. Conduct direct observations.

_____ 3. Locate books on the topic.

_____ 4. Locate relevant general reference works.

_____ 5. Locate magazine and journal articles.

_____ 6. Locate newspaper articles.

_____ 7. Locate relevant government documents.

_____ 8. Locate internal documents.

_____ 9. Interview an expert on the issue.

_____ 10. Conduct and analyze a focus group session.

_____ 11. Search electronic databases.

Noting Sources:

When collecting information, make sure that you do the following:

_____ 1. Note whether you have collected primary or secondary sources of information.

_____ 2. Record your information and its complete source in a clear and organized manner.

Evaluating Information:

Make sure that each piece of information you collect meets the following criteria.

_____ 1. The sources are reliable.

_____ 2. The information is recent.

_____ 3. The information is consistent.

_____ 4. The statistics are valid.

_____ 5. There is enough information.

Recommended Readings

Booth, W. C., Colomb, G. G. & Williams, J. M. (1995). *The craft of research.* Chicago: The University of Chicago.

Harris, S. (1991). *The New York public library book of how and where to look it up.* New York: Prentice-Hall.

Harnack, A. & Kleppinger, E. (1998). *Online! A reference guide to using Internet sources.* New York: St. Martin's Press.

Notes

1. Hirokawa, R. Y. (1996). Communication and group decision-making efficacy. In R. S. Cathcart, L. A. Samovar & L. D. Henman (Eds.), *Small group communication: Theory and practice* (7th ed.). Madison, WI: Brown & Benchmark, p. 108.
2. Goodall, H. L., Jr. (1990). *Small group communication in organizations* (2nd ed.). Dubuque, IA: Wm. C. Brown, p. 55.
3. Booth, W. C., Colomb, G. G. & Williams, J. M. (1995). *The craft of research.* Chicago: The University of Chicago, pp. 76–77.
4. Bennis, W. & Biederman, P. W. (1997). *Organizing genius: The secrets of creative collaboration.* Reading, MA: Addison-Wesley, p. 71.
5. Bennis & Biederman, p. 71.
6. Dennis, A. R. (1996). "Information exchange and use in small group decision making." *Small Group Research, 27,* p. 532.
7. Dennis, pp. 534–536.
8. Propp, K. M. (1997). "Information utilization in small group decision making: A study of the evaluative interaction model." *Small Group Research, 28,* p. 428.
9. Booth, Colomb & Williams, pp. 76–77.
10. Booth, Colomb & Williams, p. 73.
11. Booth, Colomb & Williams, p. 70.
12. Engleberg, I. N. & Cohen, M. C. (1989). Focus group research in the community college. *Community/Junior College Quarterly, 13,* p. 102.
13. Engleberg & Cohen, p. 106.
14. Harnack, A. & Kleppinger, E. (1998). *Online! A reference guide to using internet sources.* New York: St. Martin's Press, pp. 69–71.
15. Maxwell, B. (1998 November 6–8). "12 tips to search the internet successfully." *USA Weekend,* p. 12.
16. Tavris, C. (1992). *The mismeasure of women.* New York: Simon & Schuster, p. 94.
17. Hirokawa, R. Y. & Scheerhorn, D. R. (1986). Communication in faulty group decision-making. In R. Y. Hirokawa & M. S. Poole (Eds.), *Communication and group decision making.* Beverly Hills, CA: Sage, pp. 73–74.
18. Hirokawa & Scheerhorn, pp. 74–75.
19. Rothwell, J. D. (1992). *In mixed company: Small group communication.* Orlando, FL: Harcourt Brace.

Resources and Tools

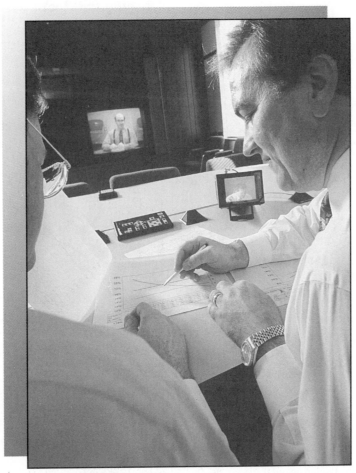

Roger Tully/Tony Stone Images

Planning and Conducting Meetings

Meetings, Meetings, Meetings

To Meet or Not to Meet

What Is a Meeting?

Planning the Meeting

Why Are We Meeting?

Who Should Attend the Meeting?

When Should We Meet?

Where Should We Meet?

What Materials Do We Need?

The Chairperson's Responsibilities

Pre-Meeting Tasks

Tasks during the Meeting

Post-Meeting Tasks

Participation in Meetings

Dealing with Difficulties

Nonparticipant

Loudmouth

Interrupter

Whisperer

Latecomers and Early Leavers

Adapting to Differences

Evaluating the Meeting

Balanced Meetings

Meetings, Meetings, Meetings

Over 10 million business meetings take place in the United States every day. The typical manager attends five meetings per week and averages two hours and fourteen minutes each day in a meeting room.[1] Odds are that you've spent your share of time in meetings. Certainly you will be attending meetings in the future. Unfortunately, many of these meetings may not be productive and rewarding group experiences. Ninety percent of managers report that half of the meetings they attend are "either unnecessary or a complete waste of time."[2] *Industry Week* estimates that time wasted in unproductive meetings costs U.S. businesses over $37 billion a year.[3]

> "I've gathered you here today because we haven't had a meeting in a while."wrong."I've called this meeting because several of you have indicated we need a better way of coordinating this team project." right.[4]

Many meetings fail to achieve their purpose. Our own observations as well as studies and expert conclusions suggest the following explanations for why so many people criticize and dread meetings:

- The meeting was unnecessary and wasted time.
- The meeting's purpose was unclear.
- The meeting failed to use or follow an agenda.
- There was not enough prior notice or time to prepare.
- The right people did not attend or were not invited.
- The meeting was held at the wrong time or place.
- The chairperson was ineffective.
- There was too much political pressure to conform or take sides.

Another significant reason meetings fail is that we take them for granted. Too often we resign ourselves to attending unproductive meetings rather than trying to improve the meetings we must attend.

To Meet or Not to Meet

In *Running a Meeting That Works*, Robert Miller offers the following counsel:

> You may hate to write reports or memos. You may feel lost without colleagues with whom to try out new ideas. You may be afraid you can't handle an assignment alone. You might prefer not to do the research yourself. . . . These are not reasons to have a meeting.[5]

The best way to ensure that your meeting does not waste time or frustrate members is to make sure that the meeting is really needed. Answering the following questions can help you decide whether to meet or not to meet:

- Is an immediate response needed?
- Is group input and interaction critical?
- Are members prepared to discuss the topic?

You may find alternative methods of communicating with other members can prevent unnecessary group meetings. A memo, fax, e-mail or voice mail message, or a one-to-one conversation may be sufficient.[6] Sometimes calling a meeting is the fastest way to inform and interact with a group of people. If an unexpected problem arises, there may not be time to write a memo or distribute a report. If a group must be made aware of a problem and has limited time to come up with a solution, a meeting is required.

As indicated in Chapter 1, one of the advantages of working in groups is that groups outperform individuals acting alone, especially when performance requires multiple skills, judgments, and experiences.[7] When the combined ideas, opinions, and skills of all members are needed to accomplish a goal, a meeting can be the best tool for generating synergy. Miller writes that meetings are the way "half-formed ideas [lead] to the generation of a fully formed concept."[8]

Even if immediate action is required and member input is critical, a meeting may not be productive if members are not prepared to discuss the issues before the group. Group decisions and action based on insufficient information or misinformation will not yield the best decisions. If members resent being called to a meeting, they may be unwilling to contribute their best effort.

What Is a Meeting?

If a group of people get together in the same room at the same time, you have a meeting, right? Wrong. You merely have a gathering of people in one place. We define a **meeting** as a scheduled gathering of group members for a structured discussion guided by a designated chairperson.

You can better understand the unique nature of a meeting by examining the three elements in the definition: schedule, structure, and chairperson. First, a typical meeting is scheduled in advance for a particular time and place; a coincidental gathering of group members does not constitute a meeting. Usually meetings begin and end at a predetermined time in a predetermined place.

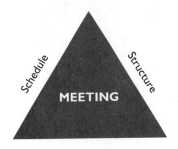

Chairperson

FIGURE 13.1 Three Essential Elements of a Meeting

The second essential element in a meeting is structure—the organization of discussion topics and tasks to facilitate the achievement of a group's goal. Meetings can be formal and highly structured or informal and loosely structured. A meeting using parliamentary procedure is an example of a formally structured meeting.

Informally structured meetings may not follow strict rules for conducting a group's business. In such meetings, members may interject their ideas and opinions at any time during the discussion of an issue. Voting may not be used as a means of making decisions; instead the group may infer majority opinion on the basis of comments made during the discussion.

The third element of a meeting is a designated chairperson. A **chairperson** is a group member appointed or elected to conduct the meeting. The chairperson is not necessarily the group leader but a person responsible for guiding the group through discussion topics or tasks in an orderly manner. The specific responsibilities of the chairperson are discussed later in this chapter.

TOOLBOX 13.1 Parliamentary Procedure

Parliamentary procedure is a systematic method for conducting a decision-making meeting in an orderly manner. The chief purpose of parliamentary procedure is to protect the rights of minority members while ensuring majority rule. Parliamentary procedure requires that members be called upon to speak by the chairperson, that voting follow set procedures, and that issues be discussed and debated in the order determined by the rules. **Chapter 15: Parliamentary Procedure** summarizes the basic rules and primary motions used in meetings.

- **Why** are we meeting?
- **Who** should attend the meeting?
- **When** should we meet?
- **Where** should we meet?
- **What** materials do we need?

FIGURE 13.2 Meeting Planning Questions

Planning the Meeting

The success or failure of a meeting largely depends on proper planning. Anderson estimates that careful planning can prevent at least twenty minutes of wasted time for each hour of a group's meeting.[9] Answering the following questions can help you begin the process of planning an effective group meeting.

Why Are We Meeting?

The most important step in planning a meeting is defining its purpose and goals as clearly as possible. Is the group meeting to share information, make decisions, solve problems, coordinate and implement tasks, or to motivate members? What does the group want to accomplish by the time the meeting is over?

Purpose is not the same as the subject of the meeting. The subject is the topic of the discussion. Purpose identifies the desired outcome of the meeting. For example, if an executive calls her assistant and says, "Call a staff meeting next Thursday at 2:00 p.m.," the assistant may ask, "What will the staff meeting be about?" "Employer-provided day care," the executive replies. Has the executive revealed the purpose of the meeting? No. We only know that the subject of the meeting is employer-provided day care. If the executive had said, "We need to determine whether our employer-provided day care system needs to be expanded," we would know the purpose of the meeting.

It is important to ensure that a group can achieve its purpose by the end of a meeting. If the objective cannot be accomplished during a single meeting, the purpose statement should be rewritten to focus on a more specific outcome. If necessary, a series of meetings should be scheduled in order to achieve the final goal.

Who Should Attend the Meeting?

The membership of many groups is predetermined. For example, you wouldn't hold a routine staff meeting and not invite the usual group of employees. However, if a task does not require input from everyone or only needs the expertise of certain people, you should select participants who can

THE success of a meeting largely depends on proper planning. What preparations do you think were necessary when planning for this meeting? (Mark Richards/PhotoEdit)

make a significant contribution. Inviting the appropriate people will save the time of individuals who do not need to attend.

When selecting meeting participants, try to include members who will be affected directly by the outcome of the meeting. In addition, choose participants with special expertise, different opinions and approaches, and the power to implement decisions. Although you may be tempted to invite only those people who agree with your point of view, individuals who disagree or who represent minority opinions can provide a more balanced and realistic discussion of issues. Diversity in your group members' backgrounds, experiences, and viewpoints can add new perspectives, ideas, and support for any actions the group agrees upon.

Another major consideration in assembling a group is to make sure that it is a manageable size. The larger a group, the more difficult it will be to manage. According to Antony Jay, an **assembly** consists of one hundred or more people gathered to listen to a speaker make a presentation.[10] Such a group is much too large to ensure the effective interaction of interdependent members working toward a common goal. A **council** is a meeting of forty or fifty people in which the group listens to several speakers. Usually, a council has too many participants for a high degree of interaction but is sufficiently small enough to allow some audience participation. A **small group meeting** is composed of twelve or fewer members who have equal opportunities to become fully involved in all discussions and decision making. Try to limit a small group meeting to fewer than twelve participants; a group of five to seven members is ideal.

When Should We Meet?

The next step is deciding what day and time are best for the meeting. Should the meeting be in the morning, in the afternoon, after work hours, or during lunch? Avoid scheduling group meetings near holidays or at the beginning or end of the week when members may be less focused on working. Determine what time the meeting should begin as well as what time it should end. Don't schedule more time than is necessary to accomplish the meeting goal. For a time-consuming and difficult goal, you may decide that more than one meeting will be necessary.

Contact your group members to find out when they are available, and schedule the meeting at a time when the most essential and productive

TOOLBOX 13.2   Meeting Through Technology

When group members are far apart, teleconferencing and videoconferencing technology may be a practical alternative to a face-to-face meeting. Careful planning is needed to take advantage of these technologies. For on-site meetings, you may be able to use computerized meeting scheduling. If you work for a company or organization with a computer network, you may have access to a calendar program with a group scheduling feature. These programs can provide an instant list of times and dates when all group members are available. The program will schedule the meeting, notify the participants by e-mail, and enter the meeting on their calendars. **Chapter 16: Technology and Groups** discusses opportunities for using computer programs to aid in scheduling meetings as well as the available technology for conducting teleconferences and videoconferences.

participants are free. A meeting that only a few members can attend will not be very productive and will waste the time of those who do show up.

Where Should We Meet?

Choose a location that is appropriate for the purpose and size of the meeting. The room should be large enough, clean, well lit, not too hot or too cold, and furnished with comfortable chairs. Although you may have little control over such features, do your best to provide an appropriate and comfortable setting. Working in an attractive meeting room can make a group feel more important and valued. Also, the meeting room should be located away from distractions such as ringing phones or noisy conversations. Finally, check to see whether the room is available at the required time and then reserve it if necessary.

What Materials Do We Need?

The most important item to prepare and distribute to the group is the meeting's agenda. The agenda tells the group what topics will be discussed and in what order. In addition to the agenda, it may be necessary to distribute reports or other reading material that the group must be familiar with in order to contribute to a productive discussion. Ask group members what materials they need. Make sure that any distributed reading material is relevant to the meeting's purpose, is essential for participation, and is not unnecessarily long. Distribute all materials far enough in advance of the meeting so that everyone has time to prepare. Plan on having extra copies available at the meeting. In addition, make sure that supplies and equipment such as markers, paper, flip charts, chalk, or projectors are available to the participants.

*T*he *Chairperson's Responsibilities*

If you are the chairperson of a meeting, you have a tremendous amount of influence over, and responsibility for, the success of the meeting. Although the chairperson may or may not be responsible for planning the meeting, it is the chairperson who must conduct the meeting and who is often responsible for following up on decisions after the meeting is over. A chairperson is not necessarily the leader of a group. In some cases, a skilled facilitator is assigned the task of chairing meetings so that the group's leader has the opportunity to function as an active participant.

Effective chairpersons maintain order during meetings and facilitate productive discussions by making sure they have fulfilled their responsibilities prior to, during, and after the meeting.

Pre-Meeting Tasks

Prior to a meeting, notify everyone who should attend, preferably in writing. Your announcement should include a clear statement of purpose, expectations of participants, and the time, location, and duration of the meeting. After the meeting has been announced, all the materials that participants need, including the agenda, should be distributed in advance. It is important to check with all members to confirm that they are planning to attend. If necessary, send a brief reminder before the meeting.

As the chairperson, you must be fully prepared for the discussion. Gather any additional information you need to participate in and understand the discussion. Think through the issues from different perspectives other than your own.

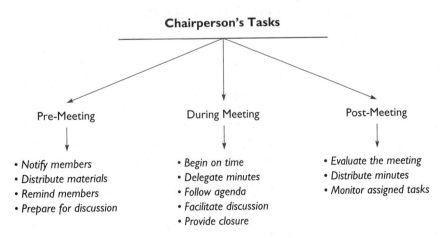

Chairperson's Tasks

Pre-Meeting
- *Notify members*
- *Distribute materials*
- *Remind members*
- *Prepare for discussion*

During Meeting
- *Begin on time*
- *Delegate minutes*
- *Follow agenda*
- *Facilitate discussion*
- *Provide closure*

Post-Meeting
- *Evaluate the meeting*
- *Distribute minutes*
- *Monitor assigned tasks*

FIGURE 13.3 Chairperson's Tasks

*Tasks during
the Meeting*

Linkemer contends that during the meeting, effective chairpersons "balance strength with sensitivity; they balance knowing where they want the meeting to go with allowing the group to sometimes take it way off course; they balance having something to say with the restraint to say nothing; they assume the role of traffic cop in discussions without coming across with stifling authority."[11]

The agenda will be your guide to keeping the discussion moving in an orderly way. The meeting should begin at the scheduled time. Starting on time establishes a norm for the group and can, in subsequent meetings, minimize late arrivals. Make sure all members have an agenda and determine who will take the minutes of the meeting. Attendance should then be taken and noted in the minutes.

If you are chairing a group's first meeting, introductions may be necessary to help reduce primary tension. Clearly state the meeting's purpose, and with that in mind, ask the group to review the agenda and make any revisions that may be needed. At the completion of such preliminary tasks, you can proceed through the agenda items as planned.

If you are the chairperson, make sure that the meeting sticks to the purpose of the discussion and the items on the agenda. Monitoring the time devoted to each agenda item and summarizing group progress keeps the meeting moving along at a reasonable pace. When the group's discussion drifts too far from the meeting's purpose, remind members of their goal.

As the chairperson, you should refrain from dominating the meeting. Your first priority is facilitating the group's discussion. When the group tackles problem solving and decision making, an open and balanced discussion of all sides of an issue should be encouraged. Recognize hidden agendas and

---

TOOLBOX 13.3   Agendas and Minutes

An agenda outlines the items to be discussed or tasks to be accomplished at a meeting. During the meeting, the agenda acts as a road map guiding the group through discussion items in an orderly way. The minutes of a meeting are the official record of your group's discussion and activities. The minutes of a meeting allow your group to review what was accomplished since the last meeting and what still needs to be accomplished. The task of taking minutes should be delegated to another group member so the chairperson is free to focus on guiding the group's discussion. **Chapter 14: Agendas and Minutes** describes how to prepare a meeting's agenda and take accurate and useful minutes. Samples of model agendas and minutes are provided.

make sure that minority viewpoints are expressed and discussed. Know when to call for a vote or final decision.

Finally, the chairperson should provide a sense of closure to the meeting by ending efficiently and effectively. Briefly summarize what was accomplished and what still needs attention and action. If work has been delegated to different members during the meeting, those responsibilities should be reviewed. If the group plans to schedule another meeting, ask for agenda item suggestions and, if possible, set the date, time, and place of the next meeting. The meeting should be adjourned by politely thanking the group for their time and contributions. End the meeting on time.

Post-Meeting Tasks

After the meeting is over, take time to evaluate the meeting's success and determine what should be done to improve the next meeting. If you are the chairperson, it is your responsibility to distribute the minutes of the meeting and any reports that were prepared. As members work on projects outside the group, you may provide assistance to group members and check their progress. A chairperson's job does not end when a meeting adjourns; it may continue right up to the minute a subsequent meeting is called to order.

Participation in Meetings

Just as a single member has the power to derail a meeting with disruptive behavior, a single member has the potential to make every meeting more productive. Plan on being an active participant by preparing for the meeting in advance, by reviewing agenda items, and by thinking about your opinions on the issues. Read any material that was distributed and be prepared to discuss it. In some cases, your role as a participant may be minimal. If a special presentation or subcommittee report is being shared, you can be most effective by listening attentively. In most small group meetings, however, everyone is expected to participate. Contribute to the discussion whenever you have something relevant to add but avoid monopolizing or dominating the discussion.

As a participant you should also be willing to share some of the chair's responsibilities. Help keep the group focused on the meeting's purpose and agenda. Don't abandon a chairperson faced with other members who are distracting or disruptive. A good chairperson will welcome your assistance; and an unprepared or inexperienced chairperson will surely need your help.

*D**ealing with Difficulties*

A carefully planned meeting can fail if the chairperson or group allows individuals to persist in behavior that disrupts the group process. All group members should address such behavior rather than assuming the chairperson can or will resolve the problem. Doyle and Straus write that "dealing with these problem people is like walking a tightrope. You must maintain a delicate balance between protecting the group from the dominance of individual members while protecting individuals from being attacked by the group."[12]

Although there can be as many potential problems as there are group members, there are a few particular behaviors that cause most of the headaches. Based on our own observations and some of the "people problems" identified by Doyle and Straus,[13] we offer several suggestions for dealing with member difficulties in meetings.

Nonparticipant

It is not necessary to have full participation at all times just for the sake of participation; the goal is to have a balanced group discussion over the course of the entire meeting. The group should be concerned, however, with members whose participation is always minimal. Are they anxious, unprepared, or uninterested? Apprehensive or introverted participants should not be forced to contribute before they are ready. At the same time, though, make sure you provide opportunities for reluctant members to become involved in the discussion. Increasing your eye contact with less talkative members may encourage their participation by signaling your interest in anything they might have to say.

When nonparticipants do contribute, respond positively to their input to demonstrate that you see the value in their ideas. Negative responses to apprehensive group members can inhibit participation for the rest of a meeting.

Loudmouth

A member who talks more than the others is not necessarily a problem. However, when a person talks so much that no one else gets a chance to speak, the group has a loudmouth problem. At first, allow loudmouths to state their ideas and acknowledge that you understand their position. It may be necessary to interrupt them to do so. Then shift your focus to other members or other issues by asking for alternative viewpoints. If a loudmouth continues to dominate, remind him or her of the importance of getting input from everyone. The next time the group meets, you may want to assign the loudmouth the task of taking minutes as a way of shifting focus from talking to listening and writing.

Interrupter   Sometimes group members are so preoccupied with their own thoughts and goals that they interrupt others when they have something to say. Although most interrupters are not trying to be rude, their impatience and excitement cause them to speak out while other members are still talking. When a group member continually interrupts others, it is time to interrupt the interrupter. Invite the previous speaker to finish making her or his point. A more aggressive option is simply not to allow the person to be interrupted, by intervening and saying, "Let Mary finish her point first, and then we'll hear other viewpoints."

Whisperer   Carrying on a confidential conversation with another group member during a meeting can distract everyone else. The interference caused by members who are whispering or snickering makes it hard to concentrate and listen to other members. Directing eye contact toward such sideline conversations may make the offenders more aware of their disruptive behavior. If the behavior persists, ask the talkers to share their ideas with the group. This action will probably stop the behavior and may uncover issues that deserve discussion.

Latecomers and Early Leavers   People coming in and out of the meeting after it has begun can distract those who have managed their time to arrive on schedule and stay through the entire meeting. If you are the chairperson, start the meeting at the scheduled time and avoid wasting meeting time by stopping to review what has already been accomplished. A government employee described his frustration with latecomers in this way:

> It irks me when the chairperson stops to review everything that was missed for a person who comes in late to a meeting. I feel like I'm being punished for being on time and the other person is being rewarded for inconsiderate behavior.

Let latecomers sit without participating until they have observed enough of the meeting to contribute to the discussion. It is not advisable to publicly reprimand or embarrass latecomers or early leavers, but you may want to talk to them after the meeting about what can be done to enable them to attend the entire meeting.

Members who come in and out of the meeting to do other work at the same time cannot be full participants. Such behavior is distracting; it communicates to the rest of the group that the meeting is not very important. These members should be asked politely either to stay for the entire discussion or to take care of other work in advance.

Whether you are dealing with a loudmouth or a latecomer, keep the group's best interests in mind. When difficulties are not addressed, participants may feel so uncomfortable they stop attending meetings altogether.

When you have to confront a dysfunctional member, be sensitive and focus on the behavior rather than making personal attacks. Point out the behavior and suggest alternative behavior, as well as the consequences if the alternative is not followed. Don't overreact; your intervention can be more disruptive than the problem member's behavior. It is best to begin with the least confrontational approach and then work toward more direct methods as necessary.

Adapting to Differences

Very often, group members from different cultural, ethnic, and age groups do not share similar expectations about group roles. Dodd reports that some cultures expect more directive leadership and control than others.[14] In countries with more socialist governments such as Denmark, Australia, or Israel, people expect there to be equality among members. In other countries such as India or Mexico, where there are strong traditional beliefs about class differences, group members may expect a leader to exert more power.

In some cultures, it would be considered disrespectful for a young group member to interrupt an older one or for a new group member to challenge a veteran member. In such cases, it may be tempting to interpret lack of participation for inattention or lack of interest when, in fact, the group member is demonstrating a high degree of respect for the group and its leader.

At one college, the president appointed an advisory council to coordinate activities designed to improve the racial climate on campus. One member of the group reported the following observation:

> One council member was a former diplomat from an African country. He rarely spoke but when he did, he always began with a very formal "Madam Chairman." After that he would deliver a three to five minute speech in which he would summarize what had been said and offer his opinion and recommendations. When he was finished, he would thank everyone for listening. At first we didn't know how to respond. It was so formal, so complex. Eventually we learned to expect at least one "speech" from this member. We learned to listen and respond to a very different style of participation.

This member defined his participant role very formally and acted accordingly. Patience on the part of other participants allowed his custom of formality to be accommodated.

Group members may represent different ages, genders, educational and work backgrounds, religions, political viewpoints, and cultures. All of these elements can affect how a meeting is conducted and how well a meeting meets its goals. Adapting to the diversity of group members involves understanding and accommodating differences while pursuing shared goals.

Evaluating the Meeting

To determine the effectiveness of meetings and identify areas for improvement, chairpersons and participants should evaluate their meetings. There are a number of ways to determine the success of a meeting:

- Throughout the meeting the chairperson may ask for comments before moving on to the next item. This practice allows the group to modify its behavior and improve interaction when discussing the next item.
- At the end of the meeting, the chairperson can briefly summarize perceptions of the meeting and ask for comments and suggestions from the group before adjourning.
- After the meeting, participants can be approached individually for their comments and suggestions for improving the group's next meeting.
- A Post-Meeting Reaction Form can be distributed to members before adjourning.

A **Post-Meeting Reaction (PMR) Form** is a questionnaire designed to collect and assess reactions from meeting participants. The chairperson should prepare the form in advance of the meeting, distribute the form at the meeting, and collect it before participants leave. Regardless of the format of the questions, a post-meeting reaction form should ask questions about the issues being discussed, the quantity and quality of group interaction, and the effectiveness of meeting procedure. The feedback from the group should then be used to improve the next meeting. The sample PMR form in the Assessment section at the end of this chapter contains many of the typical questions asked to evaluate a group's meeting. It is important to remember that the evaluation questions should match the purpose of each meeting.

Balanced Meetings

Just as every group is unique, every meeting is different. Planning and conducting effective meetings require balanced decision making. The group should strive for an ideal meeting but also understand what can realistically be accomplished in a single meeting.

To Meet
Chairperson Responsibilities
Dealing with Difficulties

Not to Meet
Participant Responsibilities
Dealing with Differences

Effective Meetings

FIGURE 13.4 Effective Meetings

The 3M Meeting Management Team describes the critical role of the chairperson as "a delicate balancing act" in which chairpersons must

> . . . influence the group's thinking—not dictate it. They must encourage participation but discourage domination of the discussion by any single member. They must welcome ideas but also question them, challenge them, and insist on evidence to back them up. They must control the meeting but take care not to overcontrol it.[15]

Effective meetings achieve a balance between the different needs of individual members and the necessity of accomplishing the group's goal. Balanced meetings result in greater productivity and member satisfaction.

*S*ummary Study Guide

- The primary characteristics of a meeting are schedule, structure, and a designated chairperson.
- All group members should understand the purpose and goals of a meeting.
- For an effective meeting, decide who should attend, where and when the meeting should be held, and what materials participants will need to be prepared.
- As a chairperson, you may be responsible for a variety of tasks including planning, preparing for, conducting, and following up a meeting.
- As a participant, you should take responsibility for the success of the meeting by being prepared, contributing to the discussion, and sharing the responsibilities of the chairperson.
- Control of disruptive behavior should focus on achieving the group's goal and maintaining group morale.

- Meetings should be adapted to the diverse needs and expectations of participants.
- Learn from experience by evaluating meetings and using such feedback to improve future meetings.

Groupwork *Meet the People Problems*[16]

GOAL   To understand the principles and apply textbook suggestions to other common people problems that arise during meetings.

PARTICIPANTS   Groups of 5–7 members.

PROCEDURE

1. Read the descriptions of the five additional people problems that often arise in meetings.
2. As a group, prepare at least two strategies for dealing with each type of people problem.
3. Groups should share their strategies with the entire class and discuss the following question: What general, overriding principles emerge as effective strategies for dealing with member difficulties?

People Problems

The Broken Record. Brings up the same point or idea over and over again. Regardless of what other members say, the Broken Record keeps "singing the same song."

The Headshaker. Nonverbally responds in a disruptive manner. Shakes head, rolls eyes, groans, slams books shut, madly scribbles notes after someone has said something. Members begin reacting to what the Headshaker does rather than what is said.

The Know-It-All. Uses age, seniority, credentials, and experience to argue a point. Know-It-Alls declare "I've been here for twenty years, and I know this won't work"; or "I'm the only one here with an accounting degree, so you'd better listen."

The Backseat Driver. Keeps telling everyone what they should do or should have done. "If we'd met earlier this week, we could have avoided this problem"; "I would have let everyone read the report rather than summarizing it."

The Attacker. Launches personal attacks on other group members or the chairperson. Purposely zeros in on and criticizes the ideas and opinions of others.

A S S E S S M E N T

Post-Meeting Reaction (PMR) Form

Directions   After a selected meeting, complete the following PMR form by circling the number that best represents your answer to each question. After compiling the answers from all participants, including the chairperson, use the results as a basis for improving future meetings.

1. How clear was the purpose of the meeting?
   unclear   1   2   3   4   5   clear

2. How useful was the agenda?
   useless   1   2   3   4   5   useful

3. Was the meeting room comfortable?
   uncomfortable   1   2   3   4   5   comfortable

4. How prepared were group members for the meeting?
   unprepared   1   2   3   4   5   well prepared

5. Did everyone have an equal opportunity to participate in the discussion?
   limited opportunity   1   2   3   4   5   ample opportunity

6. Were different viewpoints listened to?
   not listened to   1   2   3   4   5   listened to

7. How would you describe the overall climate of the meeting?
   hostile   1   2   3   4   5   friendly

8. Were assignments and deadlines made clear by the end of the meeting?
   unclear   1   2   3   4   5   clear

9. How would you rate this meeting overall?
   unproductive   1   2   3   4   5   productive

Additional Comments

Recommended Readings

Levasseur, R. E. (1994). *Breakthrough business meetings: Shared leadership in action.* Holbrook, MA: Bob Adams.

Miller, R. F. (1991). *Running a meeting that works.* Hauppauge, NY: Barron's Educational Series.

3M Meeting Management Team with J. Drew. (1995). *Mastering meetings: Discovering the hidden potential of effective business meetings.* New York: McGraw-Hill.

Notes

1. 3M Meeting Management Team with J. Drew. (1995). *Mastering meetings: Discovering the hidden potential of effective business meetings.* New York: McGraw-Hill, p. 11.
2. Wiggins, D. (1998). "How to have successful meetings." *Journal of Environmental Health, 60,* p. 1. Available: http://db.texshare.edu/ovidweb/ovidweb.cgi.
3. Sheridan, J. (September 4, 1989). The $37 billion waste. *Industry Week,* p. 11.
4. Adapted from Miller, R. F. (1991). *Running a meeting that works.* Hauppauge, NY: Barron's Educational Series, p. 3.
5. Miller, p. 13.
6. Anderson, K. (1997). *Making Meetings Work: How to plan and conduct effective meetings.* West Des Moines, IA: American Media Publishing, p. 17.
7. Katzenbach, J. R. & Smith, D. K. (1993). *The wisdom of teams: Creating the high-performance organization.* New York: HarperBusiness, p. 9.
8. Miller, p. 11.
9. Anderson, p. 18.
10. Jay, A. (1991). How to run a meeting. In *The articulate executive: Improving written, interpersonal, and group communication.* Boston: Harvard Business Review, p. 100.
11. Linkemer, B. (1987). *How to run a meeting that works.* New York: American Management Association, p. 42.
12. Doyle, M. & Straus, D. (1976). *How to make meetings work.* New York: Jove, p. 105.
13. See Doyle & Straus for additional people problems, pp. 107–117.
14. Dodd, C. H. (1995). *Dynamics of intercultural communication* (4th ed.). Madison, WI: Brown & Benchmark, p. 91.
15. 3M Meeting Management Team, p. 78.
16. Based on the people problems developed by Doyle & Straus, pp. 107–117.

*A*gendas and Minutes

The Importance of Agendas

> The agenda is one of the two most powerful tools in meeting management. The other [is the] minutes of the meeting.[1]

An **agenda** is the outline of items to be discussed and the tasks to be accomplished at a meeting. A well-prepared agenda can serve many purposes. First and foremost, the agenda is an organizational tool—a road map for the discussion that helps group members remain focused on their task. When used properly, an agenda helps participants prepare for a meeting by telling them what to expect and even how to prepare. As a time management tool, Thomsett suggests that "you can use the agenda to plan the time required for a meeting . . . and then to control the total amount of time spent on each topic."[2] An agenda also provides a sense of continuity for a group—it tracks member assignments and provides status checks for work in progress. After a meeting, the agenda can be used to assess a meeting's success by determining the extent to which all items on the agenda were addressed.

When you are very busy or when a meeting is routine and predictable, writing up an agenda for a future meeting may seem like a waste of time.

MOST public groups—such as this city council meeting—use agendas and minutes to document their work. What are the benefits to this group of recording meeting minutes on a computer during the meeting? (Spencer Grant/PhotoEdit)

Just the opposite is true. Failure to plan and prepare an agenda denies a chairperson and a group one of the most powerful tools in meeting management. Burleson notes that "although agendas can be formal, informal, or anywhere between . . . the operative rule is: If there is a meeting, there ought to be an agenda."[3]

Agendas are an absolute must for every meeting. One study reported that nearly one-third of participants blamed the failure of meetings on the lack of an agenda; nearly two-thirds (63 percent) said no written agenda was distributed in advance.[4] A carefully prepared agenda is one of the best ways to make meetings more productive.[5] The Software Engineering Institute, a federally funded research and development center at Carnegie Mellon University in Pittsburgh, considers agendas so important "that employees are allowed to walk out of meetings that convene without one."[6] The 3M Management Team concludes that a "written agenda, distributed in advance, is the single best predictor of a successful meeting."[7]

Elements of an Agenda

While it is the chairperson's responsibility to prepare and distribute an agenda in advance of the meeting, group input can ensure that the agenda covers topics important to the entire group. Asking group members to suggest items for an agenda ensures that important issues are discussed and that members feel involved in the process of planning the meeting.

A traditional business meeting agenda will include the following items:

- *Purpose of the Meeting.* A clear statement of the meeting's objective and topics for discussion allows members to come prepared to focus on a particular objective.
- *Names of Group Members.* A list of all invited participants lets members know who will be part of the discussion.
- *Date, Time, and Place of the Meeting.* Clearly indicate the date, time, duration, and precise location of the meeting.
- *Call to Order.* This is the point at which the chairperson officially begins the meeting.
- *Approval of the Agenda.* Members are given the opportunity to correct or modify the agenda before approving it for the meeting.
- *Approval of Previous Meeting's Minutes.* For groups that meet on a regular basis, the minutes of the previous meeting are reviewed, revised if necessary, and approved by the group as an accurate representation of the last meeting's business.
- *Reports from Individuals and Subcommittees.* Individuals and subcommittees within a group report on the progress of their activities. When organizations hold formal business meetings, the officers of the group report on their work, after which subcommittee reports are presented.
- *Unfinished Business.* This section of the meeting includes any topics that require ongoing discussion from meeting to meeting or issues the group was unable to resolve during the last meeting.
- *New Business.* New discussion items are outlined in this category. If the issue needs to be addressed again at the next meeting, it will be listed as unfinished business on the next agenda.
- *Announcements.* Any items of information that the group needs to know but that do not require any discussion are announced.
- *Adjournment.* The chairperson officially dismisses the participants and ends the meeting.

Not all meetings will follow the traditional sequence of agenda items. The customs of the group and the purpose of the meeting will determine the format of the meeting's agenda. For example, if the purpose of the meeting is to solve a problem, the agenda items may be in the form of questions rather than the key word format of a more formal agenda. The questions would be determined by the problem-solving method the group has decided to use.

— PARKVIEW CONDOMINIUM ASSOCIATION —

Parkview Condominium Board of Directors
May 18, 1996, 7:30 p.m. – 9:00 p.m.
Community Center Recreation Room

Purpose: Monthly Business Meeting

    I. Call to Order

   II. Approval of Meeting Agenda

  III. Approval of April 20, 1996, Minutes

  IV. Officers' Reports
      A. President's Report
      B. Treasurer's Report

   V. Committee Reports
      A. Finance Committee
      B. Facilities and Operations Committee
      C. Architectural Advisory Committee
      D. Activities Committee
      E. Landscape Committee

  VI. Unfinished Business
      A. Compvuter System Upgrade (For Decision)
      B. Management Fee Contract (For Decision)
      C. Fall Maintenence (For Decision)

 VII. New Business
      A. Parking Tickets (For Information)
      B. Recycling Program (For Discussion)

VIII. Announcements

  IX. Adjournment

FIGURE 14.1   Sample Business Meeting Agenda

Additional Options

In addition to identifying topics to be addressed during the meeting, agenda items should include any information that helps group members prepare for the meeting.

- Note the amount of time it should take to complete a discussion item or action. This will let the group know the relative importance of the item and help them manage the time available for discussion.

Recycling Task Force
September 14, 1996, 1:00 p.m. – 3:00 p.m.
Conference Room 352

Purpose: To recommend ways to increase the effectiveness and participation
in the company's recycling program.

  I.   What is the goal of this meeting? What have we been asked to do?

 II.   How effective is the company's current recycling effort?

III.   Why has the program lacked effectiveness and full participation?

IV.   What are the requirements or standards for an ideal program?
       A. Level of Participation
       B. Reasonable Cost
       C. Physical Requirements
       D. Legal Requirements

 V.   What are the possible ways in which we could improve the
      recycling program?

VI.   What specific methods do we recommend for increasing the
      recycling program's effectiveness and level of participation?

VII.   How should the recommendations be implemented? Who or what
       groups should be charged with implementation?

FIGURE 14.2   Sample Discussion Meeting Agenda

- Identify how the group will deal with each item by noting whether information will be shared with the group, whether the group will discuss an issue, or whether a decision must be made. The phrases "For Information," "For Discussion," and "For Decision" can be placed next to appropriate agenda items.
- Include the name of any person responsible for reporting information on a particular item or facilitating a portion of the discussion. Such assignments remind members to prepare for a specific topic or action item.

Double Checking the Agenda

Once you have determined what items need to be included in the agenda, check them against the meeting's original purpose.

- Are there any items that don't relate to the purpose and can be delayed until another meeting? If so, they should be eliminated from the agenda.

- Can all of the items on the agenda be addressed within the allotted meeting time? If there isn't enough time to cover all of the items, rephrase the meeting's purpose to be more specific, and eliminate some items.

Hawkins cautions against "overloading agendas by trying to do too much in a single meeting."[8] For example, the group may not have time to discuss the causes of a problem and start identifying possible solutions in the same meeting. The number of meetings and their purpose should then be reconsidered. For instance, "Identify the causes and effects of the lack of sufficient parking on campus" could be the purpose of one meeting. "Recommend solutions to the campus parking problem" could be the purpose of a follow-up meeting.

Determining the Order of Items

After you have identified all the agenda items, carefully consider the order in which topics should be discussed. When several different topics must be addressed within a single meeting, agenda items should be put in an order that will maximize productivity and group satisfaction. For example, a controversial issue that *must* be discussed should not be placed last on an agenda. If the topic is left until the end of a meeting, a group may not have enough time to discuss it and make an important decision. Furthermore, ending with an item that could produce conflict may not leave members feeling positive about the group experience.

The following guidelines should help you determine how to balance the sequence of discussion topics in an agenda:

- Begin the meeting with simple business items and easier-to-discuss issues.
- Reserve important and difficult items for the middle portion of the meeting.
- Use the last third of the meeting for easy discussion items not requiring difficult decisions.

This sequence provides the group with a sense of accomplishment before it launches into more controversial, tension-producing issues. If a difficult but important decision is taking more time than anticipated, the group may be able to deal with those less important discussion issues at the next meeting.

Using the Agenda

The chairperson should distribute the agenda to all group participants in advance of the meeting and make sure that all those present at the meeting have an agenda to follow. Cynthia Ward, Vice President of Marketing for a computer documents corporation, suggests handing out the agenda "at least a week beforehand, so there's no reason for anyone to come unprepared."[9] At the beginning of a meeting the group should review the agenda and make any revisions before proceeding with the discussion. The agenda is then used to guide the meeting. Time spent carefully planning the agenda will have been wasted if the group doesn't agree to follow it during the meeting.

The Importance of Minutes

The **minutes** of a meeting are the written record of a group's discussion and activities. Minutes become a group's long-term memory by documenting its activities from one meeting to the next. McEachern points out that minutes can reinforce group norms because they are a record of group behavior.[10] By looking through a group's minutes over a period of time, you can learn about a group's activities, measure how productive it has been, learn about individual member contributions to the group, and know whether group meetings tend to be formal or informal.

In formal meetings, minutes are legal documents as well as the historical records of an organization. In such cases, minutes should be very accurate because they can be used in a court of law to verify an action or document a person's statements. Within some organizations, signed copies of minutes are kept in a secure place for reference.

The minutes record discussion issues and decisions for those who attended a meeting and provide a way to communicate with those who didn't attend. Because the minutes of a meeting are often read by others, they are also an opportunity to reward members by officially recognizing their good work. For example, the minutes could state that: "The officers officially thanked Marla and Kevin for chairing the annual Fourth of July picnic com-

The Relationship of Agendas and Minutes

FIGURE 14.3 The Relationship of Agendas and Minutes

> **TOOLBOX 14.1**   Parliamentary Procedure and Minutes
>
> The designated clerk (or secretary) of a group plays an important role before, during, and after meetings that use parliamentary procedure to conduct business. Parliamentary rules specify that the clerk keep accurate records of the proceedings of an organization, be prepared to read aloud all motions and their amendments during a meeting, prepare a roll call of members and call it when necessary, and preserve all important meeting documents. **Chapter 15: Parliamentary Procedure** provides a summary of the rules and practices that should be understood by the person assigned the task of recording minutes.

mittee." Of most importance, however, the minutes help prevent disagreement over what was decided in the meeting and what tasks individual members agreed to do.

Select a Recorder

The chairperson is ultimately responsible for the accuracy and distribution of the minutes. However, during the meeting the chairperson must be free to facilitate the group's discussion. The task of taking minutes should be delegated to another group member. The group may designate a recorder or secretary to take minutes at every meeting or have members take turns volunteering to do the minutes. Regardless of who takes the minutes, the chairperson is responsible for checking their accuracy and distributing a copy to all group members.

Determine What Information to Include

For the most part, the format of the minutes should follow the format of the agenda. If you are assigned to take minutes, you will probably include much of the following information:

- Name of the group
- Date and place of the meeting
- Names of those attending
- Name of person who chaired the meeting
- Names of absent members
- Exact time the meeting was called to order
- Exact time the meeting was adjourned
- Name of the person preparing the minutes
- Summary of the group's discussion and decisions using agenda items as headings
- Specific action items

Action items are tasks that individual members have been assigned to do after the meeting. An action item includes the person's name, the assignment, and the deadline. For example, an action item might look like this: "Action: M. Smith will review the prices charged by competing companies by the next meeting." It is helpful to underline action items in the minutes to make it easier to refer back to them when reviewing the group's progress.

Formal and Informal Minutes

The more formal the meeting, the more information must be included in the minutes. For example, if a group is using parliamentary procedure, the minutes must include all proposed motions and the results of any votes. In order to take accurate minutes for such meetings, the recorder or secretary should be familiar with parliamentary procedure. The minutes from informal meetings normally don't include such details. The samples in Figure 14.4 and Figure 14.5 illustrate the difference between formal and informal meeting minutes.

Taking Minutes

Well-prepared minutes are brief and accurate. When summarizing a group's discussion, it is important to remember that the minutes are not a word-for-word record of everything that every member has said. To be useful, they must briefly summarize the discussion. The following guidelines should be used when taking minutes:

- Instead of describing the discussion in detail, write clear statements that summarize the main ideas and actions.
- Make sure to word decisions, motions, action items, and deadlines exactly as the group makes them in order to avoid future disagreements and misunderstandings.
- If there is any question about what to include in the minutes at any point during the meeting, ask the group for clarification.
- Obtain a copy of the agenda and any reports that were presented to attach to the final copy of the minutes. These documents become part of the group record along with the minutes.

Sometimes it is useful to tape-record the group's discussion so the secretary can refer to it when preparing the minutes. A tape recorder can ensure accuracy, but before choosing to use one, you should carefully consider its potential effect on the group discussion. Group members should be informed that the minutes will be taped. Understand that some people feel uncomfortable being recorded and may limit their participation.

Be Objective. Although the minutes of a meeting should be brief, they also must be accurate and impartial. Burleson contends that "minutes should never contain personal reflections, opinions, insights, or be written from a

**Draft Summary Minutes for the
SCA Legislative Council Meeting—1994**

Presiding: Bruce Gronbeck, SCA President
Parliamentarian: Gaut Ragsdale
Recording: James L. Gaudino, Executive Director
Location: Acadia Room
Marriott, New Orleans, LA

Note: The following material represents a summary of actions taken by the 1994 Legislative Council. Attendance reports are included in Appendix A.

Call to Order: The meeting of the 1994 Legislative Council was called to order by Bruce Gronbeck, SCA President, at 1:10 P.M. on Friday, November 18, 1994, in the Acadia Room of the New Orleans Marriott, New Orleans, LA.

Opening Remarks: Gronbeck welcomed the Council members and offered opening remarks. The President presented an overview of the agenda and an estimated schedule for conducting the Council's business. He then reminded the Council members to sign the attendance sheets and to pick up handouts distributed at the meeting. The President asked that all members of the council speak loudly or use wireless microphones so that all could be heard.

Announcements: Gronbeck made the following announcements:

Judith Trent will be the new SCA 2nd Vice President (assumes position following the Annual Meeting).

The newly elected LC Members-at-large are Judith C. Espinola, Guo-Ming Chen, and Kelly S. McNeilis. They will serve on the 1995–97 Legislative Councils.

Approval of Minutes from the 1993 Legislative Council Meeting: The minutes of the 1993 Legislative Council meeting were approved as distributed by voice vote.

Approval of Standing Rules: A motion was made and seconded establishing the following as Standing Rules of the 1994 Legislative Council (LC): 1) LC members must sign the roll for each LC meeting. 2) Only LC members shall offer motions and vote. 3) Substantive motions and amendments must be provided in writing when presented to the LC. 4) No LC member may move the previous question (close debate) prior to an opportunity for one pro and one con speech on a debatable motion. The motion carried.

NEW BUSINESS

Review of the FY 93/94 Financial Reports: The SCA Income and Expense Report, the SCA Balance Sheet, SCA Investment Summary, and the Report of Independent Auditor were distributed to Council members prior to the meeting. Finance Board Chairperson Trent presented a summary of each report. A motion was made and seconded to accept the FY 93/94 reports as presented. The motion carried.

Requests for SCA affiliate status: A motion was made and seconded that the Legislative Council grant the status of affiliate organization to the Association for Chinese Communication Studies. After discussion, the motion carried.

Resolutions: The following resolutions were considered (see Appendix B for the text of the resolutions):

Statement on Language Arts: A motion was made to adopt the Resolution Endorsing Comprehensive Language Arts. After brief discussion, the motion carried.

Statement of Principles on Information Highway: A motion was made to adopt the Resolution establishing a Credo for Free and Responsible Use of Electronic Communication Networks. After discussion, a motion was made and seconded to amend the resolution by changing "We support freedom of expression and condemn attempts to limit any form of information processing or electronic communication" to "We support freedom of expression and condemn attempts to constrain information processing or electronic communication." Some concern was expressed about overly general language in the resolution and inadequate treatment of copyright issues. The motion to amend carried. After discussion, the original motion carried.

Adjournment: The first Council meeting was adjourned at 5:40 P.M., November 18, 1994.

(This sample is composed of edited *excerpts* selected from 14 pages of minutes recorded at the Speech Communication Association's 1994 Legislative Council meeting that took place at the association's annual convention. For clarification of parliamentary actions recorded in the minutes, see Chapter 15.)

FIGURE 14.4   Sample of Formal Minutes

Domestic Violence Class Discussion Group Meeting
February 10, 1995, in Library Conference Room 215

Present: Gabriella Hernandez (chairperson), Eric Beck,
Terri Harrison, Will Mabry, Tracey Tibbs
Absent: Lance Nickens

Meeting began at 2:00 P.M.

Group Topic: The group discussed whether emotional and verbal abuse should be included in the project. Since we don't have much time to do our presentation, we decided to limit the topic to physical abuse only.

Research Assignments: Since the assignment is due in two weeks, we decided to divide the issue into different topics and research them on our own.

Action: Eric will research why people stay in abusive relationships.

Action: Gabriella will research the effects on the children.

Action: Terri will find statistics and examples of the seriousness of the problem.

Action: Will is going to find out why and how the abuse happens.

Action: Tracey will find out what resources are available in the area for victims.

Members will report on their research at the next meeting.

Absent Members: Lance has not been to the last two class meetings. We don't know if he is still going to participate in the group. Action: Gabriella will call Lance.

Class Presentation: We need to think of creative ways to make a presentation to the class. The group decided to think about it and discuss it at the next meeting.

Next meeting: Our next meeting will be at 2:30 on Tuesday, February 14th, in the same place. Action: Terri will reserve the room.

The meeting ended at 3:15 P.M.

(Meeting notes taken by Tracey Tibbs)

FIGURE 14.5   Sample of Informal Minutes

position. Minutes are factual. Minutes are neutral."[11] If you are the recorder of the minutes, you must be objective. Report the facts and all sides of a discussion accurately and never insert your own personal opinions. The minutes must reflect the experience of the entire group, not just the person chosen to document it.

Be Discreet.   There are times when the group may have a discussion or make comments they want kept "off the record." The group may need to blow off steam or feel comfortable discussing a sensitive matter. Reporting such comments would only serve to create a less open communication climate, in which members guard what they say for fear of being held accountable for it later. If the group determines that something should not appear on record, that decision should be honored by whomever is responsible for taking the minutes.

Prepare the Minutes   Immediately after the meeting, the minutes should be prepared for distribution. The longer you delay, the more difficult it will be to remember the details of the meeting. For this reason, you should report not only the date the

CLOSE TO HOME   JOHN McPHERSON

As soon as Mrs. Felster began to read the minutes of the last meeting, the board members knew she was not going to work out as the new secretary.

meeting took place but also the date you prepared the minutes. If a discrepancy is later found in the minutes, members may conclude that too much time elapsed before the minutes were prepared. One way to reduce elapsed time is to compose the minutes during or immediately after the meeting. In some meetings, minutes may be taken on a laptop computer.

Once the minutes have been prepared, they should be given to the chairperson for review. The chairperson will either request that corrections be made or distribute the minutes to group members for review before coming to the next meeting. Once the group has officially approved them, the minutes are final and become the official record of the meeting.

Agendas	**Minutes**
Organization	Organization
Information	Information
Distribution and Use	Preparation and Distribution

Agendas and Minutes

FIGURE 14.6 Agendas and Minutes

Balanced Agendas and Minutes

Agendas must be designed to promote maximum participation and productivity during a meeting without including more items than the group can realistically manage. A group will accomplish little if too few items are placed on a meeting's agenda. An agenda with too many items may require the group to make hasty decisions without adequate discussion.

The most difficult part of taking minutes is balancing the need to accurately report the group's discussion against the need to be brief. Including too many details of the meeting is unnecessary because the minutes would be difficult for the group to use later. Minutes that contain too little information will not accurately represent what the group has accomplished. If the minutes are referred to later, any vagueness in their preparation will confuse the group. Agendas and minutes must contain a balance of information in order to be useful tools for group meetings.

Summary Study Guide

- An agenda is an outline of the items to be discussed and the tasks to be accomplished at a meeting.
- The traditional business agenda will include the following information: purpose, names, date, time, place, call to order, approval of agenda and minutes, reports, unfinished business, new business, announcements, and adjournment.

- Agenda items should be ordered in a sequence that permits the group to complete all of the tasks.
- The minutes of the meeting are the written record of the group's discussion and actions.
- Although the chairperson is responsible for the accuracy and distribution of the minutes, another group member should be designated to take the minutes.
- The format of the minutes will generally follow the format of the meeting's agenda; the formality of the minutes will depend on the nature of the meeting.
- Well-prepared minutes are brief, accurate, objective, and appropriately discreet.

Groupwork *Designing an Agenda Form*

GOAL   To highlight the essential elements in a meeting agenda and create a useful agenda form for future meetings.

PARTICIPANTS   Groups of 5–7 members.

PROCEDURE

1. As a group, use the textbook's list of essential elements and additional options for an agenda to create an original, standardized agenda form.
2. Make sure that your fill-in-the-blank agenda form reminds your group of things that should be noted or covered before, during, and after a meeting.
3. In addition to the topics for discussion and action, your agenda should include items and information that help group members prepare and participate effectively. Examples are the names of participants, invited guests, material needed for the meeting, action item assignments and deadlines, time allocated for discussion or action, and scheduled oral presentations.

ASSESSMENT

Agenda and Minutes Checklist

Directions   Use the following checklist to assess the extent to which a meeting's agenda and minutes helped your group work toward achieving its goals.

Agenda

_____ The agenda was prepared and sent to all participants in advance of the meeting.

_____ The purpose of the meeting was clearly stated on the agenda.

_____ Depending on the purpose and formality of the meeting, the agenda contained essential elements such as the date, time, place, and duration of the meeting, names of participants, and discussion and action items.

_____ All the agenda items could be discussed during the allotted time of the meeting.

Minutes

_____ A recorder was assigned or volunteered to take minutes.

_____ Depending on the purpose and formality of the meeting, the minutes contained essential elements such as the time and date of the meeting, names of the chairperson, recorder, and participants, a summary of the discussion and decisions, and action items.

_____ The recorder accurately summarized the key ideas and action items.

_____ The minutes were objective and discreet.

_____ The minutes were prepared and distributed to group members within a short time after the meeting.

_____ The minutes would be understandable to people who did not attend the meeting.

Recommended Readings

Burleson, C. W. (1990). *Effective meetings: The complete guide.* New York: John Wiley.
Doyle, M. & Straus, D. (1976). *How to make meetings work.* New York: Jove.
Thomsett, M. C. (1989). *The little black book of business meetings.* New York: AMACOM.

Notes   1. Burleson, C. W. (1990). *Effective meetings: The complete guide*. New York: John Wiley, p. 25.
2. Thomsett, M. C. (1989). *The little black book of business meetings*. New York: AMACOM, pp. 91–92.
3. Burleson, p. 206.
4. 3M Management Team with J. Drew. (1995). *Mastering meetings: Discovering the hidden potential of effective business meetings*. New York: McGraw-Hill, p. 9.
5. Hawkins, C. (1997). "First aid for meetings." *Public Relations Quarterly* [on-line], 42, p. 2. Available: http://db.texshare.edu/ovidweb/ovidweb.cgi. Accession Number: 03528854.
6. Dressler, C. (December 31, 1995). We've got to stop meeting like this. *The Washington Post*, p. H2.
7. 3M Management Team, p. 26.
8. Hawkins, p. 2.
9. Ligos, M. (1998). "Why your meetings are a total bore." *Sales and Marketing Management* [on-line], 150, p. 2. Available: http://db.texshare.edu/ovidweb/ovidweb.cgi. Accession Number: 03713802.
10. McEachern, R. W. (1998). "Meeting minutes as symbolic action." *Journal of Business and Technical Communication* [on-line], 12, p. 3. Available: http://db.texshare.edu/ovidweb/ovidweb.cgi. Accession Number: 03683385.
11. Burleson, p. 88.

Parliamentary Procedure

The Rules of the Game

No one questions the need for rules in sporting events. Even the simplest schoolyard basketball or softball game follows a set of basic rules. Without them, playing the game would be impossible, and players could end up in a brawl. The same is true for certain kinds of group discussions and meetings. As discussed in Chapter 2, most groups develop informal rules and procedures. In small, casual groups, these rules can be a simple set of group norms about what members should do during the discussion.

In large, formal groups, rules can be as detailed and complicated as official baseball rules. In such groups, the official rule book is usually *Robert's Rules of Order, Newly Revised* or adaptations of it.[1] When J. J. Auer wrote that "parliamentary rules are just as necessary, and no more technical, than rules governing baseball or football,"[2] he was inviting his readers to become responsible players in a serious game that can determine whether a group achieves its goal.

What Is Parliamentary Procedure?

Parliamentary procedure is a systematic method used by groups to determine the will of the majority. For group members new to parliamentary procedure, the experience can be confusing and intimidating. Not only are there hundreds of rules, the language of parliamentary procedure seems old fashioned: "Mr. Chairman, I call for the previous question" or "Madam Chairman, I rise to a point of order."

One of our students told us that learning parliamentary procedure is something like mastering the proper etiquette for a formal dinner. Courses progress in a ritualized order: an appetizer and/or soup, a light fish course, the main dish, a small salad, a cheese course, and sweets. Surrounding your plate is an armament of utensils: several different types of knives, forks, and spoons. Three or four empty glasses stand near your plate. The formality and splendor can be overwhelming. But with practice and by observing other diners, you soon get the hang of how to get through and even enjoy a fancy meal. The same is true when learning and using parliamentary procedure.

One reason the rules may seem old-fashioned is that the roots of parliamentary procedure are found in the British Parliament's House of Commons. Like the House of Representatives in the U.S. Congress, Parliament's House of Commons meets to debate and eventually make legislative decisions. Much older than the U.S. Congress, the British Parliament has a stormy history—so stormy that it was necessary to develop standard operating procedures for conducting business. These procedures were exported to the American colonies and then developed by Thomas Jefferson into a set of procedural rules for the U.S. Senate. In 1876, Colonel Henry M. Robert used the British Parliament's procedures and Jefferson's code of rules as sources for

Robert's Rules of Order, still considered "the parliamentary bible" by many organizations.

One of the most important obligations of group members is to know the purpose, principles, and rules of parliamentary procedure. An interesting analogy describing the value of knowing parliamentary rules is provided by Gray and Rea:

> Parliamentary procedure might be compared with our traffic laws. The traffic laws tell us when to *stop,* and parliamentary procedure tells us when to be *silent.* The traffic laws tell us when to *go,* and parliamentary procedure tells us when to *speak.* Without parliamentary procedure, we often find ourselves "running into one another"—speaking at the same time. Parliamentary procedure will help "direct our traffic," and prevent our speaking at the same time.[3]

No one questions the need to learn traffic rules before being licensed to drive. In the same sense, discussants should learn the parliamentary rules before participating in a meeting or discussion that uses parliamentary procedure.

Who Uses Parliamentary Procedure?

Most organizations and associations specify in their constitution or **bylaws** (rules governing how an organization operates) that parliamentary procedure must be used to conduct meetings. Weitzel and Geist note that of the 23,000 national voluntary associations, 11,000 international associations, and 53,000 regional, state, and local associations in the United States, most use some form of parliamentary procedure to determine the will of their members.[4] Even though it can be difficult to follow the many rules specified in a manual such as *Robert's Rules of Order, Newly Revised,* organizations have learned that agreed-upon rules can ensure reasonable and civil debate as well as a timely group decision accepted by supporters and opponents alike.

In a study of how parliamentary procedure is used by community groups, Weitzel and Geist reached several interesting conclusions about the people and groups who rely on these rules:[5]

- Parliamentary procedure is widely used but not well understood by its users.
- Most users report that they feel comfortable with and like the way parliamentary procedure is used in their groups.
- Most group members feel "competent" in using parliamentary procedure.
- Parliamentary procedure is seen as a useful communication tool for group decision making.
- There is no evidence of parliamentary maneuvering by members trying to achieve some ulterior goal.
- Parliamentary procedure, even when used in an informal or limited way, seems to foster rational decision making.

In all likelihood, you belong or will belong to an association, organization, or business group that uses the rules of parliamentary procedure to govern discussion and debate. Whether such groups follow the "letter of the law" in Robert's famous rules or use the basic principles of parliamentary procedure to ensure fair and efficient discussion, parliamentary procedure can help a group engage in more time-efficient discussion in order to achieve its goals.

When to Use Parliamentary Procedure

If your group has a record of accomplishing its goals without much controversy, confusion, or waste of time and effort, parliamentary procedure may not be needed. In fact, you may want to avoid parliamentary procedure. Unless used properly, parliamentary procedure can discourage participation and hinder decision making. When a group is small enough to permit face-to-face, cooperative interaction, decision making may be easier without the restrictions imposed by the rules of parliamentary procedure. If, however, your group is either large or formal, or is forced to make critical decisions in a short period of time, parliamentary procedure can help maintain order while your group is engaged in important debate.

Parliamentary procedure helps a group determine the will of the majority by making sure that there is fair and orderly debate. Determining the majority will, however, is not the same as taking a vote; it is the result of meaningful communication that follows the rules of parliamentary procedure.

Principles of Parliamentary Procedure

Whether your group uses the most formal parliamentary rules or adapts its basic principles as a set of group norms, agreed-upon procedures can improve the quality and efficiency of decision making. *Robert's Rules of Order, Newly Revised* maintains that the rules of parliamentary procedure are "constructed upon a careful balance of the rights of persons or subgroups within

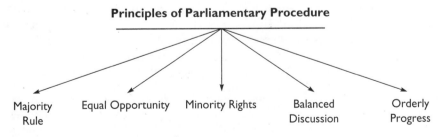

Principles of Parliamentary Procedure

Majority Rule   Equal Opportunity   Minority Rights   Balanced Discussion   Orderly Progress

FIGURE 15.1 Parliamentary Procedure

an organization's . . . total membership."[6] These rules are based on the following ideals: majority rule, equal opportunity to participate, protecting individual and minority group rights, balanced discussion, and orderly progress.

Majority Rule

First and foremost, parliamentary procedure is based upon the most basic principle in a democracy—majority rule. When groups agree to abide by the rules of parliamentary procedure, they are agreeing to accept the will of the majority. On many issues, achieving total agreement or consensus is impossible. Parliamentary procedure lays out strict rules for achieving majority rule and, in the case of critical issues, requires that decisions represent two-thirds rather than a simple majority of group members.

Equal Opportunity

Although parliamentary procedure requires that the majority rules, it also guarantees that every group member has an equal right to be heard before a vote is taken. Regardless of whether you agree or disagree with other members, you have the right to address the group with your ideas, opinions, and arguments. Parliamentary procedure also grants every member the right to vote, run for office, and have the same rules applied to all members.

Minority Rights

Many parliamentary rules are designed to protect the rights of all members whether they represent the majority or not. By using the rules of parliamentary procedure, a well-organized minority may try to block, postpone, or defeat an idea proposed by the majority of members in a group. This capability can be viewed both positively and negatively. To majority members, parliamentary tactics can create gridlock and erode good relationships among group members. However, from the point of view of minority members, these rules guarantee that a group cannot ignore minority viewpoints. All members should recognize, though, that parliamentary rules are designed to assure that the majority ultimately prevails.

Balanced Discussion

Parliamentary procedure guarantees the right of all members to speak on different sides of an issue. Several rules help a chairperson decide which members should be recognized and allowed to speak. These rules guarantee that discussion is balanced between frequent and infrequent contributors as well as between members who are for and those who are against a proposal. Sturgis is very specific about this guarantee:

> A member who has not spoken has prior claim over one who has already discussed the question. Similarly, a member who seldom speaks should be given preference over one who claims the attention of the assembly fre-

quently. . . . The presiding officer should alternate between proponents and opponents of a motion whenever possible.[7]

Orderly Progress

For groups using parliamentary procedure, the meeting's agenda provides for orderly business actions while permitting the necessary flexibility that may be needed by a decision-making group. In order to be prepared for a fair and orderly meeting, everyone should know which issues and items of business are scheduled for discussion. Many groups using parliamentary procedure require that the meeting's agenda be prepared and distributed to all members well before the day of the meeting. Such a rule guarantees that members have the time to prepare for the meeting and the debate that may accompany discussion of controversial issues.

Other Principles

The principles of majority rule, equal opportunity to participate, individual and minority rights, balanced discussion, and orderly progress are fundamental principles of parliamentary procedure and democratic action to determine the majority will. There are, however, other principles that support these basic standards. The following represents an incomplete but illustrative list of additional principles that safeguard the rights of all group members:

- Only one person may speak at a time.
- Only one proposal or subject may be discussed at any one time.
- Members must limit their remarks to the topic being discussed.
- The chairperson has the primary task of seeing that parliamentary rules are followed, but every member shares that responsibility.
- A group may not make a decision unless the meeting is properly called and the rules of parliamentary procedure are followed.

TOOLBOX 15.1   Effective Meetings

Many of the unwritten rules that are taken for granted in meetings owe their existence to parliamentary tradition. Parliamentary rules determine the specific order of business for all meetings. Parliamentary procedure also grants the chairperson the power to balance the needs of the group with the rights of individual members. Chapter 13 and Chapter 14 provide detailed information describing how to plan and conduct effective meetings as well as how to prepare agendas and take minutes during a meeting. Many of the guidelines described in these chapters have a basis in parliamentary procedure.

Parliamentary Players

Under parliamentary procedure, discussants must be approved as official voting members. For example, when a condominium association meets, each unit has only one vote regardless of how many people live in that unit. Usually when a club holds a regular business meeting, you have to be a member of the club to vote.

In addition to certifying that discussants are eligible to vote, most parliamentary groups require what is known as a **quorum,** a minimum number or percentage of voting members who must be present at a meeting in order to transact business. Without the requirement of a quorum, a small group of members could meet and make decisions that go against the wishes of most members. The most fundamental principle—majority rule—would be compromised. At the simplest level, a quorum may be 51 percent of the members. For meetings at which the level of attendance is unpredictable, groups may set the quorum at 25 or 30 percent of the membership. Even a subcommittee can require a quorum to conduct its business. When a quorum is present, a majority of those voting can make decisions for the entire group. It is worth repeating that unless a quorum is present, the group should not take any action.

IN large groups, parliamentary procedure helps maintain order while members engage in important debate. What might happen to this group's discussion if no procedures were followed? (Paul Conklin/PhotoEdit)

Chair Parliamentary procedure requires that someone "chair" the meeting. Thus, the very first order of business for a new group using parliamentary procedure is to nominate and elect a chair. In some organizations, the bylaws specify that the president shall chair all meetings. In either case, the **chair,** who may be referred to as the chairperson, presiding officer, or president, has the responsibility of ensuring that parliamentary rules are followed and enforced. Like a police officer stationed at a busy intersection, a chair controls the flow of communication and protects the rights of all members to participate. Naturally, a chair must know the rules and remain separate from the congestion caused by the "communication" traffic.

Whether compared to those of a traffic cop, a baseball umpire, or a courtroom judge, the responsibilities of a chair are awesome. As chair of a formal parliamentary meeting, you should not join the discussion or express your personal opinions on the matters being discussed. Your job is to make sure that the meeting progresses according to the agenda and that the rights of all members are upheld, that debate is encouraged, and that the majority ultimately prevails. Chairing a meeting, however, does not take away your rights as a member of the assembly. The chair can vote when a vote is taken by secret ballot and can vote to make or break a tie. For example, if there is a tie vote, the proposal is defeated unless the chair votes to break the tie in favor of passage. The chair can also vote to create a tie that, in effect, defeats the proposed action.

Parliamentarian When meetings are formal and large, when the issues are highly controversial and may require the stamp of legality, or when the chair or the assembly is unsure of the rules, the chair may appoint or hire someone to serve as an official parliamentarian. Like an umpire, the **parliamentarian** has a thorough knowledge of the rules and can apply them to specific situations. Congress employs parliamentarians, as do national organizations such as labor unions and political parties. In less formal organizations, a member who knows parliamentary procedure may be asked to serve as the parliamentarian. Although good parliamentarians and umpires know their rules inside out, the parliamentarian does not have the final word—the chair does. The parliamentarian advises the chair and, when asked by the chair, explains the basis for parliamentary rulings to the entire group.

Clerk In a parliamentary setting, the group's clerk plays a very important role. When the rules of parliamentary procedure are strictly followed, the clerk serves several functions. In addition to taking accurate minutes, the **clerk** must keep a careful record of the status of all items, including the proposed wording of motions and amendments that may or may not be passed. If the debate will be summarized for another audience or for members who do not attend, or if the minutes are to become the basis for building future reports, the clerk must provide detailed records of the discussion. When a vote count is ordered or a written ballot is taken, the clerk must record the numerical results in the minutes.

*B*asic Rules of Order

Robert's Rules of Order, Newly Revised consists of over seven hundred pages and includes hundreds of rules for conducting business. This chapter includes only a simplified and condensed version of some key rules and practices. If you are interested in becoming better informed, consult the books listed as references at the end of this chapter. For starters, however, you should learn how to make and debate a motion and how to request a privilege.

Like any other complex procedure, parliamentary procedure has its own unique vocabulary. Rather than saying "Let's vote," parliamentary procedure asks that you "call the previous question." Rather than saying "Don't interrupt me while I'm talking," parliamentary speakers say "I believe I have the floor." As with any new procedure, it takes time to get used to the terms and customs required of participants.

Making a Main Motion

Robert's Rules of Order, Newly Revised states that "... a **motion** is a formal proposal by a member, in a meeting, that the assembly take certain action."[8] In other words, if you want the group to make a decision or agree to do something, you must state your proposed action as a motion. A motion is introduced with the words, "I move that...." In order to make a motion, a member must address and be recognized by the chair.

MEMBER: Madam Chair.

CHAIR: The chair recognizes (the member's name).

MEMBER: I move that we hold our 1998 annual convention in Chicago.

At first, you may feel awkward using a phrase such as "I move that...," but soon such language becomes second nature in a parliamentary session.

In order to make and debate a motion, you must know the rules governing different types of motions and the requirements for getting a motion voted on and passed.

Main Motions.   A motion that proposes a new action or decision is called a **main motion.** Main motions are the very reason why people assemble in groups. A proposal to build a tennis court for a condominium, to increase a college's tuition, or to downsize a business as part of a Board of Directors' restructuring plan are recommendations for new action that require the vote of assembled members. A motion is introduced, debated, and voted upon by following six basic steps:

1. Obtain the floor.
2. State the motion.
3. Second the motion.
4. Debate the motion.
5. Amend the motion if needed.
6. Vote on the motion.

Before you can make a motion or speak in a parliamentary session, you must obtain the **floor.** This phrase means that you cannot speak until the chair recognizes you and grants you the right to address the group. Although the word *floor* refers to standing before the group on the floor of the meeting room, it has come to mean that only one member is authorized to speak at that time. Thus, when an interrupted member says, "I have the floor!" she is referring to her right to speak. In order to present any motion, you must have the floor.

When you are preparing to state a main motion, it is important to word it as clearly as possible and state it in the affirmative. Good motions are clear, objective, and brief. Hours of discussion and debate can be wasted by a poorly expressed motion. The following examples illustrate how a main motion can be worded:

> Mr. President, I move that we adopt the Peregrine Falcon as our official mascot.
> Madam Chair, I move that we give $5,000 to our county's community college for scholarships.

Seconding a Motion.   Once a main motion has been offered by a member, it must be seconded. A **second** is just what the word implies—support for consideration of a motion by a second member. After all, if only one person wants to pass a motion, why would a group take valuable time to discuss it? The person who seconds a motion does not have to agree with the motion; seconding a motion only indicates that the member wants to see the group consider the motion.

MEMBER #1:	Madam President.
CHAIR:	The chair recognizes (the member who addressed the chair).
MEMBER #1:	Madam President, I move that we give $5,000 to our county's community college for scholarships.
MEMBER #2:	Second.
CHAIR:	It has been moved and seconded that this organization give $5,000 to our county's community college for scholarships. Is there any discussion?

Notice that the chair does not have to recognize the person who seconds the motion. As soon as someone makes a main motion, anyone may second it. If there is silence after a main motion is made, the chair should ask for a second. If there is no second, the motion "dies for lack of a second" and cannot be considered by the group.

Once a motion has been made and seconded, the chair will "open the floor" for discussion and debate, giving first priority to the member who made the motion. During this period, members may argue for or against the motion.

Amendments.   In addition to using the period of debate to argue for or against the main motion, members may offer an **amendment** to the motion. If you wish to change another member's main motion, you can do so by saying, "I move that we amend the motion by. . . ." For example, you can *substitute* one word or number for another, such as "I move that we amend the motion by substituting the amount of $25,000 for the $5,000 in scholarship funds." You can amend a motion by *adding*, such as "I move that we amend the motion by inserting the word 'honors' before the word 'scholarship.'" Finally, you can amend a motion by *subtracting*, such as "I move that we amend the motion by deleting the words 'for scholarships.'" Like a main motion, amendments must be seconded to be considered and debated by the group. Only one amendment may be considered at a time.

Voting on a Motion.   Finally, when a motion and all proposed amendments have been fully debated, a group may vote to accept or reject the final form of the motion. At this point either the chair or a member of the group can ask for a vote. The chair may ask, "Are we ready to vote on the question?" In parliamentary sessions, the word **question** refers to any motion or proposal before a group that will require a vote. In a sense, a vote determines the answer to a question such as, "Should we give $25,000 to the community college?" Those in favor would vote "yes" or "aye," while those opposed would vote "no" or "nay."

If the chair does not ask whether the group is ready to vote, any member may ask for a vote by saying, "I move the previous question." This motion must be seconded, cannot be debated or amended, and requires a two-thirds vote to pass. In other words, if two-thirds of the group decide that they want to vote on the motion, the vote must occur.

CHAIR: Are you ready to vote?

MEMBERS: Yes!

CHAIR: All those in favor of the motion that this organization give $25,000 to our local community college say "Aye."

MEMBERS: Aye.

CHAIR: Those opposed "No."

MEMBERS: No.

CHAIR: The motion is passed (or defeated).

If a chair cannot determine whether a motion has been approved or defeated by listening to the "yes" and "no" votes, the chair may choose other voting options such as raising hands or secret ballots.

Others Types of Motions

If main motions were the only kind of motion that came before a group, *Robert's Rules of Order, Newly Revised* would be a much shorter book. Instead, there are many different kinds of motions, all of which come with special rules on how to introduce, debate, amend, and vote on them. Regardless of which set of parliamentary rules you use, motions are given a **precedence,** an order in which they must be considered by the group. When more than one motion arises, rules of precedence determine which motion is discussed first. The table shown in Figure 15.2 includes twelve of the most common motions listed in their order of precedence, along with an example of the phrasing used to introduce each motion.

Robert's Rules of Order, Newly Revised lists over eighty different kinds of motions. Learning how to handle the twelve common motions shown in Figure 15.2, however, can help you deal with the others.

When a motion is being considered, only motions of higher precedence may be proposed. For example, during debate on a main motion, one member may first move to limit debate to a certain period of time and then another may move to recess. Because the motion to recess is ranked higher than the other two motions, it must be considered first. If the motion to recess fails, then the group may consider the motion to limit debate.

To complicate matters even further, some motions are debatable, whereas others are not; some are amendable, but others are not; and although some require a second and/or a vote, some do not. The chart shown in Figure 15.3 summarizes these common motions and the rules that govern their use.

Requesting Privileges

Among the many kinds of motions that can be proposed during a parliamentary session, one type deserves special attention—privileged requests. The word *privilege* means "a special right" or "a benefit granted to an individual or group member." Thus, in parliamentary terms, a **privileged request** asks the chairperson to grant you immediate consideration of a right or benefit due to every member of the group.

Privileged requests can be used to clarify parliamentary rules, correct procedural errors, and accommodate personal needs. They are so important you have the right to interrupt another member in order to introduce a privileged request and you do not have to be recognized by the chair to speak. Moreover, it is not necessary to have a second to put your request on the floor. None of these requested privileges is debatable or amendable. Among these privileges are these two frequently used requests: questions of privilege and a point of order.

Precedence and Purpose	Phrasing and Example
1. **Adjourn.** To end or dismiss a meeting.	"I move that we adjourn."
2. **Recess.** To adjourn for a short and specific time.	"I move that we recess 90 minutes for lunch."
3. **Question of Privilege.** To secure an immediate ruling on issues related to the personal needs and rights of members.	"I rise to a point of privilege. Will the speaker please use the microphone so we can hear in the back?"
4. **Call for the Orders of the Day.** To force the group to conform to its agreed-upon agenda and timing of business.	"I call for the orders of the day. According to the agenda, we should be discussing the funding resolution."
5. **Table the Question.** To put off discussion or defer action for reconsideration in order to take up an urgent issue.	"I move that we table the main motion in order to let Raphael present his report because he must leave to catch a plane."
6. **Move the Previous Question.** To end the debate of a motion and move to an immediate vote.	"I call for the previous questions" OR "I move that we close debate and vote immediately on the motion."
7. **Limit or Extend Debate.** To limit or extend the amount of time devoted to discussion.	"I move that each speaker be limited to three-minute statements on this motion."
8. **Postpone Definitely.** To defer action to a specific time or date.	"I move that this matter be postponed until our next meeting."
9. **Refer to Committee.** To send a motion to a committee for further study, to postpone debate, or to develop recommendations.	"I move that the motion to raise membership dues be referred to the Finance Board."
10. **Amend.** To change the wording of a motion being considered by the group.	"I move that we amend the motion by striking out the word 'honors' before the word 'scholarship.'"
11. **Main Motion.** To propose that the group take a certain action.	"I move that we adopt the Peregrine Falcon as our official mascot."
12. **Point of Order.*** To call attention to a violation of the rules or an error in procedure.	"I rise to a point of order. It is out of order to vote on the main motion before we vote on the amendment."

*There is no precedence for a point of order; it should be raised immediately after a mistake or error occurs regardless of a motion's precedence or the action being considered by group.

FIGURE 15.2 Common Motions

Questions of Privilege. Questions of privilege are used when conditions affect the health, safety, and operation of the meeting. They can be directed toward personal problems or room conditions. They also can be used to uphold the privileges of the group as a whole or the personal privileges of an individual member.

Order of Precedence	Recognized by Chair?	Requires Second?	Debatable?	Amendable?	Can Interrupt the Speaker?	Vote Required?
1. Adjourn	Yes	Yes	No*	No	No	Majority
2. Recess	Yes	Yes	No	No	No	Majority
3. Question of Privilege	No	No	No	No	Yes	Chair†
4. Orders of the Day	No	No	No	No	Yes	Chair
5. Lay on the Table	Yes	Yes	No	No	No	Majority
6. Previous Question (End Debate)	Yes	Yes	No	No	No	2/3
7. Limit/Extend Debate	Yes	Yes	No	Yes	No	2/3
8. Postpone Definitely	Yes	Yes	Yes	Yes	No	Majority
9. Refer	Yes	Yes	Yes	Yes	No	Majority
10. Amend	Yes	Yes	Yes	Yes‡	No	Majority
11. Main Motion	Yes	Yes	Yes	Yes	No	Majority
12. Point of Order§	No	No	No	No	Yes	Chair

* Depends on the situation
† Decision usually made by chair
‡ Debatable if the motion being amended is debatable
§ No order of precedence; should be raised immediately after an error occurs.

FIGURE 15.3 Summary Chart of Twelve Basic Motions

MEMBER: Mr. President, I rise to a question of personal privilege.
CHAIR: State your question of privilege.
MEMBER: May I be excused to meet our keynote speaker?
CHAIR: Your privilege is granted.

The following examples demonstrate other ways in which this privilege can be used:

Will the chair use the microphone so those of us sitting in the back can hear?
Will the clerk make copies of the amended motion and distribute them to all members before tomorrow's meeting?

Questions of privilege are so important that they take precedence over all motions except those to adjourn or recess. After all, if members can't hear a speaker, there isn't much point in continuing the discussion.

Point of Order. **A point of order** can be raised if, at any time, you believe that the rules of parliamentary procedure or its basic principles are not being followed. If you say "I rise to a point of order" you are asking the chair to rule on a procedural question. A point of order must be raised immediately after the error or mistake is made even if it means interrupting someone who "has the floor." If a chair has difficulty determining whether a parliamentary rule has been broken, he or she may consult the group's parliamentarian for advice. Also, the chair can ask the entire group to vote on the ruling.

MEMBER: Point of order.

CHAIR: State your point of order.

MEMBER: The motion just passed is out of order because we need a two-thirds vote in order to limit debate.

CHAIR: Your point is well taken. The motion does not pass. We will vote again to determine whether there is a two-thirds vote.

A point of order also can be applied to member behavior. Keesey suggests that a point of order should be used to "call a speaker to order for the inappropriate use of language or other breach of decorum."[9]

MEMBER: Madam President, I rise to a point of order.

CHAIR: State your point.

MEMBER: I object to the insulting language of the speaker and his personal attacks upon the motives of members who oppose his motion.

CHAIR: Your point is well taken. The speaker will please confine his remarks to the motion and refrain from behaving in an unprofessional manner.

Like a question of privilege, a point of order is a way of making the chair and group aware of an immediate problem that must be resolved before the meeting can progress in an orderly fashion.

Informal Rules

Most groups do not need parliamentary procedure to conduct business or achieve their goals. At the same time, there is great value in borrowing the basic principles of parliamentary procedure to guide the deliberations of any group.

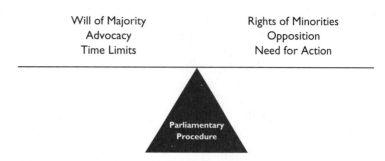

Will of Majority	Rights of Minorities
Advocacy	Opposition
Time Limits	Need for Action

Parliamentary
Procedure

FIGURE 15.4 Parliamentary Procedure

Weitzel and Geist's research reveals that group members often use a modified form of parliamentary procedure rather than adhering to the "letter of the law" espoused in *Robert's Rules of Order, Newly Revised*.[10] In an informal group, parliamentary rules can be relaxed. Agendas can be simple and brief. It may not be necessary to count the number of times a person speaks or the number of minutes a person talks. At the same time, a commitment to the principles of parliamentary procedure gives group members the right to ask for an agenda as well as the authority to curb a member who tries to monopolize a discussion.

In an informal group, the chairperson's task is somewhat different from what it is in a formal assembly. Sturgis provides a sports analogy to clarify this difference. She writes that in an assembly, "the role of presiding officer is somewhat comparable to that of referee," whereas in a committee or small group, "the chair's role is closer to that of a team captain."[11] In other words, in an assembly, the chair remains neutral on controversial issues, avoids participating in debate, and concentrates on upholding parliamentary rules. In a less formal group, the chair participates freely, joining the discussion and making motions while ensuring that everyone is treated fairly.

Sturgis notes a second difference between parliamentary procedure in formal groups and small work groups:

> Probably the most important difference . . . is that in an assembly one can speak only to a motion that has been made and seconded. In a committee the procedure is usually reversed: a matter may be discussed at great length before a specific proposal is even formulated.[12]

Small groups have the luxury of going about the problem-solving process in a way that is more likely to produce consensus.

Balanced Procedures

Despite its lofty principles, parliamentary procedure is disliked and distrusted by many people. For those who are unfamiliar with its many rules, parliamentary procedure may appear to be an old-fashioned, unnecessary, and intimidating way to conduct business. Those who know parliamentary procedure can manipulate it to distract members and disrupt meetings. These negative perceptions are justified when parliamentary procedure is not used properly and ethically. What is needed is a balanced approach— one in which parliamentary procedure is used to help a group achieve its goals without getting bogged down in rules.

When a chair fails to enforce the rules of parliamentary procedure, the group process can become chaotic. For instance, a biased chairperson can recognize friends rather than foes. Such a bias was suggested when Newt Gingrich, speaker of the U.S. House of Representatives, declared that "The power of the speaker is the power of recognition, and I will not recognize any proposal that will appropriate money for. . . ."[13]

The chair is not the only person who can cause chaos in a parliamentary session. A well-organized minority can block and delay an action until it no longer has any chance of being passed by the assembly. Like any other tool, parliamentary procedure can be used improperly.

When a chair balances the needs of the majority with the interests of each minority, respect for both sides is more likely to be generated. When everyone has an equal opportunity to speak, a sense of fairness is more likely to prevail. And when members on both sides of an issue believe they have had equal opportunity to present their case, future cooperation will be more likely to occur.

Summary Study Guide

- Parliamentary procedure originated hundreds of years ago as a set of rules for doing business in the British Parliament's House of Commons.
- *Robert's Rules of Order, Newly Revised* is considered the "parliamentary bible"; in addition, many other authors have simplified, adapted, and revised these rules for use by various types of groups and organizations.
- Parliamentary procedure's basic principles are the following: majority rule, equal opportunity to participate, protection of individual and minority rights, balanced discussion, and orderly progress.
- A chair conducts the meeting and has the responsibility of ensuring that parliamentary rules are followed and enforced.
- A group or chair may appoint an official, expert parliamentarian who advises the chair on parliamentary issues.
- A motion is a formal, carefully worded proposal made before a group for the members' consideration and action; it is introduced with the words "I move that. . . ."

- Making a motion involves six steps: obtain the floor, state a motion, second the motion, debate the motion, possibly amend the motion, and vote on the motion.
- Twelve common motions are ranked in order of precedence as follows: adjourn, recess, question of privilege, orders of the day, table the question, call the previous question, limit or extend debate, postpone definitely, refer to committee, amend, main motions, and point of order.
- Two important requests available to all members that must be considered immediately are personal privileges and points of order.
- The principles and rules of parliamentary procedure can be adapted to meet the needs of informal work groups.

Groupwork *The Mascot Debate*

GOAL   To provide groups with experience in using parliamentary procedure.

PARTICIPANTS   Four equal-sized groups.

PROCEDURE

1. An assembly has been called to debate the following motion: The college's mascot should be changed from the _____ (fill in the college's current mascot) to the _____ (fill in another animal, person, or object as the mascot).
2. Each group will advocate a separate position on the motion.
   - Group #1: The mascot should be changed to _____ .
   - Group #2: The mascot should not be changed and should remain as is.
   - Group #3: The motion should be amended to _____ (add a specific characteristic to the mascot—for example, a *blue and gold* buffalo, a *fighting* fish).
   - Group #4: Members are free to advocate any of the preceding positions.
3. Each group should be given a short period of time to discuss its position on the motion and develop a strategy to achieve its goal.
4. The instructor will serve as chair or appoint a member of the assembly to act as chair.
5. The assembly must debate and vote on the motion.

ASSESSMENT

Parliamentary Procedure Assessment Instrument[14]

Directions   The actions on this assessment instrument identify some of the most common mistakes made by chairpersons and members when using parliamentary procedure. When observing a parliamentary session, use this list to explain why a group is experiencing procedural problems or is not achieving its goal.

Chair

_____ Is unfamiliar with the rules of parliamentary procedure.

_____ Cuts off discussion without permitting the group to decide when debate should end.

_____ Fails to prevent members from making out-of-order remarks, irrelevant comments, or personal attacks on other members.

_____ Is either too formal or too informal—discussion becomes bogged down in parliamentary details, or important rules are ignored.

_____ Fails to remain impartial when a controversial matter is being discussed.

Member

_____ Is unfamiliar with the rules of parliamentary procedure.

_____ Fails to seek and obtain recognition before speaking.

_____ Does not limit remarks to the issue being discussed.

_____ Fails to raise a point of order if procedures infringe on member rights or rules.

_____ Uses trivial parliamentary technicalities to prevent the group from focusing its attention on the issue being discussed.

Recommended Readings

Jones, O. G. (1971). *Parliamentary procedure at a glance.* New York: Penguin.

Robert, H. M. with H. M. Robert, III, W. J. Evans & J. W. Cleary. (1990). *Robert's rules of order: Newly revised* (9th ed.). New York: Scott, Foresman.

Sturgis, A. (1988). *The standard code of parliamentary procedure* (3rd ed.). New York: McGraw-Hill.

Notes

1. See the following titles: Jones, O. G. (1971). *Parliamentary procedure at a glance.* New York: Penguin; Sturgis, A. (1988). *The standard code of parliamentary procedure* (3rd ed.). New York: McGraw-Hill.

2. Auer, J. J. (1959). *Essentials of parliamentary procedure* (3rd ed.). New York: Appleton Century Crofts, p. 3.

3. Gray, J. W. & Rea, R. G. (1974). *Parliamentary procedure: A programmed introduction* (Revised Edition). Glenview, IL: Scott, Foresman, p. 4.

4. Weitzel, A. & Geist, B. (1998). "Parliamentary procedure in a community group: Communication and vigilant decision making." *Communication Monographs, 65,* p. 244.

5. Weitzel & Geist, pp. 247–259.

6. Robert, H. M. with H. M. Robert, III, W. J. Evans & J. W. Cleary. (1990), *Robert's rules of order: Newly revised* (9th ed.). New York: Scott, Foresman, p. xliv.

7. Sturgis, A. (1988). *The standard code of parliamentary procedure* (3rd ed.). New York: McGraw-Hill, p. 115.

8. Robert, p. 26.

9. Keesey, R. E. (1974). *Modern parliamentary procedure.* Boston: Houghton Mifflin, p. 65.

10. Weitzel & Geist, p. 256.

11. Sturgis, p. 229.

12. Sturgis, pp. 229–230.

13. *The Washington Post,* February 17, 1995, p. F1.

14. Assessment items are based on our own observations as well as Sturgis's list of mistakes most commonly made by presiding officers and members, pp. 236–237.

Technology and Groups

Technology and Communication

Well-respected business publications, academic journals, popular magazines, and newspapers agree that technology is changing the way people work in groups. A *Wall Street Journal* headline declared that "Computerizing Dull Meetings Is Touted as an Antidote to the Mouth that Bored."[1] A headline in *Presentation Products Magazine* dubbed "Computers the Key to More Productive Meetings."[2] Major corporations such as the Boeing Company and IBM have reported that special computer software has cut meeting time by more than 50 percent.[3] On and off college campuses, computer-aided and computer-managed instruction as well as electronic discussion groups are becoming an integral part of the learning process.[4] We are participating in more and more meetings that take place on the telephone and Internet. Computers and presentation software have successfully invaded and improved our meetings. Like it or not, technology is changing the way we communicate in groups.

In this chapter, our goal is to provide sufficient information about communication technologies so you can understand and make informed decisions about their use. We also provide technical advice for communicating more effectively when using these technologies. What we cannot do is describe or recommend specific hardware and software because such information is guaranteed to be obsolete by the time this textbook is published. We do, however, encourage you to explore the potential of new technologies as tools for enhancing and improving your ability to communicate and work in groups.

The Age of Cybermeeting

Today it is possible to wake up in Los Angeles, join a meeting in London in the morning and another in Tokyo in the afternoon—all without leaving your home or office. Communication technology has made it possible for us to interact with other people anywhere in the world at nearly the speed of light. New technologies also have redefined the concept of a "meeting place." Place does not have to be a physical location such as a conference room. Instead, the place for a meeting can be virtual. This virtual place is often referred to as **cyberspace.**

Creighton and Adams discuss the role of technology in groups through the concept of **cybermeeting.** This term symbolizes "new ways of integrating information technology with innovations in management and group process to produce more effective forms of collaboration."[5] We now live in the age of cybermeeting; an era in which technology is not separate from group communication but an integral part of the group process. The goal of using technology in groups is not to keep up with the latest fad but to produce more effective collaboration. Cybermeeting innovations include a growing list of new and improved technological tools:

- Software to schedule meetings;
- Meetingware and groupware to work electronically and simultaneously on a group project;
- Interactive meeting facilities with full electronic and technical support;
- Working walls (electronic whiteboards) that can record and display information in multiple locations;
- Internet access from meeting rooms so participants can draw on organizational databases and external databases; and
- Facilities to augment social interaction, with full electronic support (computer, fax, printer, and whiteboard table).[6]

By the time you are reading this chapter, many of these so-called innovations will be quite common in some group settings. The key to using any of these innovations will be a group's willingness to understand each technology's potential to help the group achieve its goal. In this chapter, we will look at how different technological media are used to enhance group effectiveness and how specific technologies can be harnessed to improve group process.

Tools, Not Toys

For group members who look forward to the latest technological innovation, there is an eagerness to enlist their power to enhance group effectiveness. For those who fear that cybermeeting will erode group morale and productivity, the parade of new technologies seems overwhelming and even threatening. Regardless of your perspective, it is important to acknowledge several things. First, there is no question that technology has become an inevitable and, in some cases, indispensable component of groupwork. Second, these technologies are tools, not toys. Embracing a new technology because it's "new and nifty" can have just as negative an effect on group work as rejecting new technology for fear it could erode group morale and productivity.

As much fun as it may be to surf the web, the practice can become an obsession rather than a tool for information seeking and discussion. As creative as it may be to use the latest multimedia software to design a briefing, such presentations can take valuable time and attention away from issues that need immediate discussion and decision making. Throughout this chapter, we emphasize that using technology is a choice, not a mandate. New technologies should be adopted when they enhance group efficiency and effectiveness. Understanding the attributes and potential of each technological tool will help a group determine if and how it can be used to achieve a group's goal.

Group Communication Media

In the first fifteen chapters of this textbook, we have been discussing how groups interact and solve problems in a face-to-face setting. Face-to-face communication, however, is only one of several communication media available to a group. Other group-based media include teleconferences, videoconferences, and computer conferences.

Teleconferences

The teleconference is probably the most familiar and easiest type of electronic meeting to convene. Frequently referred to as a "conference call," a **teleconference** is a coordinated phone call among three or more group members. All it requires is a telephone with service that supports conference calling. Almost all business telephone service and some residential phone service provide teleconference capability.

In its simplest form, the person charged with setting up the teleconference places phone calls to those members who will be part of the conference call. The number of participants may be restricted by the availability of multiple telephone lines. Another limitation is that the sound quality of teleconferences tends to degrade as more people are added.

A second option is to have the teleconference set up by an outside company that specializes in teleconferences. Most phone companies offer this service, and other companies can be found in the telephone directory. The audio quality of teleconferences put together by these companies is generally far superior to teleconferences set up on a standard telephone. Because teleconference service can be expensive, some organizations provide their own in-house system. Group members telephone a "bridge" number and are automatically connected to the conference. In-house teleconference systems are becoming more common because they allow maximum participation at a reasonable cost.

Participating in Teleconferences. Teleconferencing is the easiest form of electronic meeting to understand because we are familiar with the basic technology—the telephone. However, author and businessman Clyde Burelson offers the following caution: "Do not think of teleconferencing as talking on the telephone. This is a meeting."[7] A group should plan for a teleconference just as it would for a face-to-face meeting. This means developing an agenda and making all other preparations appropriate for the meeting.

The following techniques can help make teleconferences more successful:

- Prepare and follow an agenda.
- Adapt to the oral-only channel.
- Introduce yourself before talking.

> **TOOLBOX 16.1**   Conducting Meetings
>
> Meetings are structured interactions, usually confined to a particular time and place, with a specified purpose and goal. Regardless of whether people meet face-to-face or in cyberspace, the success or failure of a meeting still depends on planning. Make sure you ask the following questions: (1) **Why** are you meeting? (2) **Who** should attend the meeting? (3) **When** should you meet? (4) **Where** should you meet? (5) **What** materials will you need before or during the meeting? In a teleconference the "where" of the meeting is expanded to the limits of telecommunications technology. **Chapter 13: Planning and Conducting Meetings** provides guidelines for successful meetings.

Phone calls don't require agendas; teleconferences do. Not only does a teleconference agenda provide the benefits normally associated with a meeting agenda, it also reinforces the idea that a teleconference is an organized and purposeful meeting.

The most obvious difference between a teleconference and a traditional meeting is the fact that the participants cannot see each other. Consequently, it can be difficult to determine who is speaking. Burelson emphasizes that "not knowing who is speaking affects how you perceive the message. It's like sitting in a regular meeting blindfolded, trying to guess who is making what point. That is bound to impact your judgment."[8] As a general rule, you should introduce yourself before making a comment during a teleconference, particularly if you have not been an active participant. A simple introduction is usually sufficient: "This is Terrence, and I think we should. . . ."

While a teleconference provides some nonverbal cues such as vocal tone and inflection, you cannot see facial expressions or gestures. As discussed in Chapter 7, a significant portion of your meaning is expressed nonverbally. For example, you might make a sarcastic remark in a meeting that everyone knows is a joke because you smile when you say it. In a teleconference, no one can see you smile. It is quite possible that your joke could be taken seriously.

Pros and Cons of Teleconferences.   The primary advantage of teleconferencing is that it is an easy procedure to set up and use. If an emergency arises that must be addressed by a group, it may be easier to bring a group together via a conference call than through other forms of electronic meetings. In fact, a teleconference may be easier to set up than a face-to-face meeting. It also requires the least investment in equipment of all the forms of electronic meetings.

Teleconferencing does have some drawbacks. Because members may feel isolated, the quantity and quality of their participation may be affected. For

ADVANTAGES OF TELECONFERENCES	DISADVANTAGES OF TELECONFERENCES
Is easy to set up and use. Has fewer and less expensive equipment needs.	May make members feel isolated. Reduces group cohesion.

FIGURE 16.1 Teleconferences

example, group members who would never think of bringing nongroup work to a face-to-face meeting might be tempted to work at their desks on other matters during a teleconference.

Another significant drawback of meeting via teleconferences is that it can reduce group cohesion. Group members may feel less a part of the group when they don't meet with each other face-to-face. Thus, while teleconferences are convenient, it is best to avoid using them as the only form of group interaction.

Videoconferences **Videoconferencing** is much like teleconferencing except that a visual component is added. Thus, videoconferencing permits both oral and visual communication. The visual element of videoconferencing eliminates many of the drawbacks associated with teleconferencing. In its most general sense, videoconferencing is teleconferencing with pictures. Unlike teleconferences, however, videoconferences rely on much more sophisticated and expensive equipment.

Setting up a videoconference is more complicated than setting up a teleconference. The most sophisticated videoconferences take place in specially designed studios equipped with professional lighting, cameras, and a crew. It is also possible to conduct videoconferences using less expensive digital cameras connected to personal computers. As technology improves, the cost of videoconferencing will continue to drop, and the equipment will become easier to use.

The high cost of videoconferencing must be balanced against the costs of a face-to-face meeting. If the members of a group have to travel from various parts of the country, the time lost in traveling must be accounted for as well as the cost of airfare, hotel accommodations, meals, and other expenses associated with the face-to-face meeting.

Participating in Videoconferences. Here are a number of guidelines to use when preparing for a videoconference:

- Brief all members on the operation of the videoconferencing system.
- Use the microphone discreetly.
- Dress appropriately.

Although videoconferences are becoming more popular, they are still relatively uncommon and can produce anxiety for participants. For many people, the thought of being "on television" during a videoconference generates a great deal of communication apprehension. If an effective meeting is to take place, this anxiety should be addressed before the videoconference. All group members should be fully briefed on how the videoconference works and what to expect. The more group members know about the process, the more comfortable they will be during the meeting.

Always be aware of the microphone. In videoconferences a microphone will be attached to your clothing, set on a table in front of you, or suspended above you. Regardless of how the microphone is set up, remember that it is always listening. Avoid the temptation to lean over and whisper something to the person sitting next to you. Although the people across the room may not be able to hear you, the microphone and everyone at the other end of the videoconference can.

Consider what you are going to wear to a videoconference. If your clothing is distracting, you will create a barrier to effective communication. Narrow, contrasting stripes should be avoided because video monitors can make striped clothes appear to pulsate. Also avoid wearing shiny or reflective clothing. Finally, clothes that fit poorly will appear to fit even worse when magnified on the screen.

Pros and Cons of Videoconferences. The primary advantage of videoconferencing is its combination of sight and sound. Sophisticated videoconferencing systems allow group members to see and hear each other much as

ADVANTAGES OF VIDEOCONFERENCES	DISADVANTAGES OF VIDEOCONFERENCES
・ Combine sight and sound. ・ Closely simulate face-to-face meeting. ・ Can save travel and lodging costs.	・ May make members feel apprehensive. ・ Are difficult to set up. ・ Require expensive equipment and staff costs. ・ May be difficult for members to adapt to camera and microphone.

FIGURE 16.2   Videoconferences

they would in a face-to-face meeting. Once the initial apprehension about being on camera passes, a videoconference can operate as efficiently and effectively as a traditional meeting.

Unlike teleconferences, however, videoconferences require more effort to plan and set up and are likely to be much more expensive. Although members feel less isolated in a videoconference than they do in a teleconference, everyone knows that seeing the images on the screen is not the same as having real people in a real room.

Computer Conferences   Computer conferencing is the third type of electronic meeting. Unfortunately, there is no simple definition of computer conferencing because it covers a wide variety of activities and can even be combined with videoconferencing or teleconferencing. It is probably best to think of **computer conferencing** as using a computer to communicate and interact with a group. Today, more and more people are using their computers as communication tools. Linked together via modems, local area networks, and the Internet, computers provide a "place" for groups to communicate and work together.

Synchronous and Asynchronous Communication. When group members use computers to interact simultaneously in real time, they are engaged in **synchronous communication.** In essence, the group holds a meeting via computer, and members type to each other instead of speaking. Internet Relay Chat (IRC) and the chat rooms on various on-line services are examples of synchronous communication.

Because synchronous communication requires real-time group interaction, it allows a group to work together as a cohesive unit and thus promotes synergy. Synchronous communication is spontaneous and dynamic; it can enhance certain group processes like brainstorming or solution development and analysis. Unfortunately, some of this advantage is lost because most of us type more slowly than we speak. Consequently, there can be a significant lag time between a comment and a response.

Another problem that can disrupt synchronous conferences is that the message sequence can become confused. Statements and responses may not arrive in the order in which they are sent.

Asynchronous communication is the opposite of synchronous communication. Asynchronous communication is linear and not interactive. Immediate feedback is not received when a message is sent. In an asynchronous conference, one person makes a statement and posts it for the group to see. Group members, at their convenience, look at the message and post responses. Asynchronous communication does not require the group members to hold a meeting. Instead, group members read and respond to messages as their schedules permit. Electronic mail (e-mail), bulletin boards, and USENET are all examples of asynchronous communication. Groups working for Boeing often use asynchronous communication as they work through complex issues. Group members from all over the world are able to discuss an issue, but they don't all have to take part in the discussion at the same time.[9]

Asynchronous communication is more deliberate than synchronous communication. Group members can take time to give serious consideration to each other's messages and offer thought-out responses. Asynchronous communication is particularly useful for completing certain types of group tasks such as developing and editing written reports. For example, sending out a document via e-mail to an entire group may require no more effort or expense than sending it to a single person.

The advantages and disadvantages of these two types of computer-based group communication are summarized in the table shown in Figure 16.3.

*Working
with Text*

If you use networked computers at work or use the Internet to communicate with friends, family, or distant colleagues, you know that this is a very different medium for communicating with groups of people. One of the biggest differences is that this type of communication depends on writing as the only form of communication. There is no spoken or nonverbal component—no

Synchronous Communication	**Asynchronous Communication**
Advantages:	Advantages:
• Group cohesion and synergy.	• More time to compose responses.
• Spontaneous and dynamic interaction.	• Facilitated document review and editing.
Disadvantages:	Disadvantages:
• Typing speed is slower than speaking speed.	• Lacks spontaneity.
• Messages might be received out of order.	• Linear rather than interactive.

FIGURE 16.3 Synchronous and Asynchronous Communication

vocal tone, no inflection, and no visual cues to add meaning to the communication. The focus is solely on the words. Because computer conferencing relies on the written word instead of the spoken word, an Internet novice may approach the task just as he or she would approach more traditional writing. As anyone who frequents the Internet knows, this can be a mistake. The communication involved in computer conferencing, particularly synchronous conferencing, tends to be a substitute for spoken, face-to-face interaction. There is an informality and immediacy in computer conferencing that separates it from other writing we do. As Bob Johansen of the Institute for the Future notes, "The personal computer is gradually becoming the interpersonal computer.[10]

Because we tend to communicate interpersonally in computer conferences, there is a tendency to write down the same words that we would say. The quick turn-around time requested on computer conferences all but requires that we write in an informal style. Some e-mailers don't capitalize any letters; they don't use "proper" punctuation or worry about grammatical rules. Rather than taking time to craft a response, communication often is spontaneous and personal. Some researchers have suggested that when computer conference participants haven't met or don't know one another very well, this abbreviated and personal writing style helps create stereotypical impressions of participants who use this medium.[11] If you write something amusing, you are more likely to be perceived by receivers as a person with a good sense of humor. If you provide much-needed information, you are more likely to be seen as an expert. If you help edit a working document, the group may turn to you for advice about report writing. All this happens because readers have nothing else to rely on in making judgments about those sending messages. Remember, however, that while the communication styles may be more informal than traditional writing, errors in spelling and grammar may (but not necessarily will) create a negative impression.

Because nonverbal elements such as vocal tone, inflection, facial expressions, and gestures are missing from a text-only message, people who frequently communicate via computers use a set of symbols to convey an

MEETINGS that rely on technology may be as simple as a telephone conference or as sophisticated as this video conferencing suite. What are some of the advantages and disadvantages of meetings conducted via technology? (Robert Reichert/Tony Stone Images)

emotional subtext to written messages. These symbols are referred to as **emoticons.** You may be familiar with the <g> symbol that is a shorthand for "grin" and indicates that a preceding statement was made in jest. Bracketing a word with asterisks gives emphasis to *important* words and often takes the place of underlining. Using all capital letters can be used to indicate forcefulness or ANGER. A message typed in all capital letters may be perceived as rude when the novice Internet user's only intention was to improve the readability of the type.

Whenever you are participating in a computer conference, carefully read your messages before sending them and rewrite them if you think they might be misunderstood. Consider the real-life example of a group that received an important report via the Internet in which one member responded to the group e-mail with the concluding sentence, "I resent the report." What she meant was that she was re-sending the report to someone who, because of a computer glitch, didn't get it the first time. For days, however, committee members assumed that she resented (was offended by) what was written in the report and no one could figure out why. The more frequently you engage in computer conferencing, the more comfortable you will become communicating in a text-only environment.

Multiple-Media Methods

For complex or long-term projects, a group may use more than one kind of communication media: face-to-face meetings, teleconferences, videoconferences, and computer conferences. Take time to decide which media match the group's needs and circumstances. The following example illustrates the advantages of using multiple media for groupwork. In 1998, the National Communication Association conducted a national survey titled *How Americans Communicate*. The team responsible for the project included members from Washington, D.C., Texas, Indiana, and Maryland. The first meeting was held face-to-face in Chicago. At the first meeting the group developed a questionnaire on a series of flip chart sheets. Minutes were kept on a laptop computer and later e-mailed to everyone in the meeting for revision and approval. A representative from the Roper-Starch polling company then became involved in transforming the questionnaire into a form suitable for a national telephone poll. Those involved in discussions with the Roper-Stark agent communicated via telephone, through teleconferences, and the Internet. When the first draft of the survey was ready, it was e-mailed to the original committee, some of whom were attending a conference in Rome. The members at the Rome meeting met face-to-face but also interacted with other committee members in the United States via e-mail. By the time the survey was conducted and the results disseminated, the group had relied on several types of technology to complete the project. If the group had relied on traditional, face-to-face meetings, the project would have taken several years to complete rather than several months. Using multiple media improved the group's ability to interact and make decisions by allowing the group to work together even though members were spread across the globe.

Computerized Meetings

In addition to using technology to facilitate communication among group members who are physically separated, groups also are using computers and specialized software to facilitate collaboration in face-to-face meetings. As the technology becomes more affordable and user friendly, these methods will soon be as well accepted as flip charts for facilitating group interaction and decision making.

Group Support Systems

In addition to different media for cybermeeting, an increasing number of technology-based group support systems are designed to promote more efficient and effective groupwork. Whether they are called group decision support systems (GDSS), group support systems (GSS), or computer-mediated communication (CMC), their purpose is to improve the group process and product. According to Contractor, Seibold, and Heller, **group support systems** include a large number of communication and decision-making tools that are available to interacting group members through the use of computer and communication technologies. GSS communication tools augment face-to-face interaction in group meetings with text and graphics. They also provide group members with the ability to generate and evaluate ideas, make decisions, and use different voting procedures.[12] Contractor and his colleagues describe several features offered in group support systems:

- Brainstorming tools, including the private input of ideas prior to sharing with other members
- Voting schemes such as preference weighting and ranking; synchronous electronic communication to one or more other members in the group
- Public display of members' individual and collective contributions.[13]

Meetingware. One specialized type of group support system, **meetingware**, includes electronic meeting tools designed to utilize group process technologies in the meeting room setting. Most meetingware tools are built around two capabilities: simultaneous (and anonymous) generation of ideas, and use of keypads for scoring or rating.[14]

In order to appreciate the utility and versatility of this type of group support system, consider this example involving a community-based, decision-making group. A small county purchased 75 acres of land on which to build a new campus for its community college. The county appointed a building committee composed of college officials, board members, and county administrators. The committee was adamant that it needed input from a variety of county constituents: students and staff at the existing campus, the college's advisory board, business interests needing workforce training, board of education officials, and community groups interested in a community center for public activities.

The building committee decided to sponsor a series of focus groups facilitated by a trained researcher using specialized meetingware. Each focus group included 7–12 group members. Upon entering the meeting room, each focus group member was assigned a laptop computer. The computers were networked and connected to a display screen at the front of the room. Focus group participants were asked a series of questions about the new campus—what should it include, who should be served, what should be built first? One question at a time, the participants typed in their answers. As soon as they were written, the ideas appeared on the screen at the front of the room. Because the ideas were anonymous, no one worried about being criticized for a bad idea or a misspelled word. No one could monopolize the group's time, show off, or criticize others. As ideas began appearing on the screen, the benefits of brainstorming kicked in. Some ideas spawned new ones; others produced a piggy-back effect in which initial suggestions were expanded and further developed.

Once the idea generation phase had slowed, software was used to support a nominal group technique (NGT) session. Focus group participants were asked to provide a rating for each idea on the screen. As members entered their responses, software processed the ratings into rankings and created a group-based list of ideas in the order of importance as decided by the entire group.

At this point in the process, there had been very little face-to-face interaction among focus group participants. Now the facilitator switched to a more traditional focus group discussion. Participants were asked to discuss the computer-generated list. Did it reflect an acceptable list of priorities? If not, what needed to be changed? Was something missing from the list? Was more detail needed?

The results and comments from each focus group were recorded. After a dozen of these focus group meetings had been completed, there was a rich database of ideas and suggestions to review. The data was analyzed and refined into a set of countywide priorities for the new campus. The final results were shared with all groups and provided to the architectural firm selected to design the campus. By combining the virtues of a group support system, brainstorming, nominal group technique, and face-to-face interaction, the building committee had confidence that its results reflected the interests, desires, and needs of the community it served.

The advantages of using meetingware to generate ideas and assist in decision making are numerous. Time isn't wasted writing and recording ideas on a board or flip charts. Instead, group members can spend time thinking about and generating their best ideas. Because ideas are generated anonymously, participants can make suggestions without interruption or fear of disapproval. (Although some research suggests that the more a group uses a group support system, the less anonymous the members feel.[15]) Time is saved because the computer automatically counts votes and prioritizes rankings. The results may even help a group reach consensus without having to spend hours talking and arguing.[16]

Groupware.   The terms groupware and meetingware are often used interchangeably. By the time this textbook is published, there may be a new word that encompasses both terms. As we see it, groupware has become a concept much broader than meetingware. Whereas meetingware is usually used in specific, face-to-face meetings, groupware is a much broader concept. The 3M Meeting Management Team offers a definition of groupware that, while still broad, focuses on some key concepts: **Groupware** is "software and hardware that meeting participants use at workstations to perform group tasks such as brainstorming, problem solving, and decision making."[17]

Groupware typically involves computers linked over the Internet or some other network, allowing group members to collaborate and engage in group tasks when they are at separate locations. For example, if a group wanted to edit a report without groupware, one person would prepare a first draft and it would be passed from person to person for review and suggestions. With a groupware system, everyone would review the document at the same time. Creighton and Adams describe how this process works:

> Using groupware, everybody can bring up the same document on the screen of their individual PC. They can either attach notes to the document or make actual corrections on the document, with changes from each person shown in a different color. . . . The group can discuss which changes have group consensus. As agreed-upon changes are keyed in, everybody will see the changes in the document on their screens. . . . Part of the power of groupware is that people can show each other what they mean, in real time, rather than trying to communicate everything orally.[18]

Group support systems—whether in the form of meetingware, groupware, or the next generation of group support technology—are designed to overcome several common problems encountered in groups. Frequently group members do not participate fully because of unequal status, unresolved conflict, and communication anxiety. By using group support systems to overcome such inhibitions, "groups can transcend characteristics of individual group members and use the members' combined knowledge, expertise, and experience to reach decisions which combine the best ideas of the individual group members."[19]

Information Gathering and Presentation

Computers are also improving the ability of a group to locate, retrieve, and present information. As we have indicated, well-informed groups make better decisions. What happens, then, when a group discovers that it lacks a vital piece of information? Before the era of cybermeeting, the meeting would be recessed or someone would have to leave the meeting to find the information. Even worse, the group might move ahead and make a poor decision because it lacked a critical piece of information. Today, information can be located, retrieved, and presented almost instantaneously. With appropriate software, browsers, and search engines, information can be as close as the nearest computer screen. In some cases, the information may be available from an organization's database. In other cases, members may retrieve information from a document filed in their PCs. Through an e-mail system, fax, or the telephone, a group can contact someone who has access to the information and have the document e-mailed, faxed, or delivered to the meeting. A group might even venture out onto the Internet in search of information. The introduction of computers to help groups locate and retrieve information has enabled groups to work more efficiently.

Computers also assist group members in presenting information. It is now common to attend meetings where presentation software and computer hardware are used to prepare and present slides. Slides—whether projected on an LCD screen or imprinted on transparencies—can present budget details, provide proposal specifications, graph recent trends, summarize the outcome of a vote or survey, list options, present alternate layouts for reports and publications, and display photographs and graphics. By using presentation software, groups can modify budgets, proposals, graphs, summaries, lists, and layouts within minutes. Presentation software does more than provide fancy ways to present information; it also gives members equal access to the same information. By accessing and displaying information electronically, groups can devote more time and attention to collaboration and decision making.

Whiteboard Technology

Once upon a time groups relied on chalk and blackboards to record ideas. Flip charts made life easier because they were portable and could be posted on walls. Today, whiteboard technology has combined the advantages of blackboards and flip charts into a versatile, cybermeeting tool. Whiteboard technology is not the same as a classroom whiteboard, which does little to improve upon the traditional chalk and blackboard system. When we use the term **whiteboard technology,** we are referring to whiteboards that are fully linked to a computer system. Anything written on the whiteboard is instantly digitized and can be processed the same way as any other information stored in the computer. This means that it can be stored, printed, and displayed in remote locations. Thus, a group member can sketch a flow chart or design on an electronic whiteboard and it can be seen and altered by other group members thousands of miles away. Thus, whiteboard technology allows groups to obtain the benefits of text-based computer conferencing while working with information that is better displayed graphically. It will become more common for high-tech meeting rooms to "have coated the walls with whiteboard panels or some other surface that allows people to write and draw to their heart's content."[20] Meeting centers with whiteboard technology are already operating and saving groups time and energy.

Pros and Cons of Computerized Meetings
Computerized meetings, just like teleconferences, videoconferences, and computer conferences, have advantages and disadvantages. Many of the disadvantages have as much to do with members' attitudes as they do with the technology itself. The advantages are only inhibited by a group's financial ability and willingness to stay current with the latest technology.

ADVANTAGES OF COMPUTERIZED MEETINGS	DISADVANTAGES OF COMPUTERIZED MEETINGS
Technology can save time.	More time is needed to implement and maintain the technology.
Technology can provide immediate access to vital information.	Technology will become more important than people and process.
Technology can do mundane tasks and allow groups to concentrate on substantive issues.	Technology will be difficult for some members to learn and use.
Technology can create an environment in which introverted members will participate and disputants will feel free to express their opinions.	Technology costs too much.

FIGURE 16.4 Advantages and Disadvantages of Computerized Meetings

Matching Technology to the Task

At the beginning of this chapter, we emphasized that technology is a tool, not a toy. The reason to integrate technology into the group process is to improve collaboration, not to show off with the latest gizmo. The question is not, "Should we use computer conferencing?" but "What technology, if any, will enable us to communicate more effectively and achieve our goal?" We believe that decisions about using technology in groups should be based on matching group needs with the capabilities of specific technology. We suggest that technology should be used only when it matches the purpose, the participants, and the process selected by a group.

Match the Purpose

As was the case with decision-making models and methods, a group's purpose should be the guide in selecting an appropriate technology. If the group's purpose is to review and edit a report, a computerized meeting or e-mail may be a better method than a face-to-face meeting. If, however, group members strongly disagree about what should be put in a report, generating and prioritizing ideas through the use of meetingware may be more appropriate. If the task is not the issue but the group's morale and member relationships are in jeopardy, a good old-fashioned, low-tech, face-to-face meeting may be the only way to establish or reestablish trust.

Match the Participants

Not everyone is comfortable with technology. A focus group using laptop computers may not work if group members have never used such equipment or cannot type—even using the hunt-and-peck method. We have found that fear of technology can be alleviated if there is enough support staff to help the novice or apprehensive group member through the process. In the electronic focus groups conducted to establish priorities for the community college campus, an assistant dubbed an "angel" attended every session. The angel moved among participants helping them overcome any technical difficulties they encountered. In some cases, a technical angel can type in suggestions for a techno-phobic or disabled participant.

Some group members who are quite comfortable using technology on an individual basis may worry that the technology will diminish the group's ability to achieve its goal and erode group relationships. Fear of losing the social advantages of group membership may convince participants that doing it the old-fashioned, face-to-face way is the best way to perpetuate group cohesiveness and harmony. Interestingly enough, there is research suggesting that under certain conditions and using appropriate technology, groups using computer-mediated communication will be as affectionate, appreciative, and hard working as groups working face-to-face.[21] As with any innovation, it may be necessary to spend time and effort training group members before letting them sink-or-swim in a cybermeeting.

Match the Process

Creighton and Adams emphasize that the use of technology is more likely to be effective when there "is a synergy among the type of meeting, the technology used, the meeting processes used, and the meeting facility."[22] They also emphasize that some groups and meetings require more than one process. An information-gathering phase may require technology different from a decision-making phase. Resolving a dispute may require face-to-face mediation whereas arguments for or against a proposal may be charted and evaluated on an electronic whiteboard. A PERT chart may be easier to adjust if it is displayed at a meeting on an overhead projector or LCD screen whereas the group members assigned to oversee project teams may be selected through an e-mail discussion among senior officers or group leaders. As a meeting's agenda and processes change, so should the technology selected to produce more effective forms of collaboration.

Balancing Technology in Groups

In the preface to *CyberMeeting: How to Link People and Technology in Your Organization*, the authors emphasize the need to balance the advantages and disadvantages of using technology for working in groups. On the one hand, they note that organizations will spend billions of dollars "connecting their employees through technology that will permit collaboration and electronic participation in meetings." On the other hand, "hundreds of millions of those dollars will be wasted chasing fads and installing technology that people will use to work the same way they worked before the technology was installed."[23] As important as it is to understand how to use technology in group settings, it is even more important to understand why and when to choose technology as a tool for enhancing group efficiency and effectiveness. In the end, the real issue is collaboration; technology is simply a valuable tool for helping to bring it about.[24]

The explosion in communication technology has released dozens of high-tech devices into the marketplace. In some businesses and organizations, teleconferences have replaced business trips and meetings. Felt-tip markers have given way to computer-generated graphics. Technology has changed the way many meetings are scheduled and conducted. Yet, in the rush to embrace new technologies, there has been a downside. Teleconferences have removed important human dimensions from group meetings. In many cases, presentation software has substituted slickness for substance.

Face-to-Face
Synchronous Communication
Human Potential

Cyberspace
Asynchronous Communication
Technological Power

FIGURE 16.5 Technology

Groups with access to every modern technology are not necessarily better groups. A nubby piece of chalk in the hands of a conscientious group member can do more to help a group achieve its goal than can a team of graphic designers. Robbins and Finley observe that a "team is still a team, no matter how much hardware and software it drags behind it; and prone to all the human frailties that all teams are prone to. A computer will not impose clarity on a fuzzy notion, that is something only we can do."[25] Technology is but a tool. Like any of the other tools used by groups, technology is "a means to pursue particular objectives."[26] As emphasized in Chapter 1, when the application of methods and the use of tools are based on strong theories, they have the power to transform a gathering of individuals into a powerful and effective group. In our eagerness to grab the latest piece of software, hardware, or groupware, we may seize the wrong tool—one that neither addresses the group's goal nor stretches our group's thinking in important new directions.

Effective groups learn to use technology to enhance communication when and where it is appropriate. Technology cannot achieve a group's goal; only a group can. Technology cannot satisfy a member's need for affection, control, or affiliation; only other group members can. Technology cannot lead a group or solve complex problems; only active group participants can. Effective groups take advantage of technology but do not substitute technology for the effort and wisdom of its members. Perhaps the most important balance that groups must achieve is that of balancing the marvels of technology with the untapped potential of their members.

Summary Study Guide

- The availability of cybermeeting tools allows groups to conduct much of their work in cyberspace.
- Groups should use technology only when it enhances efficiency and effectiveness.

- Group-based media include teleconferences, videoconferences, and computer conferences.
- Successful teleconference participants use an agenda, adapt to the oral-only channel, and introduce themselves before talking.
- Teleconferences, which are easy to set up and use, require the least investment in equipment of all the forms of electronic meetings.
- Videoconferences rely on advance planning as well as on the use of sophisticated and expensive equipment.
- When group members are briefed for a videoconference, they should be told to use the microphone discreetly, and dress appropriately.
- Computer conferences link group members through modems, local area networks, and the Internet.
- Computer conferences can be synchronous (simultaneous and real-time communication) or asynchronous (nonconcurrent, linear communication).
- Effective group members learn the norms for communication via technology and use emoticons appropriately.
- Group support systems (GSS) provide members with the ability to generate and evaluate ideas, make decisions, and use different voting procedures.
- Technology allows groups to locate and retrieve information quickly. It also assists groups in effectively presenting information.
- Whiteboard technology allows whatever a group writes on it to be stored, printed, or displayed.
- Technology should be used when it matches the group's purpose, participants, and process.

Groupwork *Computer and Teleconference Simulation*

GOAL   To demonstrate the advantages and disadvantages of computer conferencing and teleconferences.

PARTICIPANTS   Four groups of at least three members.

PROCEDURE

1. Each group will simulate a different type of conferencing.
    - Group 1 will simulate teleconferencing. The group members will sit with their backs to each other and communicate orally. Group members should not look at each other.

- Group 2 will simulate synchronous computer conferencing. The group members will sit with their backs to each other and communicate by writing messages on index cards. Group members are encouraged to send messages whenever they choose. Messages should be passed to all members of the group and can be passed to the left or right. Group members should not look at each other.
- Group 3 will simulate an asynchronous computer conference. Group members will sit with their backs to each other and communicate by writing on a piece of paper. One individual will start the conference by writing an initial message. The paper will be passed to the left. The next group member will respond by writing a message on the same piece of paper and then will pass the paper to the left. The process continues in this fashion. Group members should not look at each other.
- Group 4 will engage in a face-to-face discussion.

2. Each group will be asked to solve the following puzzle: Your group has eight balls, one of which is slightly heavier than the others. Your group also has a balance scale that may be used only twice. Devise a method of finding the heavier ball.*

3. After 10–15 minutes, the class should discuss the following:
   - How did the conference method help or hinder resolution of the puzzle?
   - Would the conference method be better suited to other types of tasks?
   - What communication problems did the conference method create? Can they be resolved?
   - Did the group members work as a group or individually?

*The textbook's *Instructor's Manual* explains how to solve this puzzle.

Electronic Meeting Evaluation

Directions   When you participate in or witness a teleconference, videoconference, or computer conference, use the following criteria to evaluate how well these types of electronic meetings were planned and conducted. Circle the number that best represents your assessment of each statement.

Teleconference

1. A teleconference was appropriate for this meeting.
   Poor 1 2 3 4 5 6 7 Excellent
2. The sound quality was satisfactory.
   Poor 1 2 3 4 5 6 7 Excellent
3. A meeting agenda was provided and followed.
   Poor 1 2 3 4 5 6 7 Excellent
4. Members introduced themselves before speaking.
   Poor 1 2 3 4 5 6 7 Excellent
5. Members adapted to the oral-only channel.
   Poor 1 2 3 4 5 6 7 Excellent

Videoconference

1. A videoconference was appropriate for this meeting.
   Poor 1 2 3 4 5 6 7 Excellent
2. A meeting agenda was provided and followed.
   Poor 1 2 3 4 5 6 7 Excellent
3. The video quality was satisfactory.
   Poor 1 2 3 4 5 6 7 Excellent
4. Members used the microphones effectively.
   Poor 1 2 3 4 5 6 7 Excellent
5. Members dressed appropriately.
   Poor 1 2 3 4 5 6 7 Excellent

Computer Conference

1. A computer conference was appropriate for this meeting.
   Poor 1 2 3 4 5 6 7 Excellent
2. A meeting agenda was provided and followed.
   Poor 1 2 3 4 5 6 7 Excellent
3. Members typed clear and succinct messages.
   Poor 1 2 3 4 5 6 7 Excellent
4. Members used emoticons appropriately.
   Poor 1 2 3 4 5 6 7 Excellent
5. Delays between messages were reasonable.
   Poor 1 2 3 4 5 6 7 Excellent

(continued)

(Electronic Meeting Evaluation, *continued*)

Comments:

Recommended Readings

3M Meeting Management Team with J. Drew. (1994). *Mastering meetings: Discovering the hidden potential of effective business meetings.* New York: McGraw-Hill.

Burelson, C. (1990). *Effective meetings: The complete guide.* New York: John Wiley.

Creighton, J. L. & Adams, J. W. R. (1998). *Cybermeeting: How to link people and technology in your organization.* New York: AMACOM

Notes

1. Bulkeley, W. M. (January 28, 1992). "Computerizing dull meetings is touted as an antidote to the mouth that bored." *Wall Street Journal*, p. B1.
2. "Computers: The key to more productive meetings" (August, 1989). *Presentation Products Magazine*, p. 48.
3. Ober, S. (1995). *Contemporary business communication* (2nd ed.). Boston: Houghton Mifflin, p. 503.
4. Berge, A. L. (1994). Electronic discussion groups. *Communication Education, 43*, pp. 102–111.
5. Creighton, J. L. & Adams, J. W. R. (1998). *Cybermeeting: How to link people and technology in your organization.* New York: Amacom, p. 13.
6. See Creighton & Adams, pp. 1–13.
7. Burelson, C. (1990). *Effective meetings: The complete guide.* New York: John Wiley, p. 168.
8. Burelson, p. 171.
9. Burgess, J. (May 26, 1997), "Meeting the future of meetings? Technology can ensure everyone is heard." *The Washington Post*, p. 18.
10. Johansen, R. (1988). *Groupware: Computer support for business teams.* New York: The Free Press, p. 20.
11. Walther, J. B. (1997). Group and interpersonal effects in international computer-mediated collaboration. *Human Communication Research, 22*, p. 452.

12. Contractor, N. S., Seibold, D. R. & Heller, M. A. (1996). "Interactional influence in the structuring of media use in groups: Influence in members' perceptions of group decision support system use." *Human Communication Research, 22,* p. 452.
13. Contractor, et al., p. 453.
14. Creighton & Adams, p. 86.
15. Scott, C. R., Timmerman, C. E., Quinn, L. & Garrett, D. M. (1998 November). "Trying to make the virtual honeymoon last a little longer: The impact of facilitation on communicative changes associated with repeated usage of a computerized group decision support system." Paper presented at the meeting of the National Communication Association, New York, NY, p. 28.
16. Creigton & Adams, pp. 86–91.
17. 3M Meeting Management Team with J. Drew. (1994). *Mastering meetings: Discovering the hidden potential of effective business meetings.* New York: McGraw-Hill, pp. 115–116.
18. Creighton & Adams, p. 52.
19. Barnes, S. & Greller, L. (1994). "Computer-mediated communication in the organization." *Communication Education, 43,* pp. 137–138.
20. Creighton & Adams, p. 64–65.
21. Walther, pp. 342–369.
22. Creighton & Adams, p. 115.
23. Creighton & Adams, p. ix.
24. Creighton & Adams, p. 226.
25. Robbins, H. & Finley, M. (1995). *Why teams don't work: What went wrong and how to make it right.* Princeton, NJ: Peterson's/Pacesetter Books, p. 210.
26. Senge, P. M., Kleiner, A., Roberts, C., Ross, R. B. & Smith, B. J. (1994). *The fifth discipline fieldbook: Strategies and tools for building a learning organization.* New York: Doubleday, p. 29.

Glossary

Abdicrat. A group member whose control needs are not met; an abdicrat is submissive and avoids responsibility.

Abstract Word. A word that refers to an idea or concept that cannot be observed or touched.

Accommodating Conflict Style. An approach to conflict in which a person gives in to other group members even at the expense of his or her own goals.

Achievement Norm. A norm that determines the quality and quantity of work expected from group members.

Action Item. A task identified in the minutes of a meeting that an individual member has been assigned to do.

Ad Hoc Committee. A committee that disbands once it has completed a specific assignment or task.

Ad *Hominem* Fallacy. An irrelevant attack against a person's character rather than a response to an issue or argument.

Affection Need. The need to express and receive warmth or to be liked.

Affective Conflict. A type of conflict that focuses on the personalities, communication styles, and emotions of group members.

Agenda. An outline of the items to be discussed and the tasks to be accomplished at a meeting.

Amendment. A modification or change to a motion under consideration during a meeting using parliamentary procedure.

Analysis Paralysis. A situation that occurs when group members become too focused on analyzing a problem rather than making a decision.

Apathy. The indifference that occurs when members do not find the group and/or its goal important, interesting, or inspiring.

Appeal to Authority. The fallacy of using the opinions of a supposed expert when in fact the person has no particular expertise in the area under consideration.

Appeal to Popularity. The fallacy of claiming that an action is acceptable because many people are performing the action.

Appeal to Tradition. The fallacy of claiming that people should continue a certain course of action because that is the way it has always been done.

Appreciative Listening. A type of listening that focuses on how well a person expresses an idea or opinion.

Arbitration. A method of resolving conflict by allowing an outside person, or arbitrator, to decide the issue for the group.

Argument. A conclusion supported by evidence or reasons for accepting it.

Argumentation. A process used to advocate a position, examine competing ideas, and influence others.

Argumentativeness. The willingness to argue controversial issues with others.

Assembly. One hundred or more people gathered to listen to a speaker make a presentation.

Asynchronous Communication. Electronic communication that does not occur simultaneously or in real time; communication that is linear and not interactive.

Authority Rule. A situation in which a leader or an authority outside the group makes final decisions for the group.

Autocrat. A group member whose control needs are not met; an autocrat tries to dominate and control the group.

Autocratic Leader. A leader who uses power and authority to control a group and its discussion.

Avoidance Conflict Style. A passive and nonconfrontational approach to conflict.

Backing. The component of the Toulmin model of argument that provides support for an argument's warrant.

Brainstorming. A technique that encourages group members to generate as many ideas as possible in a nonevaluative atmosphere.

Bylaws. A document that specifies the rules governing how an organization is structured and how it conducts its official business.

Bypassing. A form of miscommunication that occurs when people have different meanings for the same words or phrases and miss each other with their meanings.

Chair or Chairperson. The person appointed or elected to conduct the meetings of a group. In meetings using parliamentary procedure, the chair may be referred to as the presiding officer or president.

Claim. The component of the Toulmin model of argument that states the proposition or conclusion of an argument.

Claim of Fact. An argument stating the existence of things, occurrence of events, classification of things or events, or the cause of an event.

Claim of Policy. An argument advocating a certain course of action.

Claim of Value. An argument evaluating the quality or worth of things or suggesting that certain values are more important than others.

Clerk. A group member or an employee assigned to take minutes, track the status of motions, and record votes during a meeting or assembly.

Climate. The group atmosphere characterized by the degree to which members feel comfortable interacting.

Codeswitching. The ability to change from the dialect of one's own cultural setting and use the dialect of the majority in particular situations.

Coercive Power. The ability or authority to pressure or punish group members if they do not follow the leader's orders and directions.

Cohesion. The mutual attraction that holds the members of a group together.

Collaborative Conflict Style. An approach to conflict emphasizing the search for solutions that satisfy all group members and achieve the group's goal.

Committee. A group given a specific assignment by a larger group or by a person in a position of authority.

Common Ground. An identifiable belief, value, experience, or point of view shared by all group members.

Communication Apprehension. An individual's level of fear or anxiety associated with either real or anticipated communication with another person or persons.

Competitive Conflict Style. An approach to conflict focusing on an effort to win even at the expense of the group and its members.

Comprehensive Listening. A type of listening that focuses on accurately understanding spoken and nonverbal messages.

Compromising Conflict Style. An approach to conflict involving the concession of some goals in order to achieve others.

Computer Conference. The use of a computer to communicate and interact within a group.

Concrete Word. A word referring to something that can be perceived by our senses.

Conflict. The disagreement and disharmony that occurs in groups when differences are expressed regarding ideas, methods, and/or members.

Conflict Phase. A group development phase in which members express their opinions and make suggestions.

Conformity. The choice of a course of action that is socially acceptable or favored by a majority of group members.

Connotation. The personal feelings connected to the meaning of a word.

Consensus. A process by which *all* group members accept and are willing to support the best possible group decision.

Constructive Conflict. A situation that occurs when group members are able to express disagreement in a way that values everyone's contributions and promotes the group's goal.

Constructive Deviation. The act of resisting conformity while still working to promote a group goal.

Counterdependency and Fight. A group development stage characterized by conflict.

Contingency Model of Leadership Effectiveness. A leadership theory claiming that effective leadership depends upon an ideal match between the leader's style and the group's work situation.

Control Need. The need to exercise power or grant power to others; the need to feel competent and confident.

Cooperative Argumentation. A process of reasoned interaction on a controversial topic intended to help participants and audiences make the best assessments or decisions.

Council. A meeting of forty or fifty people in which group members listen to a speaker but are permitted to comment and/or ask questions.

Critical Listening. A type of listening that focuses on analyzing and forming appropriate opinions about the content of a message.

Cybermeeting. The use of information technology to manage group process and interaction.

Cyberspace. A nonphysical "place" where people meet via electronic communications media.

Data. The component of the Toulmin model of argument that provides evidence or proof used to support a claim.

Decision Making. The act of reaching a conclusion; a process in which a group selects from among a set of possible alternatives.

Definition. A statement that clarifies the meaning of a word, phrase, or concept.

Democratic Leader. A leader who seeks input from followers and shares the decision-making process with group members.

Democratic Member. A person whose control needs are met and who has no problems dealing with power in groups.

Demographic Traits. Audience traits such as age, gender, race, ethnicity, religion, or marital status.

Denotation. The objective, dictionary-based meaning of a word.

Dependency and Inclusion. A group development stage characterized by reliance on the leader and polite interaction.

Description. A reference that creates a mental image of a person, event, place, or object.

Designated Leader. A leader deliberately and purposely selected by a group or an outside authority.

Destructive Conflict. A situation that occurs when groups engage in behaviors that create hostility and prevent achievement of the group's goal.

Destructive Deviation. The resistance to conformity without regard for the best interests of the group and its goal.

Deviation. Member behaviors that do not conform to the expectations of a group.

Dialect. The variations in vocabulary, pronunciation, syntax, and style distinct from the commonly accepted form of a particular language.

Emergence Phase. A group development phase in which the members search for solutions and decisions.

Emergent Leader. A person who gradually achieves leadership status by interacting with group members and contributing to the achievement of the group's goal.

Emoticon. A textual symbol used to express emotion when communicating via computer.

Empathic Listening. A type of listening focusing on understanding and identifying with a group member's situation, feelings, and motives.

Example. A reference to a specific case or instance.

Expert Power. The ability to motivate and persuade others by demonstrating personal skills or special knowledge.

Explicit Norm. A norm that is written or verbally stated.

Extemporaneous. A form of delivery presented with prior preparation but with limited reliance on notes.

Extrovert. An outgoing group member who usually talks more than others and often becomes enthusiastic and animated during a discussion.

Fact. A verifiable observation, experience, or event.

Fallacy. An error in reasoning.

Faulty Analogy. The fallacy of claiming that two things are similar when they actually differ in regard to relevant characteristics.

Faulty Cause. The fallacy of identifying the cause of an event before ruling out other possible causes.

Feedback. The verbal or nonverbal response to communication.

Feeler. A Myers-Briggs personality type who wants everyone to get along and who will spend time and effort helping other group members.

Floor. In parliamentary procedure, a reference to the right to speak before a group after being recognized by the chair, as in "I have the floor."

Focus Group. An exploratory research technique that uses a carefully selected group of people to discuss a specific research question.

Follower. A group member who is willing to accept group decisions and carry them out.

Forming Stage. A group development phase in which tasks are defined and interpersonal relationships are tested.

Forum. A public meeting in which audience members express their concerns and address questions to public officials and experts.

Functional Approach to Problem Solving. An approach in which competent communication is critical in order for members to understand the nature of the problem, the group's goal, and the pros and cons of possible solutions.

Functional Leadership Theory. An approach to leadership that assumes any member can and should help the group achieve its goals by performing leadership tasks.

Functional Participation Theory. An approach to participation that assumes any member can help a group achieve its goals by performing task and maintenance functions that match group needs.

Fundamental Interpersonal Relationship Orientation (FIRO). William Schutz's theory that three interpersonal needs (inclusion, control, and affection) affect group behavior.

Gatekeeper. A person who tries to regulate the flow of communication within a group discussion.

Goal. The purpose or objective toward which a group is directed.

Golden Listening Rule. The principle that you should listen to others as you would have them listen to you.

Governance Groups. State legislatures, city and county councils, and governing boards of public agencies and educational institutions that conduct meetings in public.

Group Support Systems. The software and hardware combinations that facilitate group functions such as planning, idea generation, problem solving, issue discussion, negotiation, and conflict resolution.

Groupthink. The deterioration of group effectiveness that results from in-group pressure.

Groupware. The software and hardware that group members use to perform tasks such as brainstorming, problem solving, and decision making.

Hasty Generalization. The fallacy of using too few examples or experiences to support a conclusion.

Hidden Agendas. An individual member's private motives and goals that conflict with and affect the achievement of a group's common goal.

Ideal Personal Member. A person whose affection needs are met and who is comfortable interacting with group members.

Ideal Social Member. A person whose inclusion needs are met and who enjoys working with people or working alone.

Ideal-Solution Model. A decision-making procedure that identifies members' ideal solutions and then asks the group to develop a solution that incorporates such ideal criteria.

Implicit Norm. A norm that is rarely discussed or openly communicated.

Impromptu. A form of delivery in which a person speaks without prior preparation or practice.

Inclusion Need. The need to express and receive acceptance and affiliation; the need to belong or be involved.

Individual Attributes. Distinctive features of group members such as job titles, status, special interests, relationships with other members, and length of membership.

Information Overload. A situation that occurs when a group receives too much information or information that is too complex for the group to adequately process.

Information Underload. A situation that occurs when a group does not possess enough information to make an effective decision.

Interaction. Communication that uses verbal and nonverbal messages to generate meaning.

Interaction Norm. A norm that determines how group members communicate with one another.

Interdependence. The extent to which group members are affected and influenced by the actions of other members.

Internal Document. A policy, procedure, manual, or memo that is specific to the operation of a particular organization or company and may not be intended for use by the general public.

Interview. A method of collecting information directly from a person with expertise or experience.

Introvert. A member who needs more time to think before speaking and who may prefer to work alone rather than in a group.

Intuitive. A Myers-Briggs personality type who likes to make connections and formulate big ideas but who may become bored with details.

Jargon. The specialized or technical language of a profession.

Judger. A Myers-Briggs personality type who is highly structured and likes to plan ahead.

Kinesics. The study of body movement and physical expression.

Laissez-Faire Leader. A leader who lets the group take charge of all decisions and actions.

Leader–Member Relations. A situational leadership factor that assesses how well a leader gets along with group members.

Leadership. The ability to make strategic decisions and use communication to mobilize a group toward achieving a shared goal.

Learning Group. A group that meets to help members acquire knowledge and develop skills by sharing information and experience.

Legitimate Power. The power that resides in a job, position, or assignment rather than in a person; the power to make decisions as an authorized or elected representative of a group.

Level of Abstraction. Word meanings that differ in their level of specificity; word choices that range from general, intangible concepts to specific, tangible items.

Listening. The process of receiving, constructing meaning from, and responding to spoken and/or nonverbal messages.

Main Motion. A motion in parliamentary procedure that proposes a new action or decision.

Maintenance Function. A positive role that affects how group members get along with each other while pursuing a shared goal.

Majority Vote. The results of a vote in which more than half the members favor a proposal.

Maslow's Hierarchy of Needs. A specific sequence of needs (physiological, safety, belongingness, esteem, and self-actualization) that can explain why people are attracted to particular groups.

Mediation. A facilitated negotiation that employs the services of an impartial third party for the purpose of guiding, coaching, and encouraging the disputants to a successful resolution and an agreement.

Meeting. A scheduled gathering of group members for a structured discussion guided by a designated chairperson.

Meetingware. A group support system that includes electronic meeting tools for use in a meeting room setting.

Method. A strategy, guideline, procedure, or technique for dealing with the issues and problems that arise in groups.

Minutes. The written record of the group's discussion and activities during a meeting.

Monochronic. An approach to time that favors deadlines and the scheduling of one thing at a time.

Motion. In parliamentary procedure, a formal, carefully worded proposal made before a group for the members' consideration and action.

Multimedia. A product or presentation that combines two or more of the following: text, still graphics, motion graphics (animation), and sound.

Myers-Briggs Type Indicator®. A widely used inventory that identifies specific personality types based on the ways in which people perceive and make judgments.

Negotiation. A method of bargaining for the purpose of settling differences or reaching solutions.

Nominal Group Technique (NGT). A procedure in which members write and report suggested ideas, after which discussion and multiple votes are used to decide the priority or value of listed suggestions.

Nonverbal Communication. The behavioral elements of messages other than the actual words spoken.

Norm. An expectation held by group members concerning what kind of behavior or opinion is acceptable or unacceptable.

Norming Stage. A group development stage in which members work to find ways of achieving the group's goal.

On-Line Search. The process of accessing information from databases on other computers.

Opinion. A conclusion regarding the meaning of facts.

Oral Presentation. A relatively uninterrupted talk to a group of people.

Orders of the Day. In parliamentary procedure, the program of business or group agenda listing the topics for discussion in the order they will be discussed.

Orientation Phase. A group development phase in which members get to know one another and the requirements of the task.

Overpersonal Behavior. The behavior of a person whose affection needs are not met and who tries to gain friendship despite the lack of interest by other members.

Oversocial Behavior. The behavior of a person whose inclusion needs are not met and who seeks attention as a way of compensating for feelings of inadequacy.

Panel Discussion. A group discussion in which participants interact with one another on a common topic for the benefit of an audience.

Paraphrasing. The restating of what a person has said as a way of indicating that the listener has understood what the speaker means and feels.

Parliamentarian. A person who advises the chair on matters concerning parliamentary procedure.

Parliamentary Procedure. A systematic method designed to determine the will of the majority through fair and orderly discussion and debate.

Perceiver. A Myers-Briggs personality type who is less rigid about time than are other group members and who is flexible and willing to try new options.

Performing Stage. A group development stage in which group energies focus on reaching decisions and determining solutions.

Personal Credibility. Listeners' positive or negative perceptions of a speaker.

Personal Space. The psychological space surrounding each person that expands and contracts in different situations.

Personality Type Theory. The concept that the way people see, understand, and make decisions about the world around them affects a group's ability to achieve its goals.

PERT (Program Evaluation and Review Technique). A procedure for charting who should do what tasks in what sequence over a specific period of time in order to implement a group's solution or plan.

Point of Order. A statement that questions whether the rules and principles of parliamentary procedure are followed correctly.

Polychronic. An approach to time that allows many things to be done at once.

Post-Meeting Reaction (PMR) Form. A questionnaire designed to assess meeting success by collecting written reactions from participants.

Power. The ability or authority to influence and motivate others.

Precedence. In parliamentary procedure, the rank order or priority governing the proposal and consideration of motions.

Presention Aids. Supplementary audio and/or visual materials used in a discussion or oral presentation.

Presentation Software. A category of computer programs created for the purpose of designing and presenting visual aids.

Previous Question. In parliamentary procedure, a motion to bring debate to a close and put the motion to an immediate vote.

Primary Group. Family members or friends who provide affection, support, and a sense of belonging.

Primary Source. The document, testimony, or publication in which information first appears.

Primary Tension. The social unease and inhibitions experienced by group members during the get-acquainted phase of a group's development.

Privileged Request. In parliamentary procedure, a motion regarding the personal needs and rights of members.

Problem Solving. A complex, decision-making process in which groups analyze a problem and decide upon a plan for solving or reducing the harmful effects of the problem.

Procedural Conflict. A disagreement over what method or process the group should follow.

Procedural Norm. A norm that dictates how the group will operate.

Proxemics. The study of how people perceive and use personal space and distance.

Public Group. A group that discusses issues and makes presentations in front of or for the benefit of a public audience.

Qualifier. The component of the Toulmin model of argument that states the degree to which a claim is thought to be true.

Question. In parliamentary procedure, a motion put before a group for a decision.

Question of Fact. A discussion question that asks whether something is true or false, or whether something did or did not occur.

Question of Policy. A discussion question that asks whether and how a specific course of action should be taken to solve a problem.

Question of Value. A discussion question that asks the group to decide whether something is good or bad, right or wrong, or worthwhile or worthless.

Quorum. The minimum number or percentage of people who, according to a group's constitution or bylaws, must be present at a meeting in order to transact business legally.

Referent Power. The personal power and influence held by people who are admired and respected.

Refutation. The act of proving an argument either erroneous or false or both.

Reinforcement Phase. A group development phase in which members agree upon a decision or solution.

Relationship-Motivated Leader. A leader whose major satisfaction comes from establishing close personal relations with the members of a group.

Research. The search, collection, and analysis of information.

Reservation. The component of the Toulmin model of argument that recognizes the conditions under which a claim would not be true.

Reward Power. The authority to give group members something they value.

Second. In parliamentary procedure, the endorsement of a motion for consideration by a second member.

Secondary Source. Source that reports, repeats, or summarizes information from one or more other sources.

Secondary Tension. The frustrations and personality conflicts experienced by group members as they compete for social acceptance and achievement within a group.

Self-Actualization Need. The need to fulfill one's own human potential; the personal reward of becoming the best that is possible.

Self-Centered Function. A negative role in which individual needs are put ahead of the group's goal and other members' needs.

Self-Concept. A person's perception of himself or herself.

Self-Help Groups. Groups that offer assistance and encouragement to members who need support with personal problems.

Self-Management Team. A small group of people with complementary skills who are committed to a common purpose, performance goals, and approach for which they hold themselves mutually accountable.

Sensor. A Myers-Briggs personality type who focuses on details and prefers to concentrate on one task at a time.

Service Group. A group that is dedicated to worthy causes, helping people both inside and outside the group.

Sexist Language. Terminology that demeans, excludes, or stereotypes people on the basis of gender.

Situational Theory. An approach to leadership that helps leaders improve by carefully analyzing themselves, their group, and the circumstances in which they must lead.

Small Group Communication. The interaction of three or more interdependent people working toward a common goal.

Small Group Meeting. A meeting in which twelve or fewer group members have equal opportunity to become fully involved in all discussions and decision making.

Social Dimension. A group's focus on the personal relationships among members.

Social Group. A group in which members share common interests in a friendly setting or participate in leisure activities.

Solution Criteria. The standards that should be met for an ideal solution.

Standard Agenda. A procedure that guides a group through problem solving by using the following steps: clarifying the task, understanding and analyzing the problem, assessing possible solutions, and implementing a decision or plan.

Standing Committee. A committee that remains active in order to accomplish an ongoing task.

Statistics. A collection of data presented in a numerical form.

Status Norm. A norm that identifies levels of influence among group members.

Storming Stage. A group development stage in which members argue about important issues.

Styles Theory. An approach to leadership that identifies specific behaviors that can be classified as autocratic, democratic, and laissez-faire leadership.

Substantive Conflict. A disagreement over ideas and issues.

Symposium. A group presentation in which participants give short, uninterrupted speeches on different aspects of a topic for the benefit of the public.

Synchronous Communication. Communication that occurs simultaneously and in real time, either face-to-face or electronically.

Synergy. The interaction of two or more agents or forces so that their combined effect is greater than the sum of their individual effects.

Table. In parliamentary procedure, a motion to set a matter aside for later consideration in order to take up an urgent or emergency issue.

Task Dimension. A group's focus on the achievement of its goal.

Task Force. A type of committee appointed to gather information and make recommendations regarding a specific issue or problem.

Task Function. A positive role that affects a group's ability to do the work needed to achieve its goals.

Task-Motivated Leader. A leader whose major satisfaction comes from successfully completing the group task even at the risk of poor interpersonal relations with group members.

Task Structure. A situational leadership factor that assesses how a group must organize or plan a specific task.

Team. A work group given full responsibility and resources for its performance.

Team Presentation. A presentation by a cohesive group of speakers who are trying to influence an audience of decision makers.

Team Talk. The nature of language that group members use as they work together.

Teleconference. A coordinated phone call among three or more group members.

Termination. A group development stage that describes how a group disbands.

Territoriality. The sense of personal ownership attached to a particular space.

Testimony. A statement expressing an authority's judgment or interpretation of facts.

Theory. A principle that tries to explain and predict events and behavior.

Thinker. A Myers-Briggs personality type who takes pride in thinking objectively and making difficult decisions.

Thought Speed. The speed (words per minute) at which most people can think as contrasted with the slower speed at which most people speak.

Tool. A resource, rule, skill, or equipment used to perform groupwork.

Toulmin Model of Argument. A model developed by Stephen Toulmin representing the structure of an argument.

Trait Theory. An approach to leadership that tries to identify common characteristics and behaviors of leaders.

Trust and Structure. A group development stage in which members define roles and determine procedures.

Two-Thirds Vote. Results of a vote in which at least twice as many group members favor a proposal as oppose it.

Underpersonal Behavior. The behavior of a person whose affection needs are not met, characterized by superficial relationships with other group members.

Undersocial Behavior. The behavior of a person whose inclusion needs are not met, characterized by withdrawal from the group or feelings of unworthiness.

Videoconference. A telecommunications system that combines audio and video media to provide both voice communication and video images.

Warrant. The rationale within the Toulmin model of argument suggesting why the data offered support a particular claim.

Whiteboard Technology. A whiteboard fully linked to a computer system, allowing information written on it to be stored, printed, and displayed.

Word Stress. The degree of vocal prominence given to a syllable within a word or a word within a phrase or sentence.

Work. A group development stage in which members perform tasks necessary for accomplishing the group goal.

Work Group. A group responsible for achieving specific tasks or routine duties on behalf of a company, an organization, an association, an agency, or an institution.

Text Credits

Chapter 3

The Least-Preferred Coworker Scale from *Improving Leadership Effectiveness: The Leader Match Concept,* 2nd edition, Fiedler, F. E. & Chemers, M. M. © 1984 John Wiley & Sons, Inc., pp. 17–42. Reprinted by permission of John Wiley & Sons, Inc.

Chapter 5

PRCA-24 reprinted with permission from the author from: James C. McCroskey (1993). *An Introduction to Rhetorical Communication,* 6th edition. Englewood Cliffs, N.J.: Prentice Hall, Inc., p. 37.

Chapter 8

Based on Gellerman, W. (1970). Win as much as you can. In J. W. Pfeiffer and J. E. Jones (eds.), *A Handbook of Structured Experiences for Human Relations Training, Vol. 2.* La Jolla, CA: University Associates (1974), pp. 66–69.

See DeWine, S. (1994). *The consultant's craft: Improving organizational communication.* New York: St. Martin's Press, pp. 268–272; Ross, R. G. & DeWine, S. (1988). Communication messages in conflict: A message-focused instrument to assess conflict management styles. *Management Communication Quarterly, 1,* pp. 389–413.

Chapter 10

Based on Beebe, S. A., Barge, J. K., and McCormick, C. (1994). The competent group communicator. *Proceedings of the 1994 Summer Conference on Assessing College Student Competency in Speech Communication.* Annandale, VA: Speech Communication Association, pp. 353–369.

Reprinted with permission from *Psychology Today Magazine,* copyright © 1971 (Sussex Publishers, Inc.).

Chapter 11

Argumentativeness Scale reprinted with permission from the authors, Dominic A. Infante and Andrew Rancer.

Chapter 13

Copyright © 1996 by Houghton Mifflin Company. Reproduced by permission from *The American Heritage Dictionary of the English Language, Third Edition.*

Index